# A Bad,
Bad Boy

READER BOOKS
Published by the San Diego Reader
1703 India Street
San Diego, California 92101 U.S.A.

First Printing, July 2009



ISBN 978-0-615-29879-5

Printed in the United States of America
Set in Bembo
Designed by Sherry Nicolai Russell

# A Bad, Bad Boy

Judith Moore

READER BOOKS

*Where Lamont Street phone booth stood*

**I offered money, far more money than I could afford, to try to get people to talk.**

CHAPTER ONE

# WHAT I DON'T KNOW

Some evening, soon, if you are in San Diego, drive out to Pacific Beach. Be there about 8:15. The sun will have been down several hours. Across the sky every last orange and violet streak will be gone. Take a jacket. I forgot my jacket. I was cold. Bone cold.

Turn south off Grand Avenue onto Lamont Street. Park along Lamont. Wander over to the gas station. The gas station, on your right, as you face away from the traffic along Grand. Back in 1977, a pay telephone stood along the side of this station. It was an Arco station then. Frank Bompensiero made his last telephone call here. "Dialed," someone told me, and then laughed a high-pitched crazy laugh, "his last number."

Nobody knows what number Bompensiero dialed. Nobody knows to whom Bompensiero talked, or, if he talked to anyone. Whomever he called, he knew the number, by heart. No one found wadded scratch paper that had numbers scrawled across it in the pockets of his dark green trousers.

Some people say Bompensiero talked to James Aladena ("Jimmy the Weasel") Fratianno. Others claim that he spoke to Joseph ("Joe Bananas") Bonnano, the former New York Mafia leader simmering in exile in Tucson. Fratianno protested: no way did Bompensiero call him. No way. Fratianno insisted that Bompensiero was returning the call of Los Angeles' Mafia overlord, Dominic Brooklier (who in a fit of Anglophilia had changed his name from Dominic Bruccoleri). Still other people said—whispered—that Bompensiero called the FBI.

When you get right down to it, it's hard to know much about Bompensiero. By the time I went that February evening to the spot where Bompensiero "dialed his last number," I had spent ten years, off and on, asking people questions about him. I had read court records and old newspaper clippings. I had sorted through shoe boxes stacked with blurry photographs. I had sat outside houses and apartments where he'd lived in Little Italy and Kensington and Pacific Beach. I had snapped photos of houses where he lived. Many times I walked past his long-obliterated bar—the Gold Rail—which had stood in the 1000 block of Third Avenue, downtown, between Broadway Credit Jewelers, the States Café, Graf's Exclusive Furs, the Hula Hut, and the Cuckoo Club. I visited San Quentin, where he stoically did five years. I went to church to sit behind one of his sisters, an elderly woman who had refused my request for interviews. I could hear her beads click as her fingers rushed across the Hail Marys strung between Our Fathers. I harried retired law enforcement guys. I harried the FBI. I filed endless Freedom of Information Act requests. When the requests were honored and papers arrived, I was as excited as any child at Christmas. I tore open the packages. I studied blacked-out, redacted reports. I listened, in those reports, for the sound of Bompensiero's gravelly voice. I wrote obsequious letters in which I begged people to talk with me. I offered money, far more money than I could afford, to try to get people to talk. I went to the post office and bought money orders and mailed them off to a man in prison who had known Bompensiero. I ordered *fiori di Sicilia* and stirred the aromatic citrus-and-vanilla concoction into my old pound cake recipe. I bought a Sicilian cookbook and made pasta with peas, which someone told me was a Bompensiero favorite. I even considered flying to Sicily and boarding a bus to Porticello, from where Bompensiero's parents came. I, who never read my own horoscope, looked up what the stars promised Bompensiero on February 10, 1977. "Don't be too critical about the conditions at home or it gets worse. Do what you can to better conditions there quietly. Try to be more cheerful and lift the spirits of others. Handle money matters wisely." Finally, I read and reread his autopsy, as if what David M. Katsuyama, pathologist for the coroner, wrote about Bompensiero's heart could tell me something about his soul. His heart, Dr. Katsuyama noted, "weighs 540 grams. Multiple sections reveal moderately severe sclerosis of the coronary vessels, reducing the lumen in some areas to 25-30% of original caliber. Complete obliteration or thrombosis is not encountered. Cut surfaces of the myocardium show no recognizable infarct. Valve appearances and sizes are normal. The aorta shows moderately severe atherosclerosis."

Even with all that and much more, I never knew—I do not know now—as much as I needed and wanted to know. I didn't know small personal details—how he smelled, how he kissed, if in his last years he (like LA's Mafia boss Jack Dragna) wore dentures, if he slept well at night. I didn't know how he felt when he put a rope around Frank Borgia's neck and pulled and Frank Borgia crumpled to his knees. I did not know if he ever tried to quit smoking his big cigars. I did not know why he married his second wife, Marie. I did not know if he ever said the Lord's Prayer, or, if he even knew the Lord's Prayer. I didn't know what, other than newspapers and magazines, he read. I didn't know how smart he was. I have a copy of his file from San Quentin: next to "Intelligence Estimate," a prison official printed "dull normal." Entire years passed during which he seemed to disappear, to leave no spoor of arrests or statements to newspapers. Yet for all that I did not know, I felt, some days, that I knew more about him than I knew about myself.

This not-knowing got me interested in epistemology, that branch of philosophy "concerned with the definition of knowledge, the sources and criteria of knowledge, the kinds of knowledge possible, and the degree to which each is certain, and the exact relation between the one who knows and the object that is known." I became interested in this "exact relation between the one who knows and the object that is known." By the time I started asking questions about Bompensiero, he was an object. He was to be known and I wanted to know him.

*Thelma Bompensiero (second from left), Marie Adamo and Momo Adamo*

**"And I said, 'Where in hell were you, Momo?' He didn't answer."**

CHAPTER TWO

# MOMO AND MARIE

That February evening, as I stood in the dark on Lamont Street, hugging myself to keep warm, I was waiting for Paul Ybarrando to show up. Ybarrando, now retired from the San Diego Police Department, was the sergeant in charge of the investigation into Bompensiero's murder. A murder, by the way, that never would be solved. So, forget knowing who waited for him behind the fence that ran along the alley that intersects Lamont. Forget that.

But you might want to drive out there and look at where it happened. You might.

What we do know is that at 8:00, on February 10, 1977, a Thursday night about three weeks after Jimmy Carter took the oath of office as our 39th president, Bompensiero had 20 to 30 minutes left to live. We can surmise that he was returning a call, or, that he was keeping a promise to call someone at or about a time between 8:00 and 8:15. We can surmise that the person whom Bompensiero called is the person who ordered the old man's assassination. I think we can make that surmise.

Bompensiero hadn't wanted to use his own telephone. He lived at 4205 Lamont, two and a half blocks from the gas station. Three years earlier, soon after the building was finished, he and his second wife, Marie, had moved from her Reed Street apartment to 4205. Set in among modest prewar houses, the four-story blue-and-white structure dominated the neighborhood. It was called "The Beach Club." Among its amenities were security doors and an underground parking garage.

Bompensiero's two-bedroom condominium—number seven—was on the third floor. His name, however, was not next to the buzzer that you stuck out your index finger and punched to announce your arrival. Frank Gavin was the name taped next to number seven's buzzer. Patrick Gavin had been Marie Bompensiero's third husband. Patrick Gavin was dead—cancer. Marie Bompensiero's second husband, Girolamo "Momo" Adamo, was dead—self-inflicted gunshot to the head. Her first husband, whom she dumped for Momo, was dead. Somebody told me, about Marie, a red-haired Sicilian who looked not unlike Rita Hayworth, "She was a little bad luck, you know. She was married to four guys, they're all dead. I used to tell her, 'Gee, anybody goes with you, gotta be crazy.' I seen pictures of her when she first come out from Kansas City to California, she was a very beautiful woman. Very beautiful. And she dressed good." Someone else told me, about Marie, that indeed she did dress well, and, that underneath foxes and minks and sequined gowns and jet-bead trimmed dresses and bugle-beaded cashmere sweaters, she wore "all-silk underwear. She had sets of it, in every color."

Bompensiero may have worried that the telephone in his apartment was tapped. That it was tapped would be a reasonable assumption. The FBI had tapped Bompensiero's telephones off and on for years. On the floor of my bedroom closet I keep a box in which someone sent me two dozen jumbo Florida pink grapefruit. That box is packed with photocopies of transcripts of telephone calls made by Bompensiero and recorded and transcribed by the FBI.

Then again, maybe Bompensiero didn't want to awaken Marie. Marie was asleep. Or, maybe, Marie had passed out. Marie drank too much. She'd been drinking too much for a long time. No wonder.

This is the story on Marie. *Née* Caldarello, Marie was born in Kansas City in 1907. She married Frank Guererra in Kansas City in 1934. She divorced Guererra and married Momo Adamo soon after her son by Guererra was born. Marie, one of whose brothers married into a mob-connected Kansas City family, the Lococos, was described as a high-spirited and tempestuous party girl who frequented Kansas City nightspots. Adamo was a dark, saturnine, and handsome playboy who did a mean tango and had a mean temper and a mean scar down one side of his jaw. He spoke a fractured, broken, heavily accented half-English, half-Italian. Marie loved Momo fiercely and by all accounts, Momo loved Marie. "Adored her," is what someone told me. I have that written, in my notebook. "He said, 'Momo adored Marie.'"

Girolamo "Momo" Adamo, born in Sicily in 1895, came to the U.S. in the early 1900s. He went first to Chicago. According to a man now long retired from Kansas City law enforcement, Momo Adamo "was brought to Kansas City from Chicago by Johnny Lazia, leader of the Kansas City Italian organized crime syndicate." In Kansas City during Prohibition, Momo ran a speakeasy called the Garden of Naples. He was seen around town during the great Kansas City Massacre, when on a summer Saturday morning in 1933, gangsters opened fire in front of Kansas City's Union Station, leaving four policemen and their prisoner dead. Lazia ruled Kansas City's northside until 1934, when he was shot down as he entered the Park Central Hotel. Lazia lieutenants, men like Momo Adamo, believed a Kansas City upstart—Michael James LaCapra—determined to take over the Lazia domain, ordered Lazia's killing.

In 1935, Momo packed up Marie and her son Paul and left bloody-hot-in-summer, cold-in-winter Kansas City behind. The Adamos settled in Los Angeles, where Momo allied himself with LA's Mafia godfather, Jack Dragna. Momo rather quickly became second-in-command, or underboss, to Dragna. He and Marie took up residence at 3911 Westside Avenue, not far from Dragna's house at 3027 Hulbert. The west side LA neighborhood was a well-kept upper-middle-class enclave of prewar Spanish-style houses. Marie bought good furniture, good china, good sterling. She was known, I heard, for setting a "beautiful table." She was a superb cook, and although she always hired in couples to serve her guests and to wash up after dinner, she prepared all the food—fish soups, intricate stuffed pastas, veal, cannelloni. ("Nobody in that crowd," someone told me, "had live-in maids. You didn't want anyone in the house.") Marie was a generous hostess. Her menus, I was told, were extensive, and no matter how much everyone ate, leftovers always heaped the kitchen counters. At most houses, children ate in the kitchen. But not at Marie's house; everybody, even children, pulled up chairs. Momo, always, governed at the table's head, pouring Italian red wines and French champagnes, lighting the ladies' cigarettes.

Marie was a prodigious shopper. She bragged to her lady friends about her ability to squeeze cash from Momo. Someone said, "She never gave anything away. She used to say, 'I told Momo, I want some money, we're going to go shopping,' and he'd say, 'Maria, you've got a closet full of clothes.' So what she would do is she'd get rid of some clothes. She never gave them away to her cleaning lady. She never gave a thing away. She would take them down to the secondhand store and sell them and then she'd go out and buy new clothes." So Marie bought the silk underwear, the furs and gowns and suits and stylish hats from Mr. John. Her nose poked through the hats' adorable veiling. She set bottles of Arpége and My Sin on her dressing table. She went twice a week to the hairdresser who arranged her auburn hair in marcelled waves. She kept her long fingernails polished a bright red. She was a student of her complexion. Even when she and Momo came home so drunk from LA nightclubs that they were stumbling, Marie sat down before her dressing table mirror and removed her makeup and massaged cold cream into her olive skin.

Momo and Marie partied. Marie got dolled up. Marie did not have what you would call a voluptuous figure. She did not have, the ladies said, behind her back, "a pretty bustline." Pretty bustline or not, when evening came, Marie nevertheless displayed what bosom she had in daringly low-cut bodices. And always the sequins, the traceries of beads glittered on these bodices. Momo, no mean dresser himself, shrugged his broad shoulders into his tuxedo jacket and set his black homburg atop his thinning hair.

Momo and Marie liked Ciro's. Momo was a big tipper and Ciro waiters and cigarette girls paid him exorbitant attention. Momo learned to cha-cha. He loved the cha-cha. Momo and Marie drank and cha-cha'ed and drank. Momo flirted with busty blondes. Someone told me about an evening in the late 1940s when Momo and Marie were visiting San Diego and entertaining in their suite at the El Cortez. "Momo was in another room and Marie says to the ladies, 'Did I ever tell you about when I was a blonde?' Everybody said, 'No.' 'Well, son of a bitch,' Marie says, 'Momo was out late late late one night and I don't know what time the bastard came home, and when he got home I got right up next to him and I said, "Where in hell were you, Momo?" He didn't answer. I looked at his jacket and I saw this long blond strand of hair right there on the dark suit. I said, "So, you son of a bitch, you like blondes?" The next morning I went out to the beauty parlor and got myself made blond. I got home and Momo, he looked at me and started screaming, "Maria, what are you doing? What are you doing?"'"

Marie flirted with everyone. Momo, in his broken English, hissed at her, "Maria Mag-a-da-lena!" By which Momo meant to indicate that Marie was a whore. More than once, Momo slugged Marie. He blacked her eyes, left green bruises on her arms. She wore dark glasses.

Joe Adamo, Momo's brother, also moved to California, settling in San Diego in the 1940s in a house on South Hempstead Circle in Kensington and setting himself up in the bar business as co-owner, with Momo, of a dark little sailor bar, the Gay Paree on Fourth Avenue. Momo and Marie often were in and out of San Diego during the years after World War II. They came to visit Joe and his family and Momo's old friend from Kansas City, a murderous thug named William "Willie the Rat" Cammisano who'd bought a house at 4134 Lymer Drive in Kensington. Willie, when he bought the Lymer Drive house, opened the trunk of his car and took from a suitcase $25,000 in cash and counted it out into the hands of the house's seller. Momo and Marie, in San Diego, liked to stay in a suite at the El Cortez and go out on the town to nightspots like Tops.

*Jack Dragna (head of table) and Frank Desimone (to Dragna's left)*

**"The ladies were not crazy about her because she flirted with everybody."**

CHAPTER THREE

# FRANK AND MARIE

Meanwhile, in Los Angeles, the Mafia's old *mahoofs* gradually lost their hold on the city. Benjamin "Bugsy" Siegel had come to town. Mickey Cohen had come to town. Endless freelancers showed up. Jack Dragna wasn't left with all that much, which meant that Momo Adamo, his lieutenant, wasn't left with much either. Except lots of trouble with Los Angeles' organized crime division. Those guys followed Dragna and his boys everywhere.

Friday morning, February 24, 1956, the banner atop the *Los Angeles Times'* front page read: "Jack Dragna Found Dead In Sunset Blvd. Hotel." Beneath the headline: "Reputed Ruler of Mafia in Los Angeles Apparently Had Heart Attack While Asleep."

Frank Desimone, a scrawny and dyspeptic Los Angeles lawyer, a chewer of Tums, succeeded Jack Dragna as LA's Mafia head. Somebody told me that after Dragna's death, Momo expected he would be made head of the LA family. Underbosses almost always moved up to boss position after a boss's death, particularly when the death was natural. Dragna's death was natural. His body was found, clad in pink silk pajamas, in the hotel bed. It was said that before his death he'd had the pleasure of feminine companionship. It was said that "Jack died under a whore."

After Dragna's death the LA family took a vote. By the time this vote was taken, Desimone already had muscled Momo out. Desimone, I was told, likely "made a move." He likely promised the guys he'd do this for them and do that, they'd get moneyed up. Maybe he told them Momo was weak, that he was old and from the Old World, that he couldn't do anything for them. Maybe he told them Momo was sick. Even Momo's brother Joe went against Momo in the vote. Maybe Momo was sick.

Joe Adamo, people will tell you, "was the quiet one. Pure Sicilian man that you would never dream was ever connected anywhere. Joe just seemed to have the bar. He was like a regular family man."

So. Momo and Marie packed up and moved to San Diego. Willie the Rat Cammisano went home to Kansas City. Momo and Marie took up residence on Lymer Drive. The neighbors, 40 years later, still remembered the couple's noisy arguments.

Then, on June 19, 1956, the *San Diego Union* noted, in a headline:

Ex-Hoodlum Shoots Wife, Kills Himself, Attempted Slaying, Suicide Climax Quarrel in Kensington Park Home

The report went on to say that Momo Adamo, part-owner of the Gay Paree Tavern and a resident at 4134 Lymer Drive, Kensington Park, during a quarrel with his wife Marie, pointed a .32-caliber pistol at her head and shot her. The bullet entered, circled around the back of her skull, and came out over her eye. She dropped to the floor. Momo then stuck the pistol behind his right ear and pulled the trigger. He fell backwards. The gun dropped at his feet. He died.

Her head veiled in blood, Marie pulled herself up and ran from the house. She collapsed in a front yard 150 feet away. Marie, the *Union* later would report, "was in critical condition at Mercy Hospital. She told police before lapsing into unconsciousness her husband attacked her during a quarrel, choking her and hitting her with a whisky bottle.... Mrs. Adamo did not disclose the cause of the quarrel."

There is a story about why Momo shot Marie and then himself. This story was not printed in the San Diego newspapers.

Ed Reid wrote in *The Grim Reapers*, "The hoodlums have always prided themselves on their respect, not only for their family boss, but also for the women of the family. There are, however, any number of exceptions to the rule. And one such occurred in 1956, when Frank Desimone, according to a police informant, raped the wife of Girolamo (Momo) Adamo in the presence of the shocked husband, who had served the Mafia longer and in more diverse capacities than Desimone. Desimone's action, according to the informant, was undertaken to show Adamo who was boss."

As I stood that chilly February evening on Lamont Street at almost precisely the moment, two decades earlier, that Bompensiero stood there, enjoying, I hope, the 10 to 15 minutes he had left to live, I wondered whatever possessed him to marry Marie. They plighted their troth in Imperial County on June 30, 1969. He was 63. She was 61. Marie had shrunk from her five-foot, four-inch height. She stooped. Where Momo's bullet made its entry, her face was scarred. She was frighteningly thin, her legs so emaciated that her stockings tended to billow about her shrunken calves. If you watched her walk, you'd be likely to describe her gait as a hobble. If you were a gentleman, you'd be likely to offer your arm.

Bompensiero's only child, his daughter Mary Ann, born in 1931 to Frank and his first wife, Thelma (*née* Sanfilippo) Bompensiero, remembered that her father walked into her Clairemont house one morning early in July, 1969. "He had a key to the house. I was still in bed. He came in and stood at the door to my bedroom. 'Honey,' he said, 'get up. I have something to tell you. I want to talk to you.' He sat down and I put some coffee on. He looked across the table at me and said, 'Marie and I got married.' I said, 'Why? Why did you marry her?'"

Mary Ann's mother, Thelma, died in June, 1955. She was 44. She died not quite two weeks after Superior Court Judge John A. ("Hanging John") Hewicker sentenced Bompensiero to serve 3 to 42 years in prison and fined him $15,000 on charges of bribery and conspiracy in liquor-license transactions. Hewicker, addressing the court, noted that Bompensiero had a record dating back to 1928, and added, "I've seldom seen a case where a man has been arrested so many times without being prosecuted."

Bompensiero was sent first to Chino State Prison, and then, for five years, to San Quentin. "Thelma," people will sigh and tell you, "Thelma died of a broken heart."

Thelma Sanfilippo Bompensiero is another story. Thelma is a story all her own.

Years later, talking about her father's second wife, Mary Ann said, "She was such a flirt, Marie was. She flirted so much with my father. My mother would say to my father, 'If anything ever happens to me, Marie is going to come after you.'

"My mother and dad were invited to Momo and Marie's house for dinner one time and they didn't ring the doorbell, because Momo and Marie were yelling and screaming at each other. My mother told me this, that she heard Marie say, 'I'll tell Frank.' And so my mother said to my father, 'What is she going to tell you, Frank?' So the ladies were not crazy about her because she flirted with everybody. She got away with murder, so to speak, compared to what the other wives would do. In other words, she really wasn't that much of a lady. She was but she wasn't."

Bompensiero had always told Mary Ann that he'd never remarry. On the July morning when he sat at the table with Mary Ann, explaining his marriage to Marie, he said, "My grandchildren are getting older, her grandchildren are getting older." He looked down at his hands. He said, "She knows the way of life." Then he laughed, relit his cigar, pulled himself up out of the chair. "Besides that," he said, "a wife cannot testify against her husband."

*Frank and Thelma Bompensiero and Marie and Momo Adamo in early 1950s*

**I like Bompensiero. I can't help it.**

**And I want you to like him too.**

CHAPTER FOUR

# HONOR AND MURDER

By the time Bompensiero exchanged I do's with Marie, he had murdered or attempted to murder or helped murder or helped plan the murder of perhaps a dozen men. Maybe a few more, maybe a few less. But he was not a serial killer or a thrill killer. Nor was he a "killer-for-hire." He did not take money for killing. To kill, for the boss and for the family, was an honor. This was "the work." People would say about Bompensiero, "He did some pretty good work in his time," and what they meant by that was that he killed people. He killed them because the boss told him to kill them. He killed them, because from the point of view of the family, they needed to be dead. He did not see himself as a murderer or a killer, you and I can be sure of that. He saw himself as a worker. So that while he did have blood, euphemistic blood, on the short hands and stubby fingers that he studied as he sat at the kitchen table with his daughter, he did not see this euphemistic blood in the same way that you and I might see this blood. He saw this blood as callus, as the hardened tissue that builds up on a worker's hands.

His daughter adored him then. She adores him now. Frank Bompensiero was a good father, a good grandfather. If he'd been my father or your father, we would have loved him, murders and all.

For years, I drew stories from reluctant and not-so-reluctant Bompensiero relatives and friends and employees and from law enforcement men. I will tell you two of these stories. One is a story Mary Ann tells. Another is a story of one of the murders. I hate to tell about the murders. One reason I hate to tell about the murders is that I don't like for Mary Ann to be reminded of them. Another reason is that I don't like to be reminded. I like Bompensiero. I can't help it. And I want you to like him too. I know I should not feel this way. But I do.

Mary Ann said that this must have happened before she started grade school. "I had done something bad, misbehaved in some way. I can't tell you, now, what I did. But I remember, my mother was chasing me around the house. I was probably driving her nuts. She wanted to smack me. She never beat me, but sometimes she would smack my butt. My father looked up from his newspaper and stood up out of his chair. I ran behind him and grabbed onto him around his knees. He said to my mom, 'Thelma, come on, honey. She's just a baby. Leave her alone. Get it out of your system. Hit me. Hit me, baby.'"

I will tell you about one of the murders. Many people already know about this murder. They know about it because it appears in Ovid Demaris's best-seller, *The Last Mafioso*. This murder took place in June, 1952, in a pretty little house set along South Hempstead Circle in Kensington. I drove by this house one day. I pulled over and stopped and looked at it and thought about the story I am going to tell you. The house, according to Demaris's book, belonged to Momo's brother Joe.

Anyway, a fellow named Frank Borgia, who'd made significant money as a "sugar man," supplying sugar to makers of whiskey during Prohibition, was invited to San Diego to a wedding of the daughter of a family friend. He got in his black Buick Roadmaster and drove from Los Angeles to downtown San Diego. He took a room at the U.S. Grant and drove to St. Joseph's Cathedral. After the wedding, guests stood about the cathedral's portal, tossing rice. In one of the photographs, Borgia can be seen, smiling. This would be the last photograph taken of Frank Borgia. Unbeknownst to Borgia, Jack Dragna had ordered him murdered for his refusal to "cut up his money" with a family member. Dragna had assigned Bompensiero to organize the killing.

Wedding over, Borgia returned to the Grant. According to what Jimmy the Weasel Fratianno years later would tell Demaris, this is what happened. Early that June evening, Tony Mirabile, a local San Diego bar owner, reputed to be San Diego's mob boss, came by to take Borgia out for the evening.

Demaris writes, "Seated in Bompensiero's office at the Gold Rail, Jimmy was listening as Bompensiero went over the plan he had worked out for the hit. 'I've got Tony Mirabile to set him up. He's his best friend. That way Frank won't suspect nothing. Tony will take him to Joe Adamo's house and we'll be there waiting for them. We get the rope around his neck and that's it.'"

And that, according to Demaris's *Last Mafioso*, is just what happened.

"At eight o'clock, Jimmy and Bompensiero were standing on either side of the door when Tony Mirabile brought his best friend, Frank Borgia, to Joe Adamo's house. Jimmy had the rope in his hands and as Bomp kicked the door shut, Mirabile wrapped his arms around Borgia just as Jimmy dropped the garrote over his head, handing the other end of the rope to Bompensiero. Within ten seconds, Borgia was sinking to his knees. Mirabile released him and he fell on his face, with Jimmy and Bompensiero dropping to the floor with him, lying beside him and holding the rope firm, squeezing out the last breath of life. Like all the other victims of the Italian rope trick, Frank Borgia died with a surprised expression on his face."

Five days later, when Borgia had not returned to his room at the Grant, a hotel employee called the police. Borgia's Roadmaster was impounded.

Borgia's body was never found. Never. "It's probably out there buried in some vineyard," someone told me.

I asked a friend of Bompensiero's, a good friend, a man who knew Bompensiero as an older man and knew him well, if Bompensiero ever expressed remorse about the murders. This man snorted. "Frank said that if God hadn't wanted 'em dead, he would've stopped the bullets. That's what Frank said."

While I waited for Paul Ybarrando, I walked south from the gas station toward what had been Bompensiero's apartment. I was walking toward the spot where Bompensiero would have taken his last step. This is the walk I hope you will want to take. I looked up. Lights were turned on in the third-floor corner windows where Bompensiero had lived. I imagined his walking along Lamont, puffing on his cigar. I'd never smoked a cigar. Did you puff? Or inhale? I imagined the dimes left from making the telephone call, the thin silver discs warm in his wide palm. I wondered if he'd had dinner that night. The autopsy didn't mention stomach contents.

I had arrived, I realized, only feet away from the fence, what 20 years earlier was described as "a tall picket fence." This would be the fence behind which Bompensiero's assailant or assailants (but probably assailant) was hiding—hiding in wait—that night. He would have held the gun in his hand. When Ybarrando arrived, I would ask him how, if you were the assailant, and were waiting, you would hold the gun. The weapon. In a way, I was not anxious for Ybarrando to arrive. Because when he did pull up and jump down out of his truck and walk to where I stood, shake my hand, and say, "Good evening," then Bompensiero would begin to seem truly dead. We would talk about the murder. I wanted to think about, to try to understand, the life. I was not as interested in the death. But only when he died did he become fully who he was. I knew that, too.

**A woman remembered Frank as a child, "He was a nice little boy, quiet, with a big round face."**

CHAPTER FIVE

# MILWAUKEE

Giuseppe and Anna Maria (*née* Tagliavia) Bompensiero were born and raised in Porticello, Sicily, a fishing village 13 miles outside Palermo, between Palermo and Messina. ("The way I understand it," said someone whose grandparents were born in Porticello, "is that Porticello is to Palermo like Mission Beach is to San Diego.") Giuseppe and Anna Maria both were children of fishermen and, according to one of their surviving daughters, "My mother and father knew each other, from the beginning."

In 1904, soon after they married, the young couple, together with members of the Balistrieri family, left Porticello and sailed to New York. They were not alone. Between 1901 and 1910, some 2,045,877 Italians and Sicilians fled economically troubled Italy for America. By 1910, so many Italians had left that Italy's Supervisor of Emigration noted that in certain parts of southern Italy, where economic conditions were direst, "it amounts to a general exodus. In some places the village priest and the doctor, having lost their flock, have followed them to America. Certain municipalities have had to be consolidated and the parish church abandoned."

From New York, the Bompensieros and Balistrieris made a two-day train trip to Milwaukee, Wisconsin, located on the shore of Lake Michigan, some 80 miles north of Chicago. First settled by non-Indians as a fur-trading post in 1795, Milwaukee was a major center of German immigration during the last half of the 19th century and noted for its breweries and meat-packing plants. Strange that this icy city on the banks of Lake Michigan, where snowfalls could measure six feet and temperatures drop below zero and stay there for days, lured Sicilians. These were people accustomed to olive, fig, citrus, and almond trees, to grapevines, to waters that offered up tuna and silvery sardines, to weather not unlike that of Southern California.

Giuseppe Bompensiero may have gone earlier than 1904 and then returned to Porticello and brought back his new wife. The 1902 Milwaukee telephone book shows a John and a Joseph Bompensiero, laborer, living at 154 Huron Street.

Most of the southern Italian immigrants had few skills, little if any schooling, and could not read and write even in their own language. Few, before leaving for the United States, had ever been outside their native village. Most were from the peasant class—*cafoni*—rubes, hicks. Some say that Giuseppe

Bompensiero shoveled coal for the railroad; some say he worked in one of Milwaukee's breweries. He may have done both. The 1913 Milwaukee telephone book lists a Joseph Buonpensiero (one of the name's earlier spellings) as living at 331 Cass, and next to employment—Saloon. Neither Giuseppe nor his wife spoke much, if any, English.

Frank Bompensiero was born September 29, 1905, in Milwaukee, his parents' firstborn. Whether he was born at home, with a midwife's help, or in a hospital, I don't know. Likely, he was born at home. During this time, Italian immigrant women were delivered at home by Italian midwives. Neither the state of Wisconsin nor Milwaukee has any record of Frank's birth. His sister Josephine was born two years later.

We do know this. As a toddler, Bompensiero was a brown-eyed blonde. His loose curls were so extraordinarily blond that his parents and their friends and neighbors called him *figlio d'oro*, "son of gold." Although no records exist to prove whether or not Frank was baptized, surely he was. His mother, who would live to be 92, attended Mass daily until she was felled, at 90, by a broken hip.

Southern Italian immigrants, unlike the Irish, tended not to send their children to parochial schools. Southern Italians were wary of the institutional church, in part because of its association with Rome and the Italian government. Once arrived in America, these immigrants found new reason for discomfort. American clerics were predominantly Irish. The Irish priests tended to look down on their Italian parishioners, feeling that the Italians' worship emphasized pageantry and pagan custom over piety. The Italian parishioners, for their part, tended to be immune to sermons whose language they barely understood.

Frank attended Andrew Jackson grade school. I talked with a woman in Milwaukee who remembered Frank as a child. "He was a nice little boy, quiet, with a big round face," she said, adding that he always had clean clothes and good manners and that she was surprised when, years later, she heard that he became "such a bad, bad boy." Frank attended school through the third grade and then quit. (According to an FBI report acquired through the Freedom of Information Act, Bompensiero, when filling out a prison form at San Quentin penitentiary in May, 1955, listed, in the blank that asked for "education," that he "completed third grade at Andrew Jackson Elementary School, Milwaukee, Wisconsin.") Milwaukee city directories for this time show a Frank Bompensiero working in a bar. This, too, wasn't unheard of in those days. Young Bompensiero might have been washing glasses or sweeping up.

An elderly Milwaukee resident, a man born in Milwaukee to Sicilian parents who also came from Porticello, told me that Sicilians began arriving in

Milwaukee in the late 1890s. The Cravello family, whose home was near Porticello, was among the first Sicilian settlers. From Palermo the Alioto clan, the same clan that eventually would produce a mayor of San Francisco, Joseph Alioto, who successfully would sue *Look* magazine for its insinuations that he associated with *mafiosi*, came and settled both in Milwaukee and San Francisco. The huge Balistrieri family, one of whose descendants who for many years would be considered Milwaukee's Mafia overlord, sent many of its members to Wisconsin.

"People would come to Milwaukee," the elderly Milwaukeean said, "and then write back and say, 'Come here. There's work.' There were jobs, menial work for the monolingual Italians. They worked for the railroads laying track, worked for the coal companies and ice companies, then also they worked for the sanitation department and they worked for the steel foundries that were here in Milwaukee on the near south side."

He said that gradually, other Sicilians, many from Porticello, made their way to Milwaukee—Guardalebenes, Busallachis, Catallanos, Tagliavias, Sanfilippos, San Filippis, Cravellos, Carinis, more Aliotos, more Balistrieris, Bompensieros. "Those guys who came to America were the more adventurous."

Once in America, immigrants moved into neighborhoods already settled by family and friends. In these Little Italys, immigrants replicated institutional arrangements that had held together their home villages—the mutual aid society, the *padrone* system, the parish, the criminal society. While the larger culture regarded anyone from Italy as simply "Italian," the immigrants, particularly among the first generation, took identity from distinctions rooted in village, provincial, and regional origins.

The Sicilians settled, my Milwaukee informant said, in Milwaukee's Third Ward. "The Third Ward was nestled right behind the downtown area in Milwaukee. It was bounded by the Milwaukee River on the west and Lake Michigan on the east. The Irish had been in first, then the Italians came. They followed the same pattern, regardless of what city they went to. They lived together. The people from my dad's hometown, Porticello, lived on Van Buren Street. They would group themselves. The Third Ward had the ambiance of a Little Italy, a grocery store on every corner, taverns, the Italian church—Our Lady of Pompeii. It was a beautiful church, which in 1957 they knocked down for urban renewal. The church went down, that was the last stand of the old Third Ward.

"These people lived only a block away from the lake. They could fish. However, they could not make a living with fishing. They would go there on their own to catch fish for themselves. All that freezing ice in the winter sent many back to Italy or to California because the winters are so harsh here.

"Once they got to Milwaukee, they started gardens. They were small, very small gardens. There wasn't much space in that Third Ward in back yards. They would have a duplex in front and then a small cottage behind. What they did was they would rent space from a farm and they would go out every Sunday or in the evenings and work these patches of land. They would get loaded up in a wagon with a horse, it takes only ten minutes in a car now, but then, God, how long it took."

Some Sicilian immigrants, said the Milwaukeean, began to sell produce. "Some of the biggest produce houses here in Milwaukee were founded by Italians. They cornered the produce market. My grandfather in the summer, he and his brothers-in-law, made ice cream. They would make it and sell it on Saturdays and Sundays. They built up quite a business in ice cream.

"Then there was lighter industry. Many Third Ward residents walked to work. Only two blocks away from Milwaukee Street there were factories that manufactured clothing and shoes. They made a lot of shoes! There were many little candy companies. My mother came to Milwaukee when she was two years old. She told me that factory managers actually came into the Third Ward and went house to house, recruiting young grade-school girls to work in the candy factory. Also to work in the shoe factory.

"The women, a lot of them, supplemented the husbands' income by doing odd jobs. Some of our stores, department stores, especially those that catered to the high society, used to sell lacy tops. My grandmother worked at home, making those tops. She tatted and crocheted. Many women did that kind of work—making lace for underwear, for bedspreads, curtains. Also, some families started little corner stores and while the husband was out working on the railroad, which many of the men did, the women minded the store.

"Our Lady of Pompeii was where they met, got married, baptized, courted, buried, everything. Right across from the church was Andrew Jackson school. It was a three-story building with a tower, built in the 1870s. The ceilings must have been 15 feet high. It was a cream-colored brick, Milwaukee brick.

"Milwaukee led the country in encouraging its immigrants to go to school. We had manual training courses and citizenship classes. Most immigrant parents worked hard to keep their kids in school. Maybe there were some parents who pulled their kids out of school to help supplement the family income. They shined shoes and sold newspapers downtown or worked on the railroad alongside their fathers. If an Italian or Sicilian youngster left school early, rest assured, it was because he had to work."

My Milwaukee friend explained that as in other American cities, there was tension in Milwaukee between Italians from northern Italy and Sicilians.

"The northern Italians lived on the south side. The majority were Piedmontese. There were also Italians from Venice and Padua and from Predappio, where Mussolini was born. They considered themselves superior to the southern Italians and Sicilians. They didn't want to have anything to do with them. Even back home they didn't want to have anything to do with them. The northern people figured southern people were backward, that they all carried knives, the usual prejudices.

"The northern Italians were pretty well settled in here by 1910. What added to tension between the northern Italians and Sicilians was that the Irish priest on the south side where they lived refused to marry and bury them. He said, 'You've got your own church. You go down there to the Italian church.' So the south side Italians all went to Our Lady of Pompeii. In 1917, the Sicilians from the Third Ward, they were antagonized by the people on the south side and the Sicilians went over there and had a big shoot-out. Well, then a couple of them died. There was an evangelistic church in the Third Ward. They were Sicilians from the Third Ward who were disillusioned with the priest and had bad experiences with the church in Sicily. These people got involved in this Methodist evangelistic church. They would get together and go over to the south side and play their portable organ and sing Methodist hymns. The south side Italians didn't like this. They said, 'We don't want you here. Get out.' That's when that fight ensued.

"Somebody put a bomb outside the Methodist church. It was a Saturday afternoon. The cleaning lady found it. She didn't know what to do with it. She had a son and went to him and told him to take the bomb to the police station, which was about three blocks away. He did. The police started looking at the bomb and it blew up. It killed nine policemen, right there in the building. It also killed some detectives, how many I don't know. But there was pandemonium after that. They arrested people in the Third Ward. They went to the south side and got those people all riled up. Oh, it was bad."

Almost half of the Italians who came to the United States early in the century eventually returned to Italy. Like many illegal and legal Mexican immigrants today, these Italians had come to America to make money. Once they had acquired their "nut," they went home, bought land, and stayed. Both of the Bompensieros, however, became American citizens. So it seems likely that they had intended to remain.

**"I used to ask my father,**

**'Daddy, what is the Mafia?'"**

CHAPTER SIX

# WE'RE SICILIANS

Mary Ann wishes she knew more about her father's early years. What she does know, she said, is that "By 1915 my grandfather Bompensiero was getting ill or wasn't feeling good, because of the weather, because it was so cold in Milwaukee, so the family went back to Porticello. After that, my father never did go to school again. He started in Sicily working with his father as a fisherman."

The Bompensieros returned to Porticello and moved into a two-story house, "a pretty house," someone said, "an old-timer's house with a beautiful marble stairway." Four more children, a son, Sam, and three daughters were born.

Of the four or five years Frank spent in Sicily, one can learn next to nothing. From 1914 to 1918 the war that began as a fracas between Austria-Hungary and Serbia became a global war that mired 32 nations in battle. Italy joined forces with Great Britain, France, the United States, and Russia to oppose Germany, Austria-Hungary, Turkey, and Bulgaria. Frank could read and write. Mary Ann reports that he always was interested in the news. Certainly, he must have followed the war's progress. Perhaps he was aware that in Milan, after the war's end, Mussolini founded his *Fasci di Combattimento* party, a party that would by 1922 have gained sufficient power that Italy's King Victor Emmanuel III would invite Mussolini to form a coalition government. Perhaps he was not interested in what went on up north. Like many Sicilians, he would always be somewhat distrustful of northern Italians. And northern Italians, of course, looked down on the Sicilians, derisively referring to them as "Africans" and worse.

Mary Ann, talking about this distrust, one day said, "The Bompensiero side was so fair, that people thought we were from Rome. Northern Italy. They're blondes, redheads, they have blue eyes. My father always said that on the Bompensiero side of the family, there was an illegitimate child born from royal blood. This duke or whatever, along the line, got somebody pregnant and that's where the blond came from. He used to say, and this will kill Italians to hear this, but he regularly would say, 'Don't you ever be ashamed of what you are. Whatever you are, be a good one and don't ever be ashamed.' And he said, 'We're not Italian, we're not goddamn spaghetti benders, we're Sicilians and don't ever be ashamed of it."

A San Diegan of Sicilian extraction told me, one day, about differences between northern and southern Italian. "The northern speak a different dialect. Sicilians speak Sicilian, not the real Italian. We have a dialect. If someone talks to me in the real Italian, I could not understand them. The old language, the Sicilian dialect, I understand. The northern part of Italy, they are more to themselves, they stick with their own group. The Sicilians are more warm than northerners. What we got, we give it to you. We are really friendly."

Bompensiero would have absorbed the attitudes of his fellow Sicilians. The Sicilians, at the toe of the boot of Italy, had been occupied, century after century, by foreigners. Their loyalties tended not to be to parties or powers but to the family and to institutions, like the Mafia, founded in the family. A Harvard University professor described the ethic produced by utter fealty to family and distrust of outsiders as an "amoral familism that placed family ahead of society." This ethic, he wrote, produced "excellent criminals."

The Mafia was strong in Palermo. Bompensiero would have heard the stories. He would have met, or seen, from a distance, the "men of respect." He would have been interested in them, interested in the stories. He might well have felt drawn to them.

"When I was growing up," Mary Ann said, "I used to ask my father, 'Daddy, what is the Mafia?' And he'd say, 'Honey, what are you talking about? That's the olden days. No such thing anymore as the Mafia. No such thing. All a bunch of bullshit.' He would say things, drop things, to me. Like in 1974, when Patty Hearst was kidnapped, he told me, 'The FBI contacted us to get help finding Patty Hearst. We have some connections and we asked around, but she doesn't want to come home.' And when Hoffa was missing, along in 1975, Daddy said, 'They'll never find him.' But he never said, 'There is or isn't a Mafia,' only that there used to be a Mafia, that it was in the olden days, and that it was no more."

# Liquor Tanks Hidden in Ceiling Of Apartment, Piped to Ordinary Taps; How to Get Them Out Is Problem

What was said to be one of the most cleverly concealed liquor plants uncovered here since the advent of prohibition, was discovered last night when members of the police dry detail, led by George Sears, lieutenant of detectives, raided an apartment house at 1907 Columbia street. The officers seized 60 gallons of wine, 25 gallons of whisky, 25 gallons of gin and 20 gallons of alcohol. Frank Buonpensiero was arrested as the owner of the liquor.

Four large copper tanks in which the liquor was stored, were concealed between the second floor and the ceiling of the first floor apartment. From each tank led copper pipes, all concealed either in the walls or the floors of the building to a secret compartment in a closet in a ground floor apartment occupied by Buonpensiero. Each tank was a separate compartment for the storage of liquor and in the compartment in the closet was fitted with a neat faucet. Thus, the liquor could be drawn from the storage tanks as one would draw a glass of water.

The officers who made the raid were Lieutenant Sears, Sergt. R. W. Chadwick and Patrolmen T. E. Osborne and Mike Shea.

When the officers entered the apartment house they searched it from the roof to the basement without finding any trace of liquor, or a spot where it might have been hid. They were about to give up the search when the keen eyesight and acute sense of smell of Lieutenant Sears led to the discovery.

Sears was alone in an unoccupied apartment on the second floor. He smelled what he was certain was the odor of whisky. Then he opened a small compartment used for keeping cooking utensils. It was bare, but he noticed the flooring of the compartment, adjoining the flour bin, was slightly stained. Calling the other officers, Sears tore out the flour bin and beneath it found the tops of four pipes. Each pipe had a neat screw top.

Under questioning by Sears Buonpensiero admitted the presence of the storage tanks and explained how they had been placed between the flooring and ceiling of two apartments. He also led the officers to the secret

*From the San Diego Union, May 15, 1930*

**They got husbands down on their knees and made them "take the pledge."**

CHAPTER SEVEN

# WHY WE WENT DRY

Had Congress in 1919 not ratified the 18th Amendment to the Constitution, which prohibited "the manufacture, sale, or transportation of intoxicating liquors" within all 48 states and then passed the National Prohibition Act, which provided for enforcement of the 18th Amendment, Frank Bompensiero might well have become a fisherman and died in his sleep in the back bedroom of a little house on Columbia Street. You may not want to read the next few paragraphs, about Prohibition and prohibitionists, but they are important to understanding how Bompensiero came to do what he did.

From the time of the settlement of the American colonies, there had been movements to end the sales of spirits. By the first quarter of the 19th Century, alcohol abuse had come to be considered a serious social problem in the United States. Statistics gathered during the 1830s indicate that Americans were heavy drinkers; per capita, hard liquor consumption was 7.1 gallons (given that male abstainers, and women, children, and slaves would not have consumed their per capita portion makes likely that drinkers drank far more than the 7.1 gallons). More and more of the nation's leaders began to comment publicly on the evils of drink. Abraham Lincoln, while still serving in the Illinois legislature, noted with more eloquence than most, that during his youth alcoholic beverages "had come forth like the Egyptian angel of death, commissioned to slay, if not the first, the fairest born in every family." By 1852, prohibition laws that permitted cities and counties to vote for dry status as a local option had been enacted in Louisiana, Maine, Massachusetts, and Vermont. Thirteen of the 31 states, including New Hampshire, Delaware, New York, Michigan, Iowa, had such laws by 1855.

After the Civil War's end women increasingly involved themselves in temperance activities. In 1869, the National Temperance Convention met in Chicago and formed the Prohibition Party. In 1874, delegates from 17 states met in Cleveland, Ohio, to form the Woman's Christian Temperance Union (WCTU), the first national broad-based women's group in America. The union's president, Frances Willard, encouraged women (who would not be given the vote in all states of the Union until 1920) in their role as protectors of the home to take to the streets and demand that saloon doors be closed. They did, and WCTU women held prayer vigils in streets outside saloons in almost every major American city. They marched from churches to saloons and demanded that saloon owners close their doors. They got husbands down on their knees and made them "take the pledge" to never again let liquor pass their lips. Hatchet in hand, Carry Nation, in 1890, began leading groups of similarly armed women through Kansas saloons and spirit shops where they smashed glasses and bottles.

More than alcohol fueled temperance movements. As immigrants to the United States increased in number, so did criminal activity, unemployment, out-of-wedlock births, wife-beating, and general mayhem. Many of the new immigrants were from countries where the Roman Catholic Church held ascendancy and where wine, regularly, was drunk. These new immigrants and drunkenness quickly became associated in the minds of America's older, more settled Protestant majority.

Prohibitionists gradually transformed themselves from reform groups to political activists. The Anti-Saloon League (ASL) in 1895 held its first national convention. ASL leaders enrolled mainline Protestant churches in the prohibition effort, encouraging local political action on the part of individual congregations. Guided by ASL leadership, these congregations organized support for pro-prohibition political candidates and succeeded in electing dry men to Congress and state legislatures. By 1900 millions of women and men in the United States were expressing hostility toward alcohol use and had come to regard alcoholic beverages as the most dangerous threat to the nation.

As Americans grew increasingly concerned about social instability, moral decline, and the growing numbers of immigrants (in 1911, 637,003 immigrants entered the United States), there was no political question as treacherous for politicians as prohibition. And, to many voters there was then no more important political question. Prohibitionists organized noisy and effective campaigns for state and local bans on liquor sales. More than half the states, led by the South and West, had dry laws of varying degrees of strictness. Congress outlawed liquor sales on Indian reservations and in the District of Columbia. In 1916 national elections returned a Congress in which dry members outnumbered wets two to one.

April 2, 1917, President Woodrow Wilson asked Congress to declare war on Germany. "The world," he said, in a phrase upon whose irony Americans would long reflect, "must be made safe for democracy." As one after another American unit was landed in France (180,000 American soldiers were fighting in Europe by the end of 1917), prohibitionists added to their numbers by equating prohibitionism with patriotism, anti-prohibitionists with anti-Americanism, and German brewers with the German enemy. A wartime temperance pamphlet vociferated against "the foreigner, alien to the principle of Americanism" who "sets a trap for the boy and girl and cultivates the appetite that is later exploited by the owner of brewery stock in Germany who uses his tainted wealth to buy poison gas or liquid fire to torture the troops of the Allies."

Before the year was out, Congress had passed the War Prohibition Act, forbidding sales of alcoholic beverages to members of the armed forces and restricting alcohol production as a grain conservation measure. So strong then had prohibition fervor become that by December, 1917, nine months after President Wilson declared war on Germany, Congress had adopted a resolution providing for submission to the states of a national prohibition amendment to the Constitution, prohibiting manufacture, sale, or transportation of beverages containing more than one-half of 1 percent alcohol within the United States, and sent the measure to the states for ratification.

January 16, 1919, three months after the Great War ended, when Nebraska cast its vote for prohibition, the amendment had been adopted by ample majorities in all but two states (Connecticut and Rhode Island). Prohibition throughout the United States then was slated to come into effect exactly one year later, on January 16, 1920.

Nationwide, various loosely and not so loosely organized groups who engaged in criminal activity were already in place when Prohibition closed down saloons and ended liquor sales. As immigrants arrived in the United States from Ireland, China, from Eastern Europe, Germany, and Italy, and settled in American cities, some among these immigrants found illegal ways to earn money. The Irish had the Plug Uglies and Dead Rabbits. The Chinese had their Tongs. From Italy associates of the Neapolitan Black Hand and Sicilian Mafia continued in America what they had learned back home. Many early ethnic criminal groups grew out of protection and influence-peddling systems. The Irish or Italian or Jewish gang member would sell "protection" to shops in his neighborhood and help find jobs for his newly arrived kinsmen or place bribes in the hands of the proper authorities in order to get a young man out of trouble. Stolen goods might be fenced through such groups and murders and disappearances arranged. But all this was petty and local compared to what happened with the advent of Prohibition. The illegal sale of liquor promised—and quickly delivered—enormous fortunes.

# Frank Bompensiero, San Diego Crime Boss, Slain Gang Style

By MITCH HIMAKA
and NEIL BALL
Staff Writers, The San Diego Union

Frank Bompensiero, 71, described as one of the top three Mafia bosses on the West Coast, was shot to death last night gangland-style, a few steps from his Pacific Beach home.

Police said Bompensiero, who lived at 4205 Lamont St., Apt. 7, appeared to have been shot four times with a .22-caliber automatic pistol, a weapon capable of being silenced and often used in gangland executions.

Officers said robbery was not the motive since his wallet was found on his body.

**FOUND ON SIDEWALK**

Bompensiero, also known as Frank Gavin, was found on the sidewalk at the head of an alley that runs west from Lamont Street, about half way between Thomas and Reed avenues.

Police said he appeared to be alive when they arrived at the scene but was pronounced dead on arrival at Mission Bay General Hospital.

Bompensiero was found about 8:30 p.m. in a pool of blood with his trademark, a cigar. Around the body were four spent .22 caliber cartridge cases.

Capt. Wesley Allen, commander of the crimes against persons detail, said there were no witnesses to the shooting. He said no one reported hearing any shots or hearing any cars speeding away. The cartridge cases indicated he had been shot with an automatic pistol.

Police said a neighbor in the 4300 block of Lamont Street called police reporting an injured man in an alley. They said Bompensiero often took evening walks in the neighborhood.

**MANY CRIME TIES**

Law enforcement intelligence officers said Bompensiero was a known associate of such organized crime figures as Joseph (Joe Bananas) Bonanno, deposed New York-New Jersey Mafia boss now living in virtual exile in Tucson, Ariz.; James (Jimmy the Weasel) Fratianno, described by a Los Angeles intelligence officer as "West Coast executioner for the Mafia"; the late Jack Dragna, once named as the state's top racket boss; the late Nick Licata; and the late Mickey Cohen.

[illegible] Joseph Valachi, the late mobster who testified before the McClellan Committee in 1957, as the Los Angeles Mafia chief.

Police listed Bompensiero as one of the three men in line for the top spot after Licata's death in October, 1974.

Others named as possible successors to Licata were Frank Reggie of Los Angeles and Bonanno.

**DATED TO '28**

Bompensiero's crime record dated back to [illegible] with a bootlegging conviction.

He also was convicted in 1954 for bribing public officials in a state liquor license scandal and served five years in prison.

Bompensiero and Fratianno both were charged in connection with an Imperial Valley trucking scandal in 1966 but charges against Bompensiero later were dismissed for lack of evidence.

**SUSPECT IN SLAYING**

In 1941, Bompensiero was arrested by Los Angeles police on suspicion of kidnaping and murder in connection with the mysterious disappearance of Victor Carlino, an employe of the [illegible]

*From the San Diego Union, Friday, February 11, 1977*

**"And then Lassie would save somebody,**

**a person or an animal.**

**While Daddy watched all this,**

**tears would roll down."**

CHAPTER EIGHT

# THE LAST DAYS

Mary Ann believes that her father returned to the United States at some point in 1921. "My father's youngest sister, Patrina, is the one who was born last," said Mary Ann, "in 1921. Soon after Patrina was born, my father came back to the United States, to Milwaukee, and then, later that year, to San Diego. He was 16."

Bompensiero lived in San Diego for most of the next 56 years, give or take a few years here and a few months there. He did time on McNeil Island. He was gone for a year or two, hiding out after a murder he helped commit in Los Angeles. He served for a year in his nation's armed forces during World War II. He spent five years in Chino and San Quentin. He lived, briefly, in El Centro.

By 1977 many years would have passed since Bompensiero last wrapped a garrote around someone's neck. He was an old man who slowly maneuvered about town in a battered light brown Mustang. He and Marie drove the Mustang the few blocks to Pacific Plaza where they shopped at Vons. Back in 1977 you could smoke just about anywhere except church, and Bompensiero, as he pushed the grocery cart down Vons aisles, always had a cigar clamped between his teeth. He chewed his cigars, hard, left teeth marks in the brown leaf.

His heart wasn't great. According to the autopsy of his body, his kidneys weren't so good, either. He had high blood pressure, for which he took medication. He wore heavy black-rimmed eyeglasses with thick lenses. He had problems with cataracts. He tired easily. Afternoons, he stretched out on the couch and napped.

Bompensiero, in January, 1977, had cataract surgery. Mary Ann remembered that he was in the hospital during Jimmy Carter's inauguration. "He called me up. He said, 'Baby, I'm watching television with my bionic eye.' Then he'd stop talking a minute and you knew something on the TV had gotten his attention. Then he said, 'I'm watching them walk down the street....' " After Bompensiero got out of the hospital, he made an effort to walk around the neighborhood during the day to get back his strength.

Early in February, columnist Neil Morgan saw Bompensiero in the elevator of a Sixth Avenue medical building. According to Morgan's account in the *San Diego Evening Tribune*, Bompensiero "quickly put out his hand with his old bright smile: 'I'm just an old man now, Mister Neil,' he said. 'No harm. No trouble. Just an old man.'"

Monday, February 7, Bompensiero met friends for lunch at Tarantino's on North Harbor Drive in Point Loma. He'd been eating at Tarantino's for years. He liked Tarantino's cracked crab. He liked the service. He liked his big table near the bar. He liked the view, out onto the water.

According to a report written, after Bompensiero's death, by the *San Diego Union*'s Mitch Himaka,

"From 12:55 p.m. to 1:30 p.m., five men sat in a booth at Tarantino's Restaurant in Point Loma enjoying their lunch and talking. The subject under discussion was a federal grand jury indictment which named two of the men."

At lunch that day with Bompensiero were Chris Petti, now in prison; a fellow named Robert Bertram Benjamin; David Gottlieb; and Larry Saunders, also known as Erwin Goldstein.

Himaka noted that "Benjamin and Gottlieb, along with Arthur F. Schulman and Earl John Rodde and Beach Cities Coatings and Construction Co., 722 Genevieve St., Solana Beach, had been indicted three days earlier by a federal grand jury. They were charged with one count of conspiracy and 10 counts of causing false statements to be filed in loan applications to federally insured lending institutions. The five men were discussing the actions that would be taken with regard to the indictment, according to intelligence sources."

Thursday, February 10, Bompensiero got up early. The sun was shining. It was going to be another pretty day. He cared about pretty days. He liked good weather. He dressed in dark green slacks, a white, short-sleeved shirt, and a rust brown cardigan. Nobody remembers what Marie wore that day, or, what her mood was, or whether she cared about the weather. Bompensiero walked around the neighborhood, smoked his cigar. At noon, he met his lawyer, Nicholas DePento, at Tarantino's. They sat at Bompensiero's usual table. In November, 1976, DePento had accompanied Bompensiero to Los Angeles for an appearance before a federal grand jury that was investigating pornography and pornographers. Bompensiero refused to testify. DePento said, after the hearing, "I never advocate talking freely to any police agency without benefit of counsel." He said, about Bompensiero, "He totally objects to pornography and he wouldn't even watch an R-rated movie in his motel room." I think that is accurate, that Bompensiero would not willingly have watched pornographic films.

Mary Ann said that her father never missed *Lassie*. "He would lie on the couch and watch *Lassie* on Sunday nights and cry like a baby. Absolutely would cry. Tears would roll down his eyes. I'm not kidding you. We had these love seats. My mother'd be on one side of the fireplace, I'd be curled up on the other side, and my dad stretched out on the couch. My mother would nudge me, to look over at Daddy. He would just be absolutely tearful. There would be Lassie's human 'mom,' June Lockhart, whose name on the show was Mrs. Martin, and Jon Provost, who played this orphan who was called, I think, 'Timmy,' was the kid in the show. There'd be maybe a weird noise that Timmy would hear or he'd smell smoke, and he'd say, 'Lassie, what is it, girl?' And then Lassie would save somebody, a person or an animal. While Daddy watched all this, tears would roll down and then when the show was over, he'd get up and chew on a cigar and go to the bathroom and come back, and something else was on and that was that."

On the evening of February 10, 1977, at 7:00 p.m., Bompensiero had only 90 minutes left to live. A *Lassie* rerun was shown on television from 7:00 p.m. to 7:30 p.m. I hope that Bompensiero stretched out on his couch and watched it. I hope he had a good cry.

When he walked out on the street that evening to go to the Arco station, skies were clear. You could see the stars. Temperatures were in the mid-50s. Lights were on in the small houses along Lamont Street. Television sets glowed from windows. People were watching *The Waltons* and *Mobil Oil Presents*. Bompensiero dialed whomever he dialed. They did or did not answer. He turned, then, and started walking south, on Lamont, back toward the Beach Club.

Somewhere, nearby, the parked car, motor humming, waits for him. The gunman, surely, by now, has stepped out of the "getaway car." He lurks, in the dark, most likely behind the fence. Gripping the .22-caliber automatic, he waits. "Gunman," "getaway car," "gripping," this, to me, is like the black-and-white gangster movies that as a child I watched on Saturday afternoons. Just the words "getaway car" make me smell popcorn. But for all that this moment is a cliché movie moment, it is not uninteresting to think about. What, for instance, goes through the gunman's mind? What does he see, as he stands here, maybe behind the fence, peering out perhaps, toward Grand Avenue. Can he see Bompensiero walk toward him? Can he hear his footsteps? Can he smell the smoke from Bompensiero's cigar? Does he think that soon he will do to Bompensiero what Bompensiero did to so many men?

Always when I get to this point, I want to slow down the action. I want to keep him alive for a few more minutes. I want him to hear a suspicious noise or see the gun's metallic glint. I want him to say, "Lassie, what is it, girl?" So, for another moment, I let him warm the three dimes in his meaty palm. I urge him to take another puff on the cigar. I suggest that he pull the rust-colored cardigan closed against the chill. I am so cold.

Even if we went back 20 years and yelled, "Run, Frank, run!" it would be too late. Besides, Bompensiero was too old to run.

Bompensiero strolled. He wasn't a rapid walker.

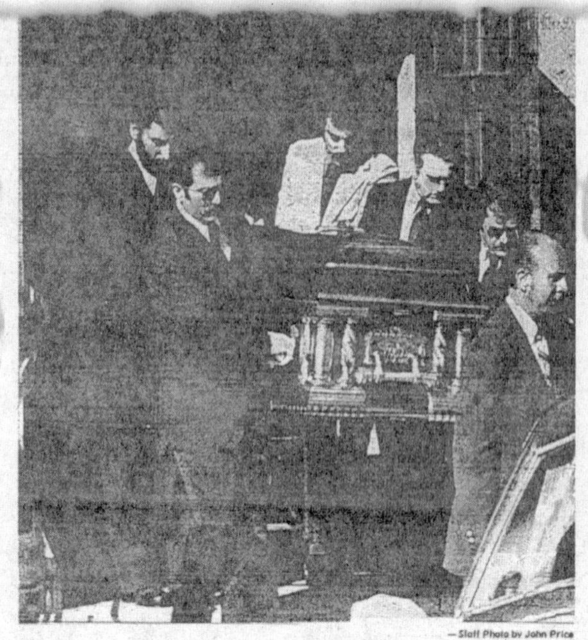

— Staff Photo by John Price

Bronzed casket bearing the body of Frank Bompensiero, who was shot to death Thursday in Pacific Beach, is carried out of Our Lady of the Rosary Roman Catholic Church following funeral yesterday.

*REPORTER TELLS OF THREAT*

# Bompensiero's Funeral Draws 300 To Church

The long, slow process of interviewing associates of the late Frank Bompensiero, reputed Mafia boss in the San Diego area, started yesterday as he was laid to rest.

Maria Bompensiero, the slain man's widow, was dressed in black and was helped by family members and close friends up the steps into the church.

McMahan said the man threatened to break the crew's camera and then threatened to hit McMahan if they did not leave.

However, the funeral

"Powder tattooing in his ear.

You only get that from a very

close-range shot."

CHAPTER NINE

# LAMONT STREET

Bompensiero translates, roughly, into English as "beautiful thought." Tagliavia, Bompensiero's mother's maiden name, in English, can mean "short street." When I first learned these meanings was when I began to think about how the "beautiful thought" and the "short street" sought each other out in the dark of Maria Tagliavia Bompensiero's womb and how on this dark night the "beautiful thought" would breathe his last breath on the comfortless "short street."

Now, it is too late. He steps from the curb at the intersection of the alley and Lamont Street.

No priest will hear his dying confession. Mary Ann said that many Sicilian men went to church every Sunday and every holy day. "But my father never did. Never saw him in church, except when I got married, and when my mother died. I never saw my father pray. He used to say that he and J.C. talked, though, all the time. This is what he said, 'J.C. and I have a talk all the time. He understands me. I understand him.' He always called him 'J.C.' He didn't say much else about religion except that."

Everyone with whom I talked said that Bompensiero was a "fatalist." They said that he knew if it was going to come to him, it would. They said he knew he could not hide. They said that he was too proud to hide. He did not say, but must have thought, that men had hidden from him. He found them. He always found them.

The gunman fires his first shot into Bompensiero's head from behind. Does the gunman whisper, politely, "Good evening, Frank"? Does the gunman hiss, "So-and-so sent me"?

We are not going to know.

The first shot is followed quickly by three more. The shots are fired into the side of his balding head, high, above his ear.

These shots brought Paul Ybarrando to this same spot some 20 years ago and these shots were what brought him out to meet me. We stand together on the sidewalk at the head of the alley that runs west from Lamont Street, about halfway between Thomas and Reed Avenues.

Ybarrando, in 1977, was a sergeant with the San Diego Police Department and the officer in charge of the investigation of Bompensiero's murder. Ybarrando was at home when the call came. "Just fooling around. I got called at 9:05. From the watch commander. A pager call."

Ybarrando shone his flashlight down on the spot where Bompensiero fell. "Right here in the center part of this alley between the two curbs here." He scuffed loose dirt with his boot tip. "By the time we got here the patrol officers had secured the scene. One of the men who responded that evening had worked vice. He recognized the victim as Bompensiero."

I asked Ybarrando what, at the time, he knew about Bompensiero.

"Everybody in San Diego, police officers especially, knew who Bompensiero was."

"Did you think of him as associated with organized crime?"

"Sure. That had been understood for years, that he was organized crime. And some people said he was the top guy in San Diego."

I asked what was going on, when Ybarrando drove up.

"It was dark. Certainly very dark when we got here. Police car was parked across the sidewalk here. They had this roped off. I think they were still letting traffic go on the other side of the street. They had another car blocking the sidewalk. They had a couple of cars down at the other end of the alley to keep you from coming this way and another one blocking the head of the alley."

Ybarrando indicated the area in the alley, near where we stood. "There were footprints, but they looked like kids' footprints. Small tennis shoes and also a bicycle track along here. All the evidence was lying right here in the alleyway. Four shell casings. The officers had taken coffee cups, white cups, and put them over the shell casings. There was a piece of his eyeglasses, three dimes. A dime is what a phone call cost then. Most likely he was carrying them and they fell out of his hand. There was the cigar, half-smoked cigar. Couldn't tell you what kind that was. It was an off brand. I never heard of it before. A Miami brand, a Florida brand."

I asked Ybarrando if he knew what time Bompensiero left his apartment to walk to the gas station.

"Not specifically. The patrol units got the call about 8:30. Basically, what happened was that a woman at one of the apartments or houses along here was taking out her trash and an elderly man approached her and said, 'Hey there's a guy lying in the alleyway.' So she called the police. That guy took off, so we never got to talk to him. He was just a passerby. The units arrived shortly after 8:30. At that time we had our own in-house ambulances. They thought he was still alive, which I doubt, and transported him. Before they took him, they'd chalked the body, so we had an outline of where the body was lying."

"How long had he been down?"

"I wouldn't say it was very long at all. He looked real fresh."

"How much blood was here when you arrived?"

"Pretty good puddle."

"How much blood comes out? A cup?"

"Oh, way more than that. Head shots usually bleed pretty good. So there was probably quite a bit of blood. Bleeding also depends on whether they live for any period of time. Because as long as the heart's pumping, you're pumping blood. Once the heart stops—no more."

"How long do you think he lived, down here in the alley?"

"Not more than a minute. Died pretty instantly."

"Is there a time you figured was pretty much the time he was killed?"

"No. We can't pinpoint it any closer than 8:30 because we don't have anybody that actually saw or actually heard the shots."

"Which way was he facing?"

"This way."

"So his head was down there, headed toward home?"

"Yeah. The way we diagrammed it, he was face down. All the shots were fired into the right side of the head and they indicated that the suspects probably hid behind this fence or the fence that was in existence at that time and stepped out and shot him as he came by."

"Was there one shooter or two?"

"No way to tell. Really don't know. One weapon. But there was probably somebody that was driving for the guy, the shooter."

"A .22?"

"Yes, a .22."

"Silencer?"

"Well, we're assuming that. There was some indication on the bullets that there could be marks that were left by a silencer. But there was no real way of telling. We don't really know. Nobody heard any shots. We interviewed everybody in the neighborhood and there were no shots heard. One guy who lived in one of these apartments thought he heard somebody running a stick across the picket fence, poppity-pop-pop. And there were a couple of other people that heard noises, but nothing that they would take to be gunshots."

I asked Ybarrando if he thought Bompensiero saw his assailant.

"I wouldn't think so. All the gunshots were at close range."

"How close?"

"Within 18 inches. Powder tattooing in his ear. You only get that from a very close-range shot."

"Do you think he knew who killed him?"

"Who knows?"

We stood quietly, then, for a minute, in the darkness. We hugged ourselves, against the cold.

"Basically, it was a simple crime scene. It wasn't very complicated. We didn't have a lot in the way of evidence except the four shell casings, all the same brand. We never got the gun. The gun was never recovered although if we had the gun we could have made the gun. He was probably walking along, smoking his cigar. Just walking along and somebody steps out and shoots him. According to the pathologist, three of the shots would have been instantly fatal. One of them he probably could have survived. They might have stood there and fired the other three after he was down, actually. The only one that showed powder tattooing was the one in his ear but that was exposed skin, where the other ones had hair and stuff around it. It was difficult to see."

"Somebody," I said, "told me that he fought."

"Well, he had some buttons torn off his shirt. So there is a possibility that he struggled, but there's nothing definitive to show that other than the fact that there's some buttons off his shirt. That easily could have been caused by his falling. He had his glasses on, a piece of the plastic from the glasses frame was here. But that was the only sign of struggle. He had bruises on his knees, which was from the fall. He had a half-smoked cigar that he was smoking when it happened and the cigar was just kind of lying there in the puddle of blood. We don't know if anything was said or not." Ybarrando looked around, again, at the fence. He looked south toward the Beach Club and north toward Grand Avenue. "I think it was total surprise. They were lying in wait for him." Ybarrando was quiet for a moment, before he spoke again. "I think maybe the ear shot was the first one. Because that was the one that had him by surprise. The one in the ear—that probably downed him."

"So it kind of sounds like, correct me if I'm wrong, it kind of sounds like some of those other shots may have been at a little more of a distance."

"Could have been."

"And that one was up pretty close?"

"Could have been. The one in the ear, that could have been the number-one shot, where the guy just stepped out and popped him, he goes down, and the guy stands back and shoots him. The ones in the ear, there was a couple just behind the ear, and there's one kind of at the base of the neck back in the back. All on the right side."

"Would you have to be a good shot to do that?"

"Not from that distance. You walk by, you just walk over, you're at an arm's length away. You shoot."

"Does it burn?"

"I've never been shot in the head so I don't know."

*Frank Bompensiero in Sicily, c. 1920*

**He was no amoral monster.**

**You or I cannot that easily dismiss him.**

CHAPTER TEN

# RETURN TO AMERICA

Frank Bompensiero jumped off a freight train in San Diego in the early 1920s. He was 16 or 17 or perhaps even 18 years old. He was five feet, six inches tall. He had hazel eyes and light brown hair. He was in trouble. Big trouble.

Mary Ann loaned me a photograph of Bompensiero that had been taken in a photographer's studio in Sicily. She guesses the photograph must have been made in Palermo. She hypothesizes that the photograph was made as a keepsake for his mother. Mary Ann does not know how old her father was when this photograph was taken. He may have not yet been 16. He may have been 15. He wears a suit that appears to be gray, a white shirt whose collar seems to set right beneath his chin. He wears a dark tie. He sits with his legs crossed. He has slicked back his hair. He has not begun to take on the weight that he will take on in later years. His dress and his posture lend him the look of the ardent, hopeful emigrant, the boy who will come to America, who will make good. I stare into the eyes that stare out of the photograph. I can read nothing from his gaze. His gaze seems entirely neutral.

Frank returned to Milwaukee from Sicily in 1921 or 1922 or even as late as 1923, without his family. No one can or will tell me why Bompensiero did not stay in Sicily. Perhaps the family needed the cash that Bompensiero could earn in the United States. Whole villages in southern Italy were being supported by Sicilians who'd come to the U.S. to work. Immigrants from Italy to the United States, during this era, were sending back as much as one million lire a year to Italian relatives. Or, perhaps Bompensiero wanted to get away from the village where, after ten years in Milwaukee, conditions must have seemed incredibly primitive. Donkeys and mules pulled wooden carts. The evil eye—*occhio malo*—was cast. Women regularly died in childbirth, and children in infancy. Mussolini was on his way to transforming all Italy, little Sicily included, into a single-party, totalitarian regime. A certain hopelessness might have infected Bompensiero in Porticello. If he stayed, all he could hope for, at best, was eventually to own his own fishing boat and to spend a lifetime hauling tuna out of the sea. In Milwaukee, Giuseppe and Anna Maria had become American citizens. Bompensiero's family remembers that Giuseppe and Anna Maria, when they left Milwaukee, had intended to return to America. Maybe the parents proposed that their eldest son return to ready a place for them, or to earn the money for boat fare. Or, perhaps

Bompensiero got himself into difficulty in Porticello or nearby Palermo, Sicily's ancient capital, where Byzantine-influenced mosaics glittered in harsh sunlight and dour men dressed in dark suits hurried to appointments in shadowy rooms. Who knows?

The Milwaukee city directory between 1918 and 1922 lists a Salvatore Bompensiero, barber, as resident in Milwaukee's Little Italy. Salvatore was Giuseppe's brother. So it is possible to imagine that after the two-week passage from Porticello to Naples and from Naples to New York and the two-day train trip from New York to Milwaukee, that Bompensiero unloaded his cardboard suitcase at his uncle Salvatore's house. The Milwaukee city directories for those years list names of many Porticello families. Any of the Guardalebenes, Busallachis, Catallanos, Tagliavias, Sanfilippos, San Filippis, Cravellos, Carinis, Aliotos, Balistrieris, might have unrolled a pallet for their young *compare*.

Mary Ann told me, "From what I understand, when Daddy was in Milwaukee, he was working with coal. I don't know how true that is, but that's what I understand."

Bompensiero may have been "working with coal." Certainly, many Sicilian immigrants—illiterate even in their own language and with only muscle to sell—went to work as manual laborers.

Bompensiero, in November, 1950, testified in Los Angeles before a closed session of the Special Committee to Investigate Organized Crime in Interstate Commerce, popularly known as the Kefauver Committee.

Mr. Halley. Where were you born?

Mr. Bompensiero. Milwaukee, Wisconsin.

Mr. Halley. In what business were you in Wisconsin?

Mr. Bompensiero. I was just working in a factory, A.O. Smith.

Mr. Halley. What kind of a plant is it?

Mr. Bompensiero. They make automobile parts.

Mr. Halley. And that was your only occupation until you came here?

Mr. Bompensiero. Yes, sir.

Bompensiero may well have been "just working in a factory." But, clearly, he had ambitions beyond grinding out engine blocks for A.O. Smith. At some point after Bompensiero arrived in Milwaukee, he became involved with a gang who made themselves useful to liquor smugglers and bootleggers. According to an old friend of Bompensiero's, Bompensiero, in Milwaukee, "was always out stealing, out bootlegging, out hijacking." Bompensiero's friend explained that Bompensiero and his gang hijacked trucks that carried illegal booze. The trucks drove down from Canada. The gang stopped the trucks and either emptied the contents of the trucks into its own vehicle or drove off with the truck and its contents. My informant did not know which. During one of these events, something went wrong and Bompensiero ended by shooting and killing one of the smugglers.

I tried to imagine Bompensiero, at this age. I hope that you will try to imagine this too. You've lived for five or six or seven years in a house with outdoor plumbing and no electricity. Your skills are a fisherman's skills. You read and write English at a rudimentary level. You may not even understand English all that well when you hear it spoken by native Milwaukeeans. Your accent is regularly mimicked. And the "native" Milwaukeeans, people not more than one or two generations away from Germany and Ireland and Scandinavia and Russian and Eastern European shtetls, look down on you. They guffaw about how your people aren't that far removed from the monkeys. In their newspapers and magazines cartoonists portray Italian men as sinister and evil, or, they draw them as comic—fat-bellied, hair slicked down with olive oil, an ornate mustache waxed upward at its ends. They sketch them as organ grinders, playing a barrel organ on corners and begging for passersby's coins. They taunt you with "wop" and "spaghetti bender" and "guinea" and "goombah" and "greaseball." They claim that you and your women are oversexed. They round up your men as suspects in sex crimes and murders. They accuse your men of Bolshevik leanings. They say they are bomb-tossers. They say they are "Black Hand" members who extort protection money from fellow immigrants. These natives warn their children against Italian and Sicilian children, claiming that they are carriers of lice, tuberculosis, typhoid, and physical and moral filth. In Massachusetts, in what all your people know is a put-up case, Sacco and Vanzetti have been sentenced to die in the electric chair. This, easily, you think, could happen to you. The hot seat.

Your father has been increasingly weak and ill and, frankly, querulous, for years. Your mother, every other year, has been pregnant or nursing a new baby. Your mother and brother and sisters look to you for help. Before you left Porticello for Naples, where you would board the ship that would bring you back to America, maybe your mother kissed both your cheeks and slipped down over your head a scapular or a miraculous medal. Certainly, she whispered that she prayed constantly for you. Surely, she begged you to be good, to be a good, good boy. But here you are, returned to Milwaukee where icy wind blows off the shores of Lake Michigan. You do not own a warm coat and you certainly do not own fur-lined gloves or flannel-lined galoshes or a wool muffler to wrap around your short neck. Maybe, like your father, you feel cold all the time; you feel as if you never will get warm again. You have been living with people who are not your family. You feel beholden to them. You never have quite enough to eat. You are trying to acquire some quick, easy, big money. You want something to send back to Porticello. You drive with your friends, out into the country on a deserted road on a dark night. Maybe you and your friends have swallowed rough grappa to build courage and body heat. The car fills up with nervous laughter and tense boasts and the odor of sweat as it soaks clothes that are not all that clean. You plan to stop the truck, grab the liquor. One of the truck's passengers jumps down out of the truck's cab. Imagine a truck, circa 1920, its cab set high off the ground, its wide running boards. Imagine the truck's headlights and how they throw a shimmering veil of light down the dark gravel road and up into the limbs of trees that grow on either side of the road. Imagine a stiff cold wind and sweat runnelling down into the small of your back. You have a gun. The man thrusts himself at you. His mouth opens wide. His teeth are white in the darkness. Everything happens faster than you thought anything could happen. The man is on the ground. Perhaps he screams. Perhaps he moans. Perhaps you gut-shot him and you smell cordite and fecal matter.

I might have asked friends who are gun experts to help me with the details of the gun—shotgun or pistol—Bompensiero carried that night. I considered querying these friends as to how, say, a pistol would have felt in Bompensiero's hand, how the bullets' entry—the hole or holes—in the dead man might have looked. Would blood pour out the bullet holes? Seep red into the dying man's linen shirtfront? Spout out the wound like water spouts out from a dolphin's blowhole? Would the dying man cry out to his mother, his wife, to the Blessed Virgin, to St. Anthony, to Jesus? If he did cry out, or, moan, would his voice spiral out into the quiet night, rise into an inky sky? Would that call, or cry or moan haunt Frank Bompensiero for months to come, for years? Would it wake him out of sleep? I do not know.

Why, finally, I did not ask gun experts about the night Bompensiero for the first time killed something other than a tuna, a sardine, a chicken or rabbit, a rat or mouse, is that details about the weapon's possible make and model, the bullet or bullets' trajectory, the size and placement of wounds, came to seem beside the point. The trajectory, if you will, of this moment, the path this moment takes through the next half century of Bompensiero's life is what all along I have wanted to understand. How this moment changed Frank Bompensiero's life is more important than are details of weapon and wound.

Frank Bompensiero knew right from wrong. What he thought was right and what he thought was wrong, likely, is different than what you think is right and wrong. He was no amoral monster. You or I, in good conscience, cannot that easily dismiss him.

After this night outside Milwaukee, Bompensiero will go on to become a soldier in a secret army, or, secret society. This army or society has its own moral code, its own rules of *onore* and *omertà*. He will follow these rules, for many years. He will kill other men. Imagine that. Certainly, that night on the dark road outside Milwaukee, Frank Bompensiero could not have imagined that, could not have foreseen his future, could not have guessed that 25 or 30 years from this night he would stand in a house in Kensington, a house along whose stucco walls red bougainvillea trailed upward. He will stand with Jimmy Fratianno behind the door of that house, on a warm summer evening. The door will open and an old bootlegger will enter, hand outstretched, thinking he has arrived for a convivial evening among *compares* who after the kisses and handshakes will pour the good Scotch. The two ice cubes will click against heavy crystal. That is not what happens. What happens is that Fratianno and Bompensiero loop a rope around the old bootlegger's throat. Fratianno and Bompensiero wrench the rope tighter and tighter until the old bootlegger crumples to his knees, until the old bootlegger's eyes pop and the trousers of his beautiful suit fill with his body's wastes. The host, the house's owner, will complain that his carpet is soiled.

## Interesting Street Car Trips

**BALBOA PARK.** Take car on Route 7 going East on Broadway, via 12th Street, passing San Diego High School and Stadium to East entrance of former Exposition Grounds, Balboa Park, now more attractive than ever. The great Spreckels Outdoor Organ Pavilion is located here and daily recitals are given by Dr. Humphrey J. Stewart, Official Organist. Returning via Laurel Street exit, taking either Car 1 or 3 on 5th Street to business district.

**MISSION HILLS, MISSION CLIFF GARDENS.** Take car on Route 3 on Broadway going East via 5th Street to Mission Hills. On return trip transfer to Car No. 1 direct to Mission Cliff Gardens. Return via car on routes 1 or 11. If transfer is desired on return trip to other points, ask for it when paying fare.

**RAMONA'S MARRIAGE PLACE, OLD TOWN.** Car on Route 8 at 3rd and Broadway, going West. Ride to end of line and visit this wonderfully interesting and historic place.

**GOLDEN HILL and EAST SAN DIEGO.** Car on Route 2 East on Broadway from Union Depot to 30th and University, transferring at last named point to car on Route 7 for East San Diego, returning via Route No. 7.

**OCEAN BEACH and MARINE BASE.** Take car on Route O. B. at 3rd and Broadway, passing in close view of Marine Base, Loma Portal to Ocean Beach. Purchase round trip tickets at San Diego Electric Ticket Office, corner 3rd and Broadway.

**CORONADO BEACH and HOTEL DEL CORONADO.** Car on Route 9 East on Broadway to 5th, via 5th and Market to ferry. Cars on Coronado side meet ferries. Take time at Coronado to roam through its beautiful parks, along the Ocean front and enjoy dinner at the famous Hotel del Coronado. Purchase round trip tickets at San Diego Electric Ticket Office, 3rd and Broadway.

**NATIONAL CITY and CHULA VISTA.** Take National City and Chula Vista car East on Broadway from Union Depot, thence South on 5th Street passing through the manufacturing district within view of the big Spreckels "Savage" Tire Plant and on through scenic and citrus producing country to National City and Chula Vista.



23

*From San Diego Greeters' Guide*

**I felt as if I had become one of those unrequited lovers who stalk their would-be sweethearts.**

CHAPTER ELEVEN

# NEED YOUR HELP

We cannot hope, now, to know what Bompensiero felt when he pulled the trigger that night outside Milwaukee. We will never know what conversation he did or did not have that night and on nights to come with that bodiless voice in his head that we call conscience.

You know how it is in a new love affair, when for the first time you tell your beloved a lie? How, with that first lie, the sweetness of relations between you and the beloved suddenly turns less sweet? How you no longer feel as easy in his company? In her embrace? I believe that Bompensiero no longer felt at ease in the world after that moment outside Milwaukee.

We do know this, for sure. According to Bompensiero's old friend, Bompensiero suddenly "was in a lot of trouble with Milwaukee people." I asked if by "people," he meant, "connected people." He did, he said. "Yes, connected people."

"Connected people" were in Milwaukee. Connected people were, indeed, by this time, in all major cities of America. The *Milwaukee Journal* for February 7, 1921, notes the death of one of them under a headline, "Little Italy Mourns Chief":

"Vito Guardalabene, 75, known as the king of Little Italy, the political ruler of the Third Ward, died Monday afternoon. He had been suffering from heart trouble. Twenty-three years ago Vito came to the United States from Palermo. He was engaged in a wholesale grocery and macaroni business. His approval was necessary to any political aspirant in the Third Ward."

Guardalabene was a *padrone*, a power in Milwaukee and nearby Madison. Other powerful families were Aliotos, and the Balistrieris, who would marry into the Alioto family. Law enforcement agencies later would refer to certain members of these families as Mafia members and would convict and send them to prison, but back in 1921, outsiders to the Third Ward's Little Italy paid them no notice. Within the Third Ward, however, there were men—Sicilian men—who could and would order your death.

Bompensiero likely met "connected people" in the Third Ward neighborhood. Maybe he shook hands with Guardalabene, whose home village also was Porticello. According to the later testimony of Aladena ("Jimmy the Weasel") Fratianno in Ovid Demaris's bestseller, *The Last Mafioso*, the Bompensiero family, while in Milwaukee, was friendly with the Alioto family. Fratianno would claim that Bompensiero, as an older man, became godfather to an Alioto child. But, perhaps Bompensiero met none of these people and only gazed at them, from a distance, and envied their tailored clothes and their Bay Rum after-shave, their cars and their women. Bompensiero may have been a gutter rat, a shabby urban Dickensian freelancer, a bottom-feeder who with other young bottom-feeders made other, slightly more powerful outlaws his victims.

We can be sure of this, too: Bompensiero was terrified. You could fry on the hot seat for killing someone. But the retribution that the law of the state might seek must have seemed mild next to the retribution his fellow Sicilians would want.

"At this point," said Mary Ann, "my dad hopped a freight train and came to California."

San Diego, since the late 1890s, had attracted families from Porticello. They sent back reports of a climate similar to that of Porticello. They mailed black-and-white photographs of fig and palm and citrus trees, of fishing boats and ocean, of stucco houses built along hillsides from the Embarcadero up to Second Street. The immigrants also sent back to relatives in Sicily money they earned from fishing and factory work.

Bompensiero arrived in San Diego certainly no later than 1923 or 1924. Mary Ann said, "I understand he went to work on the docks. First, he unloaded fish, and then he got a job as a fisherman because that's all they knew. You don't shovel coal in California."

Once Bompensiero jumps off that freight train and steps onto San Diego soil, we are—again—in the dark. I thump those years with my knuckles and the sound is the sound of hollowness. We know almost nothing. Almost everyone who might have seen or heard about what Bompensiero did during his first years in San Diego is dead. Those who aren't dead won't talk or weren't paying attention and don't know. In what local police records remain, Bompensiero's name does not appear until August 25, 1928, when Bompensiero, days away from his 23rd birthday, was arrested for violation of the State of California's Prohibition Act.

To acquire a sense of Bompensiero's life after he came to San Diego you have to take what you know, in general, about San Diego, and about Little Italy, and about fishing, and about being Sicilian, and about being young and male and on the run from Milwaukee, about Prohibition, about having killed a man, and with all that, you must patiently construct a framework. Once you build that rickety scaffolding, you can set Frank Bompensiero down within it. But you cannot do much more than that.

In 1920 San Diego's population was 74,683; 18,000 automobiles drove the one- and two-lane roads and streets. Streetcars moved up and down

Broadway. Numbers 1, 3, 7, or 11 carried you to Balboa Park where daily, at 3 p.m., you could attend free concerts played on the organ donated to the city by J.D. and A.B. Spreckels. The zoo was open. The U.S. Grant stood where it stands now. Men could order near beer and sarsaparilla at its bar. If they wanted stronger stuff, they needed connections with a bootlegger or the address of a speakeasy. San Diego Trust and Savings Bank, for $600,000, had purchased the corner of Sixth and Broadway, razed the Hotel Beacon, and begun construction. Dominic Alessio had moved to town. In 1921, Dominic's older sons, John and Russell Alessio, began polishing shoes near Fifth Avenue and E Street.

I have a pamphlet that I found in a heap of old magazines stacked in a cardboard box in a downtown used bookstore. Dated "January, 1921," and titled *San Diego Greeters' Guide for the Traveler: Up-to-date Information on San Diego,* the five- by seven-inch pamphlet offers 50 pages of information about San Diego. Advertisements take up many pages—"Dance Tonight at Ratliff's, 1029 Second Street, Dancing every night except Monday and Tuesday...Strictly First-Class." "Savoy Café at 1055-1057 Fourth St. Phone, Main 3725." "French and Italian Cuisine...G. Topuzes & Bro....Private Dining Rooms for Ladies and Small Parties, Telephone in Each Private Room, Table D'Hote Dinner, $1.00...Noon Lunch, 40 cents...Planked Steaks, Chops, Poultry and Sea Foods a Specialty." And this, "The Owl Taxi, Main 1900, Serves you Right, Day and Night! Drivers Wear Uniform and Blue Caps!"

By the time Bompensiero showed up in San Diego, Little Italy had been growing for 30 years. Its population increased after the 1906 San Francisco earthquake, when North Beach Italian residents escaped south. Families from Porticello bought and built and rented houses and apartments from the Embarcadero up the hill to Second, and from Date to Mission Hills. All along Columbia and India and State and Date and Grape and Atlantic Streets, clear down to the edge of the water, you could see houses painted pink and blue by transplanted Sicilians. Catenary arch brick ovens rose up in back yards where the women baked bread for their families and for sale as ship's stores. The fishermen went out to sea for a week at a time, then returned home, mended their nets, refitted their boats, went back out. The Sicilians mixed little, if at all, with the rest of San Diego. They had their own grocery stores, bars, outfitters for boats, net repairmen, bakeries, macaroni makers, insurance salesmen, seamstresses. They began a drive for funds to build an Italian church. Through bazaar sales, individual contributions, and a gift of the land on the corner of Columbia and Date Streets, Little Italy's residents, on August 17, 1923, were able to break ground to begin construction. The congregation's size, then, was 2000.

Many did not speak English or did not speak it well. Those who did speak English served as translators for those who didn't. Families were close. More than other immigrant groups, Sicilian-Americans held on to language, cuisine, custom, each other. A man whose parents were immigrants from Porticello said to me, "We spoke Sicilian, cooked Sicilian, married Sicilian, and acted Sicilian."

Sicilians like to say how much more friendly, outgoing, demonstrative, and generous they are than are Italians from the north. They like to say that they will give you the shirt off their back if you need a shirt. I think that is true. Sicilian-Americans whom I met over the decade during which I asked questions about Bompensiero were charming and gregarious. But they did not want to talk about Bompensiero. Some would not even admit to recognizing the name. If I contacted them by telephone, and said that I wished to ask about Bompensiero, some of these charming, generous people hung up on me. Some put the receiver down softly. Some slammed it down. Some hissed, "Don't call again."

*Omertà*: The word means "manliness," or, more generally, "silence." According to an authority on Sicilian folklore, *omertà* derives from *omoneità,* or "acting like a man." Giovanni Schiavo's 1962 book, *The Truth About the Mafia and Organized Crime in America*, explains the silence this way: "The worst insult a Sicilian can hurl at another Sicilian is that of *'nfami* or *cascittuni,* both of which mean the same thing, 'informer' or 'stool pigeon.' Calling an American 'a dirty liar' is mild compared to that."

A retired FBI agent said to me, "*Omertà*'s inbred with the Sicilians. Even the law-abiding, honest day-to-day person in that community knows better than to talk. *Omertà*'s just something that's inbred. They don't like to talk about [guys like Bompensiero]. They are embarrassed, they have to live here in these communities and the peer pressure is such that even if they are not afraid of physical violence, they are afraid of being ostracized, because the mob guys have enough influence to put out the word and make these people appear to be snitches and disloyal. So they are very concerned about talking."

A reader here can scoff at the notion of *omertà.* He or she can scoff at the notion that contemporary Sicilian-American San Diegans fear discussing Frank Bompensiero, killed execution-style in Pacific Beach in 1977. But they did and they do. They also do not want to discuss Frank Bompensiero with someone like me, an outsider, because to do so is disloyal.

A quite elderly woman, when I asked about Bompensiero, said this: "I knew him when he came out here from Milwaukee. He seemed to be a very nice guy when I knew him. Whatever people say about him I wasn't there to hold the candle, so I don't know. He was nice to me and my family, so I can't talk bad about him."

Another elderly woman, her English strongly accented, said, "I don't like to talk about the past, or to say anything about the past." Then she hung up.

A middle-aged man whose father came to San Diego several years earlier than did Bompensiero, said, "My father knew Bompensiero extremely well. We knew all these people, we knew them socially, and we never talked about their illegal activities. A lot of people tried to class them as hoodlums, and some were and some weren't. That stuff was kept secret and the people we knew were certainly never involved. It was something that was on the fringe." This man made clear to me, by his disapproving tone, that my queries about Bompensiero were intrusive, that I was a trespasser in his community.

I had lists of Sicilian names. I acquired them by squinting at old San Diego city directories and by sitting, hour after hour, in front of the downtown library's microfilm readers and studying obituaries. At home, I ran my index finger down through the telephone directory and matched names on my list with names in the telephone book. I worked up the courage to dial. I was always reluctant. I always feared failure. I had developed a spiel. Before I dialed, I practiced my spiel. "I need your help. I am a writer. I am interested in writing the true story of Frank Bompensiero. The press has misrepresented Mr. Bompensiero as nothing more than a cold-blooded Mafia hit man, who, when he was gunned down in Pacific Beach, got what he deserved. I want to write about Mr. Bompensiero in a way that shows the family man, the good neighbor, the good citizen." I would say, again, "I need your help." I always spoke of him as "Mr. Bompensiero." I hoped that the people, mostly elderly, whom I dialed would hear in my use of "Mr." that I was respectful, that I meant well.

I did mean what I said, about writing about Bompensiero. Early on in this project, I had talked by telephone with a minor hoodlum who had known Bompensiero during the 1960s. He had liked Bompensiero. He said, about what the press wrote about *mafiosi*, "Nobody looks at that side of them when they're just with their families, they just look at the shit angles." I didn't want just the "shit angles" on Bompensiero. And I truly needed help. I wonder, now, if I sounded as ardent and as earnest as I felt. Over several months I made possibly 100 telephone calls to men and women who, at least casually, had known Bompensiero or his mother or his sisters or his brother Sam or his first wife's family, the Sanfilippos. Almost everyone refused to talk.

When someone agreed to answer questions, what they did say acquired a numinous quality. That Bompensiero, for instance, as one woman told me, liked the Sicilian dish, pasta with new green peas, became to me a fact of great enormity. This fact shone. It seemed to light up entire silent, tenebrous, odorless stretches of his life. I saw him, hunched over a wooden kitchen table. Before him sat a white plate. Ivory strands of spaghetti, littered with bright green peas, coiled atop the plate. Bompensiero, using a fork, lifted long strands of the noodle to his mouth. I imagined the taste of new spring peas. I imagined pungent garlic, and hard pecorino cheese of the kind I touched in stores in Little Italy. I imagined that he grated the cheese atop the pasta. I imagined his wide hands and stubby fingers. I imagined the light through an open window falling down onto the table, onto his hair—brown now and no longer blond, as it was in childhood when everyone in his Milwaukee neighborhood called him *figlio d'oro*, "son of gold."

I felt queer, and, bad—a bad person—for trying in this way to slip into Bompensiero's skin. I felt as if I had become one of those unrequited lovers who stalk their would-be sweethearts, who hide late at night in privet hedges and gaze upward at the beloved's shadow as it drifts across bedroom windows. I felt as if I were trespassing, walking where I was not wanted. I felt as if I were transgressing, exceeding and overstepping what was permitted. I felt in love with someone who did not love me, who did not even like me. I felt I had made myself a victim of what we call "fatal attraction." I felt doomed.

When I found the pamphlet titled *San Diego Greeters' Guide for the Traveler: Up-to-date Information on San Diego*, my eyes widened when I saw the date—"January, 1921." It seemed like a sign—portentous and consequential—that this pamphlet turned up when it did. It seemed to say that I should go on and I did. I went on. I sat with my lists and I dialed more numbers. Some days, I got lucky.

*St. Anthony festival: Bompensiero's sisters, mother (center, wearing black), brother-in-law, daughter, and nephews*

**"They went to church together,**

**they danced together,**

**and they fell in love."**

CHAPTER TWELVE

# LIKE SICILY

Soon after Bompensiero first strolled down India Street, Bompensiero moved in with an uncle, Giovanni, a fisherman, who rented a small house from the Sanfilippos. They all lived within a few blocks of each other in San Diego's Little Italy. Someone told me, who knew the Sanfilippos and Bompensiero during those years, "Frank and the guys who were living there, they were all bachelors then, and a little bit wild."

I talked by telephone one morning with one of Thelma Sanfilippo Bompensiero's sisters. The sister, quite elderly, was concerned that I wished to ask about Bompensiero. She reluctantly talked with me. She told me that she was born in San Diego. She said that her mother and father had eight children—four born in San Diego, and four "back East in Milwaukee." (One of those four, Thelma, who would marry Bompensiero, was born in Milwaukee in 1911.) Her father Lorenzo, she said, was a fisherman and her mother Felipa, "a businesswoman. She owned property at the time when San Diego was nothing. When my family came here from Milwaukee, where Lindbergh Field is now, there was nothing and downtown, there was nothing.

"My folks come from Porticello, Sicily. My father was in the Italian Navy and came to San Diego. It was nothing then, empty, but my father fell in love with the climate. It was like Sicily, and then when he went back and was out of the Navy and he fell in love with my mother and they got married, they went to Milwaukee. My father had friends in Milwaukee, that's why they went there. My mother didn't like the cold there. So my father said, 'Okay, we are going to San Diego.' They came here in 1915. My mother was pregnant when she came to San Diego and then she had me and my brother and my younger sister, all four born in San Diego.

"Back then, where I grew up, all the Sicilian fishermen lived along on India Street, on Kettner, Atlantic, Date and Juniper, Union. We lived at 1971 Atlantic. Before they made the freeway, it was just dirt road and the bay. The tide goes out and comes in, it used to come up to Pacific Highway, that's how close the water was. When I was a little girl we had a skiff in the back yard in case the tide would come in. We had two big palm trees in front of our house, a beach in front of our house. There was no pier, no Anthony's, nothing at all. We could walk right to the water's edge. We used to go swimming there. When you walked by people's houses, they would be sitting on their porch, you wave to say hello and people ask, 'Where are you going?' and they would say, 'Come on over and have a cup of coffee.' But now you go by, they don't even say hello. Everyone knew everyone in the neighborhood, someone got sick and everyone ran to help. The doors were left open and no one stole anything.

"At the time the boats they didn't go far out. In the winter months the men could not go out because it was too choppy for the boats. So in the beginning the fishing was more in the spring and the summer. After they made bigger boats and were catching tuna, they would be gone two and three weeks. My father had a small fishing boat, he went out every day.

"My mother and I, we worked at the fish cannery, all hard work, getting up at two in the morning. When those little fishing boats go out for sardines and anchovies, they would blow the whistle and we had to be alert and hear that whistle blow so we could get up at midnight, two, four in the morning to go to the cannery. The Del Monte cannery was at Juniper and Atlantic. I was 11 years old. We would walk there. That was our life, working at the cannery."

Mary Ann added this to her maternal aunt's account. "My grandmother Sanfilippo, I think, really was the boss of the tribe. She was a hard businesswoman. I kind of have to believe that she was kind of the boss of everything, even over my grandfather. Which is unusual, coming as an immigrant from the old country. But she was the one with the brains. What she did is borrow money and buy property. She was a shrewd lady. She was not naïve. And she was attractive. She had gorgeous wavy hair that she wore pulled straight back from her face, in a bun. She never wore makeup.

"She had apartments at 1907 Columbia Street and then they had the big two-story house on Pacific Highway and Grape. My grandmother had three houses. On the outside of the house they lived in my grandfather Sanfilippo had a shed where he kept his fishing nets. He had all blue boats, two or three blue boats. They were for local fishing. Their house was big. Because of all the children. My grandfather Sanfilippo's mother, they'd brought her over, too, and she lived with them. She was a teeny little thing. She dipped snuff and smoked a pipe. She was past 90 when she died. And besides that, they had other families living with them, people that came over from Sicily. And when people would come in, like from Milwaukee, they also would all stay at my grandmother Sanfilippo's house until they got a job or went fishing. They all lived together until the husband would find a job and then they'd go out on their own.

"My grandmother had in her back yard on Grape and Pacific Highway—there was no Harbor Drive then—an oven that looked like an igloo. She baked all of her bread. From the leftover dough, she'd make little rolls for all the grandchildren. And she would pour a little bit of olive oil on the top and salt and pepper and it was delicious. Right out of the oven.

"Many of these houses, like my grandparents' house, had two kitchens. They had a kitchen upstairs and a kitchen downstairs in the basement. The upstairs was for company and for entertaining and the downstairs was where you really lived. They never lived in their living room. The reason for the two kitchens and the basement is because the families were so big, and where are you going to put them? Another reason they had the basements was because they didn't want to ruin the house. My grandmother had a gorgeous dining room, a beautiful kitchen upstairs, but she never cooked on the stove upstairs or had anything in the refrigerator. She never ate in the dining room, except at perhaps Christmas or Easter or weddings or funerals. Downstairs in the basement, she had a huge oak table. Every Sunday there were 15 or 20 people at that table. She also had, down there, a kitchen sink, a regular gas stove, refrigerator, a couch and radio. She used to say, 'Put on the cowboy music.' Country-western music is what she liked. And she'd sit on the couch and listen to the cowboy music. And she had a black, ebony player piano. She'd put rolls in it, and all the children and even the teenagers would pump away."

A woman in her 80s told me this, about life in Little Italy in the 1920s and early 1930s. "My mother would have down in her basement 40, 50 people. They would stay up all night playing cards, playing bingo. We would make our raviolis, our round steaks—*braciola*—where you make bread crumb with cheese and garlic and put a little oil on it and flatten it down on the steaks, then on the steaks you put salami slices and hard-boiled egg, and then we would roll the steaks up real tight and tie them and fry them and put them in the sauce and then cut them and they'd be delicious. Then we would have either baked chickens with the sauce or baked spaghetti, lasagna, a nice big salad, the antipasti—the pickers that we'd eat before dinner and all day—little pieces of lunch meat, carrot sticks, celery sticks, pieces of cheese, olives—and for dessert, we served cookies and the cannoli. One time we had 50 people down there and the whole basement was filled and we had tables all the way around. We often had almost that many people every year after the Midnight Mass."

Mary Ann said that it was difficult, now, to realize how close the families were in those days. "Cousins married cousins back then. Because they were all the same clan, they all came from Porticello, they all congregated, they all went to the same parties, they went to church together, they danced together, and they fell in love. Cousins would fall in love with each other. It was a different world. You'd think they were still in Sicily."

Full Report of Associated Press and Universal Service in The Union

The San Diego Union

FREE ORGAN RECIT

ARMY OF MEN SET TO HUGE TASK OF DRASTIC PROHIBITION ENFORCEMI

NATIONAL DRY LAW IN FORCE

Wine Interests to Test Law by Manufacturing

MORALE OF SERVICE KNOCKED TO PIECES BY AWARD SYSTEM, SAYS ADMIRAL SIMS

U. S. GOVERNMENT GIVES ITS REASONS FOR WITHDRAWING SIBERIAN TROOPS

WORDS OF PRAISE FOR FISH PATROL TO APPEAR IN COMING REPORT

Wine Uninjured When Truck Load Is Hit by Train

EXP PIN IN F

Carloads of Whisky Lose Race to Border

BRAWLEY MAKING EFFORT FOR GIN

Trying to Find Use for California Wine Grapes

Manila Is American Possession Not So Dry

Navy Yard Workers Facing Discharge

Deputy Clerk Gives Dan Cupid A Little Lift

Rodman Announces

From the San Diego Union, January 17, 1920

**"He used to come down to my mother-in-law's. That is where I met him."**

CHAPTER THIRTEEN

# THE AL CAPONE OF L.A.

All through the 1920s, San Diego's newspapers were filled with references to Prohibition, which had been in force since January, 1920. Even at the downtown library, Prohibition asserted itself. According to an issue of the *San Diego Union* published shortly after Prohibition went into effect, the *Encyclopedia Britannica* had in it a recipe for the manufacture and distillation of whiskey. The question had arisen as to whether the encyclopedia must "therefore be barred from its place on the shelves of the San Diego Public Library." The *Union* went on to note that "Miss Althea H. Warren, San Diego's chief librarian, hopes not. Officially, she will bring the question before the board of library trustees at the regular meeting today." Eventually, librarians placed behind the reference desk the volume of the encyclopedia that contained the "recipe." This is a fact I have always liked.

Mary Ann had heard stories about her maternal grandmother's defiance of Prohibition law. "Underneath my grandfather Sanfilippo's nets, there was a trapdoor. You'd open that trapdoor and go into the basement and that's where my grandparents kept the wine. Policemen used to stop by, and they'd buy wine by the shot. Also, my grandparents sold the wine in pints. When my mother was 12, which would have been in 1923, she learned how to drive a Model T Ford. She would drive my grandmother around to deliver wine. My grandmother wore long skirts and my grandmother would have under her skirt, two jugs of wine. My mother drove and her grandmother delivered the wine to their customers."

Bompensiero's old friend, the man who told me about Bompensiero's first killing, also told me that at some point after Bompensiero made his escape from Milwaukee, he went up to Los Angeles "to see Jack Dragna, to try to get Jack to straighten him out with the Milwaukee people. Jack did, and from then on in, Frank was with Jack." Bompensiero's friend said that more than once Bompensiero told him that he "loved" Jack Dragna, that Dragna, by speaking to the Milwaukee people, saved his life.

Born Anthony Rissotti in Corleone, Sicily, in 1891, Jack Dragna arrived in California with his brother Tom around 1908. The brothers set up shop in Los Angeles. Los Angeles writer Charles Rappleye and Las Vegas private eye Ed Becker in *All-American Mafioso: The Johnny Rosselli Story*, describe Jack Dragna.

"Stocky, with a broad nose, thick lips and a short temper, Dragna...had a primal instinct for power, which he exercised as sort of unofficial mayor of the Italian ghetto, settling family disputes and enforcing discipline. A conviction for extortion in 1915 and a three-year stint in San Quentin only enhanced his reputation as a man to fear and respect.

"Dragna employed as a front the offices of the Italian Protective League, located on the eleventh floor of the Law Building in downtown Los Angeles. Dragna was president of the organization formed ostensibly to promote immigrant rights, but described in police documents as 'strictly a muscle outfit, preying on various business activities,' which 'also had its fingers in gambling, bootlegging, and smuggling, and was suspected of many Black Hand killings.'

"In later years, Dragna came to be referred to in the press and in government documents as the Al Capone of Los Angeles. But in the middle 1920s, while he maintained preeminence in the affairs of his countrymen, Dragna was still an outsider in the world of Los Angeles crime. Most of the city's vice, prostitution and gambling in particular, was controlled through a well-established syndicate, a small group of businessmen who managed their rackets through payoffs to the police and city administration.... Dragna concentrated his attention to prying graft and tribute from the Italian community and on bootlegging."

Mary Ann has a more detailed account of how her father met Jack Dragna. "Sometime after my dad got to California, from what I was told, my grandmother Sanfilippo introduced him to some people in Los Angeles. That's what I was told by a close member of the family. It was Tom Dragna I was told that he was introduced to, Jack Dragna's brother. And then," Mary Ann laughed, "after he met the Dragnas, from that point on, I don't think my dad ever went back out fishing again."

When Bompensiero, in November, 1950, testified in Los Angeles before the Kefauver Committee, he testified cagily. The nation was entering into a rapt, almost hypnotic, fascination with gangsters. In May, 1950, Kefauver's committee had set up shop in Miami and grilled mob moneyman and Benjamin "Bugsy" Siegel mentor, Meyer Lansky. Bompensiero did not have the gloss and acumen with which Lansky was gifted, but he knew what to leave out. He left out entirely the five to eight years that he lived in Sicily. He mentioned nothing of his gang activities in Milwaukee or that night outside Milwaukee when his gun flared in the darkness. He changed the date of his arrival in San Diego from early in the 1920s to 1926, and the date of his first meeting with Dragna from early in the 1920s to 1927. He denied that he knew Joe Sica, a Los Angeles-based "handyman" who, with his brother

Fred, was closely connected to Mickey Cohen. Bompensiero may not have liked the Sicas, but he knew them.

Mr. Halley. What was your occupation when you came to San Diego?

Mr. Bompensiero. I used to fish for a living.

Mr. Halley. For how long did you do that?

Mr. Bompensiero. I do not—I did that for about, I should say, about, maybe, a year.

Mr. Halley. Then what did you do?

Mr. Bompensiero. Then I started selling a little liquor and I got caught at it.

Mr. Halley. Who were your associates in the liquor business?

Mr. Bompensiero. I was by myself.

Mr. Halley. Did you know Dragna at that time?

Mr. Bompensiero. At that time, no sir.

Mr. Halley. When did you first meet Dragna?

Mr. Bompensiero. About 1927.

Mr. Halley. Well, then, that was before your liquor conviction, was it not?

Mr. Bompensiero. Yes, it was. Yes, sir, before my liquor conviction.

Mr. Halley. Were you still living in Wisconsin when you met Dragna?

Mr. Bompensiero. No, sir.

Mr. Halley. Then you are here -

Mr. Bompensiero. I came out here, I guess it must have been 1926.

Mr. Halley. Now, do you know Joe Sica?

Mr. Bompensiero. No, sir.

Mr. Halley. You have never met him?

Mr. Bompensiero. Never met him.

Mr. Halley. What was your business after the prohibition conviction?

Mr. Bompensiero. With me?

Mr. Halley. Yes.

Mr. Bompensiero. I was working here and there.

Mr. Halley. Doing what?

Mr. Bompensiero. Well, fishing once in a while; peddling fish for myself.

Mr. Halley. Any other businesses?

Mr. Bompensiero. No, sir.

Mr. Halley. How did you happen to meet Dragna?

Mr. Bompensiero. I met him in San Diego through—he used to come down to my mother-in-law's. That is where I met him.

Who, you have to ask yourself, was Felipa Sanfilippo, a little Sicilian woman in San Diego who wore her hair pulled back into a bun at the back of her neck, a woman illiterate in her own language and clumsy in the New World's, to be entertaining Jack Dragna, or, to suggest that Bompensiero go to visit the

Dragnas, Jack or Tom? How did Felipa Sanfilippo come to know Tom and Jack Dragna? The Dragnas weren't from Porticello. And did Bompensiero tell Mrs. Sanfilippo that he was in trouble in Milwaukee? If he did, did he tell her the nature of his trouble? And why and for whom did Jack Dragna agree to settle things with the people in Milwaukee? And why and for whom did Jack Dragna take in a rough, perhaps impulsive, and certainly desperate teenager? Did Felipa Sanfilippo reach into her bootlegging proceeds and send "tribute" to Jack Dragna? We don't know. We won't know. Of this, I think, we can be sure: once Jack Dragna, perhaps as a favor to Felipa Sanfilippo, settled things in Milwaukee, there was no turning back for Bompensiero.

There is only one word from the Sicilian dialect of Italian which is known around the world: mafia. According to Giovanni Schiavo's *The Truth About the Mafia and Organized Crime in America*, "The adjective *mafiusu* (*mafioso*, in Italian) has been common in Sicily for at least two hundred years.... The word was common in the Borgo section of Palermo and...meant beauty, charm, perfection, excellence. Today the noun mafia commonly means criminal organization or gang, but the adjective *mafioso* still has two meanings; first, that of a member of the Mafia, and second, that of tough, or what the lower classes would call 'wise guy.' Thus, it is common to hear one say *ma chi ti senti mafiusu?* (you think you are tough?)."

Schiavo, himself Sicilian-American, notes that one "can be a *mafioso* without being a criminal." He explains, "Mafia pertains to something inherent or almost innate in the Sicilian character, the Sicilian mentality, the Sicilian way of life, such as the code of honor, *omertà*, longing for freedom, intolerance of injustice.... Such sentiments...are embodied in the word Mafia as a state of mind."

Scoff, too, if you like at the idea of Mafia and *mafioso* and secret initiation ceremonies like those we have seen in movies. But, it is likely that between 1923 and 1928, Frank Bompensiero, at the hands of Jack Dragna, became a "made man," a *soldato*, a Mafia member. Certainly, until Dragna's death in early 1956, Bompensiero would do chores, many of a deadly nature, for Dragna. With few exceptions, we will never know what these chores were. Even when they were performed in daylight, these chores were done in darkness.

*Circa 1920 fishing boat, Frank Bompensiero in foreground*

**On the night of the Jack Dempsey and Gene Tunney rematch, Capone gave a party at which he paid Jolson to entertain.**

CHAPTER FOURTEEN

# GANGLAND

In San Diego in September, 1922, U.S. Army Air Corps Lieutenant James Doolittle made the first coast-to-coast flight in a single day, flying from Pablo Beach, Florida, to San Diego in 21 hours, 28 minutes' flying time. Construction started on a second pier at the foot of B Street. By 1923, there were 30,000 cars registered in the county. East San Diego was annexed by the City of San Diego. Streetcar lines were under construction from downtown San Diego to Mission Beach and La Jolla. The command of the Pacific Fleet was transferred to San Diego.

We know that John Alessio was shining shoes in his shop at Fifth Avenue and E Street. We know that C. Arnholt Smith became director of the Bank of Italy. We know that Bompensiero's future mother-in-law was buying property in Little Italy. Mary Ann said, about her maternal grandmother, "The guy at Bank of America, where my grandmother went, said that had she been able to read and write and speak better English she would have been a multimillionaire. She was willing to take chances."

But what, precisely, Bompensiero did during these years, again, I do not know. What Mary Ann knows, is this. Her father, all his life was a graceful dancer. At some point after Bompensiero came to California, he entered and won several dance contests. "My father," she said, "won a trophy, doing the 'Black Bottom.'" He was also, at this age, said Mary Ann, "a dandy, a fancy dresser, and something of a favorite among the ladies." I have enjoyed imagining Bompensiero at Ratliff's, whose advertisement was in the 1921 pamphlet, "Dancing every night except Monday and Tuesday...Strictly First-Class."

I have a photograph, taken after Bompensiero arrived in San Diego. Dressed in shirt, bow tie, and dark vest, Bompensiero appears to be standing near a fishing boat or a dock. His face is in profile and a slight smile lifts the corners of his mouth. He does not look unhappy.

I sit with the photograph and try to see him, dressed in a dark suit and white shirt and polished shoes at the festive wedding parties held in Little Italy during this era. Mary Ann has said that her father sang in the shower, that he was fond of Al Jolson's rendition of "My Mammy." (Al Capone, by the way, also was a Jolson fan. On the night of the Jack Dempsey and Gene Tunney rematch in September, 1927, Capone gave a party at which he paid Jolson to entertain.) Exactly what Mary Ann said is this: "He used to say to me, when

I was still a little girl, 'Baby, put the Jolson records on.' He'd be in the shower and he'd sing, 'My Mammy.'" I look up titles of songs popular during the 1920s—"Way Down Yonder in New Orleans," "My Buddy," "I'll See You in My Dreams," "Yes, We Have No Bananas," "Nobody's Sweetheart," "Nobody Knows You When You're Down and Out," "Mexicali Rose." I try to guess which songs Bompensiero might have wanted to sing along with. I get him jigging to the rhythm of "Yes, We Have No Bananas." I see him on the dance floor. I see him rise to the toes of those shined shoes (did Johnny Alessio shine them?) and watch as he twirls young women who dress in pale voiles and sheer cottons hand-embroidered with the minutest of roses.

Mary Ann's maternal aunt, when we talked, described the social life in Little Italy during these years. "There were so many parties," she said, "back in those days. Mostly weddings. In the olden days the weddings were more family get-togethers and it isn't like what you see in *The Godfather.* They would rent a hall and everyone goes, but the only ones who went to the dinners were the family. In the olden days, say, for instance, the bridesmaids' families, the bride and groom's families, they all go to the dinner and the friends come later to the reception, where they had cookies, wedding cake, champagne. At the old weddings, they had bands. Six-piece bands.

"When my older brother got married to a girl from Los Angeles, he had the most beautiful wedding. My mother gave her the wedding, because my sister-in-law's family couldn't afford it. So my mother did it all, because she wanted her first son to have a beautiful wedding. I have never yet seen a wedding that could compete with that. For the dinner there were 700 people, sit-down. It was half Los Angeles and half San Diego people. My mother had two bands, a 13-piece orchestra and a black band. At ten o'clock she had a floor show. In between, one band played and then when they got tired the other one went on. They had a floor show with a Spanish tango. The wedding cake, the bride had to stand up on a chair to take off the top of the cake and three canaries flew out. And the cake was huge, it was seven layers going up. It didn't have any pillars to hold the cake up, it was seven layers, cake over cake over cake. For the dinner it was in a hotel. The dinner part was really nice. They had booths for the children, and all the grownups sat at long tables in the middle. They had a stage up there and a few people from San Diego knew how to play saxophone and sing and it was like a little entertainment up there while they were eating. The bridesmaids were dressed with dresses with beads on them and those big wide-brimmed hats. The bouquets were huge, two dozen and a half roses in each one with plumes, feathers, in them all the way around them and the bride had two dozen Easter lilies for her wedding bouquet. That wedding cost my mother a fortune, $14,000."

According to Bompensiero's old friend, the gentleman who told me about Bompensiero's first killing, Bompensiero, during his first years in California, spent considerable time in Los Angeles with the Dragnas. They introduced him to men involved in bootlegging and illegal whiskey making and what the Los Angeles Police Department described as "gangland murders and mysterious disappearances" and "the bootleg wars."

Since the late 1800s Los Angeles, like San Diego, had an Italian community. Charles Rappleye and Ed Becker write in *All-American Mafioso: The Johnny Rosselli Story*, that this community was "concentrated in the flatlands east of downtown, a fringe neighborhood of small wood-frame houses bordered on the west by the floodplain of the Los Angeles River, on the north by Lincoln Heights, and on the southeast by Boyle Heights.... Los Angeles' Italians were still an immigrant community, hemmed in by poverty and isolated by language and culture. The police were considered outsiders, and the laws of the land largely irrelevant."

Tony Mirabile, who would move to San Diego after Prohibition's end and set up in business as owner of a bar on Fourth and F, the Rainbow Gardens, by 1921 had moved from Detroit to Los Angeles. Mirabile made the acquaintance of Jack Dragna and, through Dragna, Bompensiero met Mirabile. In 1923 Mirabile opened a nightclub, the Midnight Follies, in Tijuana, but all through the 1920s, Tony Mirabile and his brother Paul were in and out of San Diego and Los Angeles. Bompensiero was introduced to Frank Borgia, the bootlegger and "sugar man" who worked with the Dragnas through the Twenties and Thirties. He came to know Biaggio Bonventre, who lived off and on in San Diego and had connections to Dragna through bootlegging. He got to know Joe Adrizzone and Joseph Bernardo, also in bootlegging with Dragna. But what Bompensiero, in these early years, did for or with Dragna, if anyone alive still knows, they are not willing to say.

"Daddy would kiss her on the forehead and say, 'Don't worry, Mama, I am in the trucking business.'"

CHAPTER FIFTEEN

# SHE WORE BLACK FOR THE REST OF HER LIFE

During his first years in San Diego, Bompensiero, at least part of the time, lived in one or another of his future mother-in-law's apartments. He didn't fish. He didn't work on the docks. An elderly Sicilian gentleman, after several hours' talk, allowed this: "Frank Bompensiero, after he'd been in town awhile, became a big bootlegger. The police were always after him. But he was pretty sly. He got away a lot. Mostly it was wine he was selling."

When I had gathered what facts I had gathered and talked with people who would talk to me, I was left, as I leave you, with an incomplete picture of Bompensiero as a young man. We can guess at some of what he did and we can be fairly sure of what and who he knew. By the time he turned 20, he was no longer the hopeful boy whose face gazes out at us from the photograph taken in Sicily. He has seen blood. He has shed blood. He is the carrier of secrets and leads a life that he must keep secret. *Omertà*: "manliness," or, more generally, "silence." I think that we would miss the point of who he is to shrug and say, "He was just after a quick, easy buck." I don't think Bompensiero simply was after easy money and I feel sure that he never looked forward to any violent act. What he looked forward to, I believe, was the act's completion, the moment when, literally and figuratively, he could wash his hands. I, continually, have tried to imagine the conversation with himself that Bompensiero carried on in his mind. I have tried to imagine how California must have appeared—downtown San Diego's tall buildings, Los Angeles' even taller structures, and the fast cars and the good paved roads and movies and movie stars and tailored suits and silk ties and flush toilets and hot showers and porterhouse steaks served at all hours in restaurants and dances where he could show himself off as the master of the Black Bottom.

The most important thing that happened to Bompensiero, once he jumped down off the freight train, was not California and was not America. It was Jack Dragna. Jack Dragna became for Bompensiero what now in our secularized, pop psychology-inflected worldview we would call Bompensiero's "mentor." Jack Dragna seemed to young Frank Bompensiero a veritable demi-god, colossus, and savior. Jack Dragna, Bompensiero would always say, had saved his life. Jack Dragna became Bompensiero's lodestar, his cynosure. "Frank," Bompensiero's old friend said, "became Jack's."

I do not think that Bompensiero talked with himself in the hyperconscious way in which so many of us carry on. I do believe, though, that during his late teens and early 20s, that at least two voices other than his own occupied his mind—Jack Dragna's and his mother's. I think that insofar as Bompensiero had what now we speak of as "goals," they were to please Dragna, to serve Dragna, and to help out his mother.

Quite how Bompensiero's family in Porticello communicated with its oldest son, I do not know. But certainly Bompensiero was aware that his father was failing rapidly. "Back in Porticello," said Mary Ann, "Grandfather Bompensiero kept getting worse. He had a sore in his mouth, and wouldn't go to the doctor. Eventually, in 1925, he died, of cancer. My father then was the head of the whole family—his mother, four sisters, and his brother Sam."

Mary Ann remembered her grandmother Bompensiero "as the typical little peasant Sicilian lady. I never saw her wear a color in my life and she died at 92. No lipstick, no perfume, nothing. Ever. Once she became a widow, she wore black, for the rest of her life. And all black, too, like the peasants. The immigrant ladies wore bandannas, tied like kerchiefs, and she wore these. She also wore tiny gold ball earrings that hung down from her earlobes. That's all the jewelry I ever saw my grandmother in. She never said much. She was more of the immigrant. She never remarried. Continued living, after my father was married, with my Aunt Grace and everybody else that came over, or got a start in life, all in one house at 2033 Columbia Street."

Mary Ann said, too, that whenever her father was in San Diego, he never failed, every morning, to go by to visit his mother. "Every single morning of her life—and she lived to be 92—if he was in town. I don't care if he stayed for five minutes, whatever. Every day he went to see his mother. Every day. That's how he started his day. Before he attended to anything else. And he gave his mother money. She didn't want for anything. They sat at the table and drank coffee. She always poured a lot of cream in his coffee. They spoke in Sicilian. She never spoke English. She was very very religious. In her bedroom, she kept an altar on top of her dresser, with the saints, the Virgin Mary, Saint Anthony, the candles, and she prayed all the time before the altar. She went early every morning to Mass at Our Lady."

I talked one day with one of Bompensiero's sisters. She spoke with me hesitantly, and, obliquely. This is what I learned. Giuseppe Bompensiero had hoped, eventually, to bring his family back to the United States. But his cancer progressed to a point that left him unable to travel. After his death, his wife, Anna Maria, left with five youngsters to support, struggled on. "When my father passed away, she didn't have any money and she had to go to work. So she decided to come over here, because that was the best thing. She said it was a better place to live. God bless America!"

Mrs. Bompensiero knew that she didn't want to live in Milwaukee again, because of the snow and cold weather which she blamed, in part, for her husband's decline and death. Some of Mrs. Bompensiero's cousins already had settled in San Diego. By 1928, she had decided she would return to the United States and chose San Diego as her destination. The family sailed from Palermo to Naples and from Naples to New York. From Naples they traveled on the *Conte Bianco Amaro*. The youngest Bompensiero daughter was ill all through the 12-day voyage, so ill that she was bedded down in the ship's hospital bunks. The family stayed in New York for several weeks with relatives and then boarded a train headed for San Diego.

They lived on Columbia Street in an apartment owned by the Sanfilippos. Bompensiero's sister remembered that "San Diego in 1928 was just a handful of people and everybody knew everybody. On India Street, on Columbia, on Union, in that area. Almost nobody had a car. If you had a car it was just a luxury."

For Anna Maria Tagliavia Bompensiero, a fisherman's widow and mother of six, a woman who never again would wear red or blue or green or yellow, this is what she found in San Diego. Her oldest son. Head of the family. Who, all her life, when he was in San Diego, would begin his day by dropping by 2033 Columbia for a cup of coffee. She found Our Lady of the Rosary Church, formally dedicated in December, 1925, where early morning after early morning for almost half a century she knelt with other women who'd made the two-week trip across the ocean from their birthplace. They muttered the prayer of St. Bernard, a fisherman's prayer: *"Quando le tempeste della vita minacciao la tua fragile barca, guarda la Stella—invoca Maria."* "When the storms of life menace your fragile boat, look to the Star, call on Mary."

Mary Ann said that her grandmother Bompensiero always worried about her oldest son, but that because she spoke little English and could not read, she remained protected from the facts. "She never knew. Her daughters and my uncle Sammie kept it a secret. When my father was gone, in hiding or in prison, they would tell her that he was working here and working there. But she never ever knew he went to jail or went to prison. When my father was home and she would ask him if everything was okay, Daddy would kiss her on the forehead and say, 'Don't worry, Mama, I am in the trucking business.'"

"*Quando le tempeste della vita*," she must have whispered to herself, "*minacciao la tua fragile barca, guarda la Stella—invoca Maria.*"

August 25, 1928, the police finally nabbed Bompensiero for selling wine. He was arrested, but never would be convicted, for violation of the state's Prohibition Act.

*Jack Dragna*

**I asked if she would tell me**

**her brothers' names.**

**"I can't tell you that," she said.**

**"I do not remember."**

CHAPTER SIXTEEN

# GAMBLING AT SEA

Jack Dragna, meantime, had become partner in a scheme to outfox Prohibition law. Liquor service and sales, as well as gambling, were legal across the border in Tijuana and on the high seas. June 23, 1928, Agua Caliente, where gambling ran 19 hours at a stretch, from 10 a.m. to 5 a.m., opened in Tijuana. Among its comforts, the resort offered the Gold Room, where wealthy gamblers were served gourmet fare from pure gold table service. *The San Diego Union* noted the next day that "Lower California's great new $1.5 million resort opened here last night with an elaborately formal dinner dance. The merry-making throng of San Diego, Los Angeles and Hollywood notables arrived early and stayed late, entranced with the magnificence of the creation of Baron Long, Wirt G. Bowman and James N. Crofton.

"The atmosphere of old Mexico added a touch lacking north of the border and the opening event was celebrated in a lively fashion. James Coffroth, race track operator, entertained a large party of friends as did John and George Burnham, San Diego capitalists. Among the Hollywood crowd at tables were Al Jolson, Dolores Del Rio, Charlie Chaplin, Joe Schenck, Lupe Velez, Harry Weber, Jack Dempsey, Jackie Coogan, Estelle Taylor."

In October, 1927, the Dragnas had entered into a partnership with a group of non-Sicilian men that the *Los Angeles Times* described as "sportsmen," a euphemism used in those days to mean "gamblers." This partnership purchased a wooden, 282-foot-long boat that had been built in Texas in 1919—the *Montfalcone*. The boat, for a year, sat in the dock in San Pedro, undergoing conversion to a pleasure boat. The *Los Angeles Times* on November 28th reported:

New Gambling Vessel Ready

"Another attempt to operate a gambling and café barge off the California coast will be made when the former barkentine *Montfalcone* leaves LA Harbor at daybreak this morning for an anchorage six and one half miles off the harbor, which her owners say they have been advised is on the high seas and beyond legal jurisdiction.

"The big windjammer, with gaudily painted top sides and her interior transformed into a café and casino that equals the best of Mexican resorts, has been converted for her new career at a cost of $58,000 and last night her operators put aboard the last of stores and paraphernalia.

"The *Montfalcone* is a ship without a country and thereby her operators believe she may operate as a gambling vessel beyond the law. She originally was documented as a coastwise fishing barge, but at the San Pedro customhouse yesterday it was announced that her papers have been canceled. The Federal statutes have no jurisdiction, it was explained, because she is undocumented.

"H.O. 'Doc' Dougherty, well-known local sportsman, who says he is one of the *Montfalcone*'s owners, explained her status and plan of operation while superintending lading of supplies.

"'We intended to begin operations Saturday night, running the gambling and bookmaking departments on the same basis as Tia Juana. You see there is nothing in the Constitution that makes gambling illegal and as far as the State and county are concerned, the boat will be on the high seas.'"

Bompensiero, according to his old friend, went to work on the *Montfalcone*. "As a card dealer, as muscle, when folks got too rowdy, when guys wouldn't pay their gambling debts, that kind of thing."

Bompensiero's sister reported that when they arrived in San Diego in 1928 that she and the other young Bompensieros enrolled in Washington Elementary and Roosevelt Junior High School. Their mother stayed home. "My mother was a terrific cook. She cooked everything—pasta, meat, fish, vegetables, you name it. She used to cook twice a day, lunch and dinner. Pasta with sauce, with garlic, with beans. She didn't have time to make her own noodles, she had a family to take care of, she couldn't do all that. There were six of us, two brothers and four sisters, a big family."

I asked Bompensiero's sister about her brothers. "My brothers," she said, "both were fishermen. They used to go out to sea."

I asked if she would tell me her brothers' names. "I can't tell you that," she said. "I do not remember. They are gone, they have been dead for a long time."

I sat, then, by the telephone. I said to myself, in clumsy Italian: "*Quando le tempeste della vita minacciao la tua fragile barca, guarda la Stella—invoca Maria.*"

*Elopement car*

**"He would lick the floors for her.**

**He would lick the floors for Mary Ann."**

CHAPTER SEVENTEEN

# FRANK AND THELMA ELOPE

"This is the Romeo and Juliet part. My father would throw pebbles at the window and then my mother would sneak out so they could spend a few hours together. This was before my mother turned 18 and when my father was 21 and 22. My father was five years older than my mother. He was born in 1905.

She was born in 1911. They were very, very much in love."

Frank Bompensiero's daughter Mary Ann is talking. She stops and wipes away a tear with the back of her hand.

Carl Sifakis in *The Mafia Encyclopedia* writes this about Mary Ann's father. "In the treacherous world of Mafia hit men, few characters proved shiftier than Frank 'Bomp' Bompensiero.... For decades regarded as one of the most efficient hit men in the West Coast mob, Bompensiero was an expert in the so-called Italian rope trick, a surprise garroting that always left the dying victim with a surprised look on his face.

"For double-dealing, Bompensiero was without peer. Once the Detroit mob gave him a murder contract involving one of two crime figures who had each approached the leadership with demands that the other be killed. The leadership discussed the matter at a sit-down and decided which man should get it. Bomp was informed and at a party he immediately approached the victim to be, whom he happened to know, and told him, 'Look here, you've been having this problem and the old man's given me the contract. I'm going to clip this guy but I'm going to need your help.'

"Naturally, the man was eager to be of aid and was overjoyed when told to help dig a hole for the body in advance. Bomp picked out a lonely spot and they took turns digging. Finally the man asked Bomp if the hole was deep enough. Bomp announced it was perfect and shot his victim in the back of the head."

I don't know if Mary Ann ever read that and I hope that she hasn't. I hope she doesn't. Her father was a good father. Her father was a good grandfather. And, Lord knows, he loved Mary Ann and, Lord knows, he loved Mary Ann's mother. "Are you kidding?" a woman who knew Mary Ann's mother said to me when I asked if Bompensiero loved his first wife. "He would lick the floors for her. He would lick the floors for Mary Ann. I was there. I saw it." You may stop right here and say that no man who loved his wife and his child would act in the way that Frank Bompensiero acted. My answer to you, then, would be, "You don't know what love is. You don't know."

Mary Ann was sitting at her dining room table in the house in San Diego where she's lived since the late 1950s. She was talking about how her mother and father's courtship.

During the mid-1920s, Mary Ann's father became interested in her mother, Thelma Sanfilippo. "They were going together," Mary Ann told me, and then added, "When I say 'going together,' it was nothing like today. They saw each other with everybody else around them. My mother was never allowed out.

"My mother was a sweet lady. Of all of the family, anybody that has anything to say about my mother said she was the saint of the family, she got along with everybody. My mother was curvaceous, with pretty legs, pretty bustline. She was petite. She had such a sweet little face and she adored my dad. She just loved him so much.

"My mother's mother, Felipa, liked my father. My mother's father, Lorenzo, did not like my father. I think he could see that my dad was sharp. My grandmother, Felipa, wanted my father and mother to get married."

They couldn't get married right away. Frank's father Giuseppe died in Sicily in 1925. "My father, then," said Mary Ann, "was head of the family. In 1928, three years after my grandfather Bompensiero died, my grandmother Bompensiero and her four daughters, two born in Porticello, and Sam came over from Sicily to San Diego. My grandmother Bompensiero and the older girls went to work in the fish canneries and my father helped them out with money and was more or less the sole support. My father told my grandmother Sanfilippo that he couldn't marry yet because he was the oldest one in the family.

"Also, by the time my father and mother wanted to marry, Aunt Grace was 18 and had met her fiancé. Before my dad could marry, he said that his sister Grace would have to marry. He could not leave his mother and family alone like that. My father said, 'I've got to give my sister her wedding.' So Aunt Grace wound up with a big Italian wedding. I mean a big Italian wedding. And my father paid for it."

The same person who told me that Frank and the "bachelors" with whom he was living were "a little bit wild," told me this story. "Frank Bompensiero and Frank Sanfilippo, before they got married, got roped into taking Thelma Sanfilippo and Frank Sanfilippo's fiancée to church at Our Lady one Sunday. The two Franks embarrassed those two girls half to death. The offering plate came around and Frank Bompensiero slipped a pint of bootleg whiskey into the plate. When Thelma asked him why he did that, he said, 'The father likes a nip now and then.'"

Mary Ann said that her father acquired "a fancy car, a LaSalle. He bought my mother a pea green suit with a red fox collar. They drove off to Santa Ana in the LaSalle and they got married—June 21, 1929. Josephine, who lived in Los Angeles, was supposed to be my mother's matron of honor, because Josie was engaged to marry my mother's older brother Frank. Josephine—who later became my godmother and my mother's best friend—said my mother sent her a postcard that said, 'Jo, I know I promised you, you would be our matron of honor at our wedding, but Frank and I eloped. What a wedding night, whoo, whoo!' Isn't that cute? I think about that and after all these years, I still get a lump in my throat."

Mary Ann handed me, across the table, a photograph of her mother taken in 1930. Thelma is gowned for Frank's wedding to Josephine. "That dress," Mary Ann said, "was lavender and the reason my mom looks plump in this photo is that she was pregnant with me and just beginning to show." Thelma—delicate and small-boned, barely five feet tall, with dark hair and wide, open hazel eyes—in this photo seems ethereally beautiful. She seems so ethereally beautiful that you're surprised she doesn't sprout wings and fly up out of the picture's frame.

Years ago, I began asking questions about Bompensiero. I queried retired policemen, retired FBI agents, residents in Little Italy, retired owners of downtown bars, retired crooks, authors of mob books. Many of these people had known Bompensiero; some spent considerable time with him at different points in his life. Most admitted, readily, that, yes, Bompensiero had murdered his share of men. Some went on to explain that most of the men Bompensiero "whacked" were not "straights." They were men "in the life." A few exceptions were named by retired lawmen: "Wife beaters," one man told me, "Frank had a thing about wife beaters. He just didn't have patience with a man who'd beat his wife." Bompensiero was suspected of killing at least one wife beater, perhaps two. What really surprised me, however, is this. Not one person with whom I talked about Bompensiero, retired policemen included, did not say how much he or she liked Bompensiero. People spoke of this short man as if he were tall. As they described him, he grew taller. As a youth he was "handsome, very handsome." His eyes were "big" and "beautiful." His skin, one woman said, was "so soft, so fair." As a young man, his hair was light, almost blond. Even later in San Diego, he kept the name *figlio d'oro*. Over the years, as he went about his affairs on the streets of San Diego's Little Italy, his fellow Sicilians would reach out to greet him and sigh and address him in an address more spontaneous outburst than greeting: "*Figlio d'oro! Figlio d'oro*!" People blinked, as if seeing bright light and spoke of Bompensiero as "immaculate," as "immaculately dressed." His white shirts were "spotless," his French cuffs "wide" and "generous." You could see your face in the toes of his shoes, so carefully were they shined. Even in 1955 when he went to San Quentin, he was "immaculately dressed." A visitor to him at the prison reported back, "Why, he looked as if he stepped off a bandbox. He didn't look like a convict." Often, a story followed the descriptions, a tale that had the air of fable, of legendary persons and exploits. Bompensiero had shown up at the home of a widow with "huge salamis, hams, a cheese so heavy you could hardly lift it, Italian bread, fruits and vegetables. He unrolled large bills from a wad of cash." He loaned new automobiles to people needing transportation. He drove drunken sailors home from his bar. He left $50 tips for lunches. He dealt with waiters and waitresses as if they were kings and queens. He was tender. He treated his mother, his sisters, his wife, his wife's girlfriends, his daughter, his daughter's girlfriends, his grandchildren with rare courtesy.

"I want you out of the house,

I want everybody to move."

CHAPTER EIGHTEEN

# YOU DIDN'T ASK QUESTIONS

How, then, I wondered, was I to explain Bompensiero? How was I to understand him? Here was a man who killed more than one man, who perhaps killed a dozen men. True, he was not always a great marksman. He botched more than one shooting. But he was clever and fast with a rope, and, frankly, if one is to believe the reports of autopsies and the notations on police reports, he was able to beat a man to death with a blunt instrument. One afternoon in the 1950s, he strode into a suite in the U.S. Grant Hotel and caused a large burred cucumber to be lodged deep in the anus of a union organizer.

Always, as I have tried to learn more about Bompensiero, I have been avid to learn facts—dates, names, incidents. I have also been avid—ardent, passionate—in my desire to know why he did what he did and how. When I first saw Thelma Sanfilippo Bompensiero's photograph I began to ask myself how the same hands that squeezed the life out of another man also caressed a woman so lovely that one could imagine her inspiring Dante. "What a wedding night, whoo, whoo!"

I think that we can be sure that Bompensiero, by the time he began to court Thelma Sanfilippo, was a trusted member of Dragna's organization. The organization, of course, wasn't "organized" in the way that the CEO of a large corporation might think of organization. We can be sure that there was no "business plan" in the modern sense. The "products" were liquor, debt collection, protection, extortion, intimidation and beatings, murder, influence, bribery, a bit of fencing of stolen goods, counterfeit immigration papers, bookmaking, a percentage of the take from the Dragnas' part ownership in the *Montfalcone*'s gambling and liquor proceeds and whatever else came along. Glossy advertisements did not sell these products and services; they were sold through word of mouth and coercion. Many actions taken were ad hoc. How Bompensiero would have acquired the LaSalle, the clothes, the money to help out his family and to support his wife would also have been ad hoc—improvised and often impromptu. He would have had no salary. There would have been no regular payday. Occasionally, often on whim, Jack or Tom Dragna (and Jack was notoriously mean with money) would have passed a stack of tens or twenties or hundreds to Bompensiero. On an irregular basis, money would have been "cut up" among Dragna's "workers"; each would have received a share, determined by the Dragnas, of this or that deal.

We can be sure of this. Bompensiero would never have been paid—at least directly—for any roughing-up or killing. Once an "enemy" or "problem" was dispatched, Jack Dragna might have handed over a stack of bills to Bompensiero and said, "Thank you, Frank, for taking care of this."

Mickey Cohen, in *Mickey Cohen: In My Own Words* (as told to John Peer Nugent) explained, about killings performed for the mob or Mafia, "You didn't ask any questions when you were told to do something, you just did it. Whenever you were asked to do something against somebody, it was always somebody in the racket world who had an in for you. And that guy would do it to you just as fast as you would do it to him. Some guys rose faster and farther in the racket world than others because they were able to do things asked of them. Some guys' feelings wouldn't let them do it. Other guys couldn't do it without bungling it up by getting caught or messing up in some way."

Described by the *Los Angeles Times* as perhaps "the only classic 'godfather' that the city has ever known," Jack Dragna was calculating and fierce. In his later years, no evidence exists that he participated in killings. Indeed, it was a standing joke among the guys that when time came for shotguns to go off, Dragna alibied himself by checking into a hospital for a physical. Evidence does indicate, however, that he didn't flinch when he ordered hits on associates who got out of line. Jack Dragna was nobody to mess with and men who crossed him could end up dead.

Bompensiero, in San Diego, was something of a freelancer. He engaged in a little bootlegging, a little stealing, whatever came along. This money would have been his money, and again, the acquisition of this money would have been on an ad hoc basis.

I asked Mary Ann how her maternal grandparents reacted to the elopement.

"Not too well. My grandmother did like my father and encouraged it, but my grandfather Sanfilippo didn't like him because my father was driving a beautiful car, wearing expensive clothes, and my grandfather Sanfilippo probably knew there was lots more than bootlegging going on. They didn't speak very much English, but they knew. There was talk.

"So, the fact is that my grandfather Sanfilippo had a fit. He wouldn't talk to my mother for six months. She adored her father. My grandfather Sanfilippo was the sweetest, handsomest man, beautiful white-gray hair, tall. This really hurt my mother, hurt her bad. He wouldn't talk to my mother, wouldn't talk to my father. And then, to make things more complicated, my grandmother Bompensiero was renting a house at 2033 Columbia Street that the Sanfilippos owned. My grandfather Sanfilippo went up to my grandmother Bompensiero's house and stood there and called her, 'Maria, come out here...' He said, 'I want you out.' She went to the door, and said, 'What is it?' And he yelled, 'I want you out of the house, I want everybody to move.' He was throwing a fit. She said to him, 'Why? I pay the rent, we pay the rent and we're not gonna move.' Of course she didn't move and my grandfather Sanfilippo got over it in six months."

Not long after the $1.9 million Fox Theatre Building was dedicated and the Bank of Italy purchased the Spreckels Building, and Thelma Sanfilippo became Mrs. Frank Bompensiero, things begin to get tougher for Bompensiero. In San Diego, tuna had gone farther out to sea and income from fishing was down. In Little Italy, according to everyone with whom I talked, the Italians and Sicilians with Prohibition still in force made and sold even more wine than they had previously, in order to supplement their lagging income. And local police, at the same time, became more alert to bootlegging and bootleggers. In October, 1929, there was the stock market crash. The crash, however, added to the income of the Dragnas' bootlegging businesses and of the *Montfalcone*. As the Depression deepened, the market for illegal liquor increased. From nickel bingo and dime bets on horses running at Agua Caliente to middle-class businessmen's late-night poker to the high rollers' games of chemin de fer on the Dragnas' *Montfalcone*, games of chance found more and new players. Bompensiero worked, off and on, on the *Montfalcone*.

We know this. According to one of Frank Bompensiero's sisters, once the Depression hit, their mother had to go to work. "She was working at the fish cannery. When we got here it was right before the Depression and then Herbert Hoover was elected president and that was it. During the Depression nobody was working so we had to go out and work, the women. There was no money circulating around, those were tough times. It was a bad time. Lord forbid, I remember. I still remember the olden days, some of these people were so lucky they came to this country, they got it made.

"When I was 16, I went to work at the fish cannery too. When I was growing up, that's all we had in San Diego was the fish cannery—Del Monte, Westgate, Van Camp, Star Harbor, Star-Kist, you name it, I worked in all of them just about. Oh my God, it was hard work, cleaning fish, packing. We started at seven and it depended how much fish they had how long we worked. We had caps, we had aprons. The factories were down on Harbor Drive where Solar is, Westgate was there and Del Monte. Women and men both worked there, cleaning fish. It was a hard job, it was very cold. But it was all we had. It was a fish town."

*Thelma, gowned for her brother's wedding, 1930*

**"I have signed my death warrant."**

CHAPTER NINETEEN

# NEW BUSINESS STRATEGY

During the years since Bompensiero had left Sicily and returned to Milwaukee and then hopped the freight train to San Diego, what we now describe as "organized crime" truly had become organized. Prohibition, more than any other factor, spurred that organization. By 1925, in California, even small towns like Upland and San Jose and San Bernardino could boast or lament the presence of gangs of men who specialized in illegal liquor supply. No major city in the United States was without a group like Dragna's, a group that specialized in rumrunning and bootlegging, in bribery and influence-peddling, and increasingly, in gambling and numbers running and bookmaking. These crime groups, however, were volatile and violent. Most spectacular of the gang wars—that between Al Capone and George "Bugs" Moran—culminated on Valentine's Day in 1929 in what has come to be called the St. Valentine's Day Massacre, when seven members of Moran's gang were lined up and shot by men believed to be from Capone's gang. After the "massacre," Capone won control of Chicago's gang activity. But murders, particularly "massacres," drew police attention.

Early in May, 1929, a meeting took place in Atlantic City, New Jersey. Crime historians report that this meeting was held, in part, to try to bring peace among warring gangs, and in part to try to organize the profitable business of illegal bookmaking. Capone, by then alleged to be worth $60 million, was there. The New York powers—Charles "Lucky" Luciano, Joe Adonis, Albert Anastasia, Meyer Lansky, Louis "Lepke" Buchalter, and Dutch Schultz attended. Cleveland's Moe Dalitz was there and Boston's Charles "King" Solomon. Detroit's Jewish Purple Gang sent Joe Bernstein. Johnny Lazia (the mentor of the man who would be Frank Bompensiero's second wife's second husband) came from Kansas City. Waxey Gordon, Max "Boo-Boo" Hoff, and Nig Rosen represented Philadelphia.

Although Jack Dragna had the support of New York's Thomas "Three-Finger Brown" Lucchese, a fellow Sicilian and associate of Luciano's, dons back East gave Dragna negligible respect. Three-Finger Brown was Dragna's only strong connection to East Coast power. Dragna was not sufficiently important to invite to Atlantic City.

The men meeting in Atlantic City planned to end city warfare by dividing each large city into territories whose boundaries would be respected.

(This division eventually culminated in establishment of New York City's five crime families.) On a nationwide basis, the country was to be divided into territories and those territories were to be allotted to various crime chiefs. The boundaries of these territories also were to be respected. Invasions of gangsters from one city into another were to stop.

The other half of the meeting's purpose was to deal with Prohibition's inevitable end. Voters and editorialists increasingly expressed displeasure with Prohibition. Rough polls showed that more Americans, not fewer, were drinking alcohol. Arrest reports for public drunkenness showed the same. The crime chiefs realized that once Prohibition ended, they would need new illegal ways to earn money. Off-track betting, of course, was illegal and a natural outlet for bootleggers. The brilliant Meyer Lansky already had begun to use phone banks to take bets from all over the United States. Capone brought along to the Atlantic City conclave a fellow named Moses Annenberg, owner of the *Daily Racing Form*, the newspaper that bettors on horses were never without. (Annenberg's son Walter, after World War II's end, would roll his father's fortune into founding *Seventeen* magazine and *TV Guide*.)

According to Jay Robert Nash's *World Encyclopedia of Organized Crime*, "Capone and Annenberg had conceived of a way in which a national crime cartel could control horse-betting results throughout the nation, achieved by Annenberg's newly formed Nationwide News Service which Capone bankrolled. This service would send over AT&T wires all the results from every track, only seconds after each race had been run, and feed this information to every betting parlor, poolroom, and gambling den in America. This was the centerpiece of discussion at the Atlantic City Conference, a plan that was universally adopted and one that established gambling as the first syndicated national vice to be promoted by the new crime cartel."

Over the years that I asked questions about Bompensiero, I talked with many retired lawmen from Los Angeles and San Diego, as well as several retired FBI agents. Among "rub-outs" mentioned in the LAPD's "Gangland Killings report," one that some retired lawmen believe may have been Bompensiero's work is the killing in November, 1929, of Los Angeles winery owner and bootlegger Frank Baumgarteker. In 1929, Baumgarteker argued in Los Angeles with a man who called himself Jimmy Fogarty, but whose actual name was Zorra. The argument was over Mr. Zorra's setting up a still to cook alcohol in Baumgarteker's winery. Baumgarteker reportedly kicked Zorra out of the winery and ordered all alcohol cooking stopped. After Zorra left the winery, Baumgarteker said to his secretary, Mrs. Day, "I have signed my death warrant." Zorra, according to Los Angeles Police Department records, was an associate of Joe Adrizzone and Jack Dragna.

Dragna and Adrizzone visited Baumgarteker at his winery in late November.

November 25, 1929, at 11:30 a.m., Baumgarteker had lunch in Los Angeles with his partner and his attorney. He left his lunch appointment, driving away in his purple 1926 Cadillac touring car, saying he was going to Wilmington. When Baumgarteker failed to return home the next day, his wife reported him missing.

The police report shows that on the evening of November 25, at 10:50 p.m., the purple Cadillac was driven into the Sixth Street Garage, at 745 Sixth in San Diego. The Cadillac was driven in and parked by an "Italian-looking man" described as 40 years, 5' 8", 160 pounds, wearing a short leather coat, khaki pants, and leather riding boots.

Baumgarteker's auto was found to be covered with the same type of dust and dirt as was found at the Riverside County Wells. These wells, noted the police report, "are called the 'Gangland's Cemetery' as some corpses were found there, and it was the suspected location of other gang killings."

Early in December, Mrs. Baumgarteker received a letter, supposedly written by her husband, and postmarked, "San Diego—7:30 a.m., November 30, 1929." The handwriting, the police report noted, "showed either great mental strain or that writer was drunk."

Baumgarteker's body was never found. He eventually was written off as "a victim of the Italian bootlegging element," or "Black Hand."

Mary Ann said that soon after her parents eloped they went to live with Mary Ann's Grandmother Bompensiero. In May, 1930, Thelma became pregnant with Mary Ann. Twenty-five-year-old Bompensiero now had a mother, sisters, and brother to help out, a wife to support, and a child on the way.

# SEIZE 4000 GALLONS WINE IN 8 RAIDS HERE; 11 HELD

## Clean Sweep of 'Little Italy' by Police and Federal Dry Agents Adds 65 Barrels and Assorted Liquors to Rum Property Room at Local Headquarters.

[illegible] through San Diego's "Lit-tle Italy" district, police and federal dry agents yesterday afternoon raided eight houses, arrested 11 persons and seized more than 4000 gallons of wine and some 40 gallons of assorted liquors.

The raids, all made with search warrants, started soon after noon and were not completed until early evening. All of the seizures, incidentally, were made within a radius of a few blocks either in or near the 1600 block on India street. Some of the addresses where raids also were made were on West Date, West Grape and Atlantic streets and Kettner boulevard. The raiding officers described the work as a general "house cleaning" of wine-selling establishments in the Italian section.

Those arrested, according to Archie Munson, federal dry agent, gave their [illegible] and Nick Coll, Sam and Frank Bompinserio, Sam Fellipi, Grace Fronterio and Sam Fronterio, Frank De Luca, Tony Pare and Mr. and Mrs. Tony Adamo.

The arresting officers, besides Munson, were George Sears, lieutenant of detectives in charge of the police vice detail, Patrolmen Mike Shea, E. Thomas Osborne, Elmer Macy and Ray Little, detective sergeant, all members of the police department, and G. K. Reynolds, federal prohibition agent.

The liquor, contained in about 65 barrels, was hauled to central police station and stacked in the liquor property room. A large truck made several trips to transport the wine to the police station.

The greater part of the liquor, about 3000 gallons, was found in two houses in the 1600 block on India street.

*From the San Diego Union, May 15, 1930*

**"People in that part of town told us that the people who lived in that house were some of Al Capone's gangsters."**

CHAPTER TWENTY

# TROUBLE

On May 15, 1930, if you'd been one of the city of San Diego's approximately 147,897 citizens and you'd picked up a copy of the *San Diego Union* you would have found this on page nine.

> Liquor Tanks Hidden In Ceiling Of Apartment, Piped To Ordinary Taps; How To Get Them Out Is Problem

"What was said to be one of the most cleverly concealed liquor plants uncovered here since the advent of prohibition, was discovered last night when members of the police dry detail, led by George Sears, lieutenant of detectives, raided an apartment house at 1907 Columbia Street. The officers seized 60 gallons of wine, 25 gallons of whisky, 25 gallons of gin and 20 gallons of alcohol. Frank Buonpensiero was arrested as the owner of the liquor.

"Four large copper tanks in which the liquor was stored, were concealed between the second floor and the ceiling of the first floor apartment. From each tank led copper pipes, all concealed either in the walls or the floors of the building to a secret compartment in a closet in a ground floor apartment occupied by Buonpensiero. Each tank was a separate compartment for the storage of liquor and the compartment in the closet was fitted with a neat faucet. Thus, the liquor could be drawn from the storage tanks as one would draw a glass of water.

"When the officers entered the apartment house they searched it from the roof to the basement without finding any trace of liquor, or a spot where it might have been hid. They were about to give up the search when the keen eyesight and acute sense of smell of Lieutenant Sears led to the discovery.

"Sears was alone in an unoccupied apartment on the second floor. He smelled what he was certain was whiskey. Then he opened a small compartment used for keeping cooking utensils. It was bare, but he noticed the flooring of the compartment, adjoining the flour bin, was slightly stained. Calling the other officers, Sears tore out the flour bin and beneath it found the tops of four pipes. Each pipe had a neat screw top.

"Under questioning by Sears, Buonpensiero admitted the presence of the storage tanks and explained how they had been placed between the flooring and ceiling of two apartments. He also led the officers to the secret compartment where the drawing spigot for each tank was concealed."

The *San Diego Sun* noted, that same week:

Raids Send Liquor Prices Soaring

"Further shortages in San Diego's supply of bootleg liquor and home brew are apparent.

"With wholesale federal and police liquor raids recently putting some of the biggest dealers out of business, the next step, it was learned today, may be to cut off supplies for materials used in making intoxicants. The next step toward making San Diego's summer unusually dry will hit at dealers handling everything from malts to machinery for making hard liquor."

And if this were not enough, there also was trouble in Los Angeles with the *Montfalcone*. The *Los Angeles Times* on May 22, 1930, reported that "rivalry between factions claiming to own the gambling ships *Montfalcone* and *Johanna Smith*, which have plied their trade for more than a year at anchor off Seal Beach, blazed into open warfare last night.

"Nick Oswald, owner of the *Montfalcone*, told the DA that James Dougherty, said to be owner of the *Smith*, and claimant to partnership in the *Montfalcone*, commandeered a water taxi belonging to the *Montfalcone* and with four men forcibly boarded the ship.

"When the five climbed over the rail of the *Montfalcone*, they fired two shots and the crew of the boat capitulated. Then the men took possession of the boat and pirated the proceeds from the gaming table."

On July 29, Dragna and three other men were arrested in downtown Los Angeles with a large quantity of cash, proceeds from the weekend take on the *Montfalcone*, and weapons enough to ward off a hijack, including four revolvers and the shotgun.

One of the men arrested was a man who called himself "Johnny Rosselli." In 1924 Johnny Rosselli, born in Italy in 1905 as Filippo Sacco, had arrived in Los Angeles from Chicago, where he had been associated with Capone. Rosselli was tubercular. Capone recommended California sunshine. In his first years in Los Angeles Rosselli worked as a general heavy for Tony Cornero, a rumrunner and bootlegger of Italian descent known as "Tony the Hat" and "King of the Western Rumrunners." Cornero was arrested in 1927, got out on bail, escaped to Canada, and left Rosselli without means of employment. Capone suggested that Rosselli ally himself with Jack Dragna, which he did.

An old friend of Bompensiero's, a man whose knowledge of organized-crime circles is impeccable, told me that from the beginning, Bompensiero did not think that highly of Rosselli. Actually, what the old friend said was, "Frank knew Rosselli was like shit: he was all over. He was a phony. Shoulda' been an actor. He wanted to be. He was in with all those guys in Chicago." But Dragna did like Rosselli, or, perhaps was impressed by Rosselli's tight Capone and Chicago connections, contacts that Dragna, at the continent's edge, badly needed. Bompensiero's friend was correct, too, in saying that Rosselli wanted to be an actor. The handsome, leonine, expensively tailored Rosselli—"Gentleman Johnny" people called him—tried for bit parts in Hollywood films and eventually made himself invaluable to several Hollywood studios, supplying them with liquor and women. Bit by bit, Rosselli made himself sufficiently useful to Dragna that he became Dragna's right-hand man, a position he would retain through the 1930s. With the ascendance of Rosselli, a man only a few months older than Bompensiero, Bompensiero may well have felt that his opportunities to rise in Dragna's group were being squelched. I don't know that he felt that, but he may have. He may have felt pushed aside by Rosselli.

The *Los Angeles Times* on July 30, 1930, reported:

> Four Arrested For Gun Toting
>
> Suspects Taken After Chase In Auto By Police
>
> Prisoners Claim Connection With Gambling Ship
>
> Permits To Carry Weapons Declared Too Old

"Activities of four men, James Russo of 5533 Hollywood Blvd., John Rosselli of 1043 West Sixth Street, John Canzoneri of 1402 East Twelfth Street and Jack I. Dragna of 3662 Mettler Street, taken into custody at an early hour yesterday morning with four revolvers and one shotgun in their possession, are being carefully checked by Detective Lieutenants Malibeau and Gibson of the police robbery detail."

The summer of 1930 must have been difficult for Bompensiero. He and Thelma were living with his mother, at 2033 Columbia Street. Thelma's pregnancy was troubled. Her blood pressure soared. She "retained water." Her shoe size, said Mary Ann, went from a five to an eight. She did not like living with her in-laws. "But," said Mary Ann, "that's what you did then, right after you married. You moved in with your husband's family. My mother hated it. My grandmother Bompensiero had migraine headaches and things could get very tense with her and my aunt Grace, my father's sister. And, they had fish every single night for dinner and my mother hated fish because fish made her deathly ill and she had to sit there and eat it anyway."

Her mother, Mary Ann continued, wanted badly to get out of Little Italy. "I think my mother must have been the first one to want to make a break from that Italian neighborhood. She was always more modern. When I was a little older and she was telling me why we eventually moved out of that area, she said to me, 'Mary Ann, you will be so glad to be out of that neighborhood. Yakity, yak, gossip, gossip. You'll thank me later on in life that you didn't have to live down here.'" Mary Ann shuddered, and said, "The talk that goes on in those Italian neighborhoods. If they see you even look at a boy, you're a tramp. Or, if you start wearing lipstick. I was always glad that she moved us."

In August, 1930, the *Montfalcone* caught fire and burned. The pleasure boat was out of commission and Bompensiero's help as a dealer and bouncer was no longer needed.

The Bompensieros moved in November, 1930, to Kensington to a house at 4307 Hilldale. The San Diego Police Department's purity squad, the men whose task it was to deal with bootlegging and speakeasies, had decided they would clean up the city's vice dens during 1930's Christmas season. Soon after the Bompensieros got settled in Kensington, Bompensiero and many Little Italy residents found themselves in trouble. The *Union* headline for December 6, 1930, read:

> Seize 4000 Gallons Wine In 8 Raids Here; 11 Held
>
> Clean Sweep Of 'Little Italy' By Police And Federal Dry Agents Adds 65
>
> Barrels And Assorted Liquors To Rum Property Room At Local Headquarters

"Through San Diego's 'Little Italy' district, police and federal dry agents yesterday afternoon raided eight houses, arrested 11 persons and seized more than 4000 gallons of wine and some 40 gallons of liquors.

"The raids, all made with search warrants, started soon after noon and were not completed until early evening. All of the seizures, incidentally, were made within a radius of a few blocks either in or near the 1600 block on India Street. Some of the addresses where raids also were made were on West Date, West Grape and Atlantic streets and Kettner Boulevard. The raiding officers described the work as a general 'house cleaning' of wine-selling establishments in the Italian section."

The *San Diego Evening Tribune*, that evening, offered under the headline, "Will Arraign 12 On Liquor Charges": "The following is a list of those against whom charges have been filed, and the addresses of the houses raided, according to a report by federal dry agents:

"Frank and Sam Bompensiero, 1907 India Street, alleged possession and sale; Tony Adamo, 518 West Date Street, alleged possession and sale; Andrean Punta, 1632 India Street, alleged possession and sale; Frank Delucca, 1470 Kettner Boulevard, and Perry Tore, alleged possession and sale; Sam and Mrs. Fellipo, 1971 Atlantic, alleged sale; Nick and Anna Coli, 914 Grape Street, alleged sale."

The *San Diego Sun* reported:

Police Capture Holiday Wine

Vice Squad House Cleans In Little Italy; 11 Arrested

"There's gloom this morning along India Street where it cuts through the heart of San Diego's Little Italy.

"Little Italy's citizens wait annually for Santa Claus with full stocked cellars. Yesterday they looked up to find the police vice squad piling 65 barrels of wine on a truck as the first blow in a drive to clean house before the holidays.

"Dozens of bottles of whisky were confiscated and 11 persons arrested during eight raids. There will be other raids before Christmas, George Sears, vice squad leader, indicated today.

"Most of the wine was found in homes in the 1600 block on India Street."

Mary Ann explained. "Somebody once told me that this all happened because somebody snitched to the police. Somebody jealous in that neighborhood. Jealous of the money that people were making, selling wine."

Then, with poor Thelma sicker and sicker, her feet swelling and hands swelling, Bompensiero and his little brother, Sam, got themselves into another mess. The *San Diego Sun* on December 9 reported:

Schoolboy Trio Uncovers $25,000 Cache Of Opium

"The Rollo Boys, Robinson Crusoe and all the other adventure books hold little interest for three San Diego lads today.

"For late yesterday the trio, investigating in a neighbor's back yard, unearthed $25,000 worth of opium and supplied information that led to the arrest of the three men.

"The three boys are Jack Allison, Nat Munn and 'Junior' Moore. They all live in the Kensington Heights district. Jack and Nat were coming home from school yesterday when Junior met them.

"His eyes were bright with excitement and he was breathless.

"'I saw a fellow burying something in a back yard near my house yesterday,' he told them. He told about a long black box that the man had stuffed into a hole in the ground. The three went into a huddle.

"A short while later they appeared with a spade, in the rear of a house at 4307 Hillsdale Road. Junior had some other errand to perform, so Jack and Nat are the real heroes of the story. They started digging where they found some damp dirt, which appeared to have been dug up recently.

"'We were sure scared,' Nat, who is 13 years old, said today in telling his story. His eyes grew wider as he explained, 'Y'see we thought it was liquor that was buried there.

"'We thought the guy was a bootlegger. And we didn't know whether he was in the house with a gun or not. Anyway, pretty soon we came to a shiny copper box. We pulled it out of the dirt, brushed it off and found that it was locked tight.

"'Then we went and found an old wrench, and managed to pry it open. Inside there were all kinds of little black balls. We didn't know what it was, so we took it over to my house.'

"Mrs. E.J. Munn, Nat's mother, who lives at 5125 Hastings Rd, suspected that it was opium, but wasn't sure. 'You take that stuff right back where you got it,' she ordered the boys.

"They returned the box, and reburied it, but first, they took out one of the black pellets and kept it.

"'After it was all over,' young Allison said, 'we were awful scared. People in that part of town told us that the people who lived in that house were some of Al Capone's gangsters. It was just fun until we began to think about it, and then we didn't know what to do.'

"After they had gotten over their fears, they walked down the street to the drug store where they met F.J. Day, a deputy sheriff.

"When they told their stories and exhibited their trophies, Day was convinced.

"'He went downtown,' Nat said today, 'and got a couple of detectives. They went into the house and arrested a man and we showed them where the opium was stored.'"

The *San Diego Evening Tribune* on December 11, reported on page two:

Suspect Faces Court On Dope Charges

"Frank Bompercerio, who was arrested recently in connection with a find of 48 bindles of opium gum in his backyard at 4305 Hillsdale Road, Kensington Park, today was arraigned on charges of violation of the state narcotics act. Sam

Bompercerio, a brother, who gave his age as 17, was bound over to the juvenile court. A preliminary hearing for Frank Bompercerio will be held December 24. Bail was fixed at $750."

No records exist of the outcome of this hearing on the opium incident. Bompensiero and his brother Sam were never convicted.

Mary Ann was born on January 16, 1931. "My mother, by the time I was delivered, had what they call 'toxemia of pregnancy.' She almost died in childbirth. I almost died. All my mother remembered of childbirth was the ambulance and sirens. She had a slight stroke at that time. Her mouth went crooked."

Thelma was hospitalized for several weeks. And then, what a homecoming! Mary Ann said, "My dad would laugh about things. He'd say, 'You know, honey, when you were born, when I brought your mother home from the hospital, we were in the house maybe an hour or so and the trucks were coming to move the furniture out, because we didn't make the payments. It was one of those things.'" Mary Ann added, "He must have made it good and then all of a sudden things went haywire and no money was coming in."

In January 1931 Bompensiero was convicted on federal charges for violations of Prohibition laws. Mary Ann's godmother and aunt, Josephine, 90 years old when I interviewed her five decades later, recalled that before Bompensiero left for prison she and Thelma took their babies to Our Lady of the Rosary to have them baptized. Frank and Thelma, she said, were her son Laurence's godparents and she and Frank Sanfilippo were Mary Ann's godparents. After the ceremony, Josephine said that the two couples went out for a "nice dinner." Where they went, she does not remember.

On April 4, 1931, before Mary Ann was quite three months old, her father was taken by train to Tacoma, Washington, and then by ferry to the United States federal prison on McNeil Island set in the midst of Puget Sound. Built in the 1880s on McNeil Island's seven square miles, the prison was notoriously cold in winter and damp and gloomy year-round. I asked through the Freedom of Information Act for any record of Bompensiero's stay at McNeil Island. I received a photocopy of a card that had been kept on file in the United States archives. Notations on the card indicate that Bompensiero applied for and was denied parole on June 17, 1931, and that he would not be released until April 12, 1932. I was able to learn nothing about Bompensiero's time on McNeil Island other than that his friend from San Diego, Biaggio Bonventre, also was incarcerated there, during approximately the same period of time and for the same offense.

PHOTOGRAPH BY SANDY HUFFAKER, JR.

*Apartments at 1907 Columbia Street*

**"My tiny little grandmother would climb down out of the car and stand there and throw rotten eggs at the woman's door."**

# CHAPTER TWENTY-ONE

# VERY SICILIAN

While Bompensiero was in prison, the Depression deepened. Bompensiero's mother and sisters labored in the fish canneries. Thelma and Mary Ann moved into an apartment at 1907 Columbia Street, near Grape, owned by Thelma's mother. "My godmother Josephine," said Mary Ann, "who was married to my mother's brother Frank lived downstairs and we lived upstairs." Mary Ann stopped in the flow of her story and told me about Frank and Josephine and how they met. "Josephine came from Los Angeles. Her father's first name was Octavio, a handsome guy, small. He was a widower. Josephine's mother died in childbirth when Josephine was a little girl. Josephine was second to the oldest of five sisters. Octavio used to bring Josephine and all his family down to San Diego. He came down to deliver olive oil and Parmesan cheese to the Sicilian and Italian families. He also knew Jack Dragna and Tom, Jack's brother. He would go to my grandmother Sanfilippo's house on Pacific Highway and Grape to deliver oil and cheese, and that's how Josephine came to meet my uncle Frank. My grandmother liked Josephine. And Josephine fell madly in love with Frank, from the moment she saw him, she said. But it was an arranged marriage, arranged by my grandmother Sanfilippo and Josephine's father, but my aunt Josephine adored Frank and I guess he loved her.

"My mother and Josephine were crazy about each other. My mother felt more love for Josephine than her sisters, I think. I was born in January. Josephine and Frank's son was born in March. We were living, by then, all of us, on Columbia near Grape Street. Josephine nursed me. I was a crybaby when I was a baby. My mom tried to nurse me and I would get sick. Given what was going on during that period—my father getting arrested and then going off to prison—my mom was upset a lot. I wouldn't eat. So Josephine had her son and she'd nurse him and then she'd say, 'Thelma, give me that baby.' And she'd nurse me. She was like a wet nurse. Josephine told me, about all this, that she'd take me in her arms and nurse me and I would start eating right away and I'd coo and coo and coo.

"Sometime during that period, while we lived there and my dad was in prison and Josephine was pregnant with her second child, my uncle Frank started running around on Josephine. He was going around with some gal. Even though my grandmother and my mother loved Frank, they both always took Josephine's side in this. My grandmother Sanfilippo adored her son Frank. But, frankly, he was a spoiled brat. Blue eyes, handsome, gorgeous man. Josephine used to say that his eyes were as blue as the ocean he fished in. Anyway, my grandmother Sanfilippo would wring her hands and say to him, 'Frank, what are you doing? You've got a wife and children. What are you doing with this *putana*?' My grandmother Sanfilippo never called this woman anything but the '*putana*,' the whore. And, my grandmother Sanfilippo believed in the evil eye and was trying to figure out some way to get this woman. She knew where this gal lived. So my grandmother Sanfilippo would make my mother get in the car and drive her over to this *putana*'s house and my tiny little grandmother would climb down out of the car and stand there and throw rotten eggs at the woman's door. Very Sicilian," concluded Mary Ann, "to do something like that."

Her grandmother Sanfilippo, Mary Ann said, wasn't like most women were in those days. "She was tough. Back when they were still living in Milwaukee my grandfather Lorenzo had a little tavern and there was this gorgeous widow, a young widow, who was head-over-heels about Lorenzo. She haunted him, was always after him. And one day she gave him the keys to her house. He knew better than to fool around on my grandmother Felipa and so he gave the keys to her. She got a billy club and went to the widow's house and knocked on the door and said to her, 'You go near my husband again and I will knock the hell out of you.' She was wiry and strong and could have done it, too."

Mary Ann said her mother and Josephine were not happy. "Aunt Jo has told me that she and my mother would sit together with their babies and cry and cry and cry. Uncle Frank was running around on Aunt Jo and my dad was in prison. Auntie Jo said they'd both cry until their eyes were red and swollen. Then when night came, they'd gather up me and Laurence, Frank and Josie's boy, and they'd get us into our bassinets in the bedroom next to the bed and then they'd crawl into bed and they'd cry some more and then go to sleep."

Bompensiero was 25 when he entered prison and 26 when he stepped onto the ferry and sailed back across Puget Sound and boarded the train and headed home. "Frank knew how to do time," an old friend of his told me. But I continue to wonder and I hope that you also will want to wonder what it must have been like for him, to leave behind his wife and baby. He could be sure that his mother-in-law Sanfilippo would see to it that Thelma and Mary Ann weren't without a roof and didn't go hungry. And they weren't and they didn't. Thelma wrote to him and he wrote to Thelma, and at least once, according to an old friend of Thelma's, Thelma was able to go on the train to Washington State to visit with Frank.

"Just as Bompensiero was pointing

the gun at the manager,

the janitor happened to walk in."

CHAPTER TWENTY-TWO

# STICK-UPS

A year is a long time to stare out between iron bars into the mist over Puget Sound. Did Bompensiero during his year on McNeil Island consider "going straight"? Did he think that perhaps he'd do better to return to San Diego and go back out fishing? Or perhaps open a small grocery store on India Street? Did he ask himself if he might find life easier if he were to live within the law rather than without? Perhaps "going straight" never occurred to Bompensiero. Mary Ann had told me that in those days nobody was embarrassed at going to prison for bootlegging. "None of the Italians," she said, "looked down on you for that." Perhaps the months on McNeil Island were time Bompensiero felt he had to put in simply as the cost of doing business. Perhaps my speculation that a year's incarceration offered Bompensiero time to reflect upon his life and that he considered changing his life, is only speculation upon a cliché.

Perhaps, too, by 1931, Bompensiero was too entangled and enmeshed with, in thrall to Jack Dragna to even consider beginning a new life, a *vita nuova*. Perhaps Bompensiero did not want a new life. Perhaps he liked this life just fine. McNeil Island's cells, during Bompensiero's year there, were filled with other men like himself, bootleggers and rumrunners. Bompensiero was gregarious. He would have sat with these men and shared stories. He would have told them about his still on Columbia Street and how you could just turn the spigot and "liquor could be drawn from the storage tanks as one would draw a glass of water." Mary Ann, many times, said her father loved to laugh. His laugh, she said, came from deep within his chest. She said that sometimes he laughed until he wept.

Mary Ann said that when she was a little girl, a toddler whose blond Shirley Temple curls fell to her shoulders, people sometimes asked her, "Where's your daddy?" Mary Ann said that she always answered this question in the same way: "Daddy," she would say, "is bye-bye, choo-choo."

In April, 1932, Bompensiero returned to San Diego. He gave himself a quasi-assumed name, and San Diego's city directory for 1932 shows an entry for: "Bompo, Frank and Thelma—San Filippo Apartments, 1907 Columbia." Mary Ann had begun to crawl and from being with her grandmothers and her maternal grandfather and aunts and uncles, she babbled in a Sicilian dialect-inflected Italian. "I used to speak Sicilian really fluently until I was five years old because I was with my grandparents who spoke no English around the house, and what English they did speak was very, very broken English." Mary Ann does not know what her father did after he returned from prison. She thinks that he may have worked as a card dealer in a card room on University Avenue. And she remembered, vaguely, something about her father working in or owning part of a restaurant. "I recall," she said, "as a very little girl going into a restaurant in San Diego, near the docks, and Daddy making me a sandwich. But that may have been later."

The only person who remembered something about that period immediately after Bompensiero left prison was Mary Ann's godmother and aunt, Josephine. She was pregnant, she said, with her second son, and almost ready to deliver. Her husband Frank was in Tijuana with his girlfriend. "Frank Bompensiero," she said, "stuck up for me. He didn't like Frank's chasing and he said so. I couldn't walk, by then, up the stairs to our apartment. Frank Bompensiero carried me up those stairs in his arms. He was as gentle with me as if I were a baby."

Again, for almost a year, we lose Bompensiero's trail. Mary Ann was too young to know what went on. It was a time in Bompensiero's life about which Mary Ann's mother apparently had not wanted to talk with Mary Ann. So that Mary Ann, when she was older, heard no stories about these years.

Franklin Delano Roosevelt in January, 1933, took the oath of office as the nation's 32nd president. His administration immediately began to organize programs to put people to work. No record exists that Bompensiero, most of whose skills were founded in violence, took part in any of FDR's Works Progress Administration programs.

When I first began to ask questions about Bompensiero, I spent several days with a gentleman then in his 80s who had been a member of several San Diego city and county law-enforcement agencies and who had always been interested in what he spoke of as the "Italian element" and the "Siciliano element." I will call him "Mr. Willis." He told me that in the early 1930s, Bompensiero had become involved with a group responsible for at least six robberies. "He was a tough guy, don't think he wasn't. We always knew about the 211 he did at the Fox Theatre. He matched the description perfectly," said Mr. Willis. He went on to say that Bompensiero and two other "characters" went to the Fox just after closing time and made their way into the manager's office, where the night's take was. "Apparently," Mr. Willis said, "just as Bompensiero was pointing the gun at the manager, the janitor happened to walk in. Bompensiero shot the janitor, bang, in the arm or the shoulder, I can't remember, now, which."

Mr. Willis believed that Bompensiero was one of the perpetrators of a robbery June 8, at the American Cut-Rate Drug Store on Fifth Avenue. The *San Diego Union* for June 9, 1933, reported:

Drug Bandits Obtain $700

"Two hold-up men, believed by police to be 'experts' from the east, robbed the American Cut-Rate drug store, 810 Fifth Avenue, last night and escaped with $700. Part of the money was $500 which the proprietor had received from a friend for deposit in the bank.

"The bandits entered the store just as Abe Brownstone, the proprietor, was about to close at 9:30 p.m. In the store also were Mrs. Brownstone and two clerks, Paul Summers and A.W. Lewis.

"'We're sorry to do this but it's a stick-up,' said one of the bandits as they both leveled revolvers at the proprietor and his assistants.

"'Where is the "pete"?' asked the other bandit. 'Pete' is a term used by eastern crooks.

"Brownstone showed them the safe and one of the men took out the box containing the money. The robbers herded the group to the rear of the store and then ran out."

Another robbery that Mr. Willis believed Bompensiero masterminded was this, reported on the front page of the June 21, 1933, edition of the *San Diego Union*:

8 Party Guests Robbed Of $2847 By 3 Bandits

"Six prominent San Diego residents and two Los Angeles citizens were terrorized by three bandits late last night, when the thugs entered the home of Irvine M. Schulman, 4353 Trias Street, Mission Hills, and robbed guests of $847 and more than $2000 in jewelry.

"Detectives Leo Magone and Ben Eichbaum, investigating the robbery, reported that the bandits entered through a rear door. Before appearing the bandits tore the telephone wires from the wall and tied the rear door open for a quick escape.

"While two of the bandits stood guard at the front door of the home, one of the thugs carefully searched the guests who had been playing cards, taking their money and jewelry. To be sure that they left no valuables on the men, a second bandit searched the guests, taking what little change the first robber missed.

"After a complete search, the three bandits tied each of the men with a small rope and forced them into a closet. They forgot to lock the closet door, however, and after the bandits had departed one of the guests freed himself and ran to a telephone on the second floor where he summoned police. All the persons robbed were men.

"Schulman, police said, was the owner of the Globe Furniture Company on Market Street."

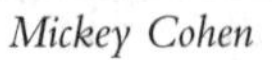

*Mickey Cohen*

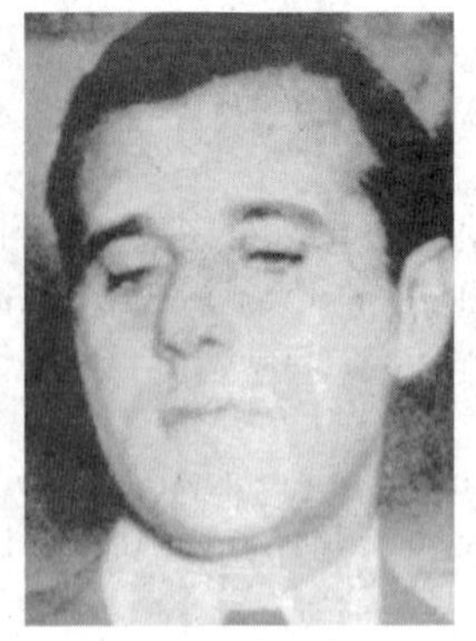

*Bugsy Siegel*

*Johnny Rosselli*

**"California was provincial, underpopulated, isolated from the mainstream."**

CHAPTER TWENTY-THREE

# JEWS TAKE ON DRAGNA

In 1933 Congress passed the 21st Amendment to the Constitution, which repealed the 18th Amendment and on December 5, 1933, lifted Prohibition. The *San Diego Union* noted on December 6, 1933: "Almost immediately there was a veritable flood of alcoholic liquors in all parts of the city. Within fifteen minutes after word had been spread through newspaper extras that prohibition officially had been repealed, drug and retail liquor stores were selling liquor over their counters and making window displays of their alcoholic stock." Men like Bompensiero, who made at least part of his money through illegal whiskey and wine, and women like his mother-in-law Felipa Sanfilippo, who made and sold wine, were now out of business.

With Prohibition's end, downtown San Diego changed rapidly. Mr. Willis said, "A fellow by the name of Tony Mirabile came to town, dear old Tony. Tony took up an old storage building, and made it into the Rainbow Gardens. He made a good living in there. Tony became the boss. His brother Paul, who came here too, was the one who had the class, the education. He was handsome, Paul was, a tall distinguished gentleman, good looking. Tony was a good-sized man too, but sinuous. And Tony was a little on the crude side. Tony would talk in four-letter words and about every third word he would utter was that type of word.

"Law enforcement was more interested in Tony than in Paul. Paul always portrayed the gentleman, always well dressed, and very polite, very courteous, his demeanor was that of a proud don, he didn't use any rough language. Tony was the rough one, but Tony was the boss. You look at the two together, you would never put them as brothers. Tony dressed well, he wasn't a slob, but the culture he had, you wouldn't say he was a cultured gentleman. Tony worked the bars and he acted and talked just like a bar owner. These bars he came to own were watering holes. Everything that Tony had and would later have was predicated on the liquor industry."

Tony Mirabile—*Mirabile* means "wonderful or beautiful to behold"—was the name everyone returned to when discussing post-Prohibition activity in downtown San Diego bars. About Mirabile, retired San Diego policeman Bill Heritage said, "It was kind of an unwritten law that you didn't mess with Tony. I can still see him coming down the street with his overcoat slung over his shoulders and his bodyguard behind him. Tony never put his arms in his sleeves. When I saw that entourage coming down the street, I got out of the way."

The "bodyguard" of whom Mr. Heritage spoke was Marco Impastato. In hearings conducted by the California Assembly Judiciary Committee's racket subcommittee in the Hotel San Diego's Continental Room in October, 1958, San Diego County Sheriff's Sgt. Robert Newsom said, describing Impastato: "He is a lackey, a hireling, you might say, an employee of Tony Mirabile. He has been around the Rainbow Gardens for a number of years. I have observed him myself on numerous occasions with Mirabile in the City of San Diego, also in the County area around the racetrack. He is, you might say, a Hollywood version of a bodyguard. He is usually about three paces behind Mirabile and has a snap brim he carries very low on his forehead. Kind of comical, as a matter of fact, to watch him."

Tony Mirabile was known to speak among friends about his association, in Detroit, with Detroit's infamous and violent Purple Gang, a group that eventually transmuted into the Detroit Mafia family. November 13, 1920, Tony became a U.S. citizen and received a certificate of naturalization. Shortly after, the Mirabile brothers left Detroit for Los Angeles.

Mirabile, who was grilled for an entire day by the rackets subcommittee, was asked: "When did you first know Jack Dragna?"

A: I told you.

Q: 1921?

A: 1921, yes.

Mirabile was asked what businesses Dragna had when the men first met. Mirabile said, "I believe he used to have a winery, or a winery farm, or something like that. Close to Los Angeles. I can't think of name. He had a winery when I met him. And also distill, some perfume, or something. I don't know what, but I know that."

In 1924, Tony and Paul crossed the border into Tijuana and opened two cabaret bars on Avenida Revolución, one called the Midnight Follies. Tijuana was a small town, then. In 1920 its population was 1028; in 1930, it had only 3300 residents. A small Italian colony existed in Tijuana during the 1920s—Cardinis, Santinis, Cardinales. Jack Dragna and other Mafia-associated Sicilians occasionally visited the Mirabiles there. A man whose family was close to the Mirabiles said his parents often went across the border to the Midnight Follies, that in addition to "stage entertainment" and ballroom dancing, the cabaret offered gambling and slot machines. Tony Mirabile's FBI report states that the Midnight Follies burned to the ground in 1933, the same year that Tony and Paul arrived in San Diego.

When Prohibition ended, Tony Mirabile opened the Rainbow Gardens.

According to articles written in 1953 in the *Los Angeles Mirror* by reporter Art White, Nick Licata loaned Tony Mirabile $7000 to help him start the Rainbow Gardens. Licata (1897-1974), like the Mirabiles, was born in Sicily and settled as a teenager in Detroit. Jay Robert Nash writes in his *World Encyclopedia of Organized Crime* that Licata soon joined the Detroit Mafia family of Joe Zerilli. "But Licata somehow offended Zerilli and was forced to flee to California. Zerilli took a contract on Licata with the boss of the Los Angeles territory, Jack Dragna. Instead of murdering Licata, Dragna convinced Zerilli to cancel the contract and took Licata into his organization."

Tony Mirabile, early on, was making enough money to allow him to buy stocks and bonds. His last will, prepared in 1952 and 1953, shows that on November 19, 1931, while still in Tijuana, he bought 3 shares in the Bancamerica-Blair Corporation. May 27, 1935, he bought 40 shares of stock in the Chicago department store, Marshall Field and Company. In 1937, on January 30, he bought 24 shares of Bancamerica-Blair. April 15, 1937, he acquired 19 shares in the National City Bank of New York. July 31, 1937, Tony bought 121 shares of common stock in the Bank of America. August 13, 1938, he purchased 605 shares in the Transamerica Corporation. By the mid-1940s Tony and Paul would be worth at least one million dollars.

Mr. Willis said that Tony Mirabile, once he settled in San Diego and opened the Rainbow Gardens, soon became known about town as the godfather of the Italian and Sicilian community, the man to go see when you had problems, when you needed a job, when you needed a loan—"Particularly," laughed Mr. Willis, "if you wanted a loan." A man long retired from law enforcement, a man who like Mr. Willis had always taken an interest in the "Italian element" in San Diego, said to me, about Mirabile, "No question in my mind that Tony was a made man." By "made man," the retiree meant that Tony, at some point, had become a Mafia member. He went on to say, about Tony Mirabile, "You don't get in a position of control like that if you aren't a made man. He was considered by the local hoods to be the one in charge. Everybody came to see him. In the middle of the night, in the middle of the day, meetings were held. Little Apalachins. Usually they went to the back room in the bar he hung around the most that he owned, the Rainbow Gardens."

The story on Tony Mirabile's being a "made man" seems to me a sad story. According to a local near-octogenarian unconnected to law enforcement, a man whose inside knowledge of organized crime is impeccable, "Tony was a joke. Tony couldn't do any work. He never did any work. He paid Jack Dragna to make him. He gave Jack $150,000, along in 1941, 1942." At best, my informant suggested, Tony Mirabile was an old-fashioned *padrone*, a distributor of petty favors to employees and other bar owners. Where Tony was a joke, he explained, was in the larger, outer world of what variously could be described as organized crime, connected people, the Mafia, or, Cosa Nostra, a world where gossip is rife. "Everyone knew about Tony," my informant said, "even back East they knew." A man who pays to be made, rather than by "doing work," or, killing, will always be looked down upon by true "workers." And so, my informant said, Tony was "a joke." My informant also told me that Bompensiero never liked or trusted Mirabile.

After Prohibition ended, Dragna's Los Angeles group began to push its way—literally—into gambling and bookmaking. According to LAPD's James E. Hamilton's "Gangland Killings" document, "When two large books in the Los Angeles area—operated by Guy McAfee and Tutor Sheerer began to be 'muscled' for a 'piece' of the 'take' by Italians, led by Jack Dragna, McAfee refused and was reported to ask 'Who the hell is Jack Dragna?' He found out! Stickupmen raided the books; runners were roughed up, all of which cost the books thousands of dollars. Soon the Italians were cut in!"

Ex-pugilist Meyer Harris (Mickey) Cohen (1913-76), beginning in the 1930s, managed a good-sized bookmaking ring in LA. Benjamin "Bugsy" Siegel (1906-47) also showed up in LA in the 1930s.

Meyer Lansky, the bookmaking mastermind, expected that Siegel's presence in California would extend syndicate control of gambling all through the West. Lansky spoke to Charles "Lucky" Luciano who spoke to Jack Dragna. Luciano told Dragna to make Siegel welcome in LA. Dragna acceded, not happily, to Lansky and Luciano's demands.

Mickey Cohen, in *Mickey Cohen: In My Own Words* (as told to John Peer Nugent) explains the LA rackets this way:

"Until Benny [Siegel] came to LA in 1936, maybe 1937, it was a syndicate, a combination like the syndicate in Chicago and the syndicate in New York. But here, gambling and everything like they did in Jersey, Chicago, and New York was completely run by cops and stool pigeons.

"Benny was part and parcel of New York. He was all-powerful and connected with the main organization back East, on a par with anybody you could mention—Joe Adonis, Lucky Luciano, Frank Costello. In Los Angeles there was this Italian man by the name of Jack Dragna. Jack was very powerful and very well respected, but he got kind of lackadaisical. He wasn't able to put a lot of things together to the satisfaction of the Eastern people, or even keep things together for himself to their satisfaction.... There was no combination; everyone was acting independently. The organization had to pour money on to help Dragna at all times. So Benny came out here to get things moving good.

"Although Benny had great respect for the Italians, he was always considered like a boss on his own. See, outside the East, like in New Jersey, the Jews and the Italians had a strong combine together, or as close as any Italian could be with any non-Italian. But Dragna was of the old school where only Italians ran things, and certainly not Jews like Benny with his Eastern ways. But that didn't bother Benny none. 'Fuck Dragna' was his attitude, and he did.

"Dragna was really from the old mustache days. The worst thing you can do to an old-time Italian Mahoff is to harm his prestige in any way, and that's what took place when Benny came out here.

"Jack Dragna didn't like to be connected with Siegel. See, Three-Finger Brown—Thomas Lucchese—in New York was Jack Dragna's goombah and a real nice guy. Benny's was Meyer Lansky. Jack Dragna was actually the complete boss out here before Siegel or I come out here. Now when Benny and I come out here, two Jews, then Meyer made trips out here. So it was really an encroachment on Dragna's Italian territory. He didn't realize it at first but I started to get wind of it when I had more meetings with Jack Dragna. He would get in a little zing all the time to Benny and Jews, and I kind of woke up to it. You gotta remember the old-time Italian outlook on things, pride is a tremendous thing with them. Dragna and Johnny Rosselli were on a pedestal by themselves. But Benny, with his takeover way, was knocking down that pedestal pretty good, and with my help."

Pete Hamill, in a February, 1992, article in *Playboy* explained Siegel's move to the West Coast this way.

"Siegel went west in 1936. The reasons were complicated. Tom Dewey was now special prosecutor in New York (later district attorney). Urged on by New York's flamboyant mayor, Fiorello H. La Guardia, he was directing the toughest investigation of organized crime in the city's history. The heat, as they said, was on. Siegel wanted to get out of the way.

"Another reason was economic. The city was bogged down in the Great Depression, and even the racket guys were beginning to feel the pinch. Of all the old bootleggers, only Siegel seemed to be without his own fiefdom. He couldn't shoot his way into personal power in New York; he didn't have the manpower and, besides, these were his friends. So when Dewey applied the big heat, Siegel—possibly at Lansky's suggestion—went to California. In 1936, that state was not the economic powerhouse it is today; in many ways it was provincial, underpopulated, isolated from the mainstream. He had a piece of a gambling ship called *The Rex* and of the race track at Agua Caliente, across the border from San Diego in Mexico. He had established himself as the Mob superior to Jack Dragna, the old boss of the L.A. rackets."

Siegel and Cohen were not good news for Dragna. Cohen was a mouthy, irascible but charming little thug. Siegel, with Lansky money behind him and Lansky acumen, was a more serious threat to Dragna's desire to take control of Los Angeles' off-track betting. According to *All-American Mafioso: The Johnny Rosselli Story*, Johnny Rosselli quickly made himself useful to Siegel by serving as "Siegel's primary contact with the Italians in Los Angeles."

During this same period, Girolamo "Momo" Adamo arrived from Kansas City with his wife Marie (who in 1969, 14 years after Mary Ann's mother's death, would marry Bompensiero). Adamo had come west to escape Kansas City's gang warfare and over the next ten years would serve as conduit between Kansas City and Los Angeles, bringing in midwestern toughs to do Dragna's dirtier dirty work. Adamo's continuing friendship with Kansas City kingpins James Balestrere, Joseph DiGiovanni, Tony Gizzo, and others, including Tano Lococo, his wife Marie's brother's father-in-law, added to his luster. Adamo rather quickly became second-in-command, or, underboss, to Dragna, and until his death by suicide in 1956, remained close friends with Bompensiero.

"I've got a forty-five automatic.
I walk right up to his table and
start pumping lead."

CHAPTER TWENTY-FOUR

# HIDING IN L.A.

In 1934, 1935, and 1936, I find no listing for Frank and Thelma Bompo or Bomp or Bompensiero or Buonpensiero or Bonpensiero in the San Diego city directory. Mary Ann feels sure that during those years she and her parents lived, at least part of the time, in Los Angeles, next door to Jack Dragna's brother Tom, Tom's wife Julia, and their sons, Frank and Louis. Mary Ann recalled Julia. "I was scared to death of her. One time one of my Patella cousins came to visit and I was being a brat and wouldn't let her play with something of mine. Julia locked me in a closet. After that I always thought of her as someone like a witch from a fairy tale. I was so scared of her that all my mom or dad had to say to me if I wouldn't finish my vegetables or take my medicine was, 'If you don't do it, I will call Julia!' And whatever it was, I'd do it right away."

In the fall of 1934, according to *All-American Mafioso: The Johnny Rosselli Story*, Jack Dragna's national standing finally was at least grudgingly acknowledged by East Coast *mafiosi*, when Dragna was invited to attend a "Mafia conference in New York. Gathered around a dinner table on the balcony of the theater café Casio de Paris were the top Italian gangsters in the country, including Paul Ricca from Chicago and Frank Costello from New York. The meeting was chaired by Charles 'Lucky' Luciano, who toasted Dragna to the others as one of 'our people.'"

Mary Ann can't remember a time when she didn't know Jack Dragna. "He was a little, squatty guy, real short. I met him when I was a little girl and he was 'Uncle Jack.' That's what I called him. Momo Adamo was Momo to me, but he was 'Uncle Jack.' Tom Dragna was 'Uncle Tom,' and Frankie Dragna, Jack Dragna's son, well," Mary Ann laughed, "Frankie was spoiled rotten with American women. But that's another matter, that's another story.

"I remember how Jack Dragna would always say, 'Come here, honey, and sit on Uncle Jack's lap.' You know in Italian, everybody is 'kiss, kiss.' If I walked in a room and my grandparents or uncles were there, you had to kiss them 'hello,' you had to kiss them 'good-bye.' Uncle Jack, I had to kiss him hello and kiss him good-bye and sit on his lap. When I got older, I didn't want to sit on his lap. So I said, 'Daddy, I don't like to sit on Uncle Jack's lap.' I didn't sit on my daddy's lap, why would I want to sit on Uncle Jack's lap? My father said, 'Well, why, honey?' And I said, 'Because I'm getting too big now. I don't want to sit on his lap.' So my father said, 'All right,' and that was it. Uncle Jack never asked me to sit on his lap again. But I knew him forever, it seems like, Uncle Jack."

Mary Ann recalled drives from Los Angeles to San Diego. "I don't know how old I was, but I remember that I'd sit in the backseat of the car and I'd sing, 'California, Here I Come,' from LA to San Diego. I remember, too, driving from Los Angeles to San Diego with my mom and dad and wanting to know what San Diego would look like. I remember asking, 'Will it look like Los Angeles?' and my father turning around in the car and answering me by saying, 'There's a lot of fishing boats there in San Diego.'"

In the summer of 1937 just before Mary Ann started first grade at Washington Elementary School, trouble that would engage her father erupted in Los Angeles. Bugsy Siegel, with Dragna and his group under his control, took on the older Los Angeles gambling syndicate. According to Charles Rappleye and Ed Becker's account in *All-American Mafioso*, "a meeting was called for the city's top game-room operators, and Siegel announced that all proceeds would have to be split with his outfit. The lone dissent was voiced by Les Brunemann...a balding veteran of the Crawford-McAfee syndicate who operated gambling clubs in the beach cities south of Los Angeles." Siegel decided to make an example of Brunemann, and "assigned Dragna to administer a dose of East Coast discipline."

On the evening of July 19, write Rappleye and Becker, "Brunemann was enjoying the perquisites that accrued to a small-time crime czar, taking a stroll on the oceanfront esplanade in Redondo Beach. On his arm was a pretty young blonde, a hostess from one of his gambling arcades.... Two men stepped up behind them, leveled automatic pistols and began shooting. His date was unharmed, but Brunemann caught three slugs in his back. He staggered 200 feet to the lobby of a local movie theater and was rushed to a local hospital."

According to the tale told Ovid Demaris by Jimmy Fratianno in Demaris's *The Last Mafioso*, Bompensiero was the shooter. His three shots only wounded the gambler. Brunemann was hospitalized for several months at the Queen of Angels Hospital. Word came, along in October, that Brunemann was sufficiently recuperated that he was visiting his old hangout, the Roost Café in Redondo Beach, in the company of his nurse. Moceri, Bonventre, and Bompensiero returned to Redondo Beach on the night of October 23. The summary of the Los Angeles Police Department notes: "Victim shot and killed while sitting at a table booth at the Roost Café—in company with his nurse, Alice Ingram, and others. Nurse Ingram wounded in legs, a bystander Frank Greuzard killed also by two gunmen who entered café and blasted at victim and party with .45 caliber automatics. Suspects fled scene in auto. There were four suspects in this case. Two gunmen who entered café and did the blasting, two others in the get-away car."

If we are to believe Jimmy Fratianno's report of this, Moceri did the final deed. Fratianno quotes Moceri as telling the story this way. "Bompensiero said, 'Okay, Leo, you take him this time and I'll cover you.' I've got a forty-five automatic and the place's packed with people. I walk right up to his table and start pumping lead. Believe me, that sonavabitch's going to be dead for sure this time." According to the police report, Moceri pumped 16 shots into Brunemann. The three men were never apprehended.

Dragna in February, 1938, asked Bompensiero to take care of Los Angeles gambler Phil Galuzo. Why Dragna wanted Galuzo dead is a fact now lost. About eight in the evening on February 28, Bompensiero and two other Dragna "workers" snapped Galuzo off the street at 636 Broadway in Los Angeles. Bompensiero apparently drove while his two sidekicks beat Galuzo. At 1674 East 83rd Street, they stopped the car, tossed Galuzo out into the gutter facedown in water, and shot him seven times. Galuzo was in the hospital a week before he died, on March 7. On March 11, the Los Angeles police put out an all-points bulletin that named Bompensiero as Galuzo's murderer. Leo Moceri, years later, would tell Jimmy Fratianno that he gave Bompensiero "some names in Detroit and they stashed him a couple years. Then he went to Tampa and stayed with Santo Trafficante."

In 1937, the year that Mary Ann started first grade, the San Diego city directory lists Thelma Bompo as a cashier at the Beverly Clothes Shop at 936 Fifth Avenue. Mary Ann said, "I started the first grade at Washington grammar school. I went to Washington up until I was in the fifth grade."

Mary Ann, living in San Diego with her mother, only knew that her father was "gone on business." Years later she would learn that for almost two years, he was hidden out by various Mafia-connected families across the United States. Her mother supported them by working as a clerk in dress shops. According to an old friend of Frank and Thelma's, "Thelma always knew where Frank was. Always. She was able to visit him sometimes, in places where he was hiding."

"Mr. Willis," the retiree from San Diego law enforcement, told me one day about the Victor Carlino killing on March 21, 1940, a murder in which Mr. Willis and other city and county men suspected Bompensiero might have had a hand. "Carlino," he said, "worked at Mirabile's joint, Rainbow Gardens. He'd only been in town from Los Angeles for about a month or so when he got wasted. His vehicle was found in La Mesa. His brains were scattered all over the dashboard and the cowling. They never did find his body. They did a real good job on him, a real permanent job. His body obviously ended up off Coronado Islands or somewhere, fish food. I think maybe Frank was questioned about it at some point, but nothing ever came of it." As to why Carlino was killed, Mr. Willis suggested that Carlino no doubt offended the wrong person. "This is the way these people think, they don't have any trust in public officials, something goes wrong, you handle it yourself."

One day in 1940 when Mary Ann was nine she came home from her fifth-grade classes at Washington Elementary School and her mother said they were moving to Los Angeles. "We moved into an apartment at Harvard and Pico and our landlady was Mrs. Rosemary. It was a Spanish-style building. I don't know how many apartments there were up and down, maybe six or eight. But the whole front was beautiful. The lawn was huge and then Mrs. Rosemary had several rows of flowers, and the beds were filled with iris, all different color iris.

"The apartment was upstairs. It was really not even a one-bedroom. It was more like a studio apartment. It was furnished. It was just one big living room, and then dead ahead from the living room was a little area for a kitchen table, and then to the right of that—as you walk into the living room, to the right, in the middle of the living room was a doorway. And that was—you couldn't call it a bedroom—like a dressing room. That was my room. The living room had one of those Murphy beds, that you fold out of the wall at night. They'd have to go into my bedroom, to go into the bathroom. And that was it. There was a big mirror with a low dresser, and I had more a cot than a bed, and on the one side of the wall—you stood up and there's a dressing table, boom.

"My dad, of course, was hiding out. He was Frank Martin, my mother was Thelma Martin, I was Mary Ann Martin. We didn't have a car. The only time we would go out as a family when we were on Harvard Street was to the movies. We walked to the movie theater. My mother got a job working for Hartfield's, a store kind of like a Lerners, in downtown Los Angeles. My mother took the bus or a streetcar to work. She got up every morning, went to work, and came home. She was the sole support of the family. My father stayed home. He did all the housework, cleaned up and dusted and washed dishes. He did all the cooking—breakfast, lunch, and dinner. He always had dinner cooked and ready when my mother got home from work. He used to make a fish soup. He made pasta. He made veal. I was so skinny. I was like Olive Oyl. My legs were skinny and long. But my father fattened me up. He made me drink two quarts of milk a day. He'd sit there at the table with me and play solitaire while I drank it.

"Sometimes, after school, he and I would take short walks around the neighborhood. We'd go five or six blocks and I'd be hot and cranky. I'd say,

'Daddy, carry me,' and he'd pick me right up and carry me. People can all say what they want to say about my father, but there never was a day when I was a child that I did not know that he loved me. I think he would have absolutely died for me.

"I don't remember ever going to church with my dad, but my mother and I would go. The only time we ever saw him in church, when I was a child, was weddings, if he had to, and maybe a funeral or when there was a baptism and he was somebody's godfather. But I was going to Catholic school. I made my first Holy Communion in Los Angeles as Mary Ann Martin. I didn't know any different.

"I had a little girlfriend at Catholic school. Her name was Patty and we'd come home from school for lunch. He always treated Patty so sweetly. Her parents were divorced and he felt sorry for her. He was home for lunch, of course, because he was home all the time, in hiding, and he would make us three-decker club sandwiches. He'd toast the bread and make the sandwich and carefully cut it into quarters, just like they did in the restaurants. He'd stick a toothpick in each quarter of the sandwich and poke an olive into the end of the toothpick. He'd lay potato chips all around it.

"Sometimes when I was home alone or didn't have girlfriends over, and my father would be playing solitaire, I'd stand in front of the mirror and sing. My dad would say, 'What are you doing?' I'd say, 'Daddy, when I grow up, I want to be a singer with a band.' 'No way!' he'd say. 'You want that kind of life? No way, baby, no way.'

"We had Christmas there, in the Harvard Avenue place. That was the first Christmas tree that I remember picking out. My father and I were a block or two from Pico Boulevard. We walked up to this lot and bought a tree. I picked out a blue tree. Maybe five feet tall. It was bigger than I was. My mother walked in the door from work that night. And she goes, 'What, my God, Frank, a blue tree?' He says, 'Honey, that's what Mary Ann wanted. She's our baby. That's what she wanted. So we got her a blue tree.'"

Mary Ann said that she remembered only one time all through her childhood that her parents seemed to quarrel in a serious fashion. "I never once, ever, heard my father call my mother names, or heard him address her in any but the most respectful way. I never heard him scream at her. And he never, not ever, laid a hand on her. I think my father would have died before he hit my mother or any woman. He looked down on men who hit women. He thought they were scum, low. But when we were living in this little studio apartment in Los Angeles and he was hiding out, I woke up one night and heard my mother talking loudly. I ran in to see what was happening. They were sitting there on the Murphy bed, both of them in all their clothes, and my mother was biting down on my father's hand and his hand was bleeding. And he was stroking her hair, whispering, 'Thelma, honey, please, honey, Thelma, baby.'"

On June 21, 1941, Mary Ann and her mother went to a movie. Mary Ann recalled the evening. "My father used to go with us all the time, but this night my mother and I went. When we came back every light in the apartment was on, there were people downstairs, and my mother goes, 'Oh my God, what happened?' Mrs. Rosemary, our landlady, was downstairs and my mother said, 'Mrs. Rosemary, Mrs. Rosemary, what's happening?' She didn't know what was going on. They had arrested my dad. Mrs. Rosemary said to my mother, 'Oh, Thelma, you could have trusted me, why didn't you tell me?' My mother was just crying and crying. She said, 'Oh, Mrs. Rosemary, how could I?' And she was sobbing. And I was screaming and crying, 'Where's my daddy?' But then, four or five days later, he came home. It was almost always like that. The police would pick him up and hold him for a while and then he'd come home."

The LAPD "Gangland Killings" document notes this: "Frank Bompensiero was arrested on June 21, 1941, in connection with the murder of Phil Galuzo. However, as there was insufficient evidence to prosecute on kidnapping and murder charges, suspect released. At this time Bompensiero was wanted for three felony counts of robbery by San Diego police. Disposition unknown."

I asked my retired friend, Mr. Willis, what he made of the Los Angeles police letting Bompensiero go. He laughed, a big laugh that rumbled up out of his big chest. He said, "It's like this. Irish policemen and *mafioso* hoods, they got along well together."

*Thelma and Frank Bompensiero*

**"She must have known, or guessed.**

**He never told her much."**

CHAPTER TWENTY-FIVE

# MY MELANCHOLY BABY

I asked Mary Ann if she recalled her parents being affectionate. She said, "My dad would always say, 'When you love somebody you don't have to display it and show it in public. Actions may speak louder than words but all of these people who are huggy, huggy, kissy, kissy all the time, that's no good. There's a time and place for things like that.' He also used to say that there were guys who were always kissing on their women out in public and then they'd take the woman home and beat hell out of her. My father never laid a hand on me or my mother. And he was affectionate with her, but at least in front of me and other people, he was not overly affectionate. He would look at her across the table, for instance, and the way he looked at her and the way she looked back at him, you knew these people were people who were in love. I'll tell you one thing that I know, for sure. My father loved my mother dearly. He worshipped the ground my mother walked on. And my mother worshipped him."

I asked Mary Ann if she thought her mother knew about the robberies, the beatings, the murders. "She must have known, or guessed. He never told her much. He said, 'What you don't know, they can't ask you.' But she must have known."

I asked Mary Ann how she thought her mother bore up under her father's absences and arrests. Mary Ann frowned, almost imperceptibly. "I don't think my mother was happy. She probably shed more tears than I ever saw. You could sense it. But she loved him. She really loved him. I don't know what else to say.

"'My Melancholy Baby,' that was their song. 'Come to me, my melancholy baby,' that's how it starts out. And then, 'Come on and smile my honey dear, let me wipe away each tear, or else I shall be melancholy too.' When we moved back to San Diego after the war and my parents went on Saturday night to Tops or Imig Manor, my father always had the band play that song for them. My mom would be wearing one of her beautiful strapless gowns that showed off her shoulders and her beautiful bustline. She'd tip her head down on his shoulder and they'd dance. They were beautiful dancers. They were in a world of their own. My dad would sing along in her ear, 'Wait until the sun comes shining through, life is always sunshine when the heart beats true.' That was their song."

*Frank Bompensiero in the Army, 1942*

**"They stopped the movie and said that the Japs had bombed Pearl Harbor and that we all were to get up out of our seats and go straight home."**

CHAPTER TWENTY-SIX

# WAR YEARS

From the Sunday in December, 1941, when the Japanese bombed Pearl Harbor to the Monday in August, 1945, when the United States bombed Hiroshima, San Diego transformed itself from town to city. Merchants and bar owners, during the war years, fattened their bank accounts. The downtown blocks back of Broadway grew fecund with what, back then, was called "vice"—whores, dope, gambling, liquor, B-girls.

"During World War II," a retired San Diego policeman told me, "the hoods in the downtown bars made plenty of money. Don't let anybody fool you. The reason they made more money than anyone else was because they could get liquor where a square couldn't. During the war, booze wasn't always available, there just wasn't enough booze to go around, sure, that's true. There were some strange names of liquor they were selling. But these hoods could get all the booze they wanted. A square had a bar, he could have a hell of a time getting beer or whiskey, but the hoods got beer and whiskey. They got bootleg stuff. What they did was to bring booze in that didn't show on any bills of lading. They'd sell that. I think mostly from the East the bootlegged whiskey would come. Some of it was hijacked liquor. During World War II, liquor was regularly hijacked. I recall a $200,000 deal, a liquor truck hijacked in Del Mar, coming into San Diego. But these hoods, they had the connections to get liquor. A straight person couldn't pick up a phone and call Cleveland and Chicago and say, 'How about we do each other a favor?' These guys had the connections.

"They had to keep decent records, but they all skimmed. No doubt in my mind that they skimmed. They would run two tapes. They would run the tape for the night and then they would rerun a tape after closing time and they would take one-third or one-fourth off that tape of their intake. A simple operation. Easy to do. Easy to run two tapes. You don't pay any tax on what you take off. It's all clean money. Dollar for dollar, it's all yours. No taxes. Every buck you take in like that is yours. Another reason these guys liked to have bars was that it gave them alibi income, so they could hide away what else they were up to. They made fortunes during the war. They moved into bigger homes in better neighborhoods. A lot of them moved into Kensington."

Frank Bompensiero got none of that money. While Bompensiero carried out Dragna's dirty work, Dragna, like Tony Mirabile and his brother Paul, carried money to the bank. Thelma Bompensiero stood on her feet eight and ten hours a day, six days a week, in retail clothing shops, to help pay rent and keep the family fed; Jack Dragna's wife Frances, during this same period, was busy decorating her Los Angeles home with European antiques and directing Mexican gardeners in planting exotic bulbs that Frances ordered from East Coast greenhouses. Dragna cohort, Girolamo "Momo" Adamo, and Momo's wife Marie, also living in Los Angeles, slipped into swank clothes and partied in LA nightclubs. Johnny Rosselli, a Dragna advisor, ordered custom-made suits, tooled about LA in expensive cars, and rented Beverly Hills apartments in buildings where movie stars lived.

In the fall of 1941, Frank and Thelma and Mary Ann, 10 going on 11, moved to Rolando Village into a house on 4573 Campo Drive. Her parents, Mary Ann said, didn't want her going from school to school. They were determined to settle down and stay in San Diego. Mary Ann enrolled in La Mesa Elementary School. Her father, as far as Mary Ann recalls, worked as a card dealer. Her mother, as she had during 1940 in Los Angeles, when Bompensiero was in hiding and the family lived under the name "Martin," took a job as a clerk in a dress shop.

December 7, 1941, Mary Ann was sure that she and her parents were in San Diego. "We always went to dinner at my grandmother Sanfilippo's at noon. And then afterwards, my cousins and I went to the movies. We were all sitting together that day at the Spreckels Theatre and they stopped the movie and said that the Japs had bombed Pearl Harbor and that we all were to get up out of our seats and go straight home." Mary Ann does not recall her father's response to Pearl Harbor.

We do not have another sighting of Bompensiero until May 20, 1942, when police knocked on the door of the La Jolla Riding Stables, an illegal gambling establishment where Bompensiero served as doorman and general enforcer. According to the police report, when plainclothes officers approached the stable's door, Bompensiero peered through the door's peephole and asked the officers to show their cards. As the plainclothesmen riffled through their wallets, Bompensiero opened the door. The police walked past him, up the stairs, and on to the second floor where they found roulette wheels, poker chips stacked on tables, a blackjack table layout and chips. Bompensiero was arrested for conspiracy to commit gambling and fined $100.

(In 1950, when called to testify in Los Angeles before the Senate Special Committee to Investigate Crime in Interstate Commerce, Bompensiero would explain this event in this way: "Once, before I got in the Army, I tried to get a job in La Jolla in a gambling house there, and as I get in there, the same night they opened, the place got arrested, and I never got the job. So I was never in the gambling business in all my life.")

Bompensiero enlisted in the Army on June 3, 1942, shortly after his gambling arrest, and received an honorable discharge on October 6, 1943. "My father," said Mary Ann, "was 37 when he went into the Army and 38 when he got out. He was older than everyone in his platoon. The guys called him 'Pops.' He was stationed in El Paso, Texas, where he used to say, after the war when all the other men who'd served would sit around and brag, 'Well, I fought the Battle of the Mosquitoes.' The platoon he was with, the rest of them were sent to Africa. I think because of his age, they kept my father in the States."

Bompensiero's sister Josephine died while he was in the Army. Mary Ann was sure that her father did not come home for the funeral. "She died in 1942 in childbirth. That was the first funeral I ever went to. At the viewing and Rosary the night before, they had the casket open. The women who came from Porticello have a group they call La Madonna del Lume—Our Lady of Light—and the ladies from that group dressed Josephine in the Madonna del Lume veil and dress. It was a pale blue, choir robe-type dress. Her infant was cradled in her arms. People were sobbing and crying. I still can see that tiny baby, cradled in her arms.

"Anyway, while my father was away, my mother and I were living in Rolando Village. What's the Army send you? Very little money. My mother was working at a dress shop in Hillcrest on Fifth Avenue called Margaret Lucas Dress Shop. My dad had left us his car, a green Buick. I came home from school and there was no car. We couldn't make the car payment. They took the car away, repossessed it. Nobody said, 'Oh, you're going to lose your car, we'll make the payment.' No Momo Adamo, no Jack Dragna, no Johnny Rosselli. No nobody came around to help out. My poor mother had to walk in heels, six or eight long blocks to the bus. My mother didn't have it that easy all of her life. We didn't live the glamorous life that some people thought we lived. No way.

"Every single Sunday that my father was in the Army for a year, every Sunday, my mother and I took two buses to go to my grandmother Bompensiero's. The bus at that time from Rolando Village took a half hour to get to Horton Plaza, then we took the bus from Horton Plaza down to Columbia Street. Had to be down there for twelve o'clock dinner because my father was in the Army and it was to show respect to my grandmother that we had to go. We didn't go to my mother's mother, to the Sanfilippos. Nope. My mother was respectful, a good wife, and that's what you're supposed to do, so she did it.

"But she didn't like doing it, and this is what I think made my mother so mad at the Bompensiero side of the family. She just couldn't get over it. On Sunday you got dressed up. My mother was always dressed and wore high spiked heels. She had a beautiful bright red suit. And because she had that red suit on one Sunday when we went to dinner at my grandmother Bompensiero's, somebody wrote my father in El Paso, 'What is your wife doing in a red suit, only *putanas* wear red.' That did it for my mother.

"When my father got out of the Army, my mother said, 'Frank, I did my duty. I'm not going down to your mother's anymore.' She said, 'I'm not going to be there every Sunday. You want to go see your mother on Sunday, you go see your mother.' She went on Sunday once in a while. But after that business with the red suit, we never again went every Sunday to the Bompensiero side of the family."

Mary Ann isn't sure what her father did for money after he received his honorable discharge. She thinks that perhaps he again worked as a dealer in card rooms. He was often gone from home.

The only other glimpse of Bompensiero that remained from 1942 and 1943 came from the long-retired member of San Diego law enforcement, "Mr. Willis." "A killing down here along in 1942 or 1943 that we thought Frank might have been involved in was this tailor. The story was, this guy had been beating on his wife. He was told, I understand, by Frank, on a couple of occasions, 'One more time.' The last time this tailor fellow was seen, he'd left the tailor shop, still wearing his apron, and he was carrying a pair of shears under the apron in his right hand and he crossed Broadway to the south side and was walking east. That's the last time anybody was conscious of his being anyplace and he was never found. No body. Kind've funny, walking with a pair of shears. Maybe he was going to cut some clothes for some guy. This killing, it had nothing to do with organized crime. I think it was a pure family problem. This guy had been beating up on his wife. Frank warned him to stop it. He didn't stop. So a lot of people thought Frank finally lost patience and took care of it."

In 1945 Bompensiero was working as bouncer and general majordomo for Tony Mirabile at the Rainbow Gardens. The only glance we get of Bompensiero in this year comes on January 21, the day after Roosevelt was inaugurated for his fourth term. Police officers stopped Bompensiero for a traffic violation as he was driving home in an automobile registered to Sam Ferrara. The officers who made the stop searched the car and found in the glove compartment a loaded and cocked .38-caliber Colt automatic. Bompensiero denied any knowledge of the pistol. Ferrara, when questioned, explained that he had bought the Colt from a sailor and that indeed Bompensiero knew nothing about it. That ended that.

PHOTOGRAPH BY SANDY HUFFAKER, JR.

*5878 Estelle Street*

**"My father could look at a bottle and know how many shots were gone out of it."**

CHAPTER TWENTY-SEVEN

# THE GOLD RAIL

To explain what happened next in Bompensiero's life needs a detour. During Prohibition Los Angeles bootleggers battled for command of the liquor business; after Prohibition's end, these same men battled for command of illegal off-track betting outlets. Benjamin "Bugsy" Siegel and his henchman Mickey Cohen in the late 1930s wrenched control of Los Angeles' bookmakers, including those dominated by Jack Dragna. From necessity rather than choice, Dragna made an uneasy peace with Siegel and Cohen.

In order to do business, bookies needed lists of odds on various races and race results at tracks around the United States. A bookie needed this data quickly. In the mid-1920s Al Capone formed a partnership with Moses Annenberg, owner of the *Daily Racing Form*, the newspaper that bettors on horses were never without.

According to Carl Sifakis's *The Encyclopedia of American Crime*, Annenberg's newly formed Nationwide News Service, which Capone bankrolled, worked this way: "The service received its information from telegraph and telephone wires hooked into 29 race tracks and from those tracks into 223 cities in 39 states, where thousands of pool rooms and bookie joints operated in violation of local laws." The wire service itself was not illegal. Nationwide did not sell its information directly to bookies. Rather, it sold its service to distributors who then sold the information to bookies. Using that information to make book was illegal.

In 1939, Moses Annenberg was about to be sentenced for income tax fraud. He sold Nationwide, by then a multimillion-dollar business, to James Ragen, a Chicago ex-newspaperman. Ragen, not involved in the mob, wished to rid Nationwide of Capone associations. He changed the wire service's name to Continental Press. The Chicago mob soon tried to muscle a piece of Ragen's business. Ragen refused. The Chicago mob then offered to buy out Ragen. He refused the offer, saying that the mob would never let him live to collect the check. Meyer Lanksy, deeply invested in illegal gambling, threw up his hands. Bugsy Siegel, with Lansky's support, in 1942 set up his own competing wire service in California—Trans-American Publishing. Siegel, with Dragna as his cohort and Mickey Cohen and Joe Sica for brawn, forced California bookies to use Trans-American rather than Ragen's Continental. By the end of World War II, Southern California bookies were paying the Siegel-Dragna combine $100 per day for data from Trans-American's wires.

In San Diego in the mid-1940s, as many as 100 bookies actively were taking bets. Some worked the bars and others took call-in bets in homes with telephone banks. The rivalry between the Siegel-Dragna Trans-American Publishing and Ragen's Continental Press Service existed also in San Diego. In San Diego, however, Continental Press Service called itself "Southwest News Service" and was managed by Leonard Brophy, whose brother, Russell Brophy, married to James Ragen's daughter, managed the Los Angeles branch of Ragen's Continental Press Service. Trans-American Service had its offices in a Sixth Avenue hotel. Brophy ran Southwest from rooms on Fourth Avenue.

According to an April 8, 1951, *San Diego Union* article, Brophy had 14 customers and Trans-American had 16. Trans-American, the *Union* reported, had been operated during the early- to mid-1940s by Johnnie and Pete O'Toole. "The O'Toole operation was controlled by the O'Toole brothers, Frank Bompensiero, Joe Russo, a politician turned petty racketeer, and Bill Wilson, a bookmaker and a former matchmaker at the Coliseum Athletic Club. Bompensiero and his associates, in an effort to force Southwest News Service out of business, called on all the bookmakers in San Diego urging them to subscribe to the O'Toole wire service.

"'They offered faster service and sometimes used veiled threats as a selling point,' intelligence sources said. 'Failing in these methods, they resorted to the practice of calling Brophy by phone and leaving the receiver off the hook to tie up his lines.'"

By 1946, Lansky and Siegel had lost patience with James Ragen's refusal to sell Continental. They ordered his death. On June 24, 1946, in Chicago, a gunman in a passing car shot Ragen. He survived the shooting and was taken to a hospital and put under police guard. Doctors considered Ragen's condition stable. He remained in the hospital, slowly convalescing. On August 24, hospital attendants were shocked to discover Ragen had died. An autopsy was performed. The coroner's report noted that there was "enough mercury in Ragen's body to kill three men. Mercury was administered in rubbing alcohol, injected, or given by enema." Someone, somehow, got past Ragen's guards and poisoned him with mercury.

The 1951 *Union* article concluded: "The Trans-American Wire operation ostensibly ended in June, 1947. 'Shortly thereafter,' intelligence sources stated, 'Brophy admitted that Frank Bompensiero was the real head of Trans-American in San Diego and he drew his authority from Tony Mirabile and Jack Dragna. Brophy admitted that he had to pay Bompensiero $60 weekly out of the Continental-Southwest operations on direct orders from his older brother, Russell Brophy.'" (The *Union* report does not mention that while Bompensiero was in the Army in 1942, Russell Brophy had been severely beaten by Mickey Cohen and Joe Sica. Cohen wrote: "We busted Brophy's head open pretty good because he got out of line a little bit.")

By the early days of World War II, according to *All-American Mafioso: The Johnny Rosselli Story* by Charles Rappleye and Ed Becker, at least 1800 illegal bookmaking outlets were doing business in Los Angeles. By war's end that number had almost doubled. But, in Nevada, gambling had been legal since 1931. Bugsy Siegel was sufficiently foresighted to recognize that the gluttonous national appetite for illegal gambling could be satisfied, legally, in Nevada. Six days after the nation celebrated World War II's end, Siegel formed the Nevada Projects Corporation. With funds from Meyer Lansky, Siegel bought 30 acres of wasteland outside Las Vegas, on which he planned to build the Flamingo. Repeatedly, until his death in 1956, Dragna would try to inveigle or grab a piece, almost any piece, of Vegas action. He never would succeed. The Dragna family would be the only big-city Mafia group that did not share in the postwar Vegas profits. Dragna would have to remain content with his interests in illegal gambling in Southern California, with control he gained over several labor unions, with extortion, and with the profit from his banana boats.

A retired Los Angeles policeman talked with me about his surveillance of the Dragna family in the years after World War II. "At that time," he recalled, "the Dragnas and Momo Adamo were importing bananas. They bought a couple of LCIs [landing craft, infantry] and converted them and put in refrigeration, bringing in bananas up from Costa Rica. They had an outfit they called Latin American Import down on Linden Street in the commercial district of LA, down by the Farmers Market."

*The Los Angeles Times* reported about the banana business that Dragna "owns the *Santa Maria*, a vessel registered in Panama. It plies in the banana trade between Long Beach and Central and South America. [Momo] Adamo reputedly is a partner in this venture."

"That building," the retired Los Angeleno continued, "was my very first assignment when I went into Intelligence. They put me in an old apartment hotel room up there that faced back onto Linden, myself and an Italian kid, taking pictures of everyone who came and went from that place—the Dragnas, the whole bunch.

"The Dragnas and Momo also had the Trans-American Wire service that provided the odds on different things. On horses, or whatever, and the usual extortion and shakedown. The wire service came on wires across Hoover

Dam. It was a real wire. They would print out the information and deliver it to bookmakers. That was the information that the bookmakers needed because back then there weren't any scratch sheets. I know that Louis Dragna, Jack's nephew, back then, was also working down at the banana warehouse, running the wire service to bookmakers, delivering it."

Bompensiero, in September, 1946, would celebrate his 41st birthday. He had served Jack Dragna loyally for 20 years. Bompensiero, with his mother to support and wife and child, still lived from day to day, dependent always on what Thelma could earn in dress shops. At last, Bompensiero was about to receive his reward. August 22, 1946, Bompensiero became partners with Frank Paul Dragna and Louis Tom Dragna in ownership of the Gold Rail at 1028 Third Avenue in downtown San Diego. He would also move his family into a home at 5878 Estelle Street.

Both Jack and Tom Dragna had sons named Frank Paul. My retired Los Angeles policeman friend explained, about the sons: "Jack's son Frank Paul lost an eye in World War II, so he was 'One-Eyed Frank Paul.' Tom's son Frank Paul never amounted to much, he drove a bread truck; he never really was involved in anything, so he was just 'Frank Paul.' Louis Tom was Tom's other son, older than Frank Paul, and he was the most active one; he, I think, was being groomed to be the boss."

The Gold Rail altered Bompensiero's life in several ways. He no longer would be so entirely dependent upon Dragna for money. He would be able to stay in San Diego, near his mother, whom he visited daily, and to make a permanent home in San Diego for Thelma and Mary Ann. And, he would become Dragna's man, the Mafia's man, in San Diego.

If San Diego had a godfather when World War II ended, Tony Mirabile, owner and part-owner of myriad bars, clearly was that man. He had garnered his power, in part, by loaning money—between 1935 and 1958, the sum accumulated to $850,000—without interest, to his Sicilian-American countrymen. But out in the world beyond San Diego's bar owners, Mirabile was nobody, or, worse than nobody. He was described by "connected men" as a man "who never did any work, couldn't do any work." Recall that he was known among these men to have paid Jack Dragna $150,000 to "make" him. After World War II's end, Mirabile's power began to ebb. Rumors had it that Mirabile loaned Bompensiero $20,000 to buy the Gold Rail and that Mirabile "gave" Bompensiero and the Dragnas $25,000 to furnish the Gold Rail; if those rumors are fact, Mirabile likely handed over the money more from fear than from generosity.

I talked one day with a gentleman in his mid-80s, a retired San Diego lawman. About Bompensiero, this gentleman said, "Frank was the only local man who had the connections and the moxie to do things. Frank had the out-of-town connections, the good stuff. Frank was a center of power, you just knew it. Frank was no dummy. You couldn't help but like the guy because he was man, this guy was all man. Oh boy, he was a little short guy, but he must have weighed 200 pounds on a short frame. I mean built right straight up from the ground, tougher than hell. A lot of difference between him and Tony Mirabile. A lot of difference."

"The only time my mother and I ever saw the Gold Rail," said Mary Ann, about her father's bar, "was when he had already closed up, everybody was out, and he was doing his final work to prepare for the next day. He didn't want us there during business hours.

"From the outside, the Gold Rail looked like one little round window stuck in a wall. Bars in those days only had a doorway and maybe one small window. Inside was just one, long straight bar, long and narrow. There weren't any booths or tables. As you walked in the front door, the bar was on the right-hand side and that's all it was, a bar. And on the left-hand side was a hallway and then a wall. You walked straight back and then you could see that staircase going upstairs.

"My father's office was upstairs. It was dinky, the size of my bathroom. It had a desk. It had a little teeny refrigerator. It had a little two-burner stove. This was all upstairs where they were supposed to cook for the steak house. My father would get a call at home, from somebody, vice squad or somebody. They'd say, 'Frank, we're coming down. You'd better get some food in that refrigerator.' My father would get up and say, 'I gotta go put some food in the refrigerator.'

"He had a bartender, Jessie. He wasn't Italian. My dad would tell Jessie, 'You get robbed like crazy at a bar. You have to know the bar business.' My father could look at a bottle and know how many shots were gone out of it. He didn't measure it with anything. He'd just look at it. He told me, 'You gonna run a business, you gotta run a business. You gotta be in charge of your stock.' He would put so many bottles out and he'd say to the guys working there, 'You see these bottles, keep the stockroom locked up, when you're through with these bottles, there's got to be so much money in that register. And if there's not—you got a problem.' In other words, he controlled his stock that way and kind of put a little fear in them.

"He was open seven days a week. I don't think my dad ate three meals a day. I don't remember his ever sitting down having breakfast, because he'd get up and shower and go. First, he'd drive over to his mother's on Columbia and have coffee and a chat and give her some money. Then he'd go to the bar. He would stay there at the bar, maybe until six in the evening. Then he'd come home, take a shower. We'd have dinner. He slept for a couple hours after dinner, smoked a cigar, lay on the couch. My mother always had pretty French furniture. She'd look at my dad, stretched out there on the couch, and she'd shake her head and say, 'Frank, you know, the oil from your hair...' and she'd want to bring him a towel. He'd say, 'I don't want a towel. When this couch gets old and used up, we'll get rid of it and we'll get another one. I want to enjoy my furniture.' He was funny, that way. He would never, ever, at home, use a paper napkin or stainless steel flatware. We didn't even have stainless steel. We had silver, we had china. My father said, 'You want a paper napkin, you have one, I want a cloth one.' He said, 'What are we saving it for, the company? Who deserves it better than we do?'

"So, after his after-dinner nap, my father got up, put on a clean shirt, and went back down to the bar at maybe eleven or twelve, sometimes as early as eight. They had one car—a blue Hudson and then a green Cadillac—and my mom was taking him, back and forth. She would take him down if she wanted the car for anything, and she'd go pick him up at two in the morning."

Her dad, Mary Ann said, was never a heavy drinker. "He enjoyed a beer. But he enjoyed beer with certain foods. At home he enjoyed a nice, cold beer, but out of a crystal glass. And he would only pour just enough beer for a few sips. Very cold. He drank scotch. Not Chivas Regal, but J&B or Johnnie Walker Red Label. He paced himself. He'd have a couple of drinks and then if he were out, or my mother and he were out, he'd have wine with dinner."

Mary Ann said that not infrequently, she meets someone who knew her father when he owned the Gold Rail. She mentioned a couple to whom she'd been introduced. "I don't know how my maiden name came into the conversation, but it did. The husband asked, 'By any chance was your father's name Frank?' And I said, 'Yeah.' He said, 'Jesus, I loved your dad. I was a kid in the Navy. I used to go into the Gold Rail and I was young and I'd get drunk. In those days, they'd roll you. Your father was like a father to me. He would take away my watch, whatever jewelry I had on, take away my money. Leave me with my ID, call a cab, put me in a cab, and tell them, "Take him back to his ship."' He said the next day or two days later when he had leave again he would go to the Gold Rail and my father would have his watch, his money, all packed into an envelope for him. He said that my dad told him, several times, 'You're not supposed to get that drunk.' He said to me, 'I would have done anything in the world for your dad. He was great. I was a kid and got stupid drunk.' So, here was this guy, he was not Italian, not Sicilian, he wasn't in the family and my dad took a liking to him and watched out for him. And that is not by any means the only story like that about my dad."

*Bompensieros, Dragnas, and Adamos celebrate in Los Angeles, 1948*

**"They wanted to do an arranged marriage between me and their son 'One-Eyed Frank Paul.'"**

CHAPTER TWENTY-EIGHT

# FAMILY LIFE

I asked Mary Ann about her father's appearance during the late 1940s. "My dad was broad shouldered, built like a V-8 engine. He was short, five-foot nine. He was a dapper dresser. He wore gorgeous suits. He had his suits made. Pinstripe, one-button roll. One-button roll was popular then. Never wore a vest. Had every color there was. I don't mean gaudy. He wore beige and navy. He tied a beautiful tie, a nice big fat Windsor knot. He always wore a hat. He liked his hats. He wore a homburg. Just like the stuff you saw in the movies in the '40s. Beautiful handkerchiefs and a topcoat. He wore two shirts a day. He had his shirts made, a dozen at a time, French cuffs, with his initials embroidered on the pocket, white on white. He never wore a sport shirt. For the summer he'd say to the guy who did his shirts, 'Make all these shirts just like you make 'em for winter.' So they'd make all these French cuff shirts and then he'd say, 'Okay, now, cut 'em off to here for the summer,' and show them where he wanted them cut just above his elbows for short-sleeved summer shirts."

Her father, said Mary Ann, "loved, absolutely loved to see my mother all dolled up. He'd say to her, 'Honey, doll up.' He wanted her to wear strapless dresses. Not that she was showing that much off. She had a darling figure. In other words, he wanted to show her off and actually show himself off too, that she had these beautiful clothes. She was so gorgeous. She wore her hair in a pompadour, because that was the style, then. But she never wore it on her face or real fluffy, it was like in a bustle-back. Not a knot but all brought up in a bustle-type back. She would sit at her dressing table, look in the mirror, look in the front, look in the back, spray cologne. She was beautiful. She wore Shalimar. She also at times would wear Coty's Emeraude. And Chanel No. 5. I think she preferred Shalimar to Chanel No. 5. She had a huge bottle of Chanel No. 5, from Tijuana, on her dressing table. My dad used to go to Tijuana and visit somebody he called 'Little Frank' [Three-Fingered Frank]. I don't know what his last name was. He must have been 4 foot 11, Little Frank. My father always went by to see him in Tijuana."

The Bompensieros went out on Saturday night. "My dad would come home in the afternoon. He'd rest for a while. My mother naturally would take longer to dress. It didn't take my dad long to get dressed. He'd take a shower. He'd turn to my mother and say, 'What tie, baby, what tie shall I wear?' He was color-blind. So my mother coordinated his colors. And she picked out his ties for him. Later on, I picked them out. He had beautiful shoes. When he dressed at night he had black patent shoes or spectators.

"Some Saturday nights at Tops, my father had people in from other towns, Chicago or wherever. Or somebody from Los Angeles would come down. Momo Adamo and Marie were still living in Los Angeles then, near Jack Dragna. At the time he was in the banana boat business with Uncle Jack. They would come to San Diego and stay at the El Cortez, but they would have dinner with Momo's brother Joe and his wife Mary and my mother and father. That's when I first met Marie. I was young—13 or 14 or 15. I was fascinated by Momo because of this scar that ran down one side of his face. And the way he would talk. How he would call Marie, 'Maa-riiii-a!!' His English was very broken, Momo's was.

"Even though they had waitresses at Tops, when my father was there he'd have this big table and they would bring the bottles out and set them right on the table. So that the drinks were there. So that you didn't have to wait or want for a drink. And if it wasn't strong enough—you could pour what you wanted in. The flower girl would go by and he'd buy everybody a flower. Everybody sitting at the table he'd buy a flower. Gardenias, usually.

"There was music at Tops. People danced. My father loved music. At home, he used to say to me, 'Baby, put the Jolson records on.' He was so cute. He was so funny. But at Tops, my dad and mom and their friends sat around and talked and maybe they danced a little bit. The night wore on and it would get to be closing time. My father would call the owner over, whisper to him, 'We don't want to go home yet.' 'Okay, Frank,' the owner would say. So two o'clock comes, they locked the door. My dad says, 'We got to have some music. Do me a favor. Go talk to the musicians and whoever wants to stay, they got a hundred dollars.' A piano player would stay, a singer might stay. In those days a hundred dollars was a lot of money. So at five o'clock in the morning, he'd give them a hundred bucks each. Waitresses and bartenders he treated very, very well. He knew it was hard to work and he appreciated that."

Often, Mary Ann said, when her father came home at night from the Gold Rail, or, he and her mother came back with friends from a night out, her father cooked. "He would cook spaghetti with garlic and oil. That's what they would have instead of going out to breakfast. He loved Italian food. And veal cutlet. He loved veal cutlet. My mother couldn't stand garlic. Isn't that crazy? From a pure Sicilian family and not to like garlic. My dad would cook the pasta with garlic, and he'd smile at her and say, 'Honey, I know you don't like it, but I enjoy it.'"

Sundays, Mary Ann said, were family days. "Everybody had families by then; the in-laws, the outlaws. My mother never had 20, 30 people. She would have 8 or 10. My mother was a good cook but every Sunday was the same meal. If you came over to the house every Sunday for six months in a row, every Sunday you would have spaghetti and meatballs. Salad, the meatballs, the veal cutlets came out with the bread, and vegetables. After dinner the fruit came out, apples, oranges, whatever was in season. We never had heavy sweets for dessert. Only time we had desserts was Italian cookies at the holidays, cannoli for Easter and holidays. We used to sit around the table and talk. We would sit and talk and peel oranges. We had orange-peeling contests. We would go round and round and try not to break the peel."

In late 1946, when Mary Ann was 16 going on 17, Jack and Frances Dragna "asked for Mary Ann." As Mary Ann explained it, "They wanted to do an arranged marriage between me and their son Frank Paul, the one they called 'One-Eyed Frank Paul' because he lost his eye in the war. Frank was seven years older than I was. This whole thing was, 'Let's put the kids together.' They wanted, so to speak, 'to keep the marriage in the family.' Nobody at the time said a word to me about this. I mean, I am just this young girl. What do I know? But my father, I learned later, said to Jack and Frances that we could give it a try but that the marriage would happen 'only if Mary Ann likes him.'

"My father said, 'I'm going to send Mary Ann to Los Angeles for a week, with the family, and if she likes him—okay.' I had no idea. I think I'm just going up to LA to visit my godmother Josie, my Auntie Jo, who had been married to my mother's brother Frank. He was still alive then, but they were divorced. I think I am just going to spend a few days in LA with her and then I'm going to go spend several days with Anna Dragna at Jack and Frances's house, and nothing ever entered my mind. So I'm sent up to LA after Christmas for Christmas vacation. I'm at my godmother's house, my Auntie Jo's. Anna Dragna, Jack's daughter, was in college at the time. She came over and picked me up from my Aunt Jo's.

"Jack Dragna's house was a pretty house. But their house was not pretentious. Everybody kind of modified things. Nobody lived to the hilt. You didn't want to live to the hilt because it called attention to you and attention was what you didn't want. Anyway, Anna's room was beautiful. She had a French bedroom set. The room wasn't round, but on the ceiling they had painted a circle all in hand-painted roses. My mother did my room like that too on LaSalle Street, a border of hand-painted roses.

"For about three or four days, Frankie and Anna in their red convertible took me here and there, all over LA. We're just being friends, not a word was spoken. Frankie, to me, he was like an older brother. I had no romantic interest in him. I didn't think he was cute at all. I thought he was ugly. He seemed really old to me and he had lost an eye in the war.

"New Year's Eve comes and I had this white lace dress, nothing gaudy, but strapless, and I was wearing a Merry Widow under it and had my hair up. I was trying to look older. Jack and Frances and Anna and some other people, we all go to some big place downtown and have dinner at this long table. Frankie's not there yet. I'm sitting with Frances and Anna and Jack Dragna. I don't know who the other people were. We're halfway through dinner and here comes Frankie Dragna and he's got this gorgeous, gorgeous gal on his arm, this terrific tall blonde. She was like a showgirl, not hard-looking, I mean she was so beautiful. You know, as a young girl you look at someone you admire and you wish you could be that beautiful. All I thought at the time was, 'Boy, I wish I could figure out how to look like that.' She was gorgeous. And that's his date. I didn't care. I was having a wonderful time.

"The next day, Frankie and Anna and I went to the Rose Bowl game. I can't remember who played [University of Illinois beat UCLA 15-14]. So then the day after that my father came to get me. I think it was a Buick he was driving then, I'm not sure. We're driving home, just me and my father. My father turns to me and says, 'So, baby, did you have a good time?' And I say, 'Yes, Uncle Jack and Auntie Frances treated me beautiful, and I really like Anna, and we had such a good time. They took me to Chinatown. We went all over in their red convertible.' And then my dad says, 'How did you like Frankie?' I looked at him, 'I liked him, but as a brother, that's all. Don't get any ideas.' Then it registered. All at once, like that old bolt from the sky, I got it. The whole thing registered.

"So then Daddy said, 'Frankie asked for you.' I said, 'Well, that's too bad, I like him but as a brother, only as a brother, I always wanted a brother.' And then I said, 'He liked me, he wants me? He's asked for me and New Year's Eve he brings this beautiful girl as his date? What's he trying to do, show me what my life's going to be like?' I got all wound up. I said, 'Is he going to show me that he wants to marry me, and he wants me to have his children, but this is what I'm going to be going out with? A guy who brings a blonde showgirl type as his date on New Year's Eve while I sit around with Jack and Frances and Anna in my white dress? If he wanted me, if they asked for me, why did he bring that girl? I don't want him anyway, Daddy. I wouldn't have him even if he hadn't brought that girl.'

"I remember that Daddy reached over and patted my hand and calmed me down and told me not to worry. I didn't think much more about it, after that. So along in the spring, that same year, Anna Dragna got engaged. We were invited up to the engagement party. Momo and Marie [Adamo] were there with her kids. I was there with my mother and father and a lot of people. Frankie Dragna, of course was there. So, by then, I've turned 17. I'm out in the yard, talking to Marie's son, Paul Adamo, and other guys my age who were there. It was a big, big party, inside and outside, maybe a hundred people. So Frances Dragna comes up to my mother and says, 'Thelma, look at your daughter over there.' My mother was so cool. She says, 'Yes, Frances, what about it?' Frances comes right back with, 'Look over there at Mary Ann talking with all those boys. She shouldn't be over there. Frankie's not gonna like it.' And my mother said, 'Frances, my daughter is not doing a thing wrong. She's right in front of our eyes, she's young, she's talking to the young boys, and besides that, my daughter doesn't want your son.' That did it with the idea I was going to marry Frankie Dragna.

"But the nice thing was, I wasn't forced. Some people, some families, they make the arrangements for the marriage and the girls just smile their way through the whole thing and they do what their daddy tells them. Not me. When I look back on all that I realize that it was the Dragnas that wanted to make that marriage and that poor old Frankie, as far as I know, never knew anything about it. Jack never brought his son in on any of this. That's how Jack was. But that's not how my dad was. If I hadn't been crazy for somebody, my mother and father would not have insisted on an arranged marriage."

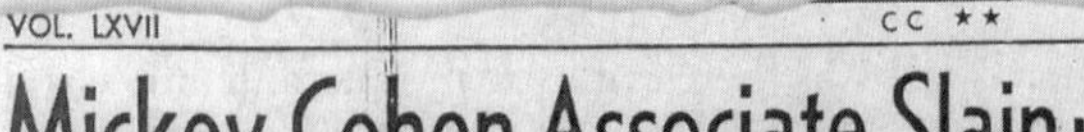

VOL. LXVII CC ★★

# Mickey Cohen Associate Slain; Gang Warfare Revival Seen

## Shotgun Blasts Wound Another in Sunset Strip Haberdashery

Shotgun blasts last night left one man dead and another wounded critically in the luxurious office of Michael (Mickey) Cohen's new haberdashery at 8800 Sunset Blvd. in the heart of The Strip.

Pronounced dead at West Hollywood Emergency Hospital was Harry (Hooky) Rothman, 36, an associate of Cohen.

Albert (Slick) Snyder, also 36, was rushed to General Hospital with numerous shotgun pellet wounds throughout his body.

**Heard Gunfire**

Cohen, a prominent figure in the sporting world here, told Sheriff's Lt. Walker Hannon that he heard what sounded like shotgun or machine-gun fire as he was in a washroom at the rear of the offices.

As he stepped from the washroom a minute later, Cohen said, he saw a man running from the front of the building. Rothman lay bleeding on the sidewalk near the door and Snyder was slumped behind a desk, Cohen added.

A final shot was apparently administered the already-dying Rothman as he struggled from the office to the street in a vain attempt to escape his murderer.

**Marks of Blast Found**

Investigators found marks of several blasts in the office itself where both men were shot and another pockmarked area near the door where a second charge was loosed at Rothman as he ran. Officers found the dead man lying in a pool of blood on the sidewalk. On the wall above him were bloody hand marks.

Another trail of blood was found on stairs leading from the office to the haberdashy above. Cohen was unable to explain its presence, but detectives theorized Rothman may have tried to make his escape over that route first.

Cohen said Snyder told him there were three men in the raiding party.

Authorities believed that the shooting may be a resurgence of gang warfare among gambling elements on the county's West Side. Cohen has long been described by police as having ex-

ESCAPES—Michael (Mickey Cohen, in whose office shotgun slaying occurred.

—he is noted among friends for his frequent hand-washing—was credited with saving his life. Had he stepped from the washroom while the slayer was still in the office, it was pointed out, the gunman undoubtedly would have turned the shotgun upon him.

The sportsman was unable to give any inkling of a motive for the shooting. When questioned about possible motives Cohen only shrugged his shoulders.

He and his two associates were alone in the office at the time, Cohen told investigators. The entrance to the office is on a small side street—Palm Ave.—and lies below the haberdashery's main portion.

Almost immediately after the arrival of Sheriff's Chief of Detectives Norris Stensland, Cohen was taken to the West Hollywood substation for a closed conference with top investigators.

*From the Los Angeles Times, August 19, 1948*

**Bompensiero swung the sawed-off shotgun in front of Hooky's face and ordered, "Get back in there."**

# CHAPTER TWENTY-NINE

# THE PLOT TO KILL MICKEY COHEN

To track Bompensiero's life, another detour is needed. In June, 1946, 33-year-old Aladena "Jimmy the Weasel" Fratianno had arrived in Los Angeles from Ohio. Fratianno, an ex-con, started making book out of the Chase Hotel in Santa Monica. He quickly made the acquaintance of Salvatore "Dago Louie" Piscopo (aka Louie Merli). A bookmaker who'd been in LA since the 1930s, Dago Louie also served as driver and bagman for Johnny Rosselli. Dago Louie introduced Jimmy to the Dragnas. Through the Dragnas, Fratianno met Rosselli, Frank and Tony Milano, James Iannone, Momo Adamo, Anthony "Tony Dope" Delsanter, Simone Scozzari, James Licavoli, "Leo the Lip" Moceri, Charles Dippolito and his son Joseph "Joe Dip" Dippolito, who owned a vineyard in Cucamonga, Sam Bruno, Nick Licata and his son Carlo Licata, Carmen Carpinelli, attorney Frank Desimone, Biaggio Bonventre, Mickey Cohen, and Frank Bompensiero.

A retired Los Angeles policeman told me about seeing Fratianno during the late 1940s, "When he first came to LA, he was just a small-town-bookie type. We watched him, but he didn't appear to be much of anything. He was just a punk from Cleveland. He worked for the Dragnas and he worked for Mickey."

On the evening of June 21, 1947, Walter Winchell began his radio newscast with "Flash! Beverly Hills, California. As Confucius say, 'Gangland gold always pay off in lead.'" Winchell went on to announce that 42-year-old Benjamin "Bugsy" Siegel had been murdered.

The question of who murdered Siegel would never be answered. Some stories have it that Dragna's family made the hit; others have it that out-of-town men, sent by Siegel's old friend Meyer Lansky, did the job.

Siegel's murder altered the Southern California crime syndicate's balance of power. In *All-American Mafioso: The Johnny Rosselli Story*, Charles Rappleye and Ed Becker postulate, "Eliminating Bugsy Siegel may have bolstered Dragna's ego, but it left the Los Angeles underworld in a state of chaos. Siegel's mercurial lieutenant Mickey Cohen was assigned control of bookmaking in 1942 with Dragna and Rosselli's consent, but with Siegel gone, Cohen renounced any ties to the Italians."

After Siegel's death, Meyer Lansky's protective hand no longer extended over what Jack Dragna called the "Jew boys." Dragna began to work out a plot to kill Cohen and break Cohen's bookmaking franchise. An operation of this size and complexity needed soldiers. Dragna would have to enlist new men.

Dago Louie, soon after Siegel's murder, set up a meeting between Jimmy Fratianno and Johnny Rosselli. The meeting took place in September, 1947, in what Jimmy described to Ovid Demaris as Dago Louie's "parlor." Fratianno explained to Rosselli that he wanted to be "made." In Demaris's *The Last Mafioso: The Treacherous World of Jimmy Fratianno,* Fratianno recalled the conversation: "Johnny, I've been wanting this since I was a kid. I knew the Italians on the Hill had something special going for them, but it's so fucking hard to crack."

To which Jimmy remembered Rosselli replying: "That's right, Jimmy, and that's the way it should be. When you get the wrong guy in there, you've got to clip him. There's no pink slip in this thing."

The scene of Jimmy's becoming a "made man" opens *The Last Mafioso.* Jimmy's "making" took place in the basement of a winery on South Figueroa Street in Los Angeles. "Made" with him, according to Demaris's book, were Dominic Brooklier, Charley Dippolito, Dago Louie, and Tom Dragna's son, Louis Tom. Jack Dragna initiated the new men, according to a further account in Rappleye and Becker's *All-American Mafioso,* "incanting in Sicilian with a dagger and a revolver lying crossed on the table before him. John Rosselli greeted the initiates at the door and led them to Dragna."

In *Vengeance Is Mine: Jimmy the Weasel Fratianno Tells How He Brought the Kiss of Death to the Mafia*, Michael J. Zuckerman uses Fratianno's testimony in a later deposition to tell the story of Jimmy's "making." Jimmy was asked, "Who decides if a person can become a member of La Cosa Nostra?"

His answer: "Well, number one, you've got to be proposed [by a member]. The boss decides if you're to become a member, the bosses of the Family.... Sometimes you have to do something significant, like kill somebody."

Then, Fratianno describes his initiation. "There were five of us.... I think at the time we had fifty to sixty members, and maybe forty to forty-five were present. They had a long table. The boss and underboss would sit on one side; the capos on the end. There was a gun and a sword in the middle of the table crossing each other.

"We would all stand up. We would hold our hands together, and the boss would rattle something off in Sicilian.... After that they would prick your finger with a sword or with a pin to draw blood. And they take you around to each member, introduce you and you kiss them on the cheek. That's the initiation."

After the ceremony, Fratianno and Rosselli celebrated in Dago Louie's parlor. "For a while there," Fratianno told Rosselli, "I felt like I was in church."

Mary Ann, meanwhile, was attending Grossmont High School. "I should have gone to Hoover High, but my father didn't like the reputation. He felt Hoover was kind of rough. We lived on Estelle, then, but I gave a different address, one of my girlfriends'.

"My girlfriends and I hung out at my house. Because my father didn't want me to spend the night at anybody's house. He wanted his daughter home. Saturday night, kids would come to my house—Beverly, Betty Dodd, and my cousin, Lorraine, and they'd spend the night. I had a small bedroom with a four-poster bed. The four of us would all sleep in that bed, two at the head of the bed and two at the foot of the bed. We'd stay up half the night.

"My mother would be home or maybe she'd go play cards with her lady friends who lived close to the Gold Rail in Little Italy. At two o'clock after the Gold Rail closed, my mother would pick up my father.

"Saturday nights, when my girlfriends stayed over, we would still all be up. We would be smoking. We were just trying it. Well, we'd be up. We were smoking, trying to smoke really was more like it. We weren't smokers. We'd have the windows open. And then we'd hear the car drive up and, boom, we'd jump into bed.

"My father would walk in the front door and you could hear him asking my mom, 'Anybody been smoking in here?' My mother smoked, she'd say, 'Frank, no, I don't smell smoke.' She covered for us.

"This one night, I remember, we're pretending we're sound asleep, right? My girlfriend, Betty Dodd, was where I usually am. My father would always come into my room when he got home and kiss me goodnight on my forehead. I don't care if he came in at three or four o'clock in the morning. He came in my room and kissed me goodnight on my cheek or my forehead. So he leans over and kisses not me, but Betty. We burst out laughing. My father, though, is truly embarrassed. He says, 'Oh my God, Betty, I'm sorry.' Betty said, 'That's okay, Mr. Bompensiero, that's okay.'"

Mary Ann said that as a teenager, she "pretty much stayed out of trouble. My dad was always warning me, 'Don't do this. Don't do that.' He would say, 'Don't ever steal anything.' He said, 'If you're going to do anything, go big, because you get the same name.' He'd say, 'Don't ever steal anything. You don't need to steal anything.' Shoplifting is what he meant. You know how kids will shoplift. Not me. Never. I would have disgraced him, are you kidding? 'Frank's daughter gotta steal, when she's got a hundred dollars in her pocket?' Which, then, in those days you could buy a whole outfit."

I asked Mary Ann if her father ever grounded her. "Never," she said. "For all he knew, I never even went out. My mother was the one who would let me go out once in a while. But my father didn't want me dating. Are you kidding? I was my daddy's pet. I could do no harm except go out with boys. He wasn't allowing anything like that. For all I knew if you French kissed you'd get pregnant. I knew about life what my mother told me. Which was not much.

"In 1948, when I was 17, I was going out with Jack Lonnie Roberts, whose nickname was Dutch. Nelson Roberts Sr., his father, was a big shot with the *San Diego Union*. He was an advertising manager. Dutch's parents were divorced. We were both the same age. Dutch was gorgeous. He looked a lot like Tab Hunter. Dutch had lied about his age and been in the military. He wasn't in school anymore. My father didn't want me seeing him or even talking to him. It wasn't that he didn't like Dutch, he just thought it was getting too serious and he thought we were too young. He also probably wanted me to be married to an Italian. I was allowed to go on dates, but they had to be highly supervised. For instance, I could go to all the Catholic formal dances. But he was very careful about who I went out with and if I went out at all.

"It was April 4. My mother knew I was going to a wedding with Dutch. Dutch was the best man in his buddy Larry's wedding. Everybody got married young in those days. I was going to the wedding with him. My father didn't know. It was on a Saturday afternoon. I wore a gray suit, and my mother said to me, 'You're not going to get any ideas and run away and get married are you?' I said, 'Mama, the day I walk out of here with my white suit on,' because I did have a white suit, 'is the day you might have to worry about it.'

"We went to the wedding and were partying afterwards. It got later and later. Dutch was driving his mother's Plymouth. He said, 'Let's go get married.' I said, 'Are you crazy?' He said, 'We're going to catch hell anyway.' So we drove all the way to Yuma. Didn't kiss. Didn't neck, pet, nothing. I swear to you. I was a virgin. I wasn't touched. I was petrified of doing anything like that. I knew my father would kill me. So we got married in Yuma, turned around, crossed the Arizona border. When we got to the border, the officers there asked us, 'You Bompensiero and Roberts?'

"The border people said, 'Bompensiero and Roberts! Congratulations, kids. You got married, right?' We nodded. We were petrified. The border officer said, 'Well, kids, you just made it, then. There's an all-out bulletin out for you two.'

"How they knew who we were of course is that when I didn't get home, my mother said to my father, 'Frank, I let her go to the wedding.' My mother knew, too, that we were driving Dutch's mother's car. So they got the license number and a description of the car and called the police and got out this all-points bulletin.

"So we drive home. I felt like I was going to die. We drive up Estelle Street and there's every car out of my family—my Aunt Grace's car, my mother's sister Annie, my grandmother, everybody was there. It was like when somebody dies in an Italian family, the whole family comes over. I said, 'Dutch, we've got to go find a phone booth and I've got to call home. I can't walk in there.' So we went to the gasoline station on El Cajon Boulevard and I called. My mother answered the phone. 'Mary Ann,' she said, 'is that you?' I said, 'Mama, Mama, yes, it's me.' Boom, she slammed the phone down on me. She was so distraught. She was relieved I guess to hear that we were alive. So we go home.

"Oh, it was bad. My father was there and my whole family was there. My grandmother Bompensiero was there, in her black dress. My father had on a white shirt, unbuttoned, he was chewing his cigar. Oh, God, he was pacing, pacing, pacing. He looked over at me, and said, 'You're okay? You're all right?' So my father, a raving maniac with everybody in the house, he told Dutch, 'Get your father. Get your father on the phone. Call your father and get him over here.'

"Meanwhile, everybody hugged me and kissed me. My mother called me in the bedroom, she wanted to know if I was pregnant. She was crying. I said, 'Mama, Mama,' and I was bawling. She said, 'Why did you do this?' And I said, 'Daddy wouldn't even let me talk to him, so history has repeated itself.' She said, 'I want to know one thing from you. Did you have to go get married?' I said, 'Mom, I'm the same girl that left here this morning. I haven't been touched.' And so she says, 'Okay, honey.' And she believed me.

"My father didn't even go in the bedroom. I went back into the living room and I said to him, 'If you want to keep me home tonight, take me to a doctor.' I told him that I was a virgin. Then my father calmed down a little with me. But not with poor Dutch.

"They had been up all night. My father was so upset, before we got home. My mother told me later that my father was saying, 'I hope they find him, the son of a bitch.' 'Goddamit.' And that my grandmother Bompensiero, trying maybe to calm him down, she said to him, in Italian, 'Frank, son of mine, didn't you run away and get married, didn't you go get married. What are you gonna do?'

"So Dutch called his father and his stepmother. He got them over there. In the meantime everybody starts dispersing. There's coffee, my aunts are gone. Dutch's father and stepmother show up. My father says to Nelson Roberts Sr., 'My daughter is a virgin. Get your son aside and tell him the goddamn facts of life because we don't want to have any babies in nine months.' Can you imagine that?

"Dutch and I spent our wedding night in a little house connected to Dutch's mother's house. A house on Kansas Street, a block off of University Avenue. It was a little house, and like a duplex, but there was a private door that didn't go into the main house, and a bedroom and bathroom and that's where we spent our wedding night.

"We never went to church. But my father gave the church a lot, donated a lot, bought a lot of tickets to this and that. My father, after we eloped and got back, said that he wanted us married in the church. I'm Catholic but Dutch wasn't. So my father went down to see the priest. The priest said, 'The young man's got to do this and that before I can marry them.' My dad said, 'Father, I think you need some new shoes.' He gave him $50. So we got married in the church and Dutch didn't have to turn Catholic. I don't know if the priests were afraid of my father, or what. I think they liked him."

In Bompensiero's FBI files, obtained through the Freedom of Information Act, I found the following notation: "On June 20, 1948, Special Agents of the Federal Bureau of Investigation observed Frank Bompensiero in attendance at a wedding of (★★★)." The three asterisks indicate that the name of the bride, surely Mary Ann, were blacked out. Did Mary Ann realize that the FBI attended her wedding? No, she said, but added that she wasn't surprised.

By early summer, 1948, Jack Dragna had decided to open his battle with Mickey Cohen and Cohen's bookmakers. In his autobiography, in Chapter 13, "The Battle of Sunset Strip," Mickey Cohen writes: "It was really a battle of recognition more than anything else. After Benny Siegel got knocked in, people like Jack Dragna kept feeling that their prestige was badly shaken.... When a war starts, it is just an understanding who fires the first shots. I wouldn't want to say that the responsibility in this war was completely on one side or the other. People just declared themselves, and that was it."

The first attempt took place on a Wednesday evening, August 18, 1948, at Michael's, Cohen's haberdashery at 8800 Sunset Boulevard. Fratianno's account in *The Last Mafioso* and *All-American Mafioso*, has Fratianno serve as point man for this first hit against Cohen. Five men were assigned to the hit team—Bompensiero, Simone Scozzari, Biaggio Bonventre, Sam Bruno, and Frank Desimone. The plan was that Jimmy, on Wednesday evening, August 18, 1948, would go by the haberdashery to visit Cohen. If everything looked right, he'd walk out onto Sunset Boulevard toward his Buick and give the okay sign to the team.

Looking back in old copies of the *San Diego Union*, a reader can learn that the weather had been chilly for August, with the low for August 18 dropping to 63 degrees and the high 74. Bompensiero would have backed the blue Hudson out of his driveway at 5878 Estelle and headed for Los Angeles. The drive, then, on old 101, took two hours.

Meanwhile, in LA, Fratianno had decided he'd take along his wife Jewel and their nine-year-old daughter Joanne. The family sat in the haberdashery office, chatting with Cohen about the hit musical, *Annie Get Your Gun*. Also in the office were Hooky Rothman, Al Snyder, and Jimmy Rist, who variously served Cohen as collectors for his bookie shops, as muscle, and "entourage." Cohen was praising *Annie Get Your Gun* as the best musical to come to a Los Angeles stage in years. Cohen offered the Fratiannos tickets. Jimmy stood from Cohen's couch, took the ticket envelope from Cohen, and then put out his hand and shook Cohen's hand.

Cohen had a hand-washing fetish. He sometimes scrubbed his small compact hands every five minutes. His office, of course, was fitted out with a bathroom.

The Fratiannos walked out. "Jimmy," Demaris writes, "spotted Frank Desimone standing on the far corner of Holloway Drive and Palm Avenue and he gave him the signal. They had taken less than a dozen steps up the sharp incline toward Sunset where their car was parked when he heard a door open behind him and he turned to see Hooky Rothman coming out.

"At that exact moment Scozzari had pulled up and three men were jumping out of the car. Bompensiero, wearing dark glasses and a white Panama hat pulled low over his forehead swung the sawed-off shotgun in front of Hooky's face and ordered, 'Get back in there.' Bruno and Biaggio ran around Hooky and into the office just as Hooky tried to hit the shotgun out of Bompensiero's hands. The explosion was deafening.

"Jewel and Joanne screamed and began running in opposite directions. Jimmy, who had just seen Hooky's face blown away, stood there for a split second, not knowing whom to chase. From the corner of his eye, he saw Bompensiero step over Hooky's body and charge into the office, his body hunched over.

"When they got back to the car, Jimmy saw Cohen run out the front door of his haberdashery and head toward an apartment building as swiftly as his short legs would take him. With wife and daughter screaming at his side, Jimmy stood there not wanting to believe his eyes. He felt ill. All that planning, Hooky dead, and there was Mickey running like a deer for cover."

When Jimmy read the newspaper account of the hit, he discovered that Cohen had escaped death because he'd rushed into the bathroom to wash the hand Jimmy had shaken. Hooky Rothman was dead, Jimmy Rist had a bullet nick on his ear, and Al Snyder took a slug in the arm.

Back home on Estelle Street, on Thursday morning, August 19, if Bompensiero picked up the *San Diego Union* off his front lawn and turned to the front-page account of the failed hit, this is what he read:

Mickey Cohen Associate Slain; Gang Warfare Revival Seen

Shotgun Blasts Wound Another In Sunset Strip Haberdashery

Shotgun Blasts Last Night Left One Man Dead And Another Wounded Critically

The shooting, he would have read, "was conducted in typical gangland style with the killers escaping in a fast automobile." He would have seen a photograph of an LAPD investigator pointing his flashlight at the holes made in the wall of Cohen's office.

Cohen noted in his autobiography, "Nobody could identify anybody in the shoot-out for the cops. That isn't the way of the racket world." Cohen regretted his old pal Hooky's loss. "He was a solid Jew. If you take a Jew that is completely solid, it makes no difference if he gets hit with a thousand-year sentence or if he's facing the loss of his life a second later. He won't be a stool pigeon. I believe a rotten cocksucker is either born a rotten cocksucker or he's not."

The Dragna-Cohen battle continued. But in the ensuing attempts to kill Mickey Cohen and his workers, Bompensiero seemed to have no part.

Miss Mary Ann Bompensiero, daughter of Mr. and Mrs. Frank Bompensiero, will recite wedding vows with Jack Lonnie Roberts, son of Mrs. Velma Roberts and Nelson Roberts, at 3 this afternoon in St. Jude's Church.

## Jack Roberts To Claim Bride

Miss Mary Ann Bompensiero, daughter of Mr. and Mrs. Frank Bompensiero, will become the bride of Jack Lonnie Roberts, son of Mrs. Velma Roberts and Nelson Roberts, this afternoon at 3 in St. Jude's Church. Father Joseph C. De Christini will officiate. The bride, to be given in marriage by her father, will wear an aqua suit with orchid corsage.

Miss Frances Signorelli, maid of honor, has selected for the ceremony a beige suit and gardenia corsage. Nelson Roberts Jr. will serve his brother as best man.

A wedding reception will be held in El Cortez Hotel for 85 guests. Mrs. Bompensiero will receive in a cocoa-colored suit trimmed with beads and Mrs. Roberts will wear a ballerina print dress.

The newlyweds will make their home in San Diego.

*Mary Ann's Wedding Announcement in the San Diego Union*

**"Instead of calling the police first, she called Frank Bompensiero."**

CHAPTER THIRTY

# HE WAS A PEACEMAKER

Del Mar brought *mafiosi* in from all over the United States. "Very seldom," said Mary Ann, "would my father go to the track. He also rarely bet on anything, including horses. He used to say, 'You can't win with those horses. You may as well just throw a dart.'"

FBI head J. Edgar Hoover, a race aficionado, first came to Del Mar in 1938. Hoover continued to visit Del Mar yearly with his longtime companion and coworker Clyde Tolson. Hoover scheduled his annual physical at Scripps Clinic to coincide with the Del Mar season.

Del Mar's 1948 meet lasted 41 days; it opened on July 27 and closed on September 11. According to Jimmy Fratianno's testimony, as recorded in Anthony Summers's *Official and Confidential: The Secret Life of J. Edgar Hoover*, Fratianno and Bompensiero were at the Del Mar track on an afternoon in 1948 when Hoover was in attendance. "I pointed at this fella sitting in the box in front," Fratianno recalled, "and said, 'Hey, lookit there, it's J. Edgar Hoover.' And Frank says right out loud, so everyone can hear, 'Ah, that J. Edgar's a punk, he's a fuckin' degenerate queer.'"

Later, according to Fratianno's account to Summers, when Bompensiero ran into Hoover in the track's men's room, "the FBI director was astonishingly meek. 'Frank,' he told the mobster, 'that's not a nice way to talk about me, especially when I have people with me.' It was clear to Fratianno that Bompensiero had met Edgar before and had absolutely no fear of him."

By Christmas, 1948, Dutch's mother had remarried and Mary Ann and Dutch had settled into his mother's house on Kansas Street. "By this time, my father's heart had softened. He had taken Dutch under his wing. He had come to love him like his own son.

"My father then called another meeting with the Robertses. I don't know exactly how the Robertses felt about my father at this time. Because he didn't ask them, he told them. Very nicely though. He says, 'Okay, now the kids have got this house on Kansas Street, and they need furniture. Mary Ann is going to take her bedroom set. A really nice set. And we're going to buy her the living room and dining room. So it looks like we've got the bedroom, living room, dining room, dishes. Now,' he said, 'they need a stove, a refrigerator, and a washing machine. That's what you're giving them for their wedding.' And Nelson Roberts said, 'Okay, Frank.'

"My father gave Dutch a job. But my dad really didn't want him in the bar, down at the Gold Rail. And I wanted my husband at home with me at night. Also, my father never wanted my husband—not because he wasn't Italian or anything, but simply because he was my husband—mixed up in anything. But I was his daughter and we were married, and he wanted him to make a decent living. So he gave him a job, with this outfit that my father owned part of, Maestro Music Company, which leased jukeboxes to bars and cafés.

"My father would tell him, 'Dutch, all you gotta do is go to the bars, you're gonna go in, you're going to get the owner or the manager, whatever it is, you're going to count all the money. You take half, you give him half. But I'm going to show you how to count it.' What I'm saying is he taught him how to count the money so he'd come out ahead.

"He told Dutch, 'If you go to a place and you don't see a jukebox there, write the name of the place down and bring it back to me. That's all you need to do.' One time I said, 'Daddy, how do you get all these jukeboxes, how come they use Maestro Music everywhere?' He said, 'Honey, it's very easy. We go in and tell them, "We've got a better jukebox, more players," and the guy says, "I'm happy with this jukebox."' So my father says, 'Pretty soon, the jukeboxes don't work anymore.' They sent people in with slugs or whatever, with gum on them. Didn't do any rough stuff, just gum. And the jukeboxes got jammed. So that was the end of that. They'd guarantee them no problems if they got the Maestro Music jukeboxes.

"My father had to prove that he had food at the Gold Rail because of the liquor license. It was called the Gold Rail Steak House. Well, my father really didn't serve any food. So he said to me and Dutch, 'There's a charge account down at DeFalco's on India Street.' And he said, 'I want you to go down, that's where you buy your food and just sign your name. Tell them to put your order on the Gold Rail account.'

"Dutch felt funny. He didn't like them doing that much for us, because my mother would go shopping and she would bring me clothes and things for the house. And Dutch would say, because he was making $125 a week now, that he worked for Maestro Music, and my father gave him a salary. But my mother would see cute things and bring them to us. Dutch said, 'I don't want your mother buying you this.' I'd say, 'I'm not going to tell my mother she can't buy me anything.' And we'd argue about that.

"Finally, I said, 'Mama, Dutch feels funny. He says, "I want to support you—your father is giving me this job, but let's live off the money I make from your father."' My father respected him for that but he said, 'Dutch, you're doing me a favor if you charge the food, because I don't serve food there, and I've got to show bills, receipts that I'm buying food.' This was when I knew, for sure, about my dad that things weren't necessarily always on the up and up."

Mr. Willis, my friend who'd retired after many years in San Diego law enforcement, one day told me a story about a murder that occurred, he believed, in late 1949. "Nobody ever knew the reason for this one. It was the Tony Regina murder out in East San Diego, in Regina's house on 43rd Street. He was in a coma for almost a year before he died. He never came out of it. The hell was beat out of him. The murder occurred while his wife was gone. She was at Mass, she went to Mass every morning at Sacred Heart Church, there at 42nd and Orange. She was a very devout Catholic. Funny thing, when she got back home and found Tony beat to a pulp, she didn't call the cops, she called Frank Bompensiero, and Frank came out. Nobody ever knew the reason for this. Her name was Vincenza Licata Regina. She was the sister of Nick Licata Sr., the aunt of Nick Licata Jr. and Carlo Licata. After her husband's murder she left San Diego and nobody could ever get to her from then on because she was in a rest home in Burbank. She wasn't culpable, she was not involved in it, she was elderly, these people were then in their 50s or 60s. San Diego Police Department investigated it." Mr. Willis shrugged, then smiled. "Instead of calling the police first, she called Frank Bompensiero. But again, this doesn't necessarily manifest culpability, this is family, this is the way these people think, they don't trust police, they trust each other to take care of things. I don't know whether her husband was beating hell out of her or if he was involved in crime, nobody knows. Nobody will ever know."

Mr. Willis, given all the years that had passed, had remembered the details of this case fairly well. When I went back into the old newspaper files and looked up Regina I found several articles. The first appeared on November 5, 1949, in a *San Diego Union* article headlined:

Wife Held As Slugged Husband Fights for Life in Hospital

"Gray-haired Mrs. Vincenza Regina, 49, was booked in the City Jail yesterday on suspicion of attempted murder, 10 hours after her husband, Tony Regina, 61, was found critically beaten in a bedroom at their home, 4383 Forty-Third Street. Regina, co-proprietor of the Melba Café, 727 Twelfth Avenue, clung to life at Mercy Hospital last night. A priest administered last rites after his arrival.

"Mrs. Regina, married to the victim for 26 years, was booked at 6 p.m. She gave conflicting statements when questioned by Detective Sgts. R.L. Ormsby and A.J. Maguire, Ormsby said. She had notified police of her husband's wounds after being unable, she said, to arouse neighbors. She said she found him in the blood-stained room upon returning from church about 8 a.m.

"The husband's condition was very poor a physician said. Regina, who suffered a compound fracture of the skull, remained unconscious last night. He had received three pints of blood in transfusions.

"In the disarrayed room at the residence, police found a large pool of blood soaking half of the top of the bed. Regina was on the floor beside the bed, wearing only an undershirt. His trousers, also on the floor, contained nine dollars. A key was beside Regina.

"During the police interview Mrs. Regina said her husband gambled and that out-of-town guests frequently came to the house at night and had access to a front door key. She said Regina kept large sums of money in a wallet, hidden in the house. Detectives found an empty wallet. No attack weapon was located.

"Mrs. Regina claimed she was not familiar with her husband's arrivals and departures, police said. Investigators did not disclose details of the conflicting versions which led to their suspicion of the wife.

"The Reginas, who have no children, have lived here 18 years and bought the house on Forty-Third Street about three years ago, neighbors said. Mrs. Regina, a native of Italy, said she had been assisting her husband in his café. Regina formerly owned the Lobby Café, Ninth and Broadway."

On November 8, 1949, the *San Diego Union* reported:

> "Mrs. Virginia [sic] Regina, 49, booked Friday in the City Jail on circumstantial evidence police gathered after her husband was found bludgeoned and near death was released yesterday from the jail. Police said evidence did not justify holding her."

And on March 28, 1950, the *Union* noted:

> Beaten Café Owner Dies in Hospital

"Tony Regina who was bludgeoned into a permanent coma nearly five months ago died yesterday at Patton State Hospital where he had been cared for since February 1.

"His wife told police that upon returning from church she found her husband beaten severely on the head and lying on a bedroom floor. He had been struck repeatedly with a weapon that never was found. No motive for the assault was uncovered. Mrs. Regina blamed enemies of Regina, but Geer said yesterday officers have not been able to trace any suspect who might have had a motive for killing him. He never regained consciousness. Mrs. Regina now lives in Los Angeles."

When I asked Mary Ann about this story, she said, "Women would come to my dad if they had trouble with their husbands. He was a peacemaker. He kept families together. They were afraid of him in a way. If a woman was having trouble, he'd talk to the woman and then go talk to the husband. He would say, 'Look, you stupido, you got a wife, you got three kids, you're not going anywhere. Your family comes first. Okay?'"

*Thelma, Frank Bompensiero, Mary Ann, and Dutch*

**He did not trust Jews,**

**any more than he trusted Americans or**

**Neapolitans or Romans or Milanese.**

CHAPTER THIRTY-ONE

# INSIDE HIS MIND

When 44-year-old Frank Bompensiero awakened at 5878 Estelle Street on the first morning of a new decade, he must have felt optimistic. He must have felt hopeful. He padded on his bare size-ten feet into the shower. He sang, as was his custom, in the manner of Al Jolson: "Mammy, how I love you, how I love you, my dear old Mammy." As he sudsed his stocky short frame, he must have added an extra warble, a rococo trill to Jolson's paean to his dear old Mammy waiting for him, praying for him, way down along the Swanee shore. On this first morning of 1950, a morning on which Harry Truman was in the White House, Earl Warren was in the state house, and Jack Butler was the city's mayor, Bompensiero had much to celebrate. More appeared to be going for than against him.

A quarter century earlier Bompensiero was in big trouble. A dead man on a dark road outside Milwaukee. He'd had to do things for Jack Dragna, and he'd done them. He accorded himself well. He had long been one of the *amici*, one of the friends, one of the family. His fealty to Dragna had been—and to this morning in January continued to be—utter, complete. He went where Jack sent him, he did what Jack said "Do." No matter how heavy the load, if Jack said carry, he carried. He screwed up the Les Brunemann thing, but he and Leo went back to Redondo Beach and finished Brunemann. Sixteen shots Leo put into Brunemann. Sixteen. That café where Brunemann was sitting with his whore looked like a butcher shop when Leo got done. Then in 1938 Jack sent him to kill Phil Galuzo. He head-shot Galuzo. Left him head down in the gutter. After Galuzo he had to go into hiding. They shipped him from *amici* in Detroit to Kansas City to Tampa to New Orleans. He met good people.

Now people were not so good. It was not what it had been. Not in California. Maybe in Chicago and in New York and even in Kansas City and Detroit, men still were good workers. Here the younger ones, the new ones coming in, were not good. They did no work. Johnny Rosselli was a fool. He impressed Jack with his Chicago connections, with knowing Capone, with knowing Paul Ricca. Rosselli had gotten himself involved with Hollywood people and gone to prison. Rosselli, he should have been an actor. That's what Rosselli wanted. Like the dead Jew Siegel. They wanted to be in movies. They pandered after the likes of George Raft and screwed blonde

American whores. Life to them was like movies. Fratianno was another one; Bompensiero never felt easy with Fratianno in a room. Fratianno had cheap feelings; his feelings did not run deep. But Momo was good people, Momo's brother Joe was good people. Biaggio was good people. Leo was good people. La Porte was good people. Three-Fingered Frank was good people. The tailor was not good people. The tailor's woman came to him many times. She begged him to do it. She showed him the marks on her arms. And Mirabile was shit. Mirabile was truly shit. A son of a bitch. All that bullshit playing the great don, the nod and smile when people addressed him as "Papa Tony, Papa Tony." Jack shamed some good money out of Mirabile, though, and everyone laughed. Laughed hard. "We will make you one of us, Tony, for a small consideration." The consideration was not small. The consideration was many fat envelopes. The consideration would end only when Mirabile found his grave. Jack knew how to get money from guys. Jack was a sly one. He had in common with Mirabile the chasing of women. Always chasing women and whores, Jack was. Always chasing women and whores, and girls, young girls, Mirabile was. The mother of one girl called Bompensiero at home. "Frank, Frank, get down here. Mr. Tony is going crazy, chasing my daughter." Bompensiero rousted Mirabile out of that house. "What?" he said to Mirabile. "Are you crazy? Gone crazy?"

Since 1946, Bompensiero had made significant money at the Gold Rail. Paydays for the sailors, you couldn't get sideways into the 25-stool bar at 1028 Third Avenue in the midst of the downtown area known as sailor row and neon row. Although, the last few years, fewer servicemen came and went through the town; their absence was hard on business. But other ways exist to earn money, ways done in the dark. Bompensiero knows many ways, as he puts it, "to alibi" income. Skimming the bar cash was best: no taxes. Every buck you take in is yours. Running two tapes—the legit tape and your own tape—that also is good. Nowadays, Bompensiero's trouser pockets always are lined with bills—20s and 50s and 100s.

Bompensiero was proud of the Gold Rail. Actually, if you are to believe the license and the Yellow Pages listing, the "Gold Rail Steak House." No steak was served. Law said you had to serve food. Bompensiero didn't serve food. Evenings, when he was home, a call sometimes came from his pal on the vice squad. The pal tipped him that vice was going to swing by. Bompensiero had to rise up off the couch and change clothes and rub the oil in his hair—hair that was receding, thinning—slip into his jacket and shoes and then sort through the refrigerator and grab a few steaks and those fennel sausages from the butcher and get Thelma to toss them in a grocery sack. Then he had to drive down to Third Avenue, park the Cadillac, and fill the refrigerator. One night he cooked a steak thick as two fingers and a dozen sausages and served them at the bar. Vice strolled in, the air was filled with the cooking smells of beef and fennel and everyone was laughing and eating. Vice rousted him several times, too, over bookmakers in the Gold Rail. Little stuff. Nothing to worry.

Beginning in the late 1940s, with various partners—Dr. Paul C. Hartman, Joseph Ernesto Matranga, Mirabile—Bompensiero owned varying numbers of shares in Southland, which did business as Maestro Music. He managed to buy a few lots. He was paying down the house on Estelle Street. Bompensiero's furniture and cars no longer were being repossessed, as they had been more than once during the 1930s and early 1940s. Certainly, he did not feel desperate for cash as he had in the past. He no longer had to go out and do stickups, as he did in 1933 at the Fox Theatre or the American Cut-Rate Drug Store or in the Trias Street home of Irvine M. Schulman.

On this first morning of 1950, while Bompensiero dried off from his shower, while he wrapped the thick towel about his hard, rounded stomach and stood before the mirror and brushed the shaving cream into his cheeks, and relit his cigar and steadied the big stogie on the sink's edge, he may have continued to count his blessings. His mother, 70, had her health. Three of his four sisters and his brother Sam still were living; they had their health. Bompensiero had wanted to kill the kid with whom Mary Ann drove off to Yuma, wanted the sob's face open-mouthed and wheezing his last breath in a watery ditch. Like Galuzo. But Jack Roberts—"Dutch" they called him—turned out to be a great kid. He wasn't Sicilian, true, but he wasn't lazy and he did not lack courage.

Cheeks shaved, skin aglow, the aroma of his lavender aftershave sharp in the steamy bathroom, Bompensiero would then have stepped into his silk boxer shorts and slipped into his paisley-printed maroon silk robe and shoved his square feet into his leather slippers. He was modest. Even before his wife of now some 21 years, he did not appear in the nude. Not even in the bed.

Bompensiero on this first morning of the new year, as he strode into his bedroom and began to slide his arms into a clean white shirt, might have pondered the miracle of his marriage. Thelma, more beautiful every year. No one but Thelma would have stayed with him. No one would have been as loyal. He told her little and she guessed everything. She understood everything. Between them, all was pure. For him, since Thelma, there had been no one. Other men in the bar business took women into back rooms. They made them perform ugly acts in order to get a job. They laughed afterwards and offered the women to the bartenders. To do such a thing, to even think of someone doing such a thing, turned his stomach. His only disappointment was that Thelma was unable to bear other children. Having Mary Ann, she almost died. She had the small stroke while Mary Ann was being born. Then when she became pregnant again, the doctor who delivered Mary Ann said, "Frank, I know you're Catholic. But you've got a wife and a daughter, she can't carry this pregnancy. Your wife will probably die and if the baby is even born, the child will have no mother and your daughter will have no mother." So he and Thelma said to him to do the abortion. For many many days after the abortion he felt such sadness he could hardly hold up his head.

Bompensiero might have thought how good it was that Thelma had the dress shop. When Thelma's mother, Felipa Sanfilippo, died last year she left money to Thelma and all Thelma's sisters and brothers. Thelma used her money to go into business. Now Thelma had Santa Ann's Moderate Shop on 30th in North Park (3912 30th Street). The dark thought about Thelma's health might then have made Bompensiero frown. She suffered still from high blood pressure and the pills the doctor gave made her feel worse. She often would not take them. She said, "They make me sick." The blood pressure worried him. Her brother Frank died at 44. Heart and blood pressure. Some evenings she was too weary to cook and her hands swelled and the diamonds on her fingers bit into her flesh. He would give his life for her. He would.

He might have said to himself that some days, now, Los Angeles seemed far away. This business of Jack's, trying to kill the dumb-ass little Jew. Jews he did not dislike just because they were Jews. He did not trust them, any more than he trusted Americans or Neapolitans or Romans or Milanese. He trusted his own; he trusted Sicilians. The business between Cohen and Jack, this business was getting to be a waste of time. This trying to control LA's bookmakers by killing the Jew, this was a waste of time. This was drawing attention. Bompensiero would have agreed with Cohen had he read what Cohen eventually wrote about the Dragna group's attempts on his life: "I think it all came about with a lot of people prodding Jack and steaming him up about him losing face in the whole community, in our way of life. Different guys wanted to make themselves look good to him in every way they could. And actually they was nothing but a bunch that kiss other people's asses, and the result was a lot of guys getting knocked off." Five of Mickey's guys were knocked off before Dragna called a halt to the war.

What we can be sure that Bompensiero thought about Jack's repeated attempts to kill Cohen was that Jack tried too many times. Bompensiero might well have reflected on the day back in 1948 when he'd driven up to LA with Biaggio Bonventre to kill Cohen.

Maybe this wasn't how Bompensiero's mind worked. Maybe it was. But surely, like all of us, as one year turned into another, Bompensiero played over his past, squinted and stared into his future. I know this: the attempt I make on your behalf and mine to enter into Bompensiero's mind is not working. I find this pretense that we are hovering within Bompensiero's mind a terrible strain. I suspect that you find it a terrible strain.

SAN DIEGO HISTORICAL SOCIETY

*Don Keller (right), c. 1954*

**"The DA at that time wasn't corrupt, he was just a naïve blue blood."**

CHAPTER THIRTY-TWO

# RUMBLINGS

So we—you and I—will try this. We will stand together outside Bompensiero's mind. We can make believe we are on a highway that begins in 1950 and ends in 1955. We can make believe that historical markers line that highway. Each of these markers is a moment in Bompensiero's life, a moment attested to by a document or a person who knew him or an event in which he became caught. We can stop at each of those moments. We can try to imagine Bompensiero—five foot eight, or, nine inches, and weighing in 1950 perhaps as much as 180 pounds, his hair beginning to thin—as an actor in these moments. That is all, now, that I know to do.

Bompensiero, like all businessmen during this era, every morning, put on a white shirt with wide French cuffs, cuff links, and a dark suit. As he walked out the door in winter, he would have placed his black homburg on his head. In summer, he would have worn his panama. He drove in his 1950 green Cadillac from Estelle Street to Columbia Street, where he began each day by drinking coffee with his mother. She spoke almost no English. She and Bompensiero spoke, always, in the version of Italian spoken then by Sicilians. After 15 minutes with his mother, or 30 minutes, after he peeled off bills for her day's shopping and urged her to buy herself something or to get something for the grandchildren, he stepped back into the Cadillac and drove to the Gold Rail. Other men in other cars also would have worn suits and hats. When Bompensiero parked in front of the Gold Rail and stepped out, there would have been no parking meters. The occasional woman who walked along Third, perhaps to shop at Graf's Exclusive Furs, would have been dressed in three-inch heels, nylon stockings, a dark or light dress or suit, depending on the season, and gloves and hat. Beneath the dress she would have worn a brassiere with strong "lift" to the cups, a slip, a girdle of some sort, perhaps one of the then-new Playtex panty girdles. Unless the woman were bold she would not have permitted her glance to meet Bompensiero's nor would Bompensiero openly have gazed at the woman. If Bompensiero knew the woman, he would have doffed his homburg, nodded, said, "Good morning."

Bompensiero, in early 1950, surely would have had worries. In January, 1948, Governor Earl Warren set up a commission to study organized crime. Warren's first charge to the committee was to scrutinize bookmaking organizations operating with the use of Western Union wires in Palm Springs. The investigations soon led to Dragna's and Cohen's Los Angeles bookmaking operations and the battle between Jack and Cohen.

I don't know what Bompensiero would have made of the announcement that on the 3rd of January, the United States Senate approved, 69 to 1, the creation of the Senate Special Committee to Investigate Crime in Interstate Commerce. I don't know what, if anything, he made of Senator Estes Kefauver, a Democrat from Tennessee, who was named the committee's chairman. In 1950 Bompensiero's Estelle Street home became one of the 3.1 million American homes that had television sets. Mary Ann said that her father bought a large mahogany console fitted with a television screen. She said her father watched television with great fascination. She said that when a newsman ventured opinions with which her father disagreed that he hissed "Dumb bastard," "Stupido," "What a pain in the fisterus" at the face staring out from the small screen. She said that "fisterus" was a word she thought her father made up. She said that "fisterus" was his word for "ass," a word he did not like to say in front of her or her mother. She said that if anyone even began to tell an off-color joke in front of her mother or herself that her father pulled what Mary Ann calls his *"funsha."* "And," said Mary Ann, "if anybody said the wrong thing in front of my mother, he would just glare at them. If anybody even started to say a dirty joke in front of my mother or me. Forget it. I mean there was cussing that went on in the house, but no one ever, ever cracked a dirty joke. They'd start a joke, and boom, they'd stop dead in their tracks. They always, then, changed the subject. Those stories never got finished."

I asked Mary Ann if her father sat at the kitchen table in the morning and read the newspaper. She said that she rarely saw her father read newspapers or magazines at home, that he did his newspaper reading at his office in the Gold Rail.

This office, by the way, which was upstairs above the bar, served as physical locus for Bompensiero's growing power. Men, many with Italian surnames and pasts that intrigued local police and the new Crime Commission, strode up the stairs to that office. What was said, we will never know. Anyone who has read transcripts of FBI tapes of *mafiosi* chitchat will know that these men gossip—who has a new Cadillac, whose daughter has married, who is having trouble with a woman, with an errant son, with the vice squad, with ulcers. Money rather endlessly is discussed—how to get it, keep it, make it grow, collect it from deadbeats. The words and phrases made familiar through films and television—"whack," "clip," "go to the mattresses"—rarely are heard.

Bompensiero in 1950 could not have guessed how far into his life the Kefauver Committee eventually would reach. The committee itself would not make much of him. But the committee's creation would cause other committees to be created. These other committees would hire investigators. The other committees' creation would provoke deputy district attorneys in the offices of San Diego County's district attorney to hire more investigators. These investigators sat on stools in dark bars and listened to conversations that drifted between English and Italian and Sicilian-inflected Italian dialect. They questioned neighbors and business associates and bartenders and waitresses. They tailed Cadillacs and Lincoln Continentals. They sorted through documents and police records stored in courthouse filing cabinets. They traded gossip with one another about who had learned what about whom. All this eavesdropping, document study, cruising up and down highways, sorting through garbage, querying, were the base metals that investigators transmuted into the gold they called "intelligence."

A gentleman, long retired from the San Diego Police Department, explained to me that as soon as the Kefauver Committee came into being that "we got word to get ready and gather intelligence and document it as best we could in preparation for that Kefauver hearing coming to Los Angeles. We were told that if we got enough down in San Diego that Kefauver might conduct a second hearing in San Diego and reveal the problems we were having here. But the local politicians talked them out of that. Their attitude was, 'We don't have any real problem here.' That was the attitude, too, of Don Keller, the DA at that time. Keller wasn't corrupt, he was just a naïve blue blood."

A second man also retired from various arms of law enforcement in San Diego County said to me about this period, "All of a sudden the Kefauver Committee is in Washington and all the states were getting into the act. Don Keller was DA then, a real political animal Don was. Everything he did had a political motivation: 'How is it going to look?' is the question he asked himself before he did anything. Don Keller was a CYA guy, no matter what you do make sure that CYA—cover your ass—is in place. But he had two deputy district attorneys, two good guys, real fighters. One of them was a lawyer fellow named Bart Sheela. Those guys were learning things. I was learning things. There was an ATF—Alcohol, Tobacco and Firearms—guy here who was learning things. There was an IRS guy here who was learning things."

*Bompensiero (left) and friends outside downtown San Diego bar*

**"We run a clean, respectable business."**

CHAPTER THIRTY-THREE

# GOOD AMERICANS

I do know that Bompensiero on the morning of February 6, 1950, certainly could not have been amused, indeed must have pulled his *funsha* when he got this news: Jack Dragna once again sent a team to tuck dynamite under Mickey Cohen's house. After this latest escapade, the Los Angeles Police Department gave orders to their Intelligence Unit to pick up on suspicion of conspiracy with intent to commit murder Jack Dragna, his brother Tom, Jack's two sons and one of Tom's sons, and Dragna's *consigliere*, Bompensiero's friend, Momo Adamo.

Bompensiero would have chomped down hard on the cigar habitually resting on his back molars, when he discovered that at Adamo's house, the police confiscated Adamo's address book and a miscellany of paper ephemera. The list of what LAPD took includes a nightclub photo of Adamo from Ciro's in Hollywood and a "snap of Mr. and Mrs. G. Adamo and small son taken in what appears to be a living room of a residence." In Adamo's address book were telephone numbers and addresses for men all across the country; the majority had criminal records. Included were Joseph Bonanno, next to whose name Adamo had written "Joe Bananas"; Joe Batters, whose given name was Joseph Accardo, a one-time bodyguard to Al Capone, considered a top man among Chicago mobsters; John Priziola in Detroit, whose daughter San Diego's Joseph Ernesto Matranga married; Santo Trafficante Sr., head of Tampa's mob; Frank Desimone, the LA attorney who in college, at USC, founded a friendship with San Diego's William Lipin; Jasper Matranga in Upland. Adamo also had the telephone number for Bompensiero's home and for the Gold Rail, for Tony and Paul Mirabile and for Tony's Rainbow Gardens, for Momo's brother Joe's house in Kensington. Also in Momo's book were Jimmy Durante, 1218 Coldwater, Apt. 263; Paramount Studios; George Raft; Fay Wilson—showgirl; and a Phil Maita, next to whose name Adamo printed, in parentheses, "dope peddler."

Additional LAPD Intelligence Unit operatives went to the home of Jack Dragna's brother Tom at 3943 Gillis Street in LA. Among items confiscated was Mrs. Tom Dragna's address book. Mrs. Dragna's lady friends' addresses and telephone numbers were listed: Mrs. Momo Adamo, Mrs. F. Bompensiero (5878 Estelle, San Diego, RAndolf 5539), and Mrs. Sam Corrao (2306 Union St., San Diego, FRanklin 2495).

Then, on Saturday morning, February 18, Bompensiero again must have hissed and sputtered and muttered about pains in the fisterus when he perused the *San Diego Union's* front page:

Dragna Gang Gets Toehold In San Diego

Names Of Mobster's Son, Nephew On Small Bar's License

"The Dragna gang, one of the two mobs the Organized Crime Commission reported is fighting for control of Southern California rackets, has at least a toehold in San Diego through a noisy 25-stool Third Avenue bar. The bar, The Gold Rail, at 1028 Third Avenue, sells liquor by virtue of a license issued to Frank Dragna, 26, and Louis Dragna, 29. Frank is the son and Louis the nephew of Jack Dragna, the 55-year-old mobster the Crime Commission labeled the Capone of Los Angeles and a member of the secret Italian Mafia.

"Third name on the license is Frank Bompensiero, a San Diegan who lives at 5878 Estelle Street. According to San Diego police records, a Frank Bompensiero served 12 months at McNeil Island for violating the National Prohibition Act and was wanted here in connection with the holdup of two theaters, a drug store and of a poker party in a private residence, all in 1933, and on suspicion of robbery and assault with intent to murder."

That morning, Bompensiero's son-in-law gave a statement to a *San Diego Evening Tribune* reporter, which was printed that afternoon beneath the headline:

Dragna Relatives Hold Liquor License For Downtown San Diego Bar

"Frank Bompensiero, through a relative, today insisted he is running a respectable business. His son-in-law Jack 'Dutch' Roberts said he was authorized to speak for Bompensiero. 'Frank's bar is well conducted. There's no shady business or misbehavior. Everything is on the up and up. Frank says the only real rap against him was for bootlegging during prohibition and they got a lot of people for that. He claims he's innocent of all the other things mentioned in the police report. Nothing has been proved against him. And there's nothing against the Dragna boys.'"

Again, the next day, February 19, the *Union* headlined:

Bompensiero: Dragna Tieup Defended By Tavern Owner

"Any blame from the activities of Dragna, described by the State Commission on Organized Crime as the 'Capone of LA,' should not be reflected on his relatives unless it is proved they are Dragna's associates in illegal activities," Bompensiero observed.

"Bompensiero admitted serving a year in a federal prison for violation of the National Prohibition Act in 1931 and 1932. But he denied being implicated in any of several crimes committed during the 1930s about which he was questioned by police.

"'Sure, I sold a little whiskey during prohibition when I was a punk kid, and I went to jail for it,' the stocky 44-year-old tavern keeper declared. 'I wasn't ever convicted of anything else and I wasn't involved in anything else. I learned that if you keep breaking the law you're going to get caught.

"'We run a clean, respectable business,' Bompensiero declared. 'We've never had any trouble. Once a fellow tried to book bets while sitting at the bar. I ran him out as soon as I found out what he was doing. It's possible that a few bets have been booked in the place, but I didn't know anything about it and I won't stand for it. I want to keep a good business.'

"Bompensiero characterized his business partners as good Americans. He said Frank Dragna lost an eye fighting in the Philippines and Louis Dragna suffered a smashed kneecap in service. Like the younger Dragna, Bompensiero served four years in the Army. They obtained the liquor license a few months after their discharges from the service, he said. Neither of the young Dragnas has been convicted of a crime, he said."

*Frank Bompensiero (right) with Kansas City friends, 1950*

**"We were like Robin Hood.**
**Then we got smart and we steal from the**
**rich and we keep it for ourselves."**

CHAPTER THIRTY-FOUR

# THREE-FINGERED FRANK

Bompensiero, of course, did not serve four years in the Army. He served a tad over one year. Whether the reporter got the years wrong or Bompensiero was engaging in patriotic hyperbole, we will never know.

In the midst of all this, Bompensiero began to drive back and forth to Tijuana to entertain guests from Kansas City and St. Louis and Sicily. Quite why these fellows in the late winter of 1950 were hanging about Tijuana, no one ever will be sure. We can be sure they were not simply getting away from wintry Kansas City blizzards. We do know that since early in the century Kansas City had been what the FBI described as a "hotbed" of vice and violence. We know that in Kansas City many of the purveyors of illegal liquor, the overlords of the bookie joints, the providers of whores, were men from villages in Sicily and Italy. We know, too, that beginning during Prohibition, these men battled one another for power. Bompensiero's friend Girolamo "Momo" Adamo left Kansas City and came west to Los Angeles to get away from these often fatal skirmishes. We know that Charles Binaggio was the most likely suspect in the 1934 killing of Kansas City boss Johnny Lazia. We know that the ruthless and inordinately crude Binaggio, soon after Lazia's death, took over the Kansas City rackets. We know, too, that at some point before World War II Binaggio added drugs to the list of items his group had for sale. These drugs came through France to Mexico and thence into the United States. Binaggio's group, by World War II's end, was making a significant amount of its money from drugs. Something of a cheapskate, Binaggio was not cutting up the money in what was perceived as a fair manner. Students of the Kansas City family hypothesize that the men in Binaggio's family who felt cheated began to plot Binaggio's death. Not wanting to be in town when that death took place, they betook themselves to Tijuana, out of reach of American lawmen and Binaggio loyalists. Another story, that told by reporter Ed Reid in his 1952 book *Mafia*, is that Binaggio, after gathering from bookmakers some $50,000 for the campaign purse of the Missouri governor Forrest Smith, was unable to convince Smith to "open up the state like a melon to the Mafia." Whatever the reason for the order to kill Binaggio, he ended up dead. On April 5, 1950, two gunmen entered Kansas City's First District Democratic Club, where Binaggio regularly held court. The gunmen left four bullets in the heads of both Binaggio and his bodyguard, Charles Gargotta. The shooter would never be identified, at least by Kansas City police.

Reid writes, about the Binaggio killing:

"It was actually committed by an assassin brought in by the Mafia from Tijuana. The man was one of a group of Mafiosi holed up at a tourist court on Revolution Street. They had come there after a previous conference at Acapulco, where members of the U.S. Mafia often meet to discuss official business. The assassin, the same one who later bumped off Willie Moretti in New Jersey, is known as 'Little Joe' to the Mafiosi because he always tries to use no more than four shells in doing any single job.

"After the assassination of Binaggio on April 5, the 14 Mafia members at the tourist court scattered to all parts of Mexico and the United States. Before they scattered they were questioned by the alert Chief of Police Francesco Kraus, who found that two of the men were recent immigrants from Palermo. One of those at the Tijuana confab was Frank (Three-Fingered Frank) Coppola, alias Frank Lamonde, brother of the infamous Trigger Mike Coppola of New York City.

"Frank, deported New Orleans gangster and friend of Frank Costello, Dandy Phil Kastel and Carlos Marcello, Mafia and narcotics king of Louisiana, is forced to live across the border but, through the good graces of his Mafia pals, gets a cut of various racket interests."

Three-Fingered Frank Coppola's brother Trigger Mike, according to Jay Robert Nash's *The Mafia Encyclopedia*, "had a reputation as one of the most vicious Mafia enforcers in New York City. In the 1930s, after Charles 'Lucky' Luciano went to prison, and Vito Genovese fled to Europe to avoid a murder charge, Coppola took over the lucrative drug trafficking empire. With the addition of the artichoke racket, a legitimate business front involving the distribution of artichokes to groceries, and the Harlem numbers racket, Coppola pushed his annual profits to $1 million."

The *Kansas City Star* wrote about Coppola in 1950 that "Coppola has been deported twice. Originally a New York gunman, he later was active under the name of Frank Lamonde in St. Louis and still later in New Orleans in association with Frank Costello. Before his last deportation in 1949, he reportedly spent several months in Kansas City, to get the help of Binaggio in staving off deportation. Binaggio, it is said, promised aid and made efforts to save Coppola, but had no success. In the summer of 1949, Binaggio, as part of a trip to California in which he visited Kansas City gamblers and racketeers who had migrated there, went to Tijuana to see Coppola."

Mary Ann recalled that as a teenager, on more than one occasion, she was with her parents when they visited in Tijuana with Francis Coppola. "Three-

Fingered Frank, we called him. I remember him as a tiny guy, very funny, a great storyteller who spoke a really broken English. I remember his talking about what life was like when he lived in Sicily and was just starting out. He said, 'Back in those days, we were like Robin Hood. We steal from the rich and give to the poor. Then we got smart and we steal from the rich and we keep it for ourselves.' He lived in Tijuana. He stayed in a hotel there. He'd been deported, I think, from Sicily, and wasn't allowed into the United States either. He also told a story about having been gone so long from Sicily that he hadn't seen his wife in many many years. She flew to Mexico. He went to the airport to meet her and coming down from the plane he sees this beautiful, beautiful woman. He said he thought to himself, 'Oh, my wife is so gorgeous.' He sees behind her this ugly skinny woman, an old woman. He runs toward the beautiful woman and she runs toward him. They embrace. He says, 'Darling, darling,' and she says, 'Daddy, Daddy.' It's his daughter and the ugly old woman behind her, of course, was his wife."

*Estes Kefauver (center) talks with Rudolph Halley during Kefauver committee hearings.*

**"I go to Caesar's all the time.**

**I was there last night."**

CHAPTER THIRTY-FIVE

# JUST A CAFÉ OPERATOR

Bompensiero would have mixed feelings in late June, 1950, when North Korean troops crossed the 38th parallel into South Korea and President Truman ordered combat forces deployed to Korea. The good news, for Bompensiero, was that downtown San Diego quickly filled up with servicemen and the lull in the bar business ended. The bad news was that Mary Ann's husband Dutch, an Army reservist, was called up and sent to Korea. Mary Ann was pregnant and frightened. Bompensiero and Thelma continued to pay rent on Dutch and Mary Ann's Kansas Street house but they moved Mary Ann home to Estelle Street, back into her old room so that Thelma could keep an eye on her.

After Labor Day, 1950, the Kefauver Committee began to show interest in the Binaggio killing, the association of the Kansas City and St. Louis mob groups in narcotics sales, and the Dragna-Cohen battles. Committee investigators began to call on Bompensiero, Dragna, Cohen, Cohen associates, and Johnny Rosselli. Figuring that local attention lighting their activities would only do harm, Rosselli, through connections in the film industry, made arrangements for Dragna and himself to testify before the committee in Chicago rather than Los Angeles.

Then, early in November the Kefauver Committee subpoenaed Bompensiero to appear in closed session. According to an old friend of Bompensiero's, Los Angeles lawyer Frank Desimone (who in 1956, after Jack Dragna's death, would become head of the Los Angeles Mafia) prepared Bompensiero to testify before the committee. Wearing a dark gray suit, white shirt, and dark tie with white polka dots, Bompensiero comported himself with dignity; he was elaborately polite, humble, and almost obsequious. Even a rapid perusal of Bompensiero's testimony shows that almost every answer he gave Rudolph Halley, Kefauver's chief investigator, was either evasion or deliberate lie. But the lies and evasions worked. When Senator Kefauver, after Bompensiero's testimony, spoke with the press, it was clear that Bompensiero succeeded in deflecting the committee's interest in him. Kefauver repeatedly referred to Bompensiero as a "San Diego café operator, who was a business partner of Frank and Louis Dragna." Kefauver told assembled newsmen that questioning of Bompensiero disclosed that he met some of the "alleged narcotics operators during a series of trips to Tijuana." The senator identified men with whom Bompensiero "had conferences" at Caesar's Restaurant: Francis Coppola, Sylvester Carrolla, Tony Lococo, Giacomo Bartolino, Carlo Sciortino, Anthony Lopiparo of St. Louis, and Sebastino Gallo of San Diego. Kefauver went on to say that while the meetings of Bompensiero with these men took place "shortly before Binaggio was killed in Kansas City, we don't know if there was any connection."

An article from the *San Diego Union* dated November 20, 1950, quoted Bompensiero as explaining his acquaintance with the so-called narcotics figures he met at Caesar's Restaurant in Tijuana the previous spring by stating: "I go to Caesar's all the time. I was there last night, after I got back from Los Angeles. I've got nothing to say. I didn't have anything to say up there in Los Angeles. I'm in the business of selling drinks, and that's all." He also stated that he had no dealings with Jack Dragna and hadn't seen him for years.

PHOTOGRAPH BY SANDY HUFFAKER, JR.

*U.S. Grant Hotel lobby*

**Bompensiero assured Gillenberg that he was getting a bargain.**

# CHAPTER THIRTY-SIX

# LIQUOR LICENSE FOR SALE–CHEAP

Early in 1951, Ernest Gillenberg, proprietor of a Jacumba café in east San Diego County, walked into the El Centro office of the State Board of Equalization and made application for a general sale liquor license that would permit him to serve beer, wine, and mixed drinks. Gillenberg, by all accounts an honest man, a man whose name never entered police blotters, was refused a license. Gillenberg drove to San Diego and walked into the San Diego offices of the State Board of Equalization and asked several clerks why he was unable to acquire a liquor license. He was told none were available.

Why Ernest Gillenberg was refused a liquor license is a complicated story that has its beginnings in America's ambivalent relationship with liquor. When Prohibition ended in the United States in 1933, the federal government and the states passed laws to regulate liquor sales. These laws varied widely from state to state. In many states, both liquor industry lobbyists and representatives and voters from Protestant temperance groups influenced these laws' contents. California's laws grew as a coral reef will, through one after another assembly session. Newly passed laws accreted, year after year, atop skeletons of old. The laws grew increasingly complex. In the mid-1930s, issuance of licenses to sell liquor became one of the perquisites of the four-man nonpartisan State Board of Equalization (SBE). This board was originally set up as a taxing and assessment agency that acted as supervisor over California's 58 county assessors. The board also fixed valuations on all corporate interests. Membership on the SBE was attained by election. Board members stood for election every four years, with each member running in his own district.

William G. Bonelli, known as "Big Bill," was first elected to the SBE in 1938. The "big" in Big Bill referred both to Bonelli's size—200 pounds on a five-feet, eight-inch frame—and his immense power. By 1950 he was chairman of the SBE, with the clout to determine tax assessments of businesses, statewide. He was also the board member representing eight Southern California counties, from Santa Barbara to the Mexican border. This position gave Big Bill final say over who got liquor licenses. In the eight counties controlled by Bonelli, there were 4500 general on-sale licenses of the kinds issued to bars and about 14,500 other classifications of permits for selling liquor. A USC graduate who sported his Phi Beta Kappa key and a lawyer,

Bonelli taught political science before entering politics. A conservative Republican, Bonelli campaigned with the support of the Los Angeles Times' Chandler family. Bonelli's SBE position made him a wealthy man. But he was not getting rich on his SBE salary. He was getting rich on graft. He boasted publicly that his $14,000-a-year state salary was insufficient to pay even his federal income taxes. In 1940 he was tried and acquitted on 23 counts of bribery, bribe solicitation, and criminal conspiracy.

In 1950 Bonelli sponsored a resolution limiting the number of liquor licenses issued in California to one per 1000 persons in each of three types of liquor license. As population grew, more licenses could be issued. The 1950 census showed Southern California counties eligible for 1300 new bar permits. This resolution's successful passage immediately increased the resale value of licenses issued years earlier. Although bribery had always been used to obtain licenses, the passage of Bonelli's resolution opened up fresh areas for graft in the acquisition of new liquor licenses and the conveyance of existing licenses from old owners to new.

Application for a liquor license for a bar like Bompensiero's Gold Rail or Ernest Gillenberg's café in Jacumba was a labyrinthine process. The annual state fee for an on-sale liquor license was $525. By the time an applicant visited a liquor license broker, the cost could rise to as much as $15,000. What, in fact, you paid the extra thousands for was influence. Who, in the end, you paid, were Big Bill Bonelli and his middlemen, the liquor license brokers and an assortment of bagmen. As one retired lawman said, "It was straight-out *mordida.* When Prohibition was repealed in 1933, up to that time all the people who were in the liquor business were bootleggers, speakeasy owners, and other people who were used to paying off for protection. They didn't see this as much different."

So that the law-abiding Ernest Gillenberg, when he initially applied at both the San Diego and El Centro SBE offices for a liquor license, was acting in the way that law-abiding citizens thought one acted. Soon after Gillenberg failed to receive his license, a Long Beach bar owner named Al Tosas called on him. Tosas explained to Gillenberg that he had been dispatched to San Diego County to rally the troops and raise funds for Big Bill Bonelli's upcoming election campaign. Tosas, according to Gillenberg's later sworn testimony, indicated that there were ways that he, Tosas, could help Gillenberg obtain his license. Gillenberg declined Tosas's offer. Several weeks after Tosas's visit another knock came at Gillenberg's door. Ira Provart, an SBE employee in the El Centro office whose immediate superior was Charles E. Berry, had come to call. Provart was bearing a message from Berry to Gillenberg. For $5000 Gillenberg could acquire a seasonal license. After a year's time passed, Gillenberg could "trade up" on this license for a general license. Gillenberg argued with Provart. Five thousand was too much. Provart suggested that Gillenberg give the matter some thought. He said that a gentleman named Frank Bompensiero soon would be coming to see him to discuss the matter further. In January, 1951, Bompensiero showed up at Gillenberg's Jacumba café. Bompensiero reiterated the message brought by Gillenberg's earlier visitors: $5000 would get him a license. Gillenberg and Bompensiero haggled over price. Bompensiero assured Gillenberg that he was getting a bargain, that licenses were selling for as much as $12,000. Gillenberg, determined to continue to try to acquire a license in the prescribed manner, again demurred.

The Kefauver Committee, through 1950 and 1951, moved from one U.S. city to another, holding hearings both closed and open. The open hearings were televised. On March 7, 1951, Kefauver began the first of eight days of open hearings in the august Foley Square Federal Courthouse in New York City. All across America, people stopped what they were doing to sit in darkened living rooms or to stand outside store windows and watch as Senate committee members and their investigators queried tough-looking guys in sharp suits. Witnesses repeatedly invoked the Fifth Amendment. On March 13, Frank Costello was queried. Costello refused to permit the cameras to show his face. His face was cropped from the necktie up. The cameras focused on Costello's hands. "Those hands," David Halberstam writes in *The Fifties*, "relentlessly reflected Costello's tension and guilt: hands drumming on the table, hands gripping a water glass, fingers tightly clenched; hands tearing paper into little shreds; hands sweating." On March 15, the late Bugsy Siegel's girlfriend, Virginia Hill, was questioned. She left the courtroom after testifying, and slugged a female newspaper reporter. She screamed at a cameraman, "I hope the atom bomb falls on you."

*Life* magazine reported: "The week of March 12, 1951, will occupy a special place in history. The U.S. and the world had never experienced anything like it....... All along the television cable [people] had suddenly gone indoors into living rooms, taverns and clubrooms, auditoriums and back offices. There in eerie half light, looking at millions of small frosty screens, people sat as if charmed. For days on end and into the nights they watched with complete absorption....... Never before had the attention of the nation been so completely riveted on a single matter. The Senate investigation into interstate crime was almost the sole subject of national conversation."

On March 19, Edward R. Murrow told the nation on CBS radio and television: The Kefauver Committee is proving that the United States has a "government within a government," and that this hidden, inner government is "organized crime."

Not as much was made, in the national news, of organized crime in California. Indeed, Dragna's little group soon became known as the "Mickey Mouse Mafia." William R. "Billy Dick" Unland was a member of the Los Angeles Police Department Intelligence Unit. "Watching Italians and Sicilians," Unland told me, "that was sort of my specialty." Unland tailed them all—the Dragnas, Frank Desimone, Simone Scozzari, Charley Battaglia, Joseph "Joe Dip" Dippolito, Sam Bruno, Nick Licata and his son Carlo, Angelo Polizzi, Bompensiero, and Momo Adamo.

"This Mafia in California," Unland said, "never was like it was in New York, Chicago, Detroit, or Cleveland." Unland suspected that, in part, the Intelligence Unit made life difficult for mobsters. "We treated them pretty rough when they came here. Tony Accardo came out and the squad met him at the train station and took him to a plane and told him to get his ass out of here and not come back. We treated 'em pretty rough.

"Also, they were so mixed up. Sometimes the same ones that worked for Mickey Cohen worked for Dragna too. Mickey had his gambling places around Hollywood, every bookmaker in LA had to pay Mickey so much for every phone he had. If they didn't pay, Mickey's Seven Dwarfs would get out and work them over, so of course they all paid up. But they were a mixed-up bunch."

Since February 6, 1950, when Jack Dragna sent his crew to bomb Cohen's house, Unland and other Intelligence Unit men had been following Dragna. "My partner and I," said Unland, "decided to make a lifetime job out of Jack. We found he was going out on his wife with a girl and we found out he had her in an apartment and bugged her and bugged him. They had some rather risqué events. Simone Scozzari and his girlfriend—Simone wasn't married—they'd get together in the apartment and play canasta. So we had 'em bugged and we knew if we could get them in some kind of sex thing, they could be deported. We caught them doing some 288-a's, it was French love, and it was against the law then." Dragna was charged and convicted of vagrancy and lewd conduct and sentenced to six months in jail. This sentence was reduced to 30 days in the county jail, which Dragna served.

Frankie, Mary Ann's first child and the Bompensieros' first grandchild, was born on Thursday, March 29, 1951, at two o'clock in the afternoon. "Dutch was in Korea with the paratroopers," Mary Ann said. "We'd kept the Kansas Street house but I had moved home, late in my pregnancy, and was living with my mom and dad. I was on one of the love seats when my labor started. I didn't say anything at first. My dad was on the couch taking a rest before he went back down to close up the Gold Rail. My dad and mother drove me to Mercy Hospital. For the first eight or ten hours, they thought it was false labor. Then, they realized it was the real thing. Mom and Dad, of course, never left the hospital. Dad paced the floor. Never took that cigar out of his mouth. Chewed it and chewed it. He'd go out and buttonhole the doctor and talk to him in that Edward G. Robinson voice of his. 'Listen, Doc, nothin' better happen to my daughter or to the baby, they better both be all right.' He'd sit by the side of the bed and hold my hand and say, 'Baby, I don't want you to have to go through this.' He was suffering right along with me. Pacing back and forth. Mom would say to him that it was going to be okay. But he just couldn't sit still. He'd get up and go pace the hall and come back and sit by me again.

"Thirty-six hours after I went into labor, Frankie was born. You'd think my father was the father. He was so proud. 'Look at that little guy,' he kept saying. 'He has the V-8–engine body, he's got those narrow hips and broad shoulders.'"

The next few days were fateful for Bompensiero. He and Thelma on Monday, April 2, took Mary Ann and Frankie to Estelle Street. "What I will always remember about that day," said Mary Ann, "is that when we got the baby home, my mother stood at the crib with my father and looked down at Frankie and she turned to my father and said, 'My new life, my new life.'"

Ernest Gillenberg, in his Jacumba café, fretted for several months. Finally, in late March, Gillenberg surrendered. He telephoned Bompensiero, who suggested that Gillenberg place $5000 in cash into an envelope. He suggested that they meet in the lobby of the U.S. Grant.

Frankie was six days old on Tuesday, April 3, when Ernest Gillenberg and his wife Gladys arrived shortly after noon in the U.S. Grant lobby. They had brought the $5000 Bompensiero said would be required, but they had not brought it in cash. They did not feel comfortable carrying that much cash. They brought a Bank of America cashier's check payable to E.M. Gillenberg and endorsed by Gillenberg. Bompensiero strolled into the lobby and took a position behind a post. The Gillenbergs approached. Hands were shaken, greetings exchanged. Gillenberg then handed over the envelope into which he'd placed the check. Gladys Gillenberg noted that Bompensiero seemed not to want anyone see him take the envelope, that Bompensiero seemed to try to hide behind the post as the envelope moved from her husband's to his hands.

The Gillenbergs' understanding, when they delivered the check to Bompensiero, was that the $5000 would allow them to obtain their long-sought-after seasonal liquor license. Gillenberg had been promised that this seasonal liquor license, eventually, could be converted into a regular or general license. Bompensiero, taking the check, assured Gillenberg that he would be able to apply for a regular liquor license at the end of a year's time without paying any additional amount. The Gillenbergs, we can presume, were happy then, when they left the downtown hotel and headed back to Jacumba. Bompensiero, check in his inside jacket pocket, walked down the street to the Gold Rail. In his office he stamped the endorsement: "The Gold Rail, 1028 Third Avenue, San Diego 1, California." Beneath the stamped endorsement, Bompensiero rapidly penned his name. Ira Provart, the SBE employee who had visited Gillenberg in Jacumba, came by later that day to pick up Gillenberg's money. Bompensiero met Provart on the sidewalk outside the Gold Rail. Bompensiero was peeved. "That stupid sob," he said, "handed me a check instead of cash." We do not know and won't ever know precisely what Bompensiero's cut of the $5000 was. What we do know from later sworn testimony by Provart is that when Provart set up the initial meeting between Bompensiero and Gillenberg, Bompensiero asked how much of Gillenberg's money he would receive for dealing with the Jacumban. Provart testified that his boss, Charles E. Berry, told Provart not to expect too much as his share of the $5000 because the money would have to be cut up 11 or 12 ways. Provart would say that for his work as a bagman, SBE liquor administrator Berry paid him $400. "This is your share of the Gillenberg case," Berry said as he passed over the money.

What we also know is that shortly after Gillenberg gave Bompensiero the aforementioned check, Gillenberg received a seasonal liquor license. We also know that Bompensiero, again, according to Provart's testimony, was not happy about his dealings with Gillenberg and said, "I hope that so-and-so sells his place; he talks too much."

Mary Ann, a month or so after Frankie was born, moved back into the home she shared with Dutch on Kansas Street. Dutch was still in Korea. Mary Ann recalled that she and her mother had "decorated the back bedroom for the baby. It was like a little picture—white shag carpet, cradle, rocker. My mother and father would come over and spend the night there in the guest room, so I wouldn't be afraid. My dad would stretch out on my couch and have me put Frankie on top of him and Frankie would fall asleep on my dad's big barrel chest and my dad would be absolutely cooing, 'Frankie boy, my baby, my little boy, my Frankie baby.' Mama and I would just stand there and admire the two of them. But forget changing diapers. My dad wouldn't do that. He said he was too scared. And he would never ever be alone with Frankie. He said he was afraid he'd do something wrong. So if my mom and I were going to the store, my dad wanted to be there with Frankie, but he also wanted a baby-sitter. But he didn't want a sitter to be alone with Frankie. Never. 'Get a baby-sitter,' he would say, 'and I will be here with him.' When Frankie was a few months old he got a terrible cold. My father would come home from the Gold Rail and rock him. He would say to Frankie, 'Let Papa take that cold away from you. Give

Papa your cold so I can have it for you.' My mom's store was just around the corner from the Kansas Street house and she would run over at lunchtime to see the baby and then come, after the store closed, and fix dinner for all of us. Those months my mom and dad were so happy. They adored that baby.

"Frankie was five months old when Dutch got out of the Army. August or September, it was, in 1951. He right away went back to work again for my dad collecting for the jukeboxes for Maestro Music. He was only home about six weeks and he called me and he was spitting up blood. We took him to the doctor and he had tuberculosis. He had to go to the VA Hospital in San Fernando Valley where they had the TB hospital. The baby and I and Mom and Dad and half the family, we had to be tested, all of us, patch tested. None of us had any signs of it. Dutch was prescribed what they prescribed for TB back in those days: bed rest. I would drive up and see him every weekend and Mom and Dad would take care of Frankie."

Mary Ann recalled about the first few months after Frankie's birth that Leo Moceri and his wife stayed for a time in the Kansas Street house. Mary Ann all her life had known Leo "Leo the Lip" Moceri as Uncle Jimmy and his wife as Aunt Marie. Mary Ann said that only years later would she learn that Moceri was a Mafia member. She said that at the time, her innocence about her father and her father's friends was so complete that when Uncle Jimmy and Aunt Marie went out and Uncle Jimmy, even on cloudy days, counseled Marie to keep on her sunglasses and put up the top of the convertible they were driving, Mary Ann thought Uncle Jimmy was being protective of Marie's complexion.

In August, 1951, two young ex-FBI agents walked into the offices of Sheriff Bert Strand. They were investigators for the state attorney general's office. The attorney general, together with the almost four-year-old California Crime Commission, was interested in the use of bribes to acquire liquor licenses. A now elderly retired San Diego policeman told me, "That's when it started. That was the genesis of the police intelligence work in San Diego. We already had the techniques, the technology in those days. We just had never had the support of the powers that be."

The state crime commission, in the fall of 1951, began to nose around to learn what it could about how liquor licenses were being bought and sold. In sworn testimony given in 1958, Captain James E. Hamilton was questioned:

Q. During your work for the Crime Commission did you have occasion to investigate a series of bar licenses owned by Mr. Tony Mirabile, or in which he had an interest?

A. One of our projects was to investigate the distribution of liquor licenses in the State of California. During that investigation down here in San

Diego in 1951 and 1952 we had access to the State Board of Equalization records here in San Diego. Those records were made available to the various organizations, and in there it gave the names and addresses of all individuals who had liquor licenses.

Q. Didn't you have occasion to inquire into 30-odd licenses, whatever the number was, to go to the State Board of Equalization at that time and look over their files on those?

A. Yes. I had complete access to their records.

Q. What happened to those records right after you looked at them?

A. The information was taken from their records and was dictated on the Soundscriber discs. The information was transcribed. I was informed shortly thereafter that those records were destroyed within about 48 hours. So I have been informed that those records do not exist after the information had been taken out of them, such as who owned these licenses, and how they were issued; investigators; reports, and that sort of thing.

Q. These records were destroyed, according to your information, on orders from who?

A. The information I had is that the order came down from Mr. William G. Bonelli, from Los Angeles, to destroy those records.

Q. Didn't you actually look at them on, like a Friday, and they were destroyed the following Monday?

A. Yes. I looked at them Friday and Saturday, and I was told that they were destroyed on Monday.

The State Board of Equalization was not the only source of corruption. My retired San Diego policeman friend said that during the early 1950s intelligence gathered about San Diego "vice"—bookmaking, whores, illegal liquor sales, irregularities in bar and alcohol management—was cautiously traded among various law-enforcement organizations. He said that it was "not uncommon knowledge" that during the 1940s and 1950s certain members of the SDPD vice squad were on the take. He said that among other investigative agencies and these agencies' intelligence arms there was an agreement that certain members of the SDPD vice squad regularly tipped off bar owners and bookmakers about upcoming raids. The gentleman who was telling me this went on to say that he himself worked vice for several years after World War II and then asked for transfer into another department. "I removed myself from vice because what I saw I didn't want to be a part of. I knew I was a puppet, allowing bookmaking to go on."

Another person in law enforcement said to me, about this period, "I got some money out of District Attorney Don Keller's secret fund and I planted a private detective in a hotel overlooking C Street because there was bookmaking going on at the Turf Club and we got movies of detectives walking right by these bookies making book in the loading zone in front of the Turf Club while they go in to get their morning toddies. But nothing ever came of it because Keller didn't want to take on the police department."

"I know who that guy is.

He won't even take a cigar."

CHAPTER THIRTY-SEVEN

# LINGERIE BRIBES

Mary Ann, one day, talking about her mother's dress shop—Santa Ann's Moderate Shop on 30th in North Park—began telling a story that had to do with the police. She said, "My mother was way ahead of her time. She wanted to be kept busy, so she opened the dress shop. She was going to specialize in large women. She was going to do this even though she was tiny; she wore her dresses in a size seven or eight when sizes were real sizes and everything was zip-up and fitted. She was open for a while, but the ladies would drop by and say, 'Don't you have anything in a smaller size?' My mother said, 'Okay, I'm going to look for a line and I'm going to bring it in.' Dresses were a headache, so she went into separates. She brought in skirts, sweaters, blouses, and catered to the working girl. Mayfair Market was across the street on 30th Street. All those girls from Mayfair, every time they got their paycheck, they'd come in. My mother said, 'Forget about the people that have a lot of money, they don't shop as often as the working girl.' She was a success in that store.

"So my mother's got her shop and Christmas comes. My father said to her, 'Honey, give me a stack of your cards.' And she said, 'Okay.' Everything was aboveboard with my mother and her shop. My father says to her, 'Anybody comes in with my name on the back of your card, give them whatever they pick out, gift wrap it, and don't charge 'em, just keep the receipt,' he says, 'and I'll pay you.' They were the cops my father was handing out these cards to. I was working in the shop then, so this is not from my mother's mouth only or my father's. I saw this myself.

"For Christmas, my mother had lingerie, she had a little bit of costume jewelry. These men, all men, came in and they'd look around and pick out things and they'd present the card and they'd say some version of 'Frank sent me.' My mother would say, 'Fine, thank you,' and gift wrap whatever they'd chosen and hand it to them and out they'd go. I don't know how many of these guys came in and did this. But there was one cop I waited on, only one, who was the exception to the rule. He asked for a box of hosiery. Then he said, 'Frank sent me in,' and gave me the card. I said, 'Would you like it gift wrapped?' He said, 'How much do I owe you?' I said, 'Nothing.' He says, 'I came in because I know Frank and I want to pay you.' I said, 'I'm not supposed to take your money.' And he said, 'Well, I don't want them then.' When I told my dad about what happened, he said, 'I know who that guy is. He won't even take a cigar.'"

*From left, Jewel Fratianno, Jimmy the Weasal Frantianno, Bompensiero (center), Thelma – at Tops, early 1950s*

**And he said, 'Why are you following my guy?' I said, 'Because I don't like him.'**

CHAPTER THIRTY-EIGHT

# HE HAD SUCH CONTROL OVER HIMSELF

In December, 1951, Bompensiero and Jimmy Fratianno, Nick Simponis, Joe Peccaro, and Nick and Carlo Licata joined forces in a business—Gold Enterprises—designed to sell and distribute fruit juice, colas, and snacks in bars and taverns. Simponis and Peccaro were local fellows, not in any way connected to Mafia circles. Fratianno and the Licatas were another matter. Fratianno, by late 1951, had been the shooter (or strangler) on at least four Mafia killings. Nick Licata, originally from Detroit, had been brought into the Los Angeles family by Dragna. Carlo Licata, Nick's son, had been one of the three shooters who gunned down Mickey Cohen's lawyer.

FBI files on Bompensiero obtained through the Freedom of Information Act note the following about Gold Enterprises:

> "Investigation conducted in 1953 in the case entitled: Gold Enterprises, San Diego, California; Frank Bompensiero; Criminal Rackets Survey, reveals that on December 31, 1951, Gold Enterprises filed Articles of Incorporation with the Secretary of State, State of California, and the County Clerk, San Diego, California. Directors were named as Frank Bompensiero, 5878 Estelle Street; Nick Gust Simponis, 4796 Panorama Drive; James Albert Fratianno, 2930 Dove Street; and Carlo Licata, all of San Diego, California.
>
> "Information was developed that this concern was set up to 'take over' the sale of citrus juices to all bars in the San Diego area, by intimidation if necessary.
>
> "The concern began operations in 1952 and (**************) found that he had lost a number of customers to this concern. (**************) reported that he had lost his accounts with My Place, Java, Barbet, Patrick's, Hi-Seas, Frolics, China Doll, the Gold Rail, and other places. All places of business which discontinued business with (**************) and subscribed to service of Gold Enterprises stated they had not been intimidated.
>
> "The investigation reflected that most of the bars which subscribed to services of Gold Enterprises were owned by Italians. After

> about one month of operation, the Gold Enterprises ceased operations because of failure to make expenses."

Mr. Willis, sipping at a tall glass of iced tea, talked one afternoon about Bompensiero. "He was very cool, had a sardonic attitude, was never contemptuous of cops, but once in a while he could be kind of sarcastic."

I asked Mr. Willis what he knew about Gold Enterprises. "Well," he sighed, "they were starting in those days, Bompensiero and his friends, to feel like big shots, like they were going to be able to take control of the city. Gold Enterprises started in 1951, the intent was to take over the condiments and all the fruit juices, not the liquor, all the related things that go into a bar, and there were a number of other companies already doing this and they cannot have been all that pleased. But you can see how for these bar owners that such a distribution plan, controlled by them, would become attractive. These dagos knew what was good to get into. So anyway, Fratianno and Licata were both living in Nate Rosenberg's house at 2930 Dove Street. This is when Rosenberg had the Navy Club and Carlo Licata was working there as some sort of manager. They opened up Gold Enterprises in a building on India Street on the east side of the street between Cedar and Date. We were getting rumbles about this. So we began tailing the delivery truck driver, Joe Peccaro—Joe Pec, old stupid Joe the Dummy.

"Joe Pec told Frank about how we were following him. Frank called the PD and started denigrating this guy who had been following his guys. The guy who answered told him to call the guy himself. Frank was at the Gold Rail. I happened to come into the PD office a short time after the call came in. The guy on duty asked me, 'Do you know this Bompensiero?' I said, yes, I did. So I called him up on the phone. Got the bartender. Told the bartender I wanted to talk to Bompensiero. 'You want to talk to me, Bompensiero? Any place, any time.' Course I was younger in those days. He said, 'Yeah, I will meet you out in front.' So I drove over there on Third Street and got out of the car and Bompensiero was standing out front of the Gold Rail and you could tell he was ready to blow. I said, 'Do you want to see me?' And he said, 'Yes. Why are you following my guy?' I said, 'Because I don't like him.' He said, 'Well, don't do that.' I said, 'Well, are you going to try and stop me?' He said, 'Well, I will get my lawyer.' I said, 'You get your goddamned lawyer. Is there anything else?' He said, 'No.' I was ready to go to fist city right there. I got in my car. That was the only time I ever saw Frank Bompensiero even remotely out of control. Frank was always controlled. That was the only time I can remember Frank being less than lucid and not having control. The guy was very perceptive. Frank was no dummy. You couldn't help but like the guy because he was man, this guy was all man. Oh boy, he was a little short guy but he must have weighed 220 pounds on a five-feet, eight-inch frame. I mean built right straight up from the ground, tougher than hell. A great dresser. He was always well dressed. A lot of difference between him and Tony. I liked the guy. I knew he was a hood, a crook. We always knew about the 211 at the Fox Theatre, that he did it, but I liked the guy. Who wouldn't?

"Bompensiero was the only local man who had the connections and the moxie to do things. This was a center of power, you just knew it. I can remember one occasion, 1952, when Eisenhower came to town. I'd never seen General Eisenhower. All I knew about Eisenhower was I'd seen him in the Movietone. I am standing out on Front Street where they had that park, 1000 block, and they've got this political parade, because Eisenhower came to town, and he was sitting up in this open car, westbound on Broadway, and, boy, people are down there. I got about halfway down, alongside the old courthouse, and here comes Eisenhower. He didn't say word one to me and he didn't look at me and I'm a half a block away but there's like a physical impact of this man on me. These people, leaders, who have so much personality that it just thrusts itself at you. I said, 'My God, Eisenhower.' Smilin' Ike, smiling like he always was. This impact he made, just looking, no wonder he was the leader he was in World War II. And Frank Bompensiero, he had it too. You look at the guy half a block away and he'd be walking along the street, not even talking to anyone, and you just knew it, here's power. He had such good control over himself and I don't know of anybody else that ever saw him any different. Except that one occasion when he called me on following old Joe Pec and he was a little hostile and about to lose it but good sense told him he'd go to jail and the hard way. He knew it, I was not about to take a physical beating from a dago hood. I would have killed him. But you like the personality anyway even though you knew what he was. I had no personal animosity toward him at all. I would have killed him if I had a chance, but hell. I liked Frank Bompensiero, you couldn't help from it."

He woke up and felt an excruciating pain,

he didn't know what it was.

CHAPTER THIRTY-NINE

# THE CUCUMBER KID

The California Crime Commission, set up by Governor Earl Warren in 1948, was still going strong in 1952. On May 11, they issued their third formal report. Bompensiero found himself named several times. Allusions were made to the 1938 Phil Galuzo murder and Bompensiero's arrest and questioning, in 1941, for that killing. "Bompensiero," the report noted, "is now located in San Diego, operating a café and bar, and poses as a legitimate business man. He is a partner of Tony Mirabile and an associate of Jack Dragna....... Jack Dragna and his associates were all connected with the notorious L'Unione Siciliano (Mafia)." The Crime Commission report also claimed that Gold Enterprises' true objective was "to gain control over the cooks and waitresses union, the bartenders union and the tavern owners association, which would have given them virtual control of that industry for shakedown purposes." When reporters from San Diego's *Union* and *Evening Tribune* called the Gold Rail to query Bompensiero about these allegations, Bompensiero insisted that the Crime Commission reports about him and about Gold Enterprises had no basis in fact.

Mr. Willis reminded me, about Bompensiero's activities in 1952, that "Bompensiero still was running this outfit called Maestro Music. Jukeboxes. It was kind of a unique deal for those days, his jukeboxes were. You punched a button and a voice would ask you what you wanted to hear. So this fellow, Hal Sherry was his name, a heavyset fellow who wore glasses, came to town along in May of 1952 from the union, the International Brotherhood of Electrical Workers, the IBEW. Hal Sherry began to make a nuisance of himself, trying to organize all the people who installed these jukeboxes and serviced them and other vending-machine operators that operated God knows what else. He was told, 'Now be a nice gentleman and leave this area alone. We don't need your help. As a matter of fact, we don't want your help.' And he was told this by Frank Bompensiero. As a matter of fact, Frank later said, 'I told the guy to stop this stuff. We don't want it.' But Mr. Sherry didn't pay attention to Bompensiero's warning. As a result Mr. Sherry got the name 'Cucumber Kid.'

"Sherry stayed in town for three or four days, trying to set up a little local, after Bompensiero spoke to him. Apparently, Bompensiero lost patience with Sherry's continued presence. Sherry was staying at the U.S. Grant. What would turn out to be his last evening in town he came back from his dinner about eight o'clock and lo and behold here are two Siciliano gentlemen in his room, waiting to talk to him. And the last thing Hal Sherry knows, he got punched. The last thing he remembered was, 'I went down.' And he was told to leave town. He woke up and felt an excruciating pain, he didn't know what it was, but he discovered he was not wearing any trousers or undershorts. The pain he felt was unbearable. He put on his clothes, and he grabbed his valise and his briefcase, he ran down, threw his money down at the desk for his room, took off in his car, and he drove all the way to the Huntington Memorial Hospital in Pasadena and from there at that point his doctor extracted from his anus, a cucumber. That's how he got the name, the Cucumber Kid.

"It's the lowest form of degradation. Anal penetration. It's the ultimate in degradation, degrade them right down to it.

"The event came to our attention several months later. Hal Sherry told our offices that after he left town he'd been sent a wire, from San Diego. So I went to the telegraph office on the south side of the plaza on the corner of Fourth and I went in and talked to the manager and said I had heard about a telegram and the manager said, 'Here's a copy of the telegram sent to Hal Sherry in LA.' I remember it as saying something about 'my condolences, I hope you had a good time in San Diego, Frank.' Hal Sherry never came back here in his organizing efforts as far as I know."

Mr. Willis laughed. "Oh, yes, we used to laugh about this. The Cucumber Kid. He did come back here once, but with a bodyguard."

*Sam and Frank Bompensiero*

**The Turkey Inn and the Valley Inn owners in Ramona needed a liquor license.**

CHAPTER FORTY

# TAKING CARE OF SAMMY

Bompensiero's brother Salvatore, or Sam or "Sammy," as friends and family called him, was eight years younger than Bompensiero. Sam, by 1952, had been a resident in San Diego for a quarter century. He had earned his living as a fisherman. Fishing, year after year, wears out the body. By the early 1950s Sammy was having back trouble and problems with hernias. Bompensiero suggested that Sammy quit fishing. "I'll set you up in the bar business," he told his brother. "Sammy," a retired San Diego city policeman told me, "was a straight. He only ran that bar for his brother. Bompensiero pulled Sammy in to run the joint." Sammy agreed to his older brother's proposal and on June 10, 1952, Bompensiero, Sam, and Leo G. Patella, a fisherman who was one of Thelma's nephews, formed a partnership to open the Spot Cocktail Lounge. The bar stood at 1046 Third Avenue, a few doors from Bompensiero's Gold Rail. The three men signed a ten-year lease on the property and a contract for $10,000 in remodeling the facilities, which previously had been a short-order greasy spoon. They acquired a liquor license that was issued in the names of Patella and Sammy.

The method by which the Bompensiero brothers acquired the liquor license for the Spot is tortuously complicated. I have accumulated my understanding of this method through newspaper clips, Crime Commission reports, and talks with Mary Ann, Mr. Willis, and Bart Sheela, a deputy district attorney in the San Diego County district attorney's office from 1951 to 1955.

During the 1950s Arthur Warnock and John Griffin owned the Turkey Inn and the Valley Inn in Ramona. The two men needed a liquor license for the Valley Inn. How Bompensiero and Patella came to meet and talk with Warnock and Griffin, we do not know. But meet and talk with them they did. Bompensiero and Patella agreed to procure a liquor license for the Valley Inn and to operate the inn as an apparently secret partnership among the four men. Griffin and Warnock's contribution to this deal was that they would supply the building and equipment. But nothing turned out as Griffin and Warnock hoped. Several days after July 25, 1952, when the license was issued to Patella, Patella returned the Valley Inn's keys to the two men. He told them he had no more use for the keys. Patella and Bompensiero, on August 28, 1952, transferred the liquor license originally issued to the Valley

Inn to the Spot. Griffin tried to talk with Patella about the transfer of the license. According to later sworn testimony by Griffin, Patella told him that he and Bompensiero never had any intention of using the liquor license at the Valley Inn. Furthermore, according to Griffin's testimony, when he asked Bompensiero and Patella to pay their half of the rent on the Valley Inn, Patella and Bompensiero refused.

Bompensiero, also in later sworn testimony, explained events in this way. He and Sam were busy remodeling the premises that would become the Spot at about the same time that Leo Patella applied for a liquor license for the Valley Inn. Bompensiero insisted that for several months he had been trying to acquire a liquor license from license broker Al Bennett. Bompensiero claimed that he made a down payment to Bennett of $500. Bennett, however, according to Bompensiero, wanted $13,500 to $14,500 to get a license for Bompensiero whereas Bompensiero was willing to pay between "$12,500 to $13,500." At the same time that he and Bennett were dickering over the $1000 difference, Sammy Bompensiero and Leo Patella decided to go in together on the Spot and transfer Patella's Valley Inn license to the Spot. "There wasn't enough for three of us so I stepped out," said Bompensiero.

"Joe Dippolito reached out
with one huge hand and whirled Russian
Louie around while Bompensiero
dropped the garrote over his head."

CHAPTER FORTY-ONE

# THE ROPE TRICK

While all the above was going on, Bompensiero helped kill Frank Borgia.

Mr. Willis, talking about the Borgia killing, said that while he does believe that Borgia was murdered he wasn't sure that he believed the story that Fratianno told of the killing. "Oh," he said, "I think Fratianno was tied in with it. Borgia was Mirabile's best friend but that Mirabile brought him to them, I can't buy this. I keep thinking of Fratianno, 'the Weasel' they call him, and for good reason. Yeah, he's a sneaky devil. I think the way he tells the story is bull, but maybe Tony Mirabile did bring Borgia to them, maybe he did, I don't know. I do know that they never did find the body. They have all these wineries and vineyards out there in San Bernardino, grape land. I suspect they dumped him there."

Ernest Gillenberg, the gentleman who, with Mrs. Gillenberg, stood in the lobby of the U.S. Grant Hotel and handed Bompensiero a Bank of America cashier's check for $5000, at this point reenters Bompensiero's story. Shortly after Gillenberg gave Bompensiero the $5000 check, Gillenberg received his seasonal liquor license. In late summer, 1952, Gillenberg applied for the general liquor license promised him by Ira Provart and Bompensiero. He was turned down. On October 24, 1952, former city councilman turned liquor license broker Al W. Bennett telephoned Gillenberg and said that he understood Gillenberg was now applying for the general liquor license. Gillenberg allowed that yes, he was. The next day Bennett showed up at Gillenberg's Jacumba café. He explained to Gillenberg that yet another payment—$2500—would have to be made if Gillenberg wanted to move up from a seasonal to a general sales license. Gillenberg argued with Bennett and then, finally, Gillenberg relented. He got out his check register and started to write a check. Bennett stopped him. He wanted cash. Gillenberg and Bennett then drove to the Bank of America in El Centro. Gillenberg took $2500 from his account and handed the cash over to Bennett. In less than a week's time Gillenberg received a telephone call from the El Centro SBE office telling him that he could come in to fill out his general liquor license application. Gillenberg prepared his application and received the license. He had paid out $7500 for what, according to state law, should have cost him, annually, $525.

Later sworn testimony before a San Diego County grand jury and in criminal trials held in San Diego courtrooms show that Gillenberg was by no means the only bar owner caught in the liquor license squeeze. San Diego County SBE administrator Charles E. Berry in 1952 alone carried some $14,000 in bribes to Big Bill Bonelli. According to Berry's testimony Bonelli told him early in 1950, that from that time on, people desirous of liquor licenses would have to pay $7000 in bribes in addition to the $525 state fee. Bennett in 1952 had handed Berry an envelope containing $7000 from Lyman Lucore, owner of Lyman's at 442 West Broadway, to get a liquor license. Berry took this envelope to Bonelli in LA. Later in the same year, Berry testified, Bennett gave him another envelope with $7000 that was paid by Max Goldfarb to get a liquor license in La Jolla. Again, the envelope was delivered to Bonelli.

Ed Reid's 1952 *The Mafia*, in a chapter entitled "Phi Beta Mafia," listed 83 names that Reid alleged were Mafia members; number 26 was Frank Bompensiero. Bompensiero continued in 1953 to expand his empire. On September 25, 1952, Bompensiero had formally removed himself from partnership in the Spot and purchased the Pirate's Cave, at 402 West Broadway. He now, not on paper but in fact, owned three bars. Where he acquired the money, we can only surmise. We know that Jimmy Fratianno told Ovid Demaris that in April, 1953, Bompensiero helped carry out Jack Dragna's contract on a gambler known in Los Angeles and Vegas as Russian Louie Strauss. Russian Louie's killing, according to Demaris's *The Last Mafioso*, took place in a house in Upland. "Joe Dippolito reached out with one huge hand and whirled Russian Louie around while Bompensiero dropped the garrote over his head, tossing one end of the rope to Jimmy. If Louie had not been struggling so desperately to breathe, he would have been surprised at the number of men interested in his execution. Besides Philly Alderieso, seated around the room were Angelo Polizzi, Charley Battaglia, Louie Dragna."

On September 29, 1952, an article in Neil Morgan's column "Crosstown" appeared in the San Diego *Evening Tribune*. Morgan's column stated that not one drink was sold at the Valley Inn in Ramona and that a liquor license valued at $14,000 was transferred to the Bompensieros' bar, the Spot, from the Valley Inn. Morgan implied that the liquor license for the Ramona area was obtained through subterfuge for the purpose of transferring it to the Third Avenue location.

"Thelma, I don't want to die.

I don't want to die."

# CHAPTER FORTY-TWO

# SHE DESERVED BETTER THAN JACK

Jack Dragna's 1951 conviction on lewd conduct—"French love"—led to his arrest in 1953 by federal immigration authorities on a charge of having illegally entered the United States. Dragna spent much of 1953 fighting the deportation order. Dragna's wife Frances in the summer of 1953 was dying of cancer. Mary Ann said that her mother regularly drove up to Los Angeles to sit with Frances. "My mother would come home from those visits and cry. She felt so sorry for Frances, in all that pain, and for the life Frances had with Jack. He had always gone out on her, Jack had. And Frances was dying and Jack wasn't even there. He was in jail. My mother would sit by the bed and hold Frances's hand and Frances would cry, 'Thelma, I don't want to die. I don't want to die.'"

Mary Ann's godmother and Thelma's best friend, Josephine, lived in LA and knew the Dragnas. "Frances," Josephine said, "was a nice woman. She deserved better than Jack. Every time Jack went to New York or someplace, he would always bring her a fur or jewelry, to appease her. She didn't have a good life with him. He was a chaser."

July 23, 1953, while Dragna was in the Terminal Island detention center awaiting deportation, Frances Dragna died. Mary Ann recalled that her parents went up to Los Angeles to the funeral. She also recalled that after Frances's death, her mother began to talk about her own death. "My mother and I were sitting on the patio. You looked out and you just saw canyon. We were having coffee. Mama said, 'When I die, I don't want to be buried in some negligee-like thing.' My mother, not long before that, had been to a wedding." Mary Ann struggled to remember the names of the people who'd married, and couldn't. She laughed. "I think my father hid out there one time with the groom's parents, you'd think I'd remember their name. They had grapes. They had a big ranch. Anyway, my mother wore an off-white, creamy white ballerina-length dress to the wedding party. Ballerina-length was fashionable then. It was a gorgeous dress. It was strapless, all bugle beads across the bodice. They wore tiaras then, too, and Mama wore a tiara. She wore pearl drop earrings. She looked better than the bride. She said, that day when we were sitting out on the patio, 'That's the dress I want to be buried in. I don't want that stiff stuff all the way up to my neck. I want to look like a princess lying on the couch. I want my tiara in my hair. I want my casket silver. I want'—she loved lavender and purple—'the casket softly draped in lavender.'"

*William Bonelli, c. 1956*

**Bonelli announced he had changed his registration from Republican to Democrat.**

CHAPTER FORTY-THREE

# THE L.A. FAMILY

Big Bill Bonelli was a longtime friend of the Los Angeles Chandler family, owners of the *Los Angeles Times* and the *Los Angeles Mirror*. In 1952 relations between Bonelli and the Chandlers soured when Bonelli set a higher tax rate on Chandler real estate than the Chandlers believed fair. The Chandlers retaliated. On October 12, 1953, *Los Angeles Mirror* investigative reporter Art White went after Bonelli.

Bonelli's Saloon Empire

"Has organized crime—particularly the sinister Mafia—moved into Big Bill Bonelli's far-flung Saloon Empire?

"Has it run away from the controls which Bonelli as elected member of the State Board of Equalization, Southern California area, is supposed to lay upon the liquor business?

"Is trouble—big trouble—brewing?

"Let's drop down to San Diego for some hints, clues and possible answers to these questions of huge civic importance.

"For here functions what one high State law-enforcement officer terms 'the best illustration of today of an "organization" of known and suspected criminals and their associates.'

"Anthony (Tony) Mirabile, husky, big-jawed, white-haired, is the 'poppa' of the 'organization.' Tony's alias is Rizzo. He has admitted, according to San Diego police, that he once served with the Italian 'muscle' element which took over Detroit's evil Purple Gang years ago.

"His name, momentarily, leads all the rest on a roster that includes Bompensiero, Dragna, Licata, Romano, Adamo, Matranga, Vitale, Pipitone, Fratianno, Secunda, Licavoli, Dia, Rizzo, Cusenza, Cavesina. All interwoven into this remarkable Saloon Empire pattern. All doing business within Big Bill Bonelli's domain.

"(note: Here, however, the Kefauver Crime Committee's windup remarks anent the Mafia should be recalled: 'It would be most unfortunate if any inferences were erroneously drawn in any way derogatory to the vast majority of fine law abiding citizens of Sicilian and Italian extraction.')

"Poppa Tony holds three Bonelli-okayed saloon licenses for his

Rainbow Gardens, Barbet and Senator, all in the dank heart of San Diego's noisome 'Jungle,' which is comparable to Los Angeles' own equally villainous Skid Row.

"Additionally, Poppa Tony is reliably known to pull the strings on at least 25 more joints besides his trio of 'on the record' dives.

"You perceive his widespread operations as you check into Mirabile's astonishing financial setup that dates back to the mid-1930s, when he made arrangements for his friends to borrow cash without red tape from the Security Trust and Savings Bank, 904 Fifth Avenue, San Diego. Poppa Tony obligingly fixed up a $50,000 fund for the boys.

"Photostats of Mirabile's account—in The *Mirror's* possession—show hundreds of loans ranging from 20 to $10,000."

Who got the loans?

"Police files observe crisply that this dossier 'contains the names of practically every known hoodlum in the San Diego–Los Angeles area.' But it also reveals loans to such persons as Lt. Nevadomsky of the San Diego Police Department (1942), Rudy Schmoke, California Highway Patrol inspector (1948), A.W. Bennett, a leading San Diego liquor license broker and (when he got his loan in 1936) a City Councilman.

"Tony Mirabile owes his start as 'poppa' of the syndicate to the notorious Nick Licata, of Dragna and Eastern Gangland ill fame, who now lives in ostensible quiet at 3523 Overland Avenue, Los Angeles.

"Because in the Great Repeal Year, 1933, Nick loaned Poppa Tony $7,000 to go into the saloon business.

"Now Mirabile's grasp is slipping.

"Up-and-coming power in the 'organization' is Frank (Bompy) Bompensiero, who once served 18 months for a prohibition rap and who has an arrest record ranging downward from murder.

"Today he rejoices in a Bonelli-granted license for the Gold Rail saloon, another San Diego 'jungle' watering hole. His partners are Frank and Louis Dragna, son and nephew of Los Angeles' Mafia chieftain, Jack Dragna.

"Bompy has other interests. He owns a piece of The Spot, just down the street from his Gold Rail, which has a brand-new Bonelli-okayed saloon license in the name of Leo Patella. With Gaspare Matranga, also a licensee, and Leo Dia, Poppa Tony's nephew-in-law, he runs Maestro Music. This pipes juke-box ditties into most of the 'organization's' dives.

"Remember Hal Sherry's painful adventure in San Diego?

"Last year Bompy, Charles Cavesina, and others of the syndicate held a powwow at the Gay Paree bar. (Which just happens to be saloon-licensed to one Jasper Curia, who has a long arrest record, and Mary J. Adamo.)

"They told Poppa Tony he was getting a little old for his heavy 'organization' responsibilities.

"Reservations were made for a vacation trip for Poppa—to Italy—but he took sick. So he's still in San Diego and, on the surface, still the Poppa.

"Here are some of the other offshoots of this amazing syndicate, involving many families with (according to police files) Mafia connections:

"The Matrangas, Gaspare, Frank, Joe, Leo, and their sister, Catherine Vitale. She lists herself as a 'widow.' But her husband, Salvatore, is very much alive, though very much incarcerated at McNeil Island Federal Penitentiary. A former runner for Dope King Lucky Luciano, Salvatore entered the United States illegally and got caught.

"Gaspare, in addition to his Maestro Music deal with Bompy, has a saloon license with Brother Joe at Kelly's Club. This 'jungle' joint used to be owned by Joe Miceli, now somewhat out of the picture owing to detention in San Quentin on a second-degree murder rap.

"Frank holds the Java Café saloon permit and, with Brother Joe, the Buccaneer.

"The Adamo girls, Maria and Mary J. The former is the wife of Girolamo (Momo) Adamo, associate of Jack Dragna and sundry other known hoodlums. Momo is wanted by federal immigration agents for questioning on his reentry into the United States, though he's been seen around San Diego lately.

"With Peter Montana, Maria holds Bonelli-granted licenses for the Panama Café and the Arizona, both 'jungle' saloons. Montana is listed by police as a 'suspected member of the Mafia.'

"Mary J., of course, co-owns the Gay Paree.

"Then there's Vic Pipitone, another ex-convict with a long arrest record (including murderous assault), who bought the Frolics Café for his wife and son. Mrs. Pipitone held the saloon license, then peddled the place to a trio including Leonard J. Brophy, of the race wire Brophys.

"And now she and son Charles operate the B&L bar, China Doll and Singapore Room, all with Bonelli-blessed licenses, with Vic hovering solicitously in the background.

"The list is almost endless.

"Poppa Tony's niece, Josephine Mirabile, has the Bonelli-okayed saloon permit for Martels. Her married name is Mrs. Leo Dia. And Leo is Bompy's other Maestro Music partner.

"Poppa Tony's brother, Paul, has the Bonelli-approved license for the Saratoga Grill.

"As another fascinating offshoot of the 'organization' you find Gold Enterprises, Inc., 'distributors of daisy fresh products.' This was dreamed up by Jimmy (the Weasel) Fratianno, the well-known ex-Cleveland hoodlum, Stanley Secunda, Carlo Licata and Nick Simponis.

"They supplied citrus juice to the 'organization's' bars. Later they provided this same lucrative service to others.

"But Gold Enterprises blew up when the Weasel left town suddenly—at Bompy's urgent request. San Diego police threatened to roust all of the 'organization's' dives if this unsavory character didn't vamoose.

"Right now the Weasel, with two liquor store licenses, is awaiting trial in Los Angeles on extortion charges."

White's article continued, listing members of Dragna's LA family and their connections to the liquor business and through the liquor business, their connections to Bonelli.

Bonelli responded to White's charges with an announcement that he had changed his registration from Republican to Democrat. "Political, economic and social enslavement is being accomplished by the aggressive Chandler family through the Republican Party and its kowtowing leadership—the picture of this scheming Chandler family……is frightening…… But, what the hell. Somebody has to have enough guts to kick a few sacred cows around here, or a man won't be able to brush his own teeth without getting the Chandlers' permissions."

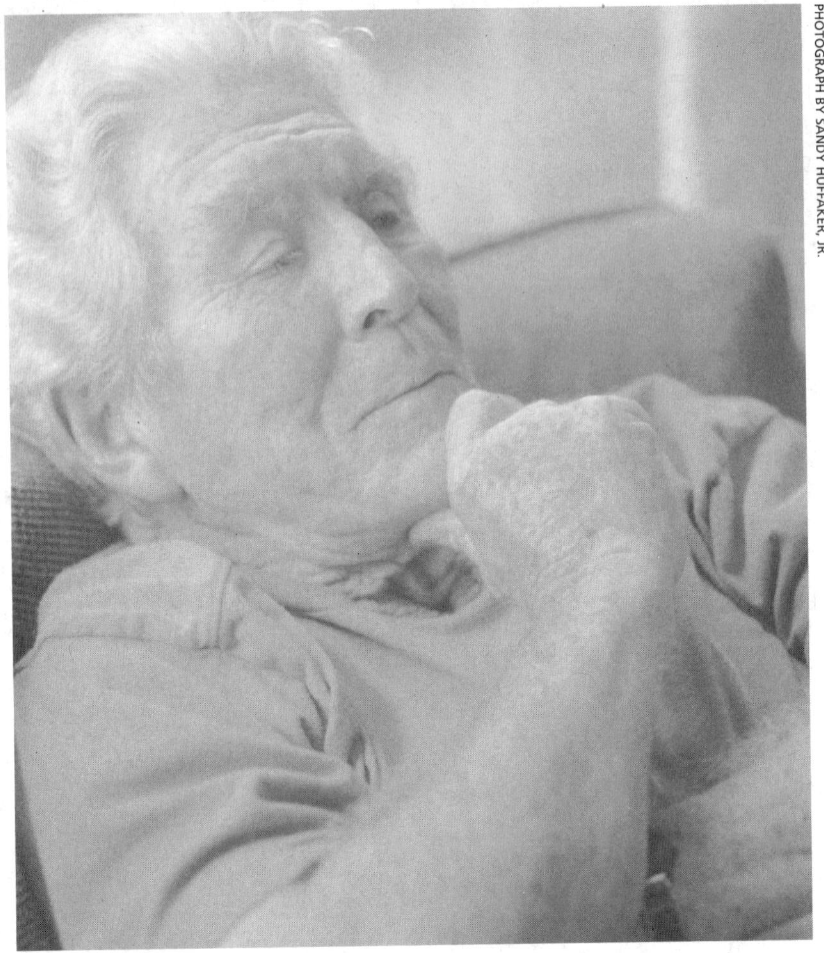

*Bart Sheela, c. 1996*

**"We figured we could get the legitimate people who had restaurants but had to pay bribes to come over to our side."**

CHAPTER FORTY-FOUR

# THE CLEAN-UP BEGINS

We cannot know what Bompensiero thought when he read Art White's exposé of Bonelli. I would guess that he pulled his *funsha*, that he paced and hissed about sobs and people who were "a pain in the fisterus." I would guess that he dropped many dimes in pay telephone boxes and made many telephone calls. He may have called Frank Desimone in Los Angeles, the Los Angeles lawyer whom all LA Mafia family members called first. But we do not know. And Mary Ann, who for various reasons was at this time beginning to find her marriage to Dutch Roberts untenable and was, therefore, unhappy and preoccupied with her unhappiness, now recalls nothing about these articles or her parents' response to them. So we do not know what Thelma Bompensiero felt when she read that her husband was the "up-and-coming power in the 'organization.'" I do know this: the only people who spoke of Bompensiero as "Bomp" or "Bompy" were not friends or "organization" associates. "If you were a friend or family member," said Mary Ann, "you called my father 'Frank' or 'Uncle Frank.' If you knew him only casually, you addressed him as 'Mr. Bompensiero.' Nobody except the police and the media ever called my father by those absurd names." Mary Ann almost sneered, then, as she said, "Bomp, Bompy," and added, "Why, no one would have dared."

What I can tell you and what you certainly have already guessed is that something bad was about to happen to Bompensiero. The bad thing that is about to happen would center on that Tuesday afternoon, six days after Bompensiero's first grandchild was born, when Ernest Gillenberg handed over to Frank Bompensiero a $5000 cashier's check.

In 1953 Caspar W. "Cap" Weinberger was a young San Francisco attorney serving his first term in the California State Assembly. Toward the end of 1953, he was made chairman of a five-man subcommittee of the Joint Legislative Interim Committee on Government Organization. The subcommittee's charge was to investigate liquor law enforcement and the work of the Board of Equalization.

By February, 1954, Weinberger's subcommittee had held hearings in various California cities, including San Diego. At the hearings' conclusion, Weinberger announced that there was strong evidence of a breakdown of liquor law enforcement. He suggested that one of the first steps in cleaning up the state's liquor law enforcement should be removal of the State Board of Equalization from any dealings with liquor law and the creation of a new department to handle these functions. According to Weinberger, it was in Bonelli's Southern California district that the subcommittee noted the greatest problems. In Los Angeles and San Diego Counties his subcommittee heard numerous complaints of illegal trafficking in liquor licenses. Attorney General of California Edmund G. "Pat" Brown, in response to Weinberger's findings, announced, "These indicated irregularities may form the basis of legal action directed toward cancellation of licenses fraudulently obtained."

Bart Sheela was a deputy district attorney, working in the office of DA Don Keller from 1951 to 1955. Over several days' time, Sheela did his best to explain how the bad thing happened to Bompensiero. "I had done a couple of little cases for the man in charge of intelligence in the sheriff's office—Bob Newsom. We were talking one day. I was getting tired in the DA's office of what I was doing. I had prosecuted a couple of murder cases, but the bulk of the work was minor narcotics cases coming out of Logan Heights and sailors who were disenchanted, who wanted to get away and see the world and then all of a sudden decided they wanted to go home, so they would rob a liquor store or steal a car. I was talking to Newsom about it and he told me about this liquor thing. He said it was an open secret that you had to pay a bribe to get a liquor license. So about that same time that Newsom and I were talking, Bonelli had his big run-in with the Chandlers over equalization on some Chandler property. You should never get in a pissing match with a skunk and that's what Bonelli did. So the Chandlers put Art White, who was a fine investigative reporter, on to Bonelli. White really was the one who caused this liquor license thing to get going."

Another of my retired San Diego law-enforcement friends told me this: "Everybody in town who kept an eye on things knew damned well that this liquor license thing was going on. Several of us finally went to Judge John Hewicker—Old Bloody John, Hanging John. In his chambers he had a goddamned hangman's knot. Hewicker was one hell of a judge. Hewicker was the most powerful judge here. And he told Keller, 'You better start doing something about this liquor license business. If you don't, I can guarantee you that judicial council is going to be talking to you.' So Don Keller then became very happy about being willing to put Sheela and his guys on to the liquor license investigation. Bonelli had to run again in 1954 and Keller knew Bonelli was going to get beat anyway that time around, so he didn't care as much what happened to Bonelli."

What Sheela refers to as this "liquor license thing" began to be brought before the county grand jury early in 1954. Keller's office trained its sights on

Bonelli, to, as Sheela said, "get some pressure on him." Sheela explained how this was done. "I was put in charge of the liquor license case. Jack Levitt, who later became a judge, worked on it too. Levitt was a good book lawyer, which I was not. He was the one who came up with the idea that eventually got Bonelli. There was a provision of law in which it was a misdemeanor for any licensee to give a gift to the Board of Equalization man who had control over the liquor licenses in this area and that man was Bonelli. So Levitt put together the theory you could get Bonelli and these other guys on a conspiracy to commit a misdemeanor, which makes it a felony. This, eventually, is what we convicted some of these guys on. Levitt was one smart lawyer.

"Shorter-range, we figured that if we could convict somebody of perjury in connection with the liquor licenses then we could get the legitimate people who had restaurants but had to pay bribes to come over to our side, which was what happened. About that time, after we started that, there was a restaurateur-tavern owner named Jack Millspaugh who had the Silver Spigot out on Morena Boulevard and was trying to get a license. Millspaugh was represented by a lawyer named Cliff Duke and Duke had been in the DA's office and so he knew about this 'open secret' of bribery to get liquor licenses.

"So Duke sent Millspaugh in, wired for sound, to talk to the Board of Equalization local chief, Charlie Berry, and to Al W. Bennett, the so-called business-opportunity broker who had his offices next door to the Board of Equalization offices. Millspaugh and Bennett talked and Bennett relayed that you had to come across with some money—a bribe—if you wanted a liquor license.

"Of course, they had Bennett and Berry on tape with Millspaugh. Anyway, they were using very rudimentary equipment and the recording wasn't that great. They were afraid to turn the tape over to law enforcement at first because this graft was so pervasive that you didn't know where you would be safe. Smith, Cliff Duke's investigator, put it into a closet. It was one of those big tape belts and he had a little child who got into it and chewed on it, so that didn't help the quality any. Finally, they brought the tape to me at the DA's office. Duke and I were classmates at Stanford and he trusted me. I gave the tape to our chief investigator. He was one of those people who had a penchant for time-stamping everything and he put it into one of those manila folders and time-stamped it. He stamped the tape. He did it so hard, he broke the goddamned thing. When we pulled it out to get ready for trial, the damned thing was a mess. We put it together and I must have listened for 30 hours until I finally could repeat word for word the first 15 seconds of this recording. I used that in my opening statement to the grand jury as a bluff."

Sheela led Millspaugh through questioning before the grand jury. Millspaugh explained that in November, 1953, he had written a letter of application to Charles E. Berry for a general on-sale license. After three weeks passed and Millspaugh received no response, he went to see Berry, who told him that the SBE was "intending to peruse all the letters carefully and all the ones they felt were the proper applicants."

Sheela: What is the next thing that happened in connection with your efforts to obtain a liquor license?

Millspaugh: Approximately three or four days later I received a call from Mr. Bennett and he wanted me to come up. I went up I think the same afternoon and he said that he had talked with Mr. Berry and that I was a No. 1 prospect for a license providing that I had four grand to give him.

Sheela: By four grand you mean $4,000?

Millspaugh: $4,000. I said, "Well, what's the $4,000 for? I either deserve a license or I don't. I have been in the business 11 years and I haven't any markers of any kind against any of the places that I have owned or that I do own." And I didn't see any reason why I should be forced to pay anybody extra money for it. He said, "Well, that's the word that we got from the top and that's the only way anybody can get a license."

"Once we had that one, had Millspaugh," Sheela told me, "we started to get the other witnesses in. Finally the case was getting so cumbersome, there were so many witnesses, we set up a special subcommittee in the grand jury. Some of the people we called would claim Fifth Amendment privileges. We had told them, of course, that we would not prosecute them if they told the truth, the standard prosecutorial ploy. But still, many of them claimed the privilege. So, first, we would take some of these people before this subcommittee. But if somebody we called was willing to talk and if what he had to say was something live and good, then we would bring them back in front of a full grand jury, so we wouldn't waste the grand jury's time.

"We started to run into some resistance, more and more of the licensees would seek lawyers and claim the privilege and not come forward. So then I planted a story that we had talked to the attorney general and that he was writing an opinion that any licensee who claimed his constitutional right and refused to testify about how his license was issued, well, that would be ground for revocation of licenses and that caused more of them to come in so by then we pretty well had it down."

Sheela and his investigators in the DA's office, by May 19, 1954, were able to get their first big indictment. The *San Diego Union's* headline on May 20, 1954, read:

Indictment Accuses Former Councilman Of Soliciting Bribes

"The San Diego county grand jury yesterday indicted Al W. Bennett, 56, former city councilman, who is now a liquor license broker, on charges of irregularities in liquor license transactions here. Bennett was arrested at his home last night and booked at the county jail. He was released later on $15,000 bail.

"Bennett was accused in the indictment returned by the grand jury yesterday of three counts of bribery, one count of grand theft, one count of conspiracy of bribery and two counts of attempted grand theft.

"He was councilman and at times vice mayor from 1929 to 1937. He has specialized in handling liquor license transfers in SD. He told a *San Diego Union* reporter he handles 80 percent of the traffic in this area. 'This is very embarrassing,' he said when taken into custody."

"In that first case with Bennett," said Sheela, "we had Millspaugh as a witness, so we had enough. Then it all started to come in and then it got hot and Governor Goodwin Knight allocated a lot of money for this investigation and of course the attorney general—Pat Brown—came into it too. The DA's office back then was small, we had 8 to 12 deputy district attorneys and four investigators. The attorney general assigned us two more: Ray McCarthy and a guy named Martino. I had Eugene Allen in our office. Part of my job was channeling where people went to talk to people. I sent McCarthy and Martino out to talk to a guy named Ernie Gillenberg in Jacumba. I could tell when these guys came back from Jacumba that they had really found something big, something they weren't telling me. I figured they were going to get it over to Pat Brown's crew, so finally I separated McCarthy and Martino and I cracked them and they told me about Gillenberg and this cashier's check he'd given Bompensiero. So that's how we got Bompensiero and we put him in the conspiracy with Bennett and Berry. Our argument to the jury was that they let Bompensiero go in and do this collection from Gillenberg because that would give the licensees the idea that the connected people were here and that would lend some muscle in case they thought about talking. I don't know if that would have happened. But that was the theory we argued to the jury."

All through the summer of 1954, the liquor license scandal produced headlines. On June 3, 1954, the *San Diego Union* reported:

Charles E. Berry, Faces 7 Bribery, Conspiracy Counts

More Prosecutions Yet To Come, DA Says As Jury Acts

"Berry appeared in Judge Howard Turrentine's court with his attorney, Leonard Wilson. He sat quietly while 16 members of the grand jury handed the indictment to Turrentine.

"After the judge signed a bench warrant, Berry surrendered to Sheriff Strand who also was in court. He was taken to county jail for booking and fingerprinting and was released on $7,500 bail."

On July 2, 1954, Charles E. Berry was suspended from his job as district liquor control administrator for the State Board of Equalization. The board met and voted four to one to suspend him for refusing on June 2 to testify before the grand jury. The board ruled this refusal was against public policy. Only Bonelli voted against Berry's suspension, a suspension Bonelli later would claim was the result of "police state and fascist action."

SAN DIEGO HISTORICAL SOCIETY

*"Hanging" Judge John Hewicker, c. 1963*

**When Judge Hewicker sentenced Berry and Bennett, spectators gasped.**

# CHAPTER FORTY-FIVE

# BOMPENSIERO TAKES THE FIFTH, BONELLI FLEES

During the spring and summer of 1954, while the county grand jury continued to meet behind locked doors in the Civic Center building and investigators from various agencies continued to sift documents and interview potential witnesses in connection with the Bonelli and the liquor license bribes, Bompensiero found himself in difficulty. Cap Weinberger's subcommittee hearings had led to State Attorney General Pat Brown's office beginning investigation into liquor license fraud. That investigation uncovered the license that Bompensiero and Leo Patella had acquired in 1952 through their dealings with Arthur Warnock and John Griffin, then-owners of the Turkey Inn and the Valley Inn in Ramona.

On July 17, 1954, the *San Diego Union* headlined its front page with:

Frank Bompensiero Named In Bar Case

"William M. Bennett, deputy state attorney general, yesterday charged that Frank Bompensiero, San Diego bar and café operator, is actually the owner of an on-sale liquor license held in the names of Salvatore Bompensiero and Leo G. Patella.

"Bompensiero, who figured in the 1953 California crime commission report as having alleged connections with the notorious Mafia, and denied them, was called as a witness in Superior Court by Bennett in a move to establish Bompensiero's connections with the license held in the name of his brother and brother-in-law. The case went to court when the Patella–Salvatore Bompensiero attorneys sought to block a license revocation hearing before Joseph Akers, Board of Equalization hearing officer. They alleged improper service of accusation notices.

"Frank Bompensiero was termed by Superior Court Judge Elmer Heald as a 'very evasive and hostile witness. The place to question him is before the grand jury,' Judge Heald said.

"Frank Bompensiero denied ownership of the liquor license and denied he bought supplies for The Spot, where the license is in operation."

Early in August, 1954, a retired lawman with whom I spoke was sent to deliver a subpoena to Bompensiero to appear before the county grand jury. "I subpoenaed him out of his bar. I knew he was in there. One of the Matrangas was with him, and Sammy Siegel, a bookmaker. Bompensiero manifested surprise, but he didn't lose control. He was perfectly polite, a gentleman. 'Here, Frank,' I said, and handed him the subpoena. He just shrugged his shoulders, took the subpoena, and thanked me and walked me to the door."

On August 4, 1954, Bart Sheela questioned Bompensiero before the grand jury. "Bompensiero," Sheela told me, "was hanging tough. He could have gotten a free ride if he'd have talked to us. All he was in that Gillenberg thing was a delivery man." Questioned by reporters after his appearance, Bompensiero said only, "I don't know what they could want me for."

Six days later, the grand jury again called Bompensiero. Again, said Sheela, "Bompensiero hung tough. We didn't have him in there even five minutes. He claimed the privilege and that was that." Sheela sighed, added, "He was on the fringes of this and had he been willing to talk to us and said to us, 'I passed this money on to Berry,' he would have gotten a free ride. No doubt about that."

Early in August, Attorney General Brown called for a "sweeping investigation." Brown and Governor Knight issued a joint statement in which Knight promised $100,000 for hiring investigators, auditors, and accountants. Bart Sheela and his assistants continued to run one after another witness before the grand jury meeting in the Civic Center. In the Chamber of Commerce Auditorium, the state attorney general's deputy William M. Bennett, at a Board of Equalization hearing, continued to hear charges that liquor licenses were issued fraudulently in San Diego County. Even then-mayor Jack Butler for a short time found himself accused of dabbling in liquor licenses. On August 17, Mayor Butler, at a city council meeting, denied the charges: "This is the first meeting of the council since the unsavory charges were made against me. I deny any direct or indirect interest in any liquor licenses. I ask that the public withhold judgment until all the evidence is in." In the end, nothing came of the charges against Butler.

On Monday, August 16, SBE liquor administrator Charles E. Berry and liquor license broker Al W. Bennett were on trial in superior court in Judge John "Hanging John" Hewicker's courtroom. Both Bompensiero and his brother Sam, during this same week, were being questioned in the Board of Equalization hearings. Bompensiero was charged with being the secret owner of the liquor license for the Spot. Bompensiero was represented by C.H. Augustine and Sam Bompensiero was represented by Frank Desimone. Leo Patella, with Sam Bompensiero the other licensee for the Spot, was at sea on a fishing boat. The *San Diego Union* reported: "William M. Bennett, deputy state attorney general, said he had heard that Patella, who left here as a seaman on the tuna clipper *Far Famed* June 12 and is reported homeward bound, might be transferred to another vessel at sea to avoid appearance at the local hearing."

On Wednesday, August 18, Ernest and Gladys Gillenberg were brought into Hewicker's courtroom under guard. They claimed that their lives had been threatened. Bart Sheela presented the Gillenbergs as witnesses for the prosecution. The Jacumba café owner testified that he handed over $5000 to Bompensiero and $2500 payoff to Al Bennett, to obtain two licenses. Mr. and Mrs. Gillenberg testified that they paid Bompensiero with a Bank of America cashier's check. The check was shown to Judge Hewicker and the jury.

A sheriff's deputy walked into the Chamber of Commerce Auditorium and subpoenaed Bompensiero to appear in Judge Hewicker's court. (The *San Diego Union* noted that Bompensiero wore "contrasting gray slacks and coat, and black and white shoes.") The Board of Equalization hearing was recessed to permit Bompensiero to testify at the trial. Sheela questioned Bompensiero, who politely gave his name but refused to answer any of the questions put to him.

Sheela showed Bompensiero the check and asked, "Is that your name on this check?"

"I stand on my constitutional grounds and refuse to testify."

Hewicker asked, "On grounds it might tend to incriminate you?"

"Yes," said Bompensiero, "that's right."

Wednesday evening Bompensiero was served with another subpoena. This subpoena came from the county grand jury. The grand jury had indicted Bompensiero on charges of bribery and conspiracy to bribe in connection with liquor licenses.

Thursday, August 19, in Judge Hewicker's courtroom, Bart Sheela led one after another tavern owner through testimony that showed a systematic attempt by Bennett and Berry to solicit bribes from applicants for liquor licenses. Bompensiero and C.H. Augustine, acting as Bompensiero's attorney, appeared in Judge Howard Turrentine's courtroom, in answer to the grand jury subpoena. Turrentine set bail at $15,000. Augustine asked for bail reduction and his request was denied. Bompensiero was booked, posted bail, and was released. Bompensiero was to appear again on September 1 to enter his plea.

By Thursday, August 26, Sheela had called 19 witnesses. Nine testified that in order to acquire liquor licenses they paid the defendants a total of $31,000. Five testified that the defendants had asked them for $11,000 in bribes which they, the defendants, were unable or unwilling to pay.

A witness whose story is typical was Ernest Esslinger, owner of the Roma Inn at 1753 India Street. Esslinger testified that he had unsuccessfully applied for a liquor license. He was then approached by Al Bennett, who suggested that $7000 was needed for a license. Esslinger gathered the money in cash, went into Bennett's office, and dropped the money on Bennett's desk. Several days later Esslinger applied for and received his license.

The jury deliberated for nine hours and delivered a unanimous verdict. They declared Bennett and Berry guilty of 17 counts of conspiracy and committing bribery in the issuance of liquor licenses. Bailiffs hustled the two men off to jail to await sentencing on September 1.

I am told that when Judge Hewicker on Wednesday, September 1, sentenced Berry and Bennett that spectators gasped. Hewicker was not known as Old Bloody John and Hanging John for nothing. Hewicker, according to the account in the *San Diego Union*, "sentenced Berry and Bennett to serve one to 14 years for each of seven counts and directed that terms for five of the counts run concurrently, recommended that Berry and Bennett each serve at least 25 years, and ordered them to pay individual fines of $14,750." Hewicker denied bail and ordered that the two men be delivered immediately to the state prison in Chino.

That same day the county grand jury returned indictments against six people, charging them with bribery, grand theft, attempted grand theft, and conspiracy to bribe. There were new indictments against Berry and Bennett and Bompensiero. Three other men were also named.

Meanwhile, Bonelli campaigned throughout his eight Southern California counties, seeking to retain his seat on the Board of Equalization. Although Bonelli, a newly minted Democrat, had managed to win the Democratic nomination in the June 8 primary, party regulars turned their backs on him. The League of Democratic Women announced that they did not even want his name on party literature. Other Democratic nominees caucused and voted to ask that their campaigns be detached from Bonelli's. And now that Bonelli was no longer a Republican, he lost support not only of his old friends the Chandlers and their Los Angeles newspapers, but also of San Diego's two Copley dailies. Bonelli added the Copley family to his list of people out to get him.

Bonelli lost his fight to hold his seat on the State Board of Equalization. He was defeated by Robert McDavid, an Altadena Republican. Bart Sheela recalled this period. "Three weeks before the election I wanted to put three subpoenas before the grand jury for Bonelli. Keller kiboshed this. He said, 'It is too close to election time, it will look like we were playing politics.' But he okayed it a week after the election, which Bonelli, after all this heat, of course lost."

February 9, 1955, the San Diego County grand jury indicted Bonelli on three charges of conspiracy in connection with issuance of liquor licenses. "We sent out the subpoena," said Sheela, "but Bonelli fled, to Arizona, where he had a ranch. We finally found him there and started extradition proceedings."

On May 16, 1955, Bart Sheela and District Attorney Don Keller and a sheriff's deputy flew to Phoenix for Bonelli's extradition hearing. "The statehouse in Arizona," said Sheela, "wasn't any bigger then than our own county courthouse. Bonelli was on the stand, testifying before Governor McFarland. Bonelli was saying, 'Look, these things may have happened, and if they did happen, they were all done by my underlings without knowledge on my part.' He said, 'Candidates have agreements not to publicize the sex life of their opponents or the supporters who supply them with campaign funds.'"

Bonelli talked for many minutes. He complained about his bad press. He told the story of his run-in with the Chandlers. He noted that as a State Board of Equalization member he had demanded that the Copley estate pay inheritance taxes. "I haven't," he said, "had a friendly press in San Diego County now for seven or eight years."

Sheela said that Keller, while Bonelli talked, kept nudging him. "He wanted me to ask this question, 'Why didn't you come to Keller and tell him this, if that is your defense, Mr. Bonelli?' I don't like to ask questions unless I know what's coming, but my boss is nudging me, so what else can I do? So finally I asked, 'Why then didn't you come to Mr. Keller and tell him this?' Bonelli was a genius. Bonelli, said, 'Well, I thought I did. I'd heard that the man closest to Mr. Keller in San Diego was C. Arnholt Smith and I did go to C. Arnholt Smith and ask him to talk to Keller and explain this and say I'd like to talk to Keller.' I looked at Keller and thought, 'What's wrong with you, asking this question?' Because it had happened that way."

As the hearing went on, Sheela repeatedly objected that Bonelli's statements were immaterial to the point at issue—Bonelli's extradition. "We had a bail of $50,000 on the thing, and Bonelli thought that was outrageous, so I said, to Bonelli, 'Why don't you come back to San Diego and we'll reduce the bond?' Bonelli said, 'I don't appreciate an angel with an axe.'"

Governor McFarland, at the hearing's end, refused to permit Bonelli's extradition. "I could not live with my conscience if my judgment was swayed by arguments in the California newspapers," said McFarland.

After Labor Day, 1954, C.H. Augustine, Bompensiero's lawyer, began filing a series of pleas. Augustine sought to have Bompensiero detached from the other men named in the two sets of indictments. He also sought to have the number of charges reduced. As 1954 ended, though, it must have been apparent to Bompensiero that eventually he would go to trial for receiving the $5000 bribe from Gillenberg. When Judge Hewicker handed down the harsh sentences to Bennett and Berry, it also must have been apparent to Bompensiero that eventually he might do time.

Mary Ann and Dutch had separated. Mary Ann was living at home with her parents. "My father came home one night and he said to my mother, 'Honey, we can leave. We can go to Mexico and we can live like kings and queens for the rest of our lives.'"

SAN DIEGO HISTORICAL SOCIETY

*Frank Bompensiero is booked into county jail, November 1, 1954*

**"The only time you'd see my dad happy was when he was playing with Frankie."**

CHAPTER FORTY-SIX

# FRANK'S WOES

I don't know how in the first months of 1955 Frank Bompensiero managed to get himself out of bed to face the day. I don't know how he slept at night. Frank and Thelma and their daughter Mary Ann and her son Frankie, in late 1954, moved from Estelle Street into temporary quarters on College Avenue and then early in 1955 into their new house on Braeburn Road in Kensington. So he had the worry of moving into the Braeburn Road house, onto which a builder was putting an addition. Then there was the Algiers, Bompensiero's restaurant. Yale Kahn had built the building, on College Avenue, next to the Campus Drive-In, with its big neon sign that depicted an Indian-headdress-wearing majorette twirling a baton. Kahn put the restaurant in for Bompensiero. The specialty was Sicilian steak. The restaurant wasn't doing well. "People don't want good food," Bompensiero told Thelma and Mary Ann. "They'd as soon eat hamburger."

Worst, though, was the fallout from the liquor license inquiries. Bompensiero may well have thought how peculiar it was, how odd, that for someone who didn't drink much, the only big trouble he'd been in was trouble over liquor. Bompensiero and his younger brother Sam and his nephew Leo Patella, since 1954, had been fighting the State Board of Equalization; the fight was over the liquor license for the Spot. Bompensiero was charged with being secret owner of the Spot's liquor license. Then, too, he was in difficulties over the Pirate's Cave, his bar at 402 West Broadway. He was accused by the Alcoholic Beverage Control Department (in 1955, authority over liquor licenses was transferred from the State Board of Equalization to the new state Alcoholic Beverage Control Department) of "running a public barroom in violation of the State Constitution." If you had, as Bompensiero did, an on-sale general liquor license, you were required to serve food. The ABC investigator charged that while the Pirate's Cave had seats for 43 patrons, he found only 4 knives, 6 forks, 3 teaspoons, 1 soup spoon, 1 plate, 1 platter, 2 salad dishes, 14 cups, 11 saucers, and 3 mugs for serving food. Plus, the investigator said that while the kitchen was of proper size, it was dirty. Also, the investigator testified that from the food on hand, a cook could prepare only one of the eight offerings on Bompensiero's menu.

Worst of the worst, the source, surely, of Bompensiero's greatest woe and worry, was the indictment brought against him in late summer 1954, by a

San Diego County grand jury. He was charged with bribery and conspiracy to bribe in connection with liquor licenses. Unbeknownst to Bompensiero, Judge Hewicker had read with zealous interest Ed Reid's 1952 *The Mafia*. Hewicker had been particularly attentive to the chapter entitled "Phi Beta Mafia" wherein Reid listed 83 men as Mafia members. Number 26 was Frank Bompensiero. Hewicker, someone told me, "was smacking his lips at the thought of getting himself the real McCoy. He finally had himself a big criminal, so he planned to really lower the boom on him."

Through 1954 and early 1955, day after day, Bompensiero saw his name blazoned across San Diego newspapers. Reporters recapitulated the old stories—his year in McNeil Island federal prison for violation of Prohibition-era liquor laws, the accusations that he'd killed Phil Galuzo, his association with Los Angeles Mafia godfather Jack Dragna. Day after day he talked with lawyers—the dyspeptic Tums-chewing Frank Desimone in Los Angeles and C.H. Augustine in San Diego. Week after week, as Bompensiero's businesses foundered, as he lost the Algiers and fell behind on payments to liquor suppliers, he paid lawyers. Paid them thousands of dollars.

Desimone tried every trick. He pled with the Fourth Appellate Court to quash the indictment. Arguing that the indictment, formally returned on September 1, 1954, referred to an act that took place on April 3, 1951, he asked the State Supreme Court to consider that a three-year statute of limitations nulled the indictment. Jack Levitt, the San Diego County district attorney's office's best "book lawyer," argued before the state court that the statute of limitations did not apply since Bompensiero's action was part of a continuing conspiracy. Desimone countered that insufficient evidence existed to show Bompensiero was a part of that conspiracy. Desimone further argued that Judge Hewicker was prejudiced against Bompensiero and that if his client's case did come to trial, Hewicker should be disqualified from hearing it. (Bart Sheela, a deputy district attorney in the San Diego County district attorney's office from 1951 to 1955, said recently when I asked him why Desimone wanted Hewicker disqualified: "Anybody that was defending anybody and had any sense at all would try to get Hewicker disqualified. He was a one-way judge.") Desimone managed to get a continuance from January 10 to March 14 to allow time for the State Supreme Court to make its decision.

Frankie, Mary Ann's son, was almost four. Mary Ann and Frankie's father were divorced. Mary Ann and Frankie were living with her parents. Mary Ann said that perhaps it was a blessing in disguise that she and Frankie were back home during this time. Her parents were edgy. Thelma Bompensiero's blood pressure had been high since she was pregnant with Mary Ann. Her blood pressure now zoomed higher. Terrific headaches practically knocked her mother over. Her father threw himself down on the couch and watched whatever came on television. In the old days, when the news came on, her father, in the midst of some political commentary, "talked" to the reporter, said something like, "What a pain in the fisterus you are!!" During the early months of 1955, however, he silently watched. "The only time you'd see my dad happy," said Mary Ann, "was when he was playing with Frankie."

About this time Mary Ann met the man who would become her second husband—Gino. I talked one day with Gino. His family was from Naples. He had grown up in Massachusetts. Early in the 1950s, at the urging of an older brother already settled in San Diego, Gino came to town. "My brother was out here, and he says, 'Come west, they're making money out here.' I went fishing. I was on a tuna boat. I'd never fished before. It is very hard work, very hard work. That's when I met Mary Ann, when I was fishing. I was living down in Little Italy on Columbia. My sister was living there too."

Did Gino know who Frank Bompensiero was?

"Well, people you hang around with, they talk and you pick up conversation and read between the lines. And then when I really met him, I knew. And then I knew from hanging around downtown. I knew who he was, what he was; I said 'Hi' to him and so forth. I was hanging out downtown. Downtown was wide open then. Third Avenue there, where all those guys owned the bars, from there, baboom, baboom, baboom, I got to know them all. These guys were older than I was. I was the young punk around the neighborhood. The Gold Rail, it was just like the rest of those bars downtown, but the Spot did a lot of business, most of the business. They depended on the Navy. They didn't have many locals. Sam, Frank's brother, I used to go talk to Sam all the time at his bar. And we used to go down to the racetrack together. And play the horses. I met Mary Ann's dad through Sam, his brother. And then when I started going out with Mary Ann, I met Mary Ann's mother. She was very nice. She was real friendly, the nicest lady in the world."

Gino met Marie and Momo Adamo. "I knew the Adamos real well. Marie drove Momo crazy back in those days. She was an attractive woman. She liked to drink. She liked to party. She liked nice clothes. Very elegant, she was, and she used to pay $200 just for a little nightgown. We used to go over to Momo's house and have dinner. Momo would have people come in from Chicago, and after dinner we'd play cards and so forth. Stupid games, you know, that women like to play."

I asked Gino what Momo did for money.

"Well, those guys, they're broke today and they got $5000, $10,000 tomorrow. That's how they operated. Frank Desimone, I remember a funny episode with him in it. This was sometime before Frank Bompensiero went to prison. It was at Momo and Marie's house. Frank Bompensiero was there and Mary Ann and Desimone and the guys. Marie was barbecuing steaks, porterhouse steaks. Frank Desimone, he comes out on the patio and he says, 'What, I gotta eat this crap? Get some good steaks.' And then Momo started in telling him, 'You go to hell.' Marie is carrying on the way Marie carried on. So Momo goes up to Marie and says, 'Marie, why don't you shut up.'"

**The jury began its deliberations**

**at ten minutes until four and returned**

**the verdict at five until eleven.**

CHAPTER FORTY-SEVEN

# THE TRIAL

District Attorney Don Keller assigned Bart Sheela as prosecutor for Bompensiero's case. "In the DA's office," said Sheela, "we'd all heard the stories about Bompensiero and the meetings that the mob guys had in their glory years, a year or so before the liquor license investigation, when they'd have these huge blowouts down at La Gloria, the hotel-rancho between Tijuana and Rosarito. We'd hear stories about rubouts. And there was no doubt that Bompensiero was a tough, tough man. If you had to have somebody killed, I would have looked to Bompensiero. I would've trusted him to get it done. No question. Then there was that Ed Reid book—it was just a little pocket paperback—about the Mafia that was out at that time. Reid listed Bompensiero as number 26 in importance in the U.S. Mafia.

"Before the trial was set to start, I went to LA and pulled the file on the Phil Galuzo case, in which Bompensiero was suspected as Galuzo's killer, because obviously if Bompensiero took the stand I wanted to wangle that in. In my judgment, the Los Angeles police had a perfect case against Bompensiero in the Galuzo thing, because they had witnesses. Bompensiero didn't do a good job of killing the guy, he lived for seven days, and in a classic dying declaration, which made it admissible, he named the two people who killed him. The declaration named his killers as Frank and a guy from the union hall, but then when it came back, a homicide detective in the LA police department said they couldn't make a case. I thought it was a bunch of baloney on their part. I thought somebody got paid off."

About Bompensiero's lawyers, Sheela said, "C.H. Augustine was a good lawyer, he'd been in the DA's office shortly before I came there. He was a trial lawyer. Then they had a guy named Bill Burns. But that case was actually being controlled by Desimone, he was making the tactical decisions. It was Desimone's job to see to it when a Mafia figure was on trial that there was no spilling over, nothing getting out that would embarrass the mob. That was my reading of it. Desimone seemed like a real nice guy. I'd never been able to go to the Turf Club, but when I got to the DA's office, then all of the judges had Turf Club passes, the DA had Turf Club passes, the jury commissioner had Turf Club passes, and they were always available. I used to see Desimone at the Turf Club, he was very pleasant. I didn't know until the Apalachin thing that he was that well connected." (Desimone was arrested in 1957 at the meeting in Apalachin, New York, of 65 men, many associated with America's crime syndicate. Others at the meeting included Vito Genovese, Carlo Gambino, Joseph Bonanno, Joseph Profaci, Joseph Magliocco, Gerardo Catena, Natale Evola, Michele Miranda, Carmine Lombardozzi, John Ormento, Joseph Riccobono, Paul Castellano, Alfred Rava, Santo Trafficante Jr., James Civello, James Colletti, Frank Zito, John Scalish, Joseph Ida, and Sam Giancana.)

March 18, the State Supreme Court in a six-to-one decision ruled that Bompensiero would stand trial and that he would do so in Judge Hewicker's courtroom. Trial date was reset for Monday, April 18. Meanwhile, Desimone reached out to the United States Supreme Court. He asked Justice William O. Douglas to receive a writ *in certioraris* review (a writ from a higher court to a lower one requesting a transcript of the proceedings of a case for review) and to stay the trial until the writ request could be argued. The Supreme Court declined and on Tuesday morning, jury selection began. Augustine, not unwisely in a city where Sunday closing blue laws still applied, queried prospective jurors about attitudes toward liquor and association with the Woman's Christian Temperance Union and Prohibition Party.

By Wednesday, April 20, the jury was chosen. Jurors were Bernice Aved, Barbara Winter, Irene Vitalich, Mrs. Burl H. Pierce, Carl A. Bertele, Mildred M. Rolph, Warren E. Wilsie, Mary Jo Molina, Rudolph Fibiger, Gwen A. Yontz, Pearl L. Collins, and Elizabeth Shukraft. Alternate jurors were Virginia R. Wroe, Lee E. Singleton, and LeRoy B. Stewart.

The *San Diego Union* noted in its April 21 issue:

Judge May Get Into Jam

"Hewicker last night took home a jar of strawberry jam, a gift from a woman juror who liked his illustration on the difference of evidence. Hewicker had told prospective jurors in the Bompensiero trial that if a youngster was caught in the jam jar, it was direct evidence. If he was caught with jam on his face, the evidence was circumstantial. Attorneys questioning jurors apparently like the illustration too. They used it frequently during the selection and questioning of the panel. Hewicker said, 'I'll have it for breakfast.'"

Jack Levitt and Bart Sheela represented the state. Their goal was to show not only that Bompensiero received a bribe but that he was involved in a conspiracy to solicit and procure bribes. To accomplish this goal, the prosecution set out to demonstrate that bribes regularly had been solicited by both State Board of Equalization employees and by the so-called business opportunity brokers who had set themselves up in business to help applicants acquire licenses. In an opening statement Levitt noted that the prosecution planned to call 18 witnesses, among them Earl Jacobs, owner of the Lakeland Resort in Cuyamaca; Silver Spigot owner Jack Millspaugh; Tony M. Silva, co-owner of the El Toreador Motel in San Ysidro; Frank Cerda, owner of the Mission Inn in Oceanside.

Charles Cameron, a State Board of Equalization employee, testified for the prosecution that he often saw Bompensiero in the SBE office at 3621 Fifth Avenue. Bompensiero, said Cameron, was in and out of the office, talking to everyone there. Augustine, cross-examining Cameron, asked, "There's nothing unusual in that, was there?" Cameron replied there was not. He admitted that Bompensiero owned several bars and had several licenses.

As the trial's sixth day began, Tony M. Silva testified that in 1949 he went three times to the State Board of Equalization offices to apply for a liquor license. "They wouldn't listen to me," Silva told the jury. "They said they had too many applications ahead of mine." Silva said that soon after his third unsuccessful attempt, he was visited by Al W. Bennett. A former San Diego city councilman (1929–1937) and vice-mayor, Bennett was a "business opportunity" broker. He had his offices at 3635 Fifth Avenue, several doors down from the SBE office. In 1954 Bennett, together with Charles E. Berry, SBE district liquor control administrator, had been tried and convicted on 17 counts of conspiracy and committing bribery in the issuance of liquor licenses. Silva said Bennett told him that a license would cost him $5000 and that he could immediately make a down payment of $1000 to get the process started. Silva said that he asked if he couldn't get a license for less. Bennett told him he couldn't. Silva went on to tell the jury that he eventually paid the $5000, in three installments, to Bennett. Payment made, Bennett then sent Silva down the street to the SBE offices to see Berry, who issued Silva's liquor license.

Earl Jacobs followed Silva to the stand. Jacobs testified that Berry himself solicited and took his money. Berry asked Jacobs for $2500. Jacobs, at Berry's instruction, slipped $1000 of the $2500 into Berry's desk drawer. Jacobs, although he never paid the balance, eventually received a license.

One after another the prosecution solicited these tales. None of these stories, however, directly involved Bompensiero. They merely revealed the climate in which bribery flourished and how bribes were solicited and money procured. Bart Sheela was ready, then, with the prosecution's last witness, Jacumba café owner Ernest Gillenberg. The café owner told his long sordid story. He had applied for and been refused a license. He then had been visited by a man who represented himself as raising funds for Bonelli's campaign chest. This man said that $5000 would get Gillenberg a liquor license.

Gillenberg demurred. Next, an SBE employee came knocking. The SBE employee said that any day, a gentleman named Frank Bompensiero would be calling on Gillenberg. Early in 1951, Bompensiero showed up and told Gillenberg that if he wanted a liquor license, he'd have to come across with $5000. Again, Gillenberg demurred. Finally, he changed his mind. Gillenberg telephoned Bompensiero and made arrangements to meet him April 3, 1951, at noon, in the lobby of the U.S. Grant.

Bompensiero must have cringed as he listened to Gillenberg confide in the jury that he and Mrs. Gillenberg—Gladys—had decided not to give Bompensiero cash. They brought a Bank of America cashier's check payable to E.M. Gillenberg and endorsed by Gillenberg. As the couple waited they saw Bompensiero stroll into the lobby and take a position behind a post. The two parties met. Gillenberg handed over the envelope. Bompensiero thanked Gillenberg and walked back to the Gold Rail.

Sheela then directed testimony that identified the check. He showed the check's stamped endorsement: "The Gold Rail, 1028 Third Avenue, San Diego 1, California." A handwriting expert identified the signature beneath the stamped endorsement: "Frank Bompensiero."

I was able to talk with one juror, Warren E. Wilsie, who remembered the trial. About Hewicker, Wilsie recalled, "A very stern-looking guy—gray hair and pointed face and steel-rimmed glasses. He would lean back in his chair while the lawyers were conducting their questioning and he would look like he was asleep and then all of a sudden he would sit bolt upright." About Bompensiero, Wilsie said, "He was a sort of roly-poly short guy. If I had to say anybody whom he looked like, in the face, I'd say Mussolini. During the trial, I certainly didn't know what his reputation was." Sheela, Wilsie remembered as "somewhat flamboyant."

Augustine seemed "a real gentleman-type attorney." Wilsie added, "The evidence that I remember was that Gillenberg had come down from Jacumba and met Bompensiero in the lobby in the Grant. I do know that the thing that was so hard to believe, if this was to be a payoff, that you wouldn't have expected Bompensiero to run it through his own books. It was pretty hard to deny that evidence. Pretty hard."

Sheela made the prosecution's closing argument. "This was a conspiracy," he told the jury, "to sell liquor licenses for all the traffic would bear. They were out to get all the money they could. You will remember that one witness testified it was common gossip in the trade that bribery was the only way to get a liquor license." Augustine countered in his closing argument that Bompensiero, by picking up the check from Gillenberg, really was only doing a favor for public officials. Then, prosecution and defense rested.

"Bompensiero," a *San Diego Union* reporter wrote, "nervously lighted large black cigars when the court took short recesses. He discarded them after only a few puffs. He was affable and joked with reporters."

That same Thursday afternoon, while Gillenberg told his story and the "affable" Bompensiero joked with reporters, county marshals seized Bompensiero's green 1950 Cadillac coupe from its parking place in front of the Gold Rail. The *San Diego Union*, beneath a headline that read "Bompensiero's auto attached as security" explained that the Cadillac was attached to satisfy a $5608.84 bill. "A writ of attachment had been filed against Bompensiero by the San Diego Wholesale Credit Men's Association on behalf of the Sunland Distributing Company, a wholesale liquor house. The bill is for liquor sold to Bompensiero's Pirate's Cave which is reported to be closed."

Mary Ann said that she and her mother never attended the trial. "We didn't know what was going on with the trial, except for what we read in the papers. My father never wanted us in the courtroom, period. But more than once, before the trial and during the trial, my father talked to my mother about simply leaving the country. He came home one night and he said to my mother, 'Honey, we can leave. But we've got Mary Ann and the baby. They're not going to want to stay there. Once we do that we can never come back. That's no life for her and the baby.' They could have gone then on the lam, they would have taken me with them. They didn't want to do it because of me and little Frank. But I know that they talked about just taking off. I know, too, that finally, sometime before he was sentenced, my father said to my mother, 'Honey, I'm tired. I made a mistake. I need a vacation. So let me go, let me take my years.'"

Mary Ann said that her mother's dizzy spells became more frequent. Thelma's brother had died several years earlier, at 44, from a heart attack. Mary Ann said that her mother began to refer to her own death as imminent. "She always said, 'I'm going to die young.' She knew she would die young. It was like she felt she was fated, that there was nothing she could do. Her blood pressure was so high that she would have headaches throbbing in the back of her head. Sometimes her head hurt so bad that her eye would swell. I remember Sundays that she couldn't even cook. She was just huddled there in bed."

At some point after the jury brought in its guilty verdict against Bompensiero and before he was sentenced, Thelma said to Mary Ann, "When I die, I don't want to be dressed in one of those awful negligees." More than once, said Mary Ann, her mother talked, almost idly, about how she wanted to be dressed for her funeral—a creamy white, strapless, ballerina-length dress that her mother had worn to a wedding party.

Friday, April 29, the jury began its deliberations at ten minutes until four and returned the verdict at five until eleven. Bart Sheela recalled, "We were waiting for the verdict at the bar in the Hotel San Diego. Seated over at another table were Bill Burns [a lawyer from Augustine's office], C.H. Augustine, Bompensiero, and Desimone. They were having drinks. Frank comes over to me and he says, 'Sheela, what they pay you in the district attorney's office?' I said, 'Six hundred sixteen dollars a month.' Frank says, 'I paid those assholes $70,000 and I think you got the best side of it. Wise up.'"

Saturday, April 30, the headline atop the *San Diego Union* read: Bompensiero Found Guilty. Bar Owner Convicted On All 3 Counts

PHOTOGRAPH BY SANDY HUFFAKER, JR.

*Holy Cross Catholic Cemetery and Mausoleum*

**"I was lying in my bunk,
with my hands behind my head
and I heard, 'Frank, Frank.'"**

CHAPTER FORTY-EIGHT

# THELMA DIES

Sentencing was set for Monday morning, May 16. Bompensiero had two weeks to arrange his business affairs. Mary Ann recalled that this period was "extremely tense. My mother cried a lot. They knew he was going away. My mother said to my father, 'Frank, put everything in Mary Ann's name.' She meant the Gold Rail, so my name would be on the license. My father says, 'Honey, what is Mary Ann going to do? She doesn't know anything about the bar business. I'm going to put everything in my brother's name.' So my father put my Uncle Sam in charge of everything so he'd have something when he came out. He knew that the vice squad had to be paid off. I didn't know those things. I was 24 and wouldn't know how to run anything. The only thing I could do is sell because I used to work in my mother's dress shop. So during those two weeks my father transferred his businesses over to my Uncle Sam.

"May 16th. The day my father was to be sentenced, I remember that day as plain as if it happened minutes ago. My mother the night before had said she wanted to go to the sentencing, but he said, 'No, I don't want you there. I want you to stay home. You'll find out. I'll get a year or so. That's all.'

"My father got up early that day. He came in the bedroom where my son and I were together. We had twin beds. My little boy slept in one bed and I was in the other. My mother was still in bed too, in their bedroom. He came into my bedroom and kissed me good-bye, and he kissed Frankie. He went into my mother's room. They kissed each other good-bye. He says to my mother, 'I'll see you tonight, honey. I'll see you later.'

"When he went out that door, my mother broke down sobbing and I was crying, and the baby didn't know what was going on. Frankie was only four years old. It was an awful, awful moment. My mother said to me, between sobs, 'Listen to your father, saying to us, "I'll see you tonight," he knows he's not coming home.' I said, 'Mama, he couldn't, don't you understand that Daddy just couldn't say good-bye? He just couldn't say good-bye.' I believe that. She knew it too, but it broke her heart. She just sobbed and sobbed, off and on all day."

According to the account in the *San Diego Union*, Bompensiero sat alone that day in the jury box and waited while his lawyers made their various motions. No one with whom I have talked recalled where Bompensiero stood when Hewicker pronounced his sentence. No one with whom I have talked remembered the expression on Bompensiero's face as Hewicker ordered Bompensiero to serve 1 to 14 years, consecutively, on each of three counts and to pay a $5000 fine on each of three counts. If Bompensiero did rapid addition in his head, a feat at which Mary Ann said he was quite accomplished, he realized that he was to go to prison for 3 to 42 years.

A longtime retiree from the sheriff's department was working in the jail on the day Bompensiero was sentenced. "I was a shift sergeant," he said. "I was the one who booked Bompensiero into the jail. He and his attorney—Augustine—came in. Bompensiero was dressed in a suit and a tie. We talked together. We bantered back and forth. Old Frank. Hard to tell with Frank. He didn't smile much that afternoon, usually a real pleasant character, but that day, he wasn't smiling. He took his diamond ring off and gave it to Augustine. Bompensiero went upstairs and then he went to the joint and that was it."

One measure of the importance granted to a U.S. Mafia figure is his inclusion in the U.S. government document *Organized Crime: 25 Years After Valachi: Hearings Before the Permanent Subcommittee on Investigations of the Committee on Governmental Affairs.* In the document's summary of U.S. Mafia activities Bompensiero's imprisonment is noted:

"May 16, 1955—Frank Bompensiero, head of LCN [La Cosa Nostra] operations in the San Diego area, was committed to California State Prison on local bribery charges. He was succeeded by Antonio Mirabile."

Mary Ann said, "Later that afternoon, Augustine and Desimone came to the house. They didn't call. They just showed up. Augustine started pacing the floor, back and forth in front of my mother and me. He didn't say anything. Then all of a sudden Desimone burst out and said, 'There's no goddamn justice—3 to 42 years.' My mother cried and sobbed and cried.

"They took my father to Chino. Mama had her dress shop—Santa Ann's Moderate Shop on 30th in North Park—and we kept that going. We were there, every day. But it was difficult. I don't even know how to tell how sad and upset my mother was. She just flipped, she just fell apart when they sentenced him. To all those years.

"A week or so after the sentencing, in the evening, I'm home with my mother and little Frankie. She and I were knitting. She had knit for years and she was teaching me how to knit. The telephone rang and it was my godmother, my Aunt Josie, my mother's best friend, calling from Los Angeles. My mother said, 'Well, Jo, I'll be up because I'm going to go see Frank at Chino this weekend. I'll come over to see you too. I'll be there unless I die.' I swear to you. 'I'll come see you, Jo, I'll be there unless I die.' My mother hung up the telephone and we went back to our knitting.

"My mother said to me, 'Honey, do you want some ice cream?' I said, 'Yeah, Mama, I'll get it.' I got the ice cream and handed a bowl to my mother. Mama walked from the kitchen to the dining room, which couldn't have been any more than from my kitchen here to my dining room over there, and she stopped at the dining room table. She said, 'Oh, my God.' I said, 'What, Mom?'

"She put the ice cream down. She said, 'Oh, my God. I'm having a stroke.' I started crying. I got her and walked her over to the sofa and she lay down. They didn't have 911 then. You know who I called? I called Marie and Momo Adamo. They lived near us. They were the closest ones to me and I will tell you—boom. I don't know what happened. I was just hysterical because my mother at this point was shivering and vomiting and crying that her head was killing her. They both came over immediately.

"When my mother was going out in the ambulance, she took off her rings, and she said, 'Here, honey, take these.' I said, 'No, Mama.' She said, 'I won't be coming back.' I said, 'Oh, Mama, yes you will.' We got her to the hospital. She was very alert and in such pain. I said, 'Mama, you're going to be okay.' She said, 'You think so, honey?' I said, 'Mama, you're gonna be fine.' She said, 'I feel like every blood vessel in my head is breaking.'"

One of the first people Mary Ann telephoned after her mother arrived in the hospital's emergency room was Josephine, her godmother. Josephine's first husband was Thelma's brother, Frank Sanfilippo, whose eyes, Josephine told me "were as blue as the sea he fished in." Josephine was not only Mary Ann's godmother, she was also Thelma's closest friend. Josephine, when I spoke to her, was in her 90s and was living in Los Angeles. "In your lifetime," she said, "you meet a lot of people. There are acquaintances and then there are friends. Thelma was my friend, my dearest and best friend. Not a day passes that I do not think of Thelma. The night Mary Ann called me and told me that Thelma had a stroke, I was having a poker party. We already were living then in LA. I told my husband what had happened and we jumped in the car and drove as fast as we could down to San Diego. I went in to Thelma's bedside. She was in terrible shape. All her veins had broken loose in her arms and you could see spots of blood underneath her skin. She knew she wouldn't live long. She couldn't say too much and she looked at me and tears were coming down her face and she said to me, again and again, 'You came, you came.' She said to me, again and again, 'Josie, don't forget my Mary Ann. Don't forget my Mary Ann.'"

Mary Ann, during the next week, drove back and forth between her mother's dress shop and the hospital. "On Monday, I had closed the shop for the day and I went to see my mother. The nurse said, 'She really had a good day today. She's finally eating something.' I said, 'Oh, good.' But my mother was restless. She was sleeping, they thought. But she wasn't sleeping. She didn't even know I was there. She kept whispering, 'Tell Mary Ann, tell Mary Ann.' I said, 'What, Mama, what do you want to tell me?'

"The nurse said to me, 'You know she really ate well. She ate creamed tuna.' My mother couldn't stand creamed anything. When my father got out of the Army, where he'd had creamed chipped beef, he loved it and he started making it at home. My mother couldn't even stand to look at the cream in creamed anything. So that when the nurse told me that my mother had eaten creamed tuna, I said, 'Oh, no, something's wrong, something's terribly wrong.'

"She never regained consciousness, never came out of the hospital, I never knew what she wanted to tell me. 'Tell Mary Ann.' Those were her last words.

"This was a Monday night. She went into a coma that night. In other words, she was really dead. She never came out of it. Monday night, Tuesday, Wednesday, Mama was in a coma. June 2nd, early Thursday morning, she passed away. It was two o'clock in the morning that they actually pronounced her dead.

"That tormented me for the longest time. What did my mom want to tell me?

"So she died June the 2nd. She didn't have a chance to go see him. She never got to see him again after that morning he left to be sentenced, and he never got to see her again. Never."

Josephine and Mary Ann dressed Thelma's body in the creamy white, strapless, ballerina-length dress and the tiara and her pearl earrings. They saw to it that her coffin was sprayed silver and softly draped in lavender. "My mother," Mary Ann said, "told me to the T what she wanted to wear and how she wanted her coffin. Can you believe that? I couldn't believe it. She must have had a premonition."

Josephine recalled that the dress was so low cut that they took some of the bustle from the back and used it to fill in around Thelma's bustline. "Oh, God," said Josephine, remembering that day, " I could not stop crying. I just couldn't. She looked like a princess, lying asleep in that coffin." Then, Josephine added, "It was a big waste when she died. A big waste."

"In those days," Mary Ann said, "you had the rosary the night before the funeral and then you had the viewing. You had this at the funeral home, the next day. The coffin's open at the funeral parlor. It's your last good-bye. My mother had flowers lined up inside, outside, all behind her, everywhere. I never saw so many flowers in my life. You could hardly breathe for the smell of roses and lilies. You went ahead and viewed, you said your last good-byes. Every Italian in the world came to my mother's viewing. Every

Italian. She looked so beautiful. I remember that I said, 'My God, she looks as if she's breathing.'

"I wanted my father to see my mother. I was told that he was going to make it to the funeral, and that he would be able to see my mother, that they were going to come to the funeral parlor, and then from there they would take him to the church. We were at the funeral home. I said, 'Uncle Sam, where's my father?' Sam said, 'Honey, he's gonna come, don't worry.' In the meantime, the funeral director is saying we've got to get to the church. The funeral was for nine o'clock. I said, 'No, I'm not going. My father has got to see my mother. Look at how beautiful she looks.' I was hysterical. My uncle said, 'We've got to go, Mary Ann, your father is not coming here. He's in the church. He's there already.' But I persisted, I wouldn't give up. 'No,' I said, 'no, he's got to see how beautiful she looks.' I was screaming.

"At the church, it was planned that my father and I would sit together in the mourner's pew in the front of the church. When I walked in, down the center aisle, I could see him: my father and the cops. I practically ran down that aisle. I sat next to him. I said, 'Daddy, give me a hug, give me a hug.' He only had one arm around me. He was handcuffed to the policeman. They had put a hat on top of my father's sleeve, to hide the handcuffs.

"I said, 'Daddy, Mama looks so pretty.'

"He said, 'Honey, if I knew I had to spend the rest of my life in jail and it would mean you could have your mother, I'd proudly do it. I know I caused this to happen to her.'

"I can't even tell you what the priest said that day, about my mother. I was crying too hard. I only remember one line. He said, 'Weep for the living, not for the dead.'

"I was able to ride with my father and the policeman in a limo to the cemetery. I was telling him again and again how beautiful Mama looked. I was determined that he was going to get to see her and to kiss her good-bye. It was all that I could think about. All.

"On the way in the car to the mausoleum, my father sat between me and the policeman. My father said to me, 'Your mother didn't die on June the 2nd.' My father, by the way, was not the type to believe in spirits. He said, 'I was lying in my bunk. I was wide awake, looking up at the ceiling. I had my hands behind my head and I was just staring, up at that ceiling. I heard her call my name. I wasn't sleeping, and I wasn't dreaming, I was lying in my bunk, with my hands behind my head and I heard, "Frank, Frank." I heard it again and again, your mother calling, "Frank, Frank." I heard her calling to me.' He said, 'That's when your mother died, honey.' That's the truth. That's what my father told me and that's the night she went into the coma. That Monday night.

"I don't think I ever saw as many people at a funeral. At the cemetery, which is on a rise, when I turned and looked down, I saw that there were miles and miles of cars in the funeral procession.

"But I was determined, no matter what I had to do, that my father was going to get to kiss my mother good-bye, that he was going to get to see her that last time. The priest comes with you to the mausoleum, to say the final words. The coffin's there. They don't immediately place the coffin into its space in the wall. They had a black velvet drape hanging over the opening to the space in which she was to be entombed. What usually happens is that the mourners go by and kiss the coffin and make the sign of the cross. But I was determined. I was shooing everybody out. I could tell people were angry, the way I was moving them back. I didn't care. I don't know how I did it but I convinced the men from the funeral home to open the coffin for my father, so that he could see her and could kiss her good-bye. Which he did. I just was so glad.

"When we left the mausoleum, my father had to get in the car with the cops and I got in with him, and we hugged each other. He had to go back to prison and I had family around me. But he had to go back to Chino.

"Back at the house, Marie and Momo had cooked. I went upstairs. I had to be by myself. My son wasn't there. Somebody took care of him. He didn't go to the funeral. I was upstairs, sobbing, I couldn't stop crying. Everybody is downstairs, Marie is cooking, everybody is drinking. 'They're having a party and I just buried my mother and my father is on his way to jail.' That's what I thought and it made me even more upset. I understand it better now, but I was so furious at the time because my mother was dead and my father was in prison. Marie came upstairs to me and she said, 'This is what you do. You come for the family and talk about things.' Someone else said to me, 'Would you have liked to gone home and been all alone? Here, the family is around you.'

"Gino was out on the boat when my mother died, and the news gets around by shortwave. He heard about my mother's death and he flew in. So he was around for the funeral."

*San Quentin*

**"Frank said that if God hadn't wanted 'em dead, He would've stopped the bullets."**

CHAPTER FORTY-NINE

# A TRAGIC CHARACTER

The *San Diego Union* on July 19, 1955, reported that the DA's office had "moved to collect the $15,000 fine imposed on Bompensiero. Keller also disclosed that Bompensiero transferred to his attorney, C.H. Augustine, three unimproved lots in the Golden Park Addition, Point Loma. Keller told a reporter the deed is dated May 15 and was recorded by Augustine on May 16, the same day Hewicker sentenced Bompensiero. Yesterday Keller filed a petition in Probate Court asking that he be granted letters of administration for the estate of Bompensiero's wife. The petition was filed to expedite settlement of the estate and the liquidation of the assets for payment of the fine. Keller said levies have been filed against Bompensiero's autos as well as abstracts of judgment against all real property believed to have been owned by him. Keller said he expects the Probate Court to act in ten days on the petition in Mrs. Bompensiero's estate."

August 3, 1955, the *San Diego Union* reported that Bompensiero's 1950 Cadillac had been sold at auction for $850. The money was seized by the federal government and applied toward an IRS lien against Bompensiero for $7000. August 6, 1955, the *San Diego Union* reported that the DA's office "planned to file liens against assets in the estate of Mrs. Thelma Bompensiero in an effort to collect the $15,000 fine assessed against her husband, Frank Bompensiero. Keller made his statement after Judge L.N. Turrentine of Superior Court approved the appointment of the Bompensieros' daughter as administratrix of her mother's estate."

In early August, 1955, Bompensiero was transferred from the Guidance Center at the California Institution for Men in Chino to the California Men's Colony in San Luis Obispo. On August 19, 1955, he arrived at San Quentin State Prison. He would remain there for almost five years. Built in 1852 on a rise above San Francisco Bay, San Quentin's barred windows look out to the Berkeley and Oakland hills on one side, Marin County on another, and San Francisco on another. During Bompensiero's stay, the brownstone and brick-walled prison was crowded, but certainly it was not the hellhole it is today. Prisoners were still housed one to a cell. Racial tension was not as high. *Mafiosi*, then as now, were treated with grave respect by guards and prisoners. Kidnapper-rapist Caryl Chessman, during Bompensiero's tenure, was ensconced on death row, typing away at his book, *Cell 2455, Death Row*.

September 29, soon after his arrival at San Quentin, Bompensiero celebrated his 50th birthday. I have wondered what he thought on that day. The woman he loved was dead. For the rest of his life, he would believe that had she not married him, or, had his way of life been different, she could have lived to see her hair turn gray and her grandchildren produce their own children. He was haunted by her voice calling to him on the night that she went into the coma. "Frank, Frank," he heard her cry out. He meant what he said, that he'd gladly give his life to bring back Thelma.

Everything he had built—the three bars, Maestro Music, the Algiers—was lost. The cars were gone, the lots he'd bought in Point Loma were gone, the money stashed in back yards was gone. Mary Ann and Frankie were unprotected. Mary Ann, who'd never worked a day in her life except in her mother's store, what would she do? And his mother? Would his brother Sam watch out for her?

I wonder, if on his 50th birthday, Bompensiero went back over his life, his association with Jack Dragna. I wonder if he regretted that association. I wonder if he regretted doing what he did for Jack. I doubt that he did.

To me, Bompensiero has come to seem a tragic character. I believe that Bompensiero became involved in Milwaukee with the group that hijacked liquor trucks coming down from Canada in an effort to raise money to send back home to Sicily to his sick father and his mother and his five siblings. I further believe that Bompensiero's first killing was accidental, that he fired wildly and out of fear in the midst of confusion. You well might say to me, "Try telling that to the family of the man your young Bompensiero shot." But that is what I believe. I believe that this first killing, outside Milwaukee, was an accident. I also believe that this accident forever altered Bompensiero's life. Because this killing angered "connected people" in Milwaukee, Bompensiero fled to San Diego. Once Bompensiero was in San Diego, Jack Dragna straightened him out with the Milwaukee people. As someone who knew Bompensiero once said to me, "After that, Frank was Jack's." That same person also told me that Bompensiero said that he "loved" Jack Dragna. I think that he did love him in the way that younger men love older, more powerful men. Bompensiero would no more have refused an order given him by Jack Dragna than a Third Army soldier would have refused an order given by George Patton. Bompensiero's fealty to Dragna was as iron strong as was his loyalty to Thelma. Bompensiero never cheated on his wife and he never cheated on Jack Dragna.

I do not think that you can apply Freudian and "pop" post-Freudian psychological templates to Bompensiero and hope to see the world as he saw it. I do not believe that you can understand him by talk of Oedipal conflicts and poor impulse control. Bompensiero was committed to the ideal of the *mafioso* as a gentleman soldier, a patrician man of honor and dignity, a man who commanded an earned respect as well as an earned fear. Men of Bompensiero's era and from his background did not engage in the self-conscious thinking that many of us do. He didn't say, "I feel," he felt. He was carried along by feeling, the way water is carried along by other water. If it "felt right," he did it; if it "felt wrong," he didn't do it.

Bompensiero often told Mary Ann about her Sicilian birthright. "We're not spaghetti benders. We are Sicilian. Don't forget, we always flew our own flag." Bompensiero failed to adjust to America in the way that Protestant, Northern European immigrants adjusted. He was born in America, but bred into his bones was the ironic Sicilian sensibility. I believe that in the quiet of his mind, he thought in the Sicilian-inflected Italian that he spoke with his mother, his sisters, and his in-laws, with Jack Dragna and others who came from Sicily. His daughter believes it likely that her father "thought" in his Sicilian version of Italian.

Like many Sicilians of his generation, Bompensiero, for good reasons, did not trust Church or State. He trusted only family. He entered into American life in ironic ways—he made and sold bootleg whiskey and wine; he held up gamblers; he handed out bribes; he became a bagman for dishonest state employees and these employees' hirelings. He pretended, along with other bar owners of every nationality, that he served food at the Gold Rail. He advertised the Gold Rail in the Yellow Pages as a steak house. He bribed the vice squad. He bribed the priests. Like a confessor who has heard every sin, he understood venality, he expected corruption, no vice surprised him. That was the way of life.

The Greeks speak of the *hamartia*, the tragic flaw. I think that Bompensiero's tragic flaw was precisely that he was Sicilian, that *onore*, for him, was more feeling than abstract idea. I think that *onore*, for Bompensiero, was a feeling stronger than fear, hunger, thirst, or any lustful drive. Bompensiero's passionate love for his family was a feeling stronger than fear, hunger, thirst, or any lustful drive.

You may say that Bompensiero was a cheap hood, a hired killer, no better, really, than any serial killer. I believe that Bompensiero understood himself as a soldier in an army. I believe that he killed in precisely the same way that soldiers kill. He did not kill civilians; he killed other soldiers. He was a healthy soldier, a good soldier, by which I mean that he did not relish killing. I think that for Bompensiero killing was an awful, an odious chore. Frankly, he did not always do it well. He was a clumsy marksman.

This was a man with a third-grade education. I suspect that he could not read easily. I do not know that, but I suspect it. He had no skills, really. He couldn't even shoot straight. He fit himself into circumstances as best he knew how. Often, the fit was awkward. But he fed his family.

I asked a friend of Bompensiero's, a good friend, a man who knew Bompensiero as an older man and knew him well, if Bompensiero ever expressed remorse about the murders. This man snorted. "Frank said that if God hadn't wanted 'em dead, He would've stopped the bullets. That's what Frank said."

What did Bompensiero mean when he said that? Was he indulging his tendency to black humor? I don't think so. I would like to suggest that Bompensiero intended no irony. I would like to suggest that Bompensiero believed that if God didn't want 'em dead, He would've stopped the bullets.

I am not here to judge Bompensiero. We are judged even as we attempt to judge. If your Bompensiero is a thoughtless id-ridden thrill killer, an idle rip-off artist, a vicious extortionist, well, then, we know something about you and rather less than but no more about Bompensiero.

San Diego Union Staff Photos

Suspects in the Tony Mirabile murder are brought to city jail after their arrest in Perris. At left is Victor Buono, escorted by Det. Harry L. Grady. At right Earnest Murray, in light jacket, is escorted by Sgt. J. H. Thompson. Police also arrested a man and a woman in Los Angeles.

Plane Crashes In N.Y.; 58 Feared Dead

(Continued from Page a-1)

ing to the river, a sailor in

4 Suspects Held In Mirabile Killing; Gunman Still Free

(Continued from Page a-1)

sent at the time of the slaying.

1. Los Angeles and San Diego police arrested Mrs

Mrs. Horton, refused to tell a reporter for The San Diego Union in Los Angeles if an identification was made.

But Blucher, here in San

ity of parole and was parolled last Oct. 15, 1958.

Thwaits once was arrested as being the fingerman, the man who put the finger or

Victor Buono (left), from the San Diego Union, Febuary 4, 1959

**Momo then stuck the pistol behind his right ear and pulled the trigger.**

CHAPTER FIFTY

# STILL IN JAIL

"Sometimes," Mary Ann said, "I thought I was really going to go crazy. After my mother's death and the funeral, I was alone in the house on Braeburn Road with a little boy, trying to save the dress shop and deal with incredible money problems. Gino was staying in the house there with me. And the talk that was going on. I was all alone. I had aunts, but they had their families. We went to see my father in Chino because Gino wanted to get married and I wanted to get married too. So, we went to see my dad and my dad said, 'Okay, the best thing for you to do is go get married quietly. Don't make any fuss.' We had to talk through a glass wall. They had phones. My father looked through the glass wall at Gino and said, 'You take good care of my daughter.'

"We'd drive to San Francisco. For a long time we went once a month. It was a long ride. Terrible. My daughter, Santa, was born in 1956, and I'd bring her. We didn't want to bring Frankie. I didn't want him to see the prison. There's a lot I think I've blocked out because I just can't handle it. Or couldn't handle it at the time. Very depressing. Believe me. Sad. I'd be happy to get up there and then, be so depressed when I'd see my dad. That big, gray prison. It was horrible. Cold.

"One of the first times we went, I asked him, 'Daddy, what do you do?' You see movies where they're breaking rocks and everything. I didn't know what the hell was going on in prison at that time. I had no idea other than you're locked up. He said, 'Oh, no, honey, I got a soft job. Nobody bothers me. Don't worry.' People would come in and he gave them their uniform. The uniforms were blue. Have you ever seen the sailors in their denim, their navy blue? That's what he wore.

"He would never be on a down trip. He was always smiling. He didn't want me to see him like that, you know. He really didn't. That was terrible. He did not want me to suffer. 'No problem, I got my cigars. Don't worry, honey. I'll be home soon.' He looked good. I think my dad just made up his mind, 'Here I am and this is what I have to do.' He had his cigars. Somebody—maybe his brother—kept money on the books for him.

"You could stay just an hour or two. That's all. You couldn't stay all day. He'd say, 'Okay, you kids, get going now.' He didn't want us to stay. It was embarrassing. I really, truly think it was embarrassing for him for me to see him like that. I'll bet if my mother had been alive he would have said, 'Don't let Mary Ann come up here to see me.' I bet anything. Because it was embarrassing for him. Humiliating. And from time to time, from what he said to me, I knew that my father's heart was broken for me. My heart was broken for my father. I wasn't locked up. He was. And he always blamed himself. I don't know how many times I said to him, 'Daddy, I don't believe that. You didn't kill her. Mama always told me she was going to die young.'

"He was glad to see us, but he didn't want us to stay long. He'd say, 'Don't come next month, honey.' But then one time he said to me, 'Honey, don't come anymore. Because you know what, I gotta go through this strip search every time I go back.' But we kept going and other people visited him too. But always, all the way home, I'd hold Santa and cry and cry."

Mary Ann's godmother Josephine and Josephine's husband often drove up from Los Angeles to San Francisco to see Bompensiero. "When we went to see him in San Quentin, he looked like he came out of a bandbox. He was immaculately clean. I remember asking him how the food was. He laughed. He said, 'You think I eat their food? I don't eat their food.' He was paying for someone to bring him other food, that's what you get when you got money. They looked the other way. He always was so glad to see you. But all that he wanted to talk about was Thelma. That was all he wanted to talk about, was her, all the time. He would bring up things we used to do. He really loved her. They loved each other. She stuck by him through everything."

Friday morning, February 24, 1956, the banner atop the *Los Angeles Times'* front page read: "Jack Dragna Found Dead in Sunset Blvd. Hotel." Beneath the headline: "Reputed Ruler of Mafia in Los Angeles Apparently Had Heart Attack While Asleep."

Frank Desimone, after Dragna's death, visited Bompensiero in San Quentin. With Dragna dead, Desimone hoped to take over the Los Angeles family. The family, apparently, had decided to elect their new chief in democratic fashion: votes were taken. Desimone returned from his visit to Bompensiero and announced that he had Bompensiero's vote. But I have been told, by an old friend of Bompensiero's, that Desimone did not get the nod from Bompensiero. Desimone soon took over as LA's boss, with Nick Licata as his closest advisor. Bompensiero's old friend Momo Adamo, Dragna's underboss, had hoped to be made the family's head man. But Desimone, somehow, convinced the other family members that Momo was not up to the job. Maybe he told them Momo was weak, that he was old and from the Old World, that he couldn't do anything for them. Maybe he told them Momo was sick. Even Momo's brother Joe went against Momo in the vote. Maybe Momo was sick. After Jack Dragna died, the army that

Bompensiero had joined seemed to Bompensiero to become corrupt, weak, venal. But he could not unjoin.

June 19, 1956, the *San Diego Union* noted, in a headline:

> Ex-Hoodlum Shoots Wife, Kills Himself, Attempted Slaying, Suicide Climax Quarrel In Kensington Park Home

Several people who knew Bompensiero well, including Mary Ann, said that Bompensiero was very fond of Momo Adamo. Mary Ann recalled that from her childhood on, her parents socialized with the Adamos. But she cannot remember now what her father's response was to Adamo's suicide or his almost fatal wounding of Marie.

Bompensiero appeared before the California Adult Authority Board on November 5, 1956. The board ordered that he be denied any parole consideration until he had served three full years in prison. He was not scheduled to appear again before the Parole Board until May, 1958. At approximately the same time Bompensiero's parole was denied, he learned that in August, 1956, Big Bill Bonelli had fled across the Arizona border into Mexico, escaping indictments brought against him in San Diego. Bompensiero also learned, at about this time, that two of the men with whom he was named as conspiring to solicit bribes—SBE employee Charles E. Berry and "business opportunities broker" Al Bennett—were to be let out of prison in early 1957. Given that Bompensiero was no more than a bagman for these two fellows, who, in turn, were bagmen for Bonelli, who was reported living in a "swanky" Mexico City apartment, it all seemed—and was—terribly unfair. Bart Sheela recalled, about this period, that he and another DA's office employee went to San Quentin to visit Bompensiero in an effort to get him to talk about what he knew of the liquor license deals. "He wouldn't talk to us though. He was pleasant and all, but he continued to hang tough. We also went to Los Angeles to see Desimone and tried to get him to talk and he wouldn't either."

"In 1957," said Mary Ann, "I'm still on Braeburn Road. I didn't have any money. I went to my uncle. I was getting $125 a week then from the Gold Rail. My mother had two lots. Augustine took those lots for the legal fees. We lost the car. They auctioned it off for the fine. The county wanted all my mother's jewelry and furs. I said, 'I don't know where they are.' I thought, 'The hell with them, they're not going to get my mother's stuff.'

"I kept trying to figure out how to save the Braeburn Road house. But there were just too many things going against me. Now, my Uncle Sam was in charge of my father's businesses and he was supposed to be helping me.

But, in the end, I felt like my father's brother never did right by my father. 'When the cat's away, the mice sure play,' I said. And that's how it seemed to me. So when we were about to lose the house, I went to my Uncle Sam and asked for $750. 'Honey, where am I gonna get it?' he said. Not, $7500; $750. But we lost that home on Braeburn Road for $750. I went to see my father and asked him what to do. He said, 'What can I do? I'm here.'

"I told my father, 'Uncle Sam is not doing right, you've lost everything.' My father hadn't put any money aside. My Uncle Sam was always sweet to me, but..." Mary Ann paused, before she went on to say, "My uncle became the number-one son because my father was gone in prison, but he did not act like the head of the family. My dad had signed everything over to him. And we were broke."

Mary Ann noted that many books and films about the Mafia emphasize that when a family member goes to prison, the Mafia family takes care of his biological family. But no one—not the Dragnas, not Johnny Rosselli, not Leo Moceri, not Frank La Porte, not Desimone, not the Adamos—offered Mary Ann any help. "What happened to 'the family takes care of the family'? I was not treated well by these people that I knew as 'Uncle Jack,' 'Uncle Jimmy.' And, of course, I didn't know how to contact these people."

In 1957, Mary Ann and Gino had to leave the Braeburn Road house. I talked one day with the people who bought the house. They had seen Bompensiero on television and knew that it had been his house. "He was in prison when we bought the house. All the neighbors," said one of the house's residents, "said they were just another family. Very nice people. Good people. Bompensiero didn't bring his business in the neighborhood. I remember that the neighborhood butcher said to me, about Mr. Bompensiero, that he was such a nice, nice man." The woman paused before she spoke again, "The neighbors told me that Mrs. Bompensiero died of a broken heart."

Mob enforcer Albert Anastasia, on October 25, 1957, while getting a shave and haircut, was murdered. The summary provided in the U.S. government document *Organized Crime: 25 Years After Valachi: Hearings Before the Permanent Subcommittee on Investigations of the Committee on Governmental Affairs* describes the killing this way:

"Albert Anastasia, Cosa Nostra Commission member, and two bodyguards walked into the barbershop of the Park-Sheraton Hotel in Manhattan. Anastasia sat down, loosened his tie, and closed his eyes as the barber covered his face with a hot towel. The bodyguards slipped away. Two other men walked in from the hotel lobby, strode up to Anastasia, and literally blasted him out of the chair. Anastasia's murder was ordered by Vito

Genovese as part of the latter's plan to eliminate his more powerful rivals and claim the long-since-discarded title 'boss of all bosses.'"

Three weeks later 65 underworld bosses from around the United States met at a country estate near Apalachin, New York. This 1957 meeting prompted J. Edgar Hoover to turn his G-men to studying organized crime. Until 1958 the FBI tended to ignore organized crime. With the exception of Captain James E. Hamilton in Los Angeles and Virgil Peterson in Chicago, little track was kept of connected men in most U.S. cities.

The FBI in 1958 began what they called (absurdly, I think) "The Top Hoodlum Program." Under the auspices of this program, the FBI in the spring of 1958 tried to tape conversations held in Balboa Park between Tony Mirabile and his friends. The FBI also began to sort through old files for Bompensiero data. The local office placed Bompensiero's name on its list of San Diego's "Top Ten Hoodlums."

April 21, 1958 Bompensiero again appeared before the California Adult Authority Board at San Quentin prison and again was denied parole. He was ordered to appear next in May, 1959. In the summer of 1958, while Bompensiero began his fourth year in prison, his co-defendants Charles Berry and Al Bennett had returned to their San Diego homes; Bonelli, working in Mexico City as a tax consultant to Americans, was still free. Not only was Bonelli free, in Mexico, but he was living well. Bart Sheela said that during the 1957 Christmas season one of his old law partners and the partner's wife were at a Mexican resort. Sheela and his wife had been there several years earlier and recommended it. "Why, the place," said Sheela, "was like the movies. For New Year's dinner they had all these courses, white wine, red wine, goat, fish, two big orchestras, dancing, two stages that revolved. I had told my partner, 'Man, you got to go there.' They did. He was an early-to-bed guy and he wanted to go home. Because at ten o'clock really nothing was going on at this nightclub, things didn't get moving until about 11:30, but his wife made him stay and they were dancing and sure as hell, they were dancing right next to Bill and Mary Bonelli. Both of them dressed up."

October 14 and 15, 1958, may have been two days when Bompensiero was not that unhappy to be sequestered in his San Quentin cell. The headline on the *San Diego Union* the morning of the 14th read: "Panel Opens San Diego Racket Probe Today," and beneath the headline the *Union* noted, "The Assembly Judiciary Committee's racket subcommittee will open a two-day San Diego County crime investigation at ten this morning in the Hotel San Diego Continental Room."

Those two days not only were the hottest mid-October days on record since 1872—94 degrees downtown at eleven in the morning and 103 degrees in El Cajon—but one of the year's heaviest smog concentrations accompanied the record-breaking heat. The Continental Room was packed, a retired San Diego lawman told me, "with Damon Runyon–type characters and their sharp-suited lawyers." He said that if Bompensiero had not been in prison, he certainly would have been subpoenaed to appear. He paused and then added, laughing, that given that Bompensiero was "locked up, everyone maybe felt more free to bandy old Frank's name about. If he'd been sitting there, I don't know they'd felt as free."

On the hearing's first day, October 14, Captain James E. Hamilton, head of LAPD's intelligence division, told the committee that the Mafia was a "hard-core" crime organization that penetrates into every great center of population, including San Diego.

San Diego County Sheriff's Sgt. Robert S. Newsom was questioned about the relationship between Tony Mirabile and Frank Bompensiero. "Do you recall any instance where one of them asked the other to move back to Italy because there was too much heat on here?"

Mr. Newsom answered, "We received information, I believe in March of 1952, of a meeting that took place in a trap—I mean an establishment known as the Gay Paree, 4th Street, San Diego. Those present were Tony Mirabile—that is, I am relating the information we received. Tony Mirabile, Frank Bompensiero, Charlie Bonisara, Nick Pepitone, who is now dead, Dominic Megale. At this meeting it was alleged that Mirabile was, it was explained to him that he had been a fine member of the community, was well respected, had done his part for his particular group of people, and that inasmuch as the State Crime Commission and the IRS, and a few others, I believe, in the police department, a few of the people who were interested in their activities were becoming too closely interested in them, they thought it would be a good idea if he would go back to Italy.

"On investigation it was found that Mirabile had, a few days later, applied for a passport and purchased a one-way ticket by plane, TWA, I think, to England, and from there across and down to Rome."

The subcommittee chairman then called Mirabile to the stand. He was asked, "Have you ever had any meetings in the Gay Paree with Bompensiero?"

A. No, never.

Q. Have you ever attended any dinners at the Gay Paree?

A. Now, wait a minute. Attend a dinner with who, and where?

Q. Anybody. Have you ever been to dinner at the Gay Paree?

A. No.

Q. And you have never met Bompensiero at the Gay Paree?

A. Now, let me get this. I didn't meet Bompensiero at the Gay Paree? No. I found him, might have. But not to meet over there.

Q. Now, wait. Now I don't understand you, Mr. Mirabile. What did you say?

A. I never made no date to go to the Gay Paree with Bompensiero.

Q. Did you ever talk with Bompensiero at the Gay Paree?

A. No.

Q. Did you ever talk with any of his men at the Gay Paree, men whom you knew were working for Bompensiero?

A. Well, now, let's get this. Work for Bompensiero. I don't know whether I know anyone that he worked for Bompensiero.

Q. Well, I will put it this way, Mr. Mirabile: Did you ever talk to anybody at the Gay Paree that you knew worked for Bompensiero?

A. No. I don't recall that. If I had been talking with someone in the Gay Paree that was work for him I wouldn't know. That I couldn't answer that. But whether they did work or not. I been talk a lot of people at the Gay Paree, but I wouldn't know if they work for Bompensiero, or who was working. But to me it is funny that word that started. See, I was told that what you refer to because I can see how you get that picture because when I went to Italy I got back and they told me that somebody chased me away from San Diego. I was laughing. My brother passed away. My God, am I entitled to go see my brother's body?

Q. By all means, you are.

A. So, who said they chased me out of San Diego. For what reason? For what? That is why I want to answer that, because I was told, and I was surprised, how come they say those words? How did they bring these things up? What was the reason?

Q. Did you ever receive a ticket in the mail for transportation to Italy? Did you ever receive in the mail a ticket to Italy?

A. Well, if I did it might have been from Los Angeles to San Diego, because when I received the telegram the same night I took a plane to go to Italy. There might have been a ticket for airplane ticket to go to Italy on account my brother pass away.

Q. Wasn't this just after you were told, Mr. Mirabile, that you were going to have to leave the San Diego area; that is when you received this ticket?

A. No. Oh, no, God, no. No. Ain't nobody would ever tell me that. There is no reason for it. Why do I have to leave San Diego? Who would be the man?

Q. I don't know. Well, I am asking you if you know that, I don't know. But I am asking you if you were told that you had to get out of San Diego?

A. No. No. No. And no man, you or no Jesus Christ tell me that. What for? I am paying my taxes. No for one is going tell me that.

When Mirabile stood down from the witness chair in the Hotel San Diego's Continental Room that October afternoon, he had 75 days left to live. In the audience that day was Victor F. Buono, an ex–San Diego policeman turned bail bondsman. Buono was the bondsman who'd made bail for Bompensiero when he was first charged with bribery in August, 1954. Buono eventually would be convicted of engineering a robbery in Mirabile's third-floor penthouse apartment overlooking Balboa Park. The robbery, bungled, would end in Mirabile's murder. Mirabile's still-warm body would be found in his bathroom; he was wearing only an undershirt and a bathrobe whose fabric was a leopard-skin print. (The *Tribune* described the robe as "shimmering." ) He was expecting a woman that evening, "a gift," he had been told, from someone in Vegas. A money clip in Mirabile's right trouser pocket—the trousers were tossed in a corner of his bedroom—contained $1597 in bills. No trace was found of the infamous $1000 bill covered with lipstick kisses that Mirabile was reported always to carry with him.

Within days, San Diego police fingered Buono as their most likely suspect. A retired lawman told me, "When we found out Buono was it, we went down to see Charlie Cavesina, one of Mirabile's oldest buddies, at Cavesina's bar. 'Look,' we said, 'Vic Buono is the guy who masterminded the killing of Tony but we don't want you people to kill him, we want to take these people to court. Do not kill him.' Charlie halfway agreed that he wouldn't. And as things turned out, they didn't make a move on Buono. I wouldn't have been surprised though if they had. Buono violated every rule in the book. We were surprised they didn't dust him."

I can't even begin to guess what thoughts crossed through Bompensiero's mind when he heard Mirabile had been murdered. Everyone to whom I posed questions about the nature of the two men's relationship said, in effect, that Bompensiero regarded Mirabile with contempt. That Mirabile paid Jack Dragna to make him a Mafia member was enough to cause Bompensiero to look down on Mirabile. Mirabile's womanizing, his taking advantage of women who worked for him, were traits Bompensiero did not admire. But as Bompensiero, to use his phrase, "took his years" in San Quentin, as he helplessly watched Mary Ann deal with problems caused by his incarceration and her mother's death, Mirabile's Midas touch with money must have rankled him. It must have seemed outrageously unfair to Bompensiero that Mirabile died a rich man while he, Bompensiero, could not even save the family home for his daughter and grandchildren. After Mirabile's death, when everything he owned was added up and his bills were paid, what remained was $504,659.79.

"Marie pushes me aside and walks

into my dad's bedroom,

and says, 'Frank, I know you're there.'"

CHAPTER FIFTY-ONE

# COMING HOME

During the same Christmas season in which Mirabile was murdered, Bompensiero's old nemesis in the race wire business committed suicide.

The *San Diego Union* on December 28, 1958, wrote:

Brophy's Suicide In Parked Car On Christmas Cited

"Leonard Brophy, 52, owner of the Frolics Tavern at 3838 Fifth Ave. shot himself to death Christmas Day as he sat with a friend in a car parked in Linda Vista. The Coroner's Office termed the Brophy death a suicide.

"Both Tony Mirabile and Brophy were subpoenaed and testified last October before the Assembly Judiciary Committee's racket subcommittee investigating crime activities in San Diego.

"In 1950, Brophy was convicted of conspiring to record and receive horse race bets. Dist. Atty. Don Keller said that at the time of his conviction, Brophy had the San Diego race track wire.

"The coroner's office reported that Brophy's suicide may have been linked to despondency over the death of his brother John, of Los Angeles, who died of natural causes a few days earlier."

A retired San Diego policeman guffawed when I mentioned the coroner's office's surmise that Brophy's suicide was caused by his brother's death. "He was in the car with his girlfriend, who had broken up with him. I knew Leonard real well. What happened is that he got a little bit impotent and he blew his brains out."

Files I received from the State of California indicate that Bompensiero was a model prisoner. At no time did he receive any "black marks." He worked in two privileged prison positions—the hospital and the commissary. In May, 1959, the Parole Board let it be known that he would be released in a year's time.

May 14, 1960, the *San Diego Union* noted on page 20:

Bompensiero Ends Prison Stay Monday

"Frank Bompensiero, 54, a former San Diego café owner, will be released Monday from San Quentin Prison. He was convicted on three counts of conspiracy and bribery in connection with efforts of a former Jacumba café owner to get a liquor license. Bompensiero was one of 11 convicted here during liquor license investigations centered around William G. Bonelli, former Southern California member of the State Board of Equalization."

Gino, Mary Ann's second husband, recalled Bompensiero's homecoming. "His brother Sam went up to San Francisco to meet him. They flew back down. We picked him up off the airplane and he came home to our house. He was just in a state where he was just thinking. He was quiet. Just talked a bit and he went to bed."

Mary Ann said that she had difficulty recalling precisely what they did in the first days her father was home. "I'm sure that everybody came over here. Family. We might have gone down to his mother's and sister's. But I don't remember." Her grandmother Bompensiero, Mary Ann said, "had been protected from the fact that her son was in prison. She was just repeatedly told that he was in the trucking business and out of town. They hid it from her. She couldn't read or write English and I don't think they brought newspapers into her house, so she would not have seen the pictures of him in the papers."

Bompensiero was paroled to Mary Ann. She was to be responsible for him. He was not to frequent places dispensing liquor nor could he have a financial interest in such a place. Gino said, "For quite a while after he got out, he was kind of quiet. He was watching his p's and q's. I think he kind of respected parole. For sure, he was watching himself."

"He looked thinner when he got out of prison," Mary Ann said. "I had some of his old suits in the closet. When he had those suits on, he looked especially thin. He looked like a smaller man, like he'd shrunk.

"The first few years he was out of prison was the worst I ever saw my dad dress. Before he went to prison? He was Dapper Dan. But when he came back, he wanted to look like he was poor. So most of the time he looked pretty shabby. 'This way,' he said, 'they don't know what's going on.' He quit wearing suits every day. He'd never worn a sweater and shirt before. But then, he did. Nights, though, if he was going out, he'd dress up. Wear a suit. Like the old days."

Mary Ann said, "People said to me, 'Gee, what are you going to do? Your father can't walk in a bar, he's got to be in by ten o'clock.' I said, 'I don't care. I want my father home. He may not be able to go out but his friends can come here and visit and they can play cards until two o'clock if they want to. I don't care. I want my dad home. I don't care if he has a nine o'clock curfew.'"

Mary Ann remembered that her father had regularly to report to his parole officers. "I remember that it was humiliating to him to tell me he was going to his parole officer. And he had to be in the house at a certain hour.

My uncle got him a little Corvair, off-white. But, at first, he didn't even want to drive much. Charlie Pepitone, in those early days, used to come over and visit with him and take him out and drive him around. He led a pretty quiet life at first. He'd get up in the morning and have his coffee, that's all, not even toast, and then later he went and had lunch.

"When he was first out, he had a girlfriend. She was a really nice woman, a cocktail waitress, just the prettiest, kindest woman. She'd buy my daughter Kate Greenaway dresses and little things, and buy my son things. She was crazy about my dad. She was a cute little petite thing. He liked little women. She was five foot one and had a darling figure. My father wouldn't drink and drive. So when they went out she came by the house and picked him up. She would be all dolled up, a pretty dress and a fox fur.

"My father, to me, was a very fair man. He dated her for many months, steady. She was a very nice lady and she didn't bug him and call all hours of the night. But she said, 'Frank, are you ever going to marry me?' And he said, 'No. I'll never marry you.' So she said, 'I met this man and he wants to marry me and take care of me and I'm not getting any younger.' And he says, 'Marry him. Because I'll never marry you.' That ended that. I think he was worried, because she was considerably younger than he was. And, she didn't know the way of life."

From the first weeks after her father's return from prison, said Mary Ann, Marie was always there, in the background. After Momo Adamo shot Marie and then turned his gun on himself, Marie gradually recovered, although she never regained the use of her right eye. She remained in the Lymer Drive house. In 1959 she met and married her third husband, a retired naval man some years her senior—Patrick Gavin. "Gavin," said Mary Ann, "was a retired attorney and worked for the Navy. He was a short fellow and he had some money.

"Marie had aged, terribly, after Momo shot her. Marie was blind in that one eye. Talk about a cat with nine damn lives. Because she was also in a terrible automobile accident with Gavin, an accident that would have killed anybody else. And she'd always been a drinker. But after Momo shot her, she really began to get into the bottle."

Mary Ann said that while her father was in prison Marie wrote to him. Whether Marie visited him or not, Mary Ann does not know. "What I do know," said Mary Ann, "is that as soon as my dad was out of prison, Marie began to hound him. She was after my father from the day he came out. She was such a flirt, Marie was. She flirted so much with my father. She hounded him. After he got out of prison, she called him here, day and night. And she was living, then, with Gavin. After he came home, Marie was always calling me and asking me what my father was doing.

"So sometime in this period after my father got out of prison Marie left Pat Gavin. She moved out of the Lymer Drive house into an apartment in Pacific Beach. She left Gavin because of my father. Not because my father was seeing her so much but because she wanted to have this freedom to be with my father, to go out with my father, and come home whenever she wanted. So she left Pat Gavin. No divorce. She just left him. So she's seeing my dad. And I think, too, that my dad was real embarrassed about the whole thing. But he didn't know what to do. I don't think my dad was ever a real chaser, chaser, chaser. Maybe when he was a young kid he was out dancing and having a good time. He was not exactly Mr. Cool with women. He was not exactly experienced with women.

"Marie was living in Pacific Beach in her apartment. My phone would ring. My father would be in bed and he'd go, 'It's Marie, tell her I'm not home.' She would call two, three times a night. I said, 'Daddy, the kids have to go to school in the morning, I've got to get up. If you don't want to talk to her, you tell her.' So that went on. He'd tell her, 'I'm tired. I'll talk to you in the morning.' He went to bed pretty early. He'd watch TV.

"So this one time she called late at night and it was obvious that she'd been drinking and I said, 'He's not home, Marie.' She said, right back, 'Oh yes he is. I know he's there.' I said, 'Marie, he's not here,' and hung up. Maybe 20 minutes later the doorbell rings. Scared the hell out of me. I answer the door and Marie walks right by me, pushes me aside and walks down the hallway into my dad's bedroom, and says, 'Frank, I know you're there.' Oh, she was screaming and yelling, just like a banshee. 'What are you doing here, Frank? I thought you were supposed to be not at home.' Then I think he lied and said, 'I just got home.' He calmed her down and whatever and then she went home."

Sam gave his brother a job as manager of Sam's Snack Bar, 2750 Midway Drive. The snack bar was located within the premises of Thrift Co., a discount store in which Sam had an interest. Mary Ann laughed when I asked her about this. She said that because her father was on parole he had to show that he was working. But she remembered the store. "It was inside a big building, like a Fed-Mart or Costco and my father had a booth concession in there. But he didn't work behind any counters."

Mary Ann said, "After my father came home, people came around the house—Leo Moceri, for one. Some picked up my dad, some visited for a while and left. Several of the guys said to me, 'Honey, why didn't you tell me that you all were having trouble?' I was very to the point, I said, 'How could I tell you? You knew where I was. I didn't know how to call you or contact you. Why didn't you contact me and see if I was all right? Why didn't you call me?' I don't know what the hell they said but they had no answer for it. How can they have an answer for it?"

*Jack Linkletter*

**"He would come by every night.**

**He would do steaks on a grill.**

**He'd make a little pasta**

**or he'd make mashed potatoes."**

CHAPTER FIFTY-TWO

# NEW JOBS

Jimmy Fratianno, on July 14, 1960, finished a 6-year sentence for extortion involving a Los Angeles oil company. With his wife Jewel's help, Fratianno began to put together a trucking company with offices in Sacramento. Bompensiero and Fratianno talked occasionally on pay telephones. Both men were disenchanted with the new LA family regime. Fratianno wanted out of the Los Angeles family and during the early 1960s Chicago family head Sam Giancana effected Fratianno's move. Johnny Rosselli, who began his career as a Capone insider, also obtained a transfer from Los Angeles and returned to the Chicago family.

December, 1960, Thrift Co. closed and Bompensiero went to work for Wright Refrigeration, 4025 Pacific Highway, a company in which Gino had an interest. Bompensiero worked as a salesman, selling fixtures for bars and stores. "This too," said Mary Ann, "was just a front, he had to show an income. He didn't really do anything down there."

In January, 1962, Bompensiero worked as assistant sales manager at the San Luis Rey Packing Company in Oceanside. Quite what he "managed," I do not know. I did discover, through FBI files I received through my Freedom of Information Act requests, that during Bompensiero's tenure with San Luis Rey, he and Jack Linkletter, Art Linkletter's son, came into contact.

"Let me tell you the story," Linkletter said. "It's a very convoluted one. I was involved in a company during this time down in San Diego, construction, and we had an insurance arm of the company and one of the accounts of that insurance business were two brothers called the Gallo Brothers—Joe and John Gallo. As I remember Joe Gallo, he was about five ten, overweight, had a roundish face, heavy through jaw to neck, flat black hair, was in his 30s then. The two brothers had a business down in the vegetable market of wholesaling produce. Through that they approached us and said, 'We have a rare opportunity here and we would like to put together a group and we are contacting you because we would be interested if you would put capital in it.' He said the Kawamuras are a Japanese family that owned the property in the San Luis Rey–Oceanside district. He said, 'What we would like to do, we think we could get some big accounts by growing tomatoes on that property. The Gallos would bring the marketing expertise, the Japanese would be the growers, and we know a guy who's a great packer and what have you.' Investigation went on and it did look like a good opportunity. The bottom line is we started growing tomatoes in that Oceanside region and selling them all over the country. The Gallos brought in another guy named Charles Gelardi who either had directly worked for them or they had worked with him somehow, kind've assisting them and one thing led to another and somehow the Gelardis and the Gallos got sideways of each other and there were threats and they were heard publicly threatening each other and I even heard from one of the guys down there in the packing plant that Gelardi was carrying a gun because he was fearful for his life. Next thing I know I get a call from an FBI agent. He introduces himself, says, 'You know a Frank Bompensiero?' And I said, 'No.' He said, 'Well, he's on your payroll.' I said, 'Help me out with this, what do you mean?' He said, 'Well, he was brought in and he's working at San Luis Rey Packing'—that was the company, and this is old memory, so I am kind of jogging it here. He said, 'To give you the feel for this guy, he's the number-one guy on our bad list in the San Diego region. He's been in prison for a long time.' The FBI fellow went on to say that Bompensiero was kind of a hit man for the Mafia group in San Diego, and the Gallos, when Bompensiero got out of prison, hired him as kind of a security guard.

"I said, to the FBI guy, 'Well, what do you want me to do?' And he said, 'I don't want to tell you what to do. We just wanted to know if you knew what he was, who he was,' and I said, 'Is there any problem with my terminating him?' And they said, 'No, I don't think so.' So I said, 'Okay, let me get into this and I'll let you know.' So, I called down there and I said, 'Joe, Joe Gallo, what is going on?' I told him I got this call from the FBI. He told me that Gelardi had threatened him and that he had Bompensiero there for protection and that they were trying to help him out and I said, 'Well, we can't have him on the payroll.' He said, 'Well, he's here.' And I said, 'Well, let me talk to him.' So Bompensiero came on the telephone and he was most polite and I said, 'I don't know you. I got this phone call from the FBI.' I told him what the phone call content was. I said, 'You know, we're public people, and it's not going to take more than a day for some reporter to get ahold of this.' I said, 'You're not in the business and you can't contribute to the business.' I said, 'I'm not taking any personal affront to you or what your background is. What you want to do is your business. I just can't take the association.' Bompensiero said, very politely, 'I understand totally, sir. Don't you worry about it. I'll leave right away.' I said, 'You're a gentleman and I appreciate it.' And that was that."

In 1962, Mary Ann and Gino separated, and Mary Ann took a job. She was no longer at home all day with Frankie and Santa. Her father by this time had an apartment that he was sharing, at least part of the time, with

Marie. "Marie had gone back to Gavin, because Gavin had cancer. She told my dad, 'Pat's dying. I've got to take care of him.' So she moved back to Lymer Drive but they kept the Pacific Beach apartment.

"He used our address," Mary Ann explained, "but he was no longer living with us. Still, he came by every morning for his coffee. Then, he drove to his mother's house to see her and to drink more coffee and to leave her off some money. When afternoon came, he made sure that he was back here when the children got home from school. He'd come by, fix the kids a steak. Hamburgers. Whatever they wanted. He'd sit with them and maybe watch the television while they did their homework, that kind of thing. And he made sure we didn't do without. He'd hand me $200 and say, 'Go get the kids some clothes.' He'd bring groceries—meat, fruit, bread, cereal, coffee.

"When I was divorced the second time and I went to work, my job opened at ten in the morning. Ten until seven, I worked. Then my father really kicked into full gear. He would come by every single night in that Mustang that he banged up. Had more dents in that car. When he was younger, he wouldn't go out unless the car was polished to the hilt and didn't have a scratch on it. But after he got out of prison, I don't think he cared that much. Anyway, he would come by every night, after he was living with Marie, and cook dinner for my kids. He would do steaks on a grill. I have the same frying pan that was my mother's. Cast iron. He used that. He'd make a little pasta or he'd make mashed potatoes. And there would be something left over for me when I got home.

"I was making peanuts. And he saw to it that we didn't do without. Like in September, it would be 'Okay, honey, here's $500, go buy clothes for Santa, whatever you need.' He brought food over all the time. He gave me money. Not a lot of money. A hundred dollars, a hundred and twenty-five. My daughter got $20 a week for doing nothing, because Papa wanted her to have money. And Frankie got $35 or $40 or $50 a week. They're like 12, 13, 14. But that was my dad.

"And he'd say to me, 'You think I can go home and eat a steak and you're going to eat hot dogs?' He always was sure that the kids had whatever they wanted or needed. He gave the kids love and he gave them time. He went to Frankie's Little League games on Saturdays. He took them to dentist appointments and doctor appointments while I was at work. And he kept them on the straight and narrow. He used to tell them the same things he told me when I was young. Like, 'Don't ever steal anything.' He said, 'If you're going to do anything go big, because you get the same name.'"

In 1963, Bompensiero opened a market at 3986 30th Street, a few doors down from his late wife's clothing store at 3912 30th Street. Mary Ann recalled the market as a produce market—"heaps of apples, oranges, lemons, asparagus, tomatoes, all produce. It was just a hole in the wall, a storefront, and I am sure that was a front too, maintained so that he could establish a source of income for the parole officers." The market didn't last long. Later in that same year Campbell Food Products in San Jose hired Bompensiero as their San Diego representative. Mary Ann laughed again. "Another front job, I'm sure."

September, 25, 1963, U.S. Attorney General Robert Kennedy and Senator John L. McClellan's 1961 Senate Permanent Subcommittee Investigation of Gambling and Organized Crime opened hearings in Washington, D.C. Although rumor had it that Bompensiero would be called to testify, he never was.

Joseph Valachi (1904–71), who claimed to be a member of Vito Genovese's crime family, testified to the existence of La Cosa Nostra—translated as "this thing of ours," or, "our thing." Valachi, a fifth-grade dropout, informed the senators and television audience that mobsters called their organization La Cosa Nostra, not the Mafia. The Mafia, said Valachi, was what outsiders called their group. Valachi went on to testify (after 15 months' coaching by subcommittee lawyers) to his initiation into La Cosa Nostra in 1930, to the existence of "families" in major American cities, including Los Angeles and San Diego.

Fascinated Valachi watchers learned the term "*omertà*," La Cosa Nostra's vow of silence. They learned that crime families were organized, that a *capo* ruled with the aid of a *sotto capo*, or, underboss. Each underboss, said Valachi, had a caporegime, or, lieutenant. Each lieutenant manned a regime, or, crew. The crew of workers were the *soldati*. A 12-man commission ruled over the families; the commission settled inter- and intra-family disputes.

Viewers heard Valachi describe his "making," or initiation into La Cosa Nostra in 1930. He told that he and three other initiates were driven to a house 90 miles upstate from Manhattan. Once in the house, Valachi claimed that he was taken into a vast room where 35 men sat at a large table. "There was a gun and a knife on the table. I sat at the edge, they sat me down next to Maranzano [at that time, according to Valachi, Salvatore Maranzano was a family *capo*]. I repeated some words in Sicilian after him."

"What did the words mean?" Senator McClellan asked.

Joe Valachi: You live by the gun and knife and die by the gun and knife.

Valachi was asked to continue to describe the ceremony.

Valachi: Then he—he—he pricks your finger.

Questioner: Who? Who?

Valachi: The godfather.

Questioner: He pricks your finger?

Valachi: He pricks your finger with a needle, makes a little blood come out. In other words, that's to express the blood relation. It's supposed to be like brothers.

Questioner: That's the letting of blood?

Valachi: That's right.

"Valachi," writes Michael J. Zuckerman in *Vengeance Is Mine: Jimmy the Weasel Fratianno Tells How He Brought the Kiss of Death to the Mafia,* "introduced America and the world to a substrata society of names that became indistinguishably mingled like alphabet soup in the Anglo mind. And in their enthusiasm at learning this once-mythic kingdom was real, Americans mistook La Cosa Nostra as a generic concept. Overnight, it seemed, every crook working in concert with another crook was a member of 'the mob.' According to news accounts, every city seemed to have a Family, and the nation was virtually overrun with crime 'soldati' doing the bidding of crime 'bosses.'

"Somewhere, the very special meaning of La Cosa Nostra was lost in translation. Americans had missed the point: La Cosa Nostra is a secret society with fewer than 5,000—recent accounts say as few as 2,500—formally initiated male members of Italian heritage, operating out of twenty-four select cities."

*Desi Arnaz*

*Sam Giancana*

**"We're going to clip Desi Arnaz, the producer of this show."**

CHAPTER FIFTY-THREE

# FRANK AND THE FAMILY

The next sighting of Bompensiero, on paper, comes in *The Last Mafioso: The Treacherous World of Jimmy Fratianno.* Fratianno told Demaris that Johnny Rosselli in 1963 telephoned him in Sacramento and asked him to meet him in Del Mar. Fratianno greeted Rosselli in Del Mar on a Saturday afternoon. Rosselli said that he had a surprise for Fratianno. The surprise was Sam Giancana. The Chicago mob boss explained to Fratianno, "We've got something we might want you to handle. Rosselli will explain it to you." Rosselli slipped into Fratianno's car. Fratianno drove along the coast. Rosselli asked Fratianno, "Have you seen the TV show, *The Untouchables*?" Fratianno said that yes, he had. Rosselli complained, then, that *The Untouchables* shows "a bunch of Italian lunatics running around with machine guns, talking out of the corner of their mouths, slopping up spaghetti like a bunch of fucking pigs. They make Capone and Frank Nitti look like bloodthirsty maniacs. The guys that write that shit don't know the first thing about the way things were in those days."

Rosselli continued. Mae Capone, Al's widow, had brought a million-dollar lawsuit against CBS when they came out with a two-part film on Eliot Ness's book, *The Untouchables*. She lost the suit and then Desilu Productions got ABC to do a series, and "since then," Rosselli concluded, "it's gone from bad to worse."

Fratianno responded, saying, "Nobody pays attention to that shit. It's like a comic book, a joke. Who cares?"

Rosselli, outraged at Fratianno's indifference, said, "I'll tell you, Jimmy. Sam [Giancana] cares, Joe Batters cares, Paul Ricca cares, and I care."

Rosselli went on, then, to tell Fratianno that Chicago's "top guys have voted a hit.... We're going to clip Desi Arnaz, the producer of this show." Further, said Rosselli, he had already talked with Bompensiero and put him in charge of the "action." Bompensiero, said Rosselli, would meet Fratianno at four that afternoon in the Grill at the U.S. Grant. They met and talked. According to Fratianno's account, Bompensiero said that Arnaz, who kept a house on the beach in Del Mar, didn't seem to be around. Plans were laid to bring in men from Chicago to do the actual shooting. Two weeks later, again, according to Fratianno's telling of the story, Bompensiero telephoned him to say that "the boys from out of town got disgusted and went back home so the deal is down the drain." Arnaz, writes Demaris, "never knew how close he came to getting clipped."

Whether Bompensiero and Fratianno ever discussed a hit on Arnaz or not, we will never know. Fratianno was a notorious liar. We can be sure, however, that Fratianno and Bompensiero were talking about Bompensiero's entry into Fratianno's trucking business, and bringing with him into the business, his old friends Leo Moceri and Frank La Porte. According to what Fratianno told Ovid Demaris, in November, 1963, Bompensiero and La Porte visited Fratianno in Sacramento. How and when Bompensiero and La Porte first met, I do not know. Mary Ann recalled meeting him soon after World War II. She recalled, too, that La Porte, his bodyguard, and La Porte's various lady friends frequently visited the Bompensieros during the late 1940s and early 1950s. "They were always spoken of by my dad and mother as 'people in from Chicago,'" said Mary Ann.

*Organized Crime: 25 Years After Valachi: Hearings Before the Permanent Subcommittee on Investigations of the Committee on Governmental Affairs* notes about La Porte that he was born "Francesco Liparota on October 7, 1907, in San Biose, Italy, that he entered the United States in 1913 and was naturalized in 1926." La Porte "frequents South Cook County, Joliet and Calumet City. Spends considerable time in California, Nevada and Arizona. Resides at 1730 Cambridge Ave., Flossmoor. Is prime suspect in at least 2 murders. Booked and held 2 days for murder in 1926. Outside investments include gold and silver mines in Calif., uranium mine in Colo., tungsten mine in Nevada, a gas well in Ariz. and real estate at Lake Geneva.

"Is syndicate overlord in South Cook and Will Counties—territory runs from Calumet City to Kankakee, and from Chicago Heights to Joliet. Operation recently extended to include Lake County, Indiana, where gambling and prostitution is a $50,000-a-day business, and a vice resort in Godley. Also operates in Central America. Controls gambling, vice, narcotics, juice, jukeboxes, extortion, vending and pinball machines, taverns, strip-joints, bail bond business (through F.L. Bail Bond Co. operated by nephew Frank Luzi, who is also his chauffeur-bodyguard), and granting of liquor licenses in his vast domain. FBI indicates that payoffs to Chicago Heights policemen are made from Cooperative Music Co. where officers pick up weekly envelopes. A top-ranking mafioso and member of the Syndicate's board of directors."

According to *The Last Mafioso* Fratianno, needing funds to expand his trucking business, was anxious to interest La Porte in being his silent partner. As the three men sat outdoors, warming themselves next to the barbecue pit, Fratianno explained his business to La Porte:

"All my drivers are union guys. If they're not Teamsters, I put them in there. But I don't pay the union a nickel. When the business agents get after me, I say I'm paying to headquarters. I never pay the pension, etc. All I pay is Workman's Comp. I've got twelve trucks and am working 40, 50 trucks on five percent commission."

John F. Kennedy was assassinated on November 22, 1963. I asked Mary Ann if she remembered her father's response to the assassination. "What I remember is that we all sat and watched the television all weekend. I do remember, about politics, that when Pat Brown ran for anything, my dad always told us, 'Vote for Pat Brown, he's a good guy.'"

April 7, 1964, Jimmy Fratianno was released from parole. He began to come and go more freely from Sacramento. Bompensiero saw him often, in San Diego, Los Angeles, Reno, and Vegas. Demaris's use of Fratianno's accounts of his meetings with Bompensiero are interesting for the background Fratianno provides about Bompensiero's unhappiness with the LA family's new regime.

"Fratianno...got wind of a possibility of getting involved with the Tallyho, in Vegas, built in 1958.... Jimmy first heard about the deal from Bompensiero. Eddie Nealis, an L.A. gambler, had sought Bompensiero's assistance when Pete Milano, son of Tony Milano, associated with the LA family, tried to muscle in.

"Here's the setup," Bompensiero told Jimmy. "Eddie's promoting this thing and he's raising big bucks. He's got two hundred grand from Shirley MacLaine and her husband. He got another bundle from a banker in Iowa. He's got this contractor building the casino and showrooms. There's this doctor who's got a pretty big chunk of money in the joint and Pete Milano's trying to take over his end for the LA family. Eddie got scared and came to me to straighten it out. I said I'd come to you. We straighten it out we get in on the ground floor." Bompensiero added, "I've got to be careful with Desimone and Licata. I'm still in the family. They know I'm with you and I hear things. I still got friends in that outfit who tell me things. All they need is some little excuse to clip me. They know I've got friends in Detroit and that's kept them away. But I don't trust them for a minute."

Fratianno cajoled Bompensiero, "What's wrong with you? These guys couldn't clip a flea. Rosselli tells me Desimone's scared of his shadow. Never goes out nights. The guy's gone bananas."

"Nick's the guy to watch," Bompensiero answered. "Rosselli," Bompensiero added, "is a flunky." The latter was an opinion that Fratianno, who was known to gaze with near worship at Rosselli, did not share.

*FBI surveillance photo of Jimmy Fratianno (left) and Frank Bompensiero, c. 1976*

**Bompensiero continued to demand that he be transferred into the Chicago family.**

CHAPTER FIFTY-FOUR

# THE FBI FOLLOWS HIM

Soon after I became interested in Bompensiero I applied through the Freedom of Information Act for his FBI files. After several years' correspondence, these files began to arrive. I had, finally, over 1000 pages of these redacted files. I had heard tales from biographers about FBI files. Clerks sat with file copies and blacked out informants' names. Clerks blacked out addresses. Clerks decided that interviews held with informants would be "withheld entirely." I had heard that by the time these files arrived in the hands of someone like me that almost nothing was left to read. I was not prepared, however, for the pages I received. Black marks ran through line after line. Notations offered: "Nine (9) pages withheld entirely at this location in file." "4 pages withheld entirely at this location in file."

For the first five years after Bompensiero left prison, I have no FBI files. Whether the San Diego office lost interest in him or whether the files were withheld, I will never know. My guess is that because Bompensiero's parole was due to end May 16, 1965, that the FBI wished to keep an eye on him. April 15, 1965, the San Diego office produced a memo.

> Federal Bureau of Investigation
> Investigative Period: 4/15/65
> Title of Case: Frank Bompensiero
> Character of Case: Anti-Racketeering
> Reporting Office: San Diego

"Bompensiero released from San Quentin Prison in May, 1960. Returned to San Diego, California, to reside with daughter. Bompensiero on parole until May, 1965. Subsequent information developed that Bompensiero is member of San Diego family of La Cosa Nostra. Close association with other known members noted."

A memo written on March 30, 1965 offered this:

> "(**************) advised that since 1961 Bompensiero has held part-time jobs with various produce companies in the San Diego area and at the present time he is listed as employed by (**************) at the Bam Produce company, 702 K Street.

> "It was further advised that there is no automobile known to be registered to Frank Bompensiero, but that he frequently uses a 1960 Chevrolet Corvair, California License KRX 142, which is registered to (**************)."

April 22, 1965, a memo from the San Diego FBI office noted:

> Frank Bompensiero Anti-racketeering

"A review of this file reveals subject was reportedly the lieutenant and 'heir apparent' to (**************) [perhaps Tony Mirabile?] prior to subject's convictions for conspiracy to commit a crime and asking or receiving a bribe from a public official in 1955. The subject's file was closed in 1958 while subject was incarcerated for the above crime and had been refused parole."

On April 28, 1965, the local FBI office sent to "Director, FBI," via "Special Delivery Airmail—Registered," a request to install a MISUR (microphone surveillance) in Bompensiero's apartment at 3838 Haines Street. The San Diego agent gave as his reason for the request:

> "Because of Bompensiero's importance in the La Cosa Nostra in San Diego, the report that he resorted to a 'Mafia' type extortion of (**************) and indications that he is attempting to regain his position of leadership among the Italian hoodlum element in San Diego, it is believed that the requested MISUR is essential to the Cosa Nostra activities in this area."

Her father, said Mary Ann, knew the FBI followed him. How did he respond to their surveillance? "He laughed that laugh of his is how he responded. He used to say, 'I am safer than I have ever been in my life. I have the cops behind me, the FBI behind me, one following the other.' But he also thought it was a big waste of taxpayers' money."

Law enforcement personnel who work organized crime often come in for criticism. The most biting I heard was this, from a local retired policeman. "The thing you have to understand about people who work organized crime is that they're fanatical about it. They would literally do anything or say anything to catch an organized-crime crook, it was like a disease with them. They want to base thousands of hours of surveillance—collecting gossip, rumor, innuendo—on the bogeyman around the corner, Mr. Organized Crime, coming to steal the city away.

"People who work organized crime intelligence have the softest job in law enforcement. They have money to spend, they can do anything they want to do to get their end accomplished, they have almost no supervision. You can't hold them accountable because you have no idea what they're doing because everything is a big secret. By and large, they are an untrustworthy lot. The way that they retain their job security is to keep their bosses paranoid at all times. They say, 'Mr. Organized Crime is coming to town to steal the city.' So the boss says, 'Gee, I don't want that to happen, so here's some more money, some more cars, some more radios, do whatever you got to do but don't let that happen.' And the intelligence guy nods, says, 'Okay, boss, I'll take care of that.'"

This same person told me that San Diego city and county law enforcement personnel tended to find the "federal boys" a "real pain in the ass." He said that G-men stationed in San Diego were always coming around to the police in various cities in the county and to sheriff's operatives and wanting information. "But they didn't want to give any information back. It was all take, take, take with the Feds. They wanted what you knew and if they got a chance, they'd take the credit for what you did, but they wouldn't give back. If you traded information with an FBI guy, you almost always came out the loser."

May 16, 1965, Bompensiero was released from parole. He celebrated with a trip to Los Angeles with Marie, where they met Frank La Porte and a woman friend. Bompensiero checked into the Beverly Wilshire Hotel. I asked Mary Ann why her father chose the Beverly Wilshire. She laughed. "Probably because they would comp him. He was comped everywhere he went."

The FBI was right behind Bompensiero that day.

> "1. Note that when Bompensiero stayed at the Beverly Wilshire Hotel on 5/25–5/26/65, he made a telephone call to (**************)
>
> "2. Note that after subject stayed at Beverly Wilshire Hotel, a note was found in the room reading, 'From The Beverly—Meet you Wood Hotel, 5:00 p.m. tomorrow.'"

May 25, 1965, J. Edgar Hoover's office gave the San Diego FBI office permission to install "MISUR coverage" in Bompensiero's apartment for a 90-day period. Memos were prepared for the attorney general's office, requesting authority for installation.

The memo from Hoover to the attorney general's office noted:

> "Bompensiero is a long-time member of La Cosa Nostra. During the time Bompensiero was in prison, (**************) promi-

nent San Diego hoodlum, became the reported leader of the La Cosa Nostra in San Diego. Indications are that Bompensiero is attempting to regain his position of leadership in the La Cosa Nostra from (**************). His activities are expected to increase greatly, inasmuch as his probation ended May 17, 1965. Early this year he was allegedly involved in an extortion of $5,000 to $10,000 from (**************) in San Diego.

"Investigation at San Diego reveals Bompensiero conducts a considerable amount of his racket affairs at his residence.

"Coverage of this apartment should provide excellent information concerning the subject's hoodlum activities, his associates and meetings, which could not be obtained from other sources. The proposed installation will involve trespass. There is no prosecutable violation against subject in existence and this microphone should provide information which will aid in development of live informants and sources who can be used to develop a prosecutable case separate and apart from the microphone.

"Bompensiero is presently attempting to regain his position of leadership in the La Cosa Nostra at San Diego which he lost while in prison. Increased activities on his part are expected inasmuch as his probation ended on May 17, 1965. In addition, he was recently contacted by (**************) prominent Chicago hoodlum [probably Frank La Porte], with respect to gambling activities in Las Vegas, Nevada. Bompensiero is regularly in contact with other La Cosa Nostra members from other parts of California.

"Authority is requested to install a microphone surveillance in the residence of Bompensiero, Apartment 2, 3838 Haines Street, San Diego, California, where he conducts most of his racket affairs. Coverage there should provide excellent information concerning his associates, activities and plans which could not be obtained from any other sources. Trespass will be involved in making this installation.

Respectfully,
John Edgar Hoover
Director"

Subsequent FBI memos noted:
"June 10, 1965, subject purchased from University Motors, San

Diego, a 1965 dark gray-blue Mustang, which now bears permanent California license RDJ 155. He registered this car in the name of (**************) and apparently gave it to her as she has been observed driving it on numerous occasions. [Mary Ann explained that this was a car that her father bought for Marie.]

"June 18, 1965, subject returned to San Diego from a trip to Sacramento, California, driving a new 1965 Pontiac Grand Prix. This car has a dark gray-blue body with a black vinyl top. It had temporary California dealer's license number 0470444, which is from the Mike Salta Pontiac Company in Sacramento, California. Later a permanent California license was assigned to this vehicle and is NSC 059. [Fratianno leased this car for Bompensiero.]

"June 23, 1965, Bompensiero was given a traffic ticket in San Diego while driving the Mustang and gave his employment at that time as the Thomas Trucking Company, Sacramento, California."

San Diego FBI agents, according to their memos, didn't find it easy to install the surveillance equipment in Bompensiero's apartment. Marie, with whom Bompensiero by this time was living, was often home. "Considerable difficulty," an agent typed, "was encountered to install as subject lives there with Marie Adamo Gavin. A long period of surveillance was necessary to insure that both subject and Marie Adamo Gavin were out of the apartment before the installation could be made. It was finally completed successfully on 7/1/65."

> The memo continued: "Upon installation the results were immediate and positive. It was determined Bompensiero was in close contact with (**************) [Fratianno] (LCN member living in the Sacramento area), (**************) [Angelo Marino] (LCN member living in the San Jose, California, area) and other fringe hoodlums and gamblers in the Las Vegas area. Investigation at San Diego and at Sacramento determined that Bompensiero, (**************) [and Fratianno] were actually in close business contact and among other things under the Fratianno Trucking Company were operating a fleet of large and expensive diesel trucks out of Sacramento."

Demaris writes in *The Last Mafioso*, "Jimmy put Bompensiero on the payroll at $150 per week and provided him with a leased automobile. One of his jobs was to ride up and down the highways to make sure the drivers kept moving at top speed. But mostly he was there as a companion for La Porte whenever he was in California and as a sounding board for Jimmy."

July 1, 1965, a memo to Hoover from the San Diego office noted:

> "On 7/1/65 surveillance of Bompensiero revealed that at 9:02 a.m. he contacted the occupant of (**************) at the (**************). After a brief conference, the three then proceeded in Bompensiero's personal car to the Club Marina, 1310 Scott Street, San Diego. Upon leaving the Club Marina, three individuals proceeded to Los Angeles, California.
>
> "Physical surveillance of Bompensiero was conducted by the San Diego and Los Angeles offices on 7/1/65. Bompensiero and (**************) and (**************) drove to Huntington Park, California. They all entered a restaurant and cocktail lounge called the Tami Ami Café, 6400 South Santa Fe, Huntington Park, California. A few moments later, Bompensiero and an unknown male strolled out of the restaurant and left the area.
>
> "The three, returned to the Islander Hotel at about 6:00 pm, 7/1/65. The three had dinner at Tarantino's Restaurant where they were joined by a fourth individual who was not identified.
>
> "July 3, 1965, Bompensiero was heard in conversation with (**************) [Fratianno] on the topic of growing potatoes. Also on this log, (**************) [Fratianno] mentions that his wife is going to file for divorce. [Jewel Fratianno subsequently did file for divorce, but for a long time the couple continued to live together when Fratianno—a flagrant womanizer—was in Sacramento.]"

A memo prepared later in the first week of July explains where Bompensiero went on July 1 after he "strolled out" of the Tami Ami Café.

> "On the early morning of 7/4/65 Bompensiero talked about taking a recent trip to Los Angeles to meet with members of the LCN. He wanted to take (**************) with him, but was refused permission. In Los Angeles he was driven by a circuitous route toward San Bernardino and then back towards Cucamonga, where he was taken to a winery. There he met several individuals, including (**************). [Charles Dippolito and his son Joe owned a vineyard in Cucamonga.] He claimed he asked for a 'transfer,' but was refused the transfer until he 'did a job.'"

Bompensiero, in this visit to the Cucamonga vineyard, may well have met with LA family head Frank Desimone. Bompensiero continued to rail against the post-Dragna LA group and continued to demand that he be transferred into the Chicago family. Why Desimone simply didn't tell Bompensiero to go, we will never know.

July 12, 1965, the FBI's DC office, by telephone, instructed the San Diego office to discontinue the MISUR coverage in Bompensiero's home. The Bureau instructed the San Diego FBI office to leave the microphone installed but to cease listening. No reason is ever given for this.

> "September 16, 1965, a surveillance of subject Bompensiero was conducted. He was observed to park a car behind the Tropics Bar in downtown San Diego and later leaving the bar with (***************). They proceeded north on U.S. 101 toward Los Angeles in (***************) car, a 1964 white Pontiac convertible, California license (***************) but turned off at a small coastal town 30 miles north of San Diego at Solano Beach. They entered the Surf and Saddle Bar and Restaurant but left about ten minutes later and returned to San Diego taking evasive tactics."

After Patrick Gavin died, then-58-year-old Marie sold the Lymer Drive house. Bompensiero and Marie rented Apartment 4 in a four-unit apartment house at 1830 Reed Street. They moved into the apartment late in September, 1965, not long after Bompensiero celebrated his 60th birthday. The FBI memo noted:

> "Subject Frank Bompensiero now residing 1830 Reed Street, San Diego, California. Subject gives no indication of employment and in frequent contact with (***************).
>
> "Subject and (************) checked into Beverly Wilshire Hotel, Beverly Hills, California, on 10/18/65, and checked out between 7:15 and 7:30 a.m. on 10/19/65. Bompensiero was observed returning to San Diego by himself driving his 1965 Pontiac Grand Prix, gray with black vinyl top, California license NSC 059, at 1:30 p.m. on October 19, 1965. Upon arrival back in San Diego he went to his daughter's home, and thereafter about 6:00 p.m., October 19, 1965, returned to his apartment residence occupied by (***************).
>
> "Spot surveillances conducted on subject Bompensiero during this period indicated frequent contact with (***************).

On several occasions Bompensiero was observed leaving his home in the morning and going directly to the Tropics Bar, downtown San Diego, which is owned and operated by (***************). On several other occasions he has been seen to drive to and enter the La Mesa Bowl on the outskirts of San Diego, a $2,500,000 bowling alley-nightclub-restaurant.

"11/16/65, when (***************) was visiting Bompensiero in this apartment, portions of their conversation was heard in the (***************) by sas (***************) and (***************). It sounded as if (***************) had come to San Diego to discuss some kind of a business deal with Bompensiero and (***************) talked about shipping lard into Mexico and paying off some Mexican senator. It is not known if (***************) was talking about anything he himself was connected with.

"It is entirely possible that (***************) might have been telling Bompensiero about this lard operation on the part of the Chicago group without actually being involved in it in any way.

"In addition to this information overheard, (*************) and Bompensiero could be heard at times talking about general problems involved in their trucking operations. From their remarks, it appeared that (***************) might also have some interest in their operations.

"It was verified on November 15, 1965, through records at the airport in San Diego, that (***************) arrived on a United Airlines flight from Sacramento to San Diego, and had made a one-way ticket purchase.

"The Los Angeles Division was alerted on November 16, 1965 and (***************) [Fratianno] and Bompensiero were surveilled into the Los Angeles Division. They traveled in Bompensiero's car. They were observed arriving at about 3:45 p.m. on November 16, 1965, at the temporary quarters of the Hess Mace Trucking Company located on Alameda Street between the freeway off ramp and the freeway in Los Angeles. This area was being utilized as a temporary office space and storage for numerous pieces of earth-moving equipment, tractors and earth-hauling trailers. After the arrival of (***************) [Fratianno] and Bompensiero, numerous individuals left the trailer office, and vehicles remaining were identified as a 1960 Ford station wagon, California license (************) a 1963 Oldsmobile, California license

(★★★★★★★★★★★★★★★★★) and a Ford panel truck, license (★★★★★★★★★★★★★★).

"Later on the evening of November 16, 1965, (★★★★★★★★★★★★★★) [Fratianno] and Bompensiero were observed at the Villa Capri Restaurant in Hollywood."

December 6, 1965, Bompensiero flew to Mexico City. I asked Mary Ann if she remembered this trip. She laughed. "No. Mexico? No. I don't remember my dad going to Mexico."

Demaris's *The Last Mafioso* provides insight into this trip. Fratianno took Bompensiero to San Francisco to meet Joseph L. Alioto, then a wealthy San Francisco antitrust lawyer, who in 1967 would be elected San Francisco's mayor. The Aliotos, Balistrieris, and Bompensieros all had come from Porticello. Many of the Aliotos and Balistrieris went directly from Sicily to Milwaukee at the same time that Bompensiero's parents immigrated to that northern city. John Alioto, a distant relative of the future San Francisco mayor, became head man of Milwaukee's mob in 1952. Alioto was succeeded by his son-in-law, Frank Balistrieri, in 1961. According to Fratianno's accounting to Demaris of the meeting between Alioto and Bompensiero, there was much talk of family the two men had in common, something Bompensiero enjoyed. But Fratianno's description of Bompensiero's conversation—"fuckin' this" and "fuckin' that" rings false. Everyone with whom I have talked has emphasized how mannerly Bompensiero was. I cannot imagine the 60-year-old Don Frank Bompensiero, dressed in his best, seated in Alioto's elegant high-rise San Francisco office, spouting "fucks."

I do think that Fratianno's explanation of Bompensiero's trip to Mexico is largely accurate. "Bompensiero and me," said Fratianno, "had a scam of our own going. Rudy Papale, you know, is Alioto's brother-in-law. Bompensiero took him to Mexico City a while back to try to work out a lard deal for Baja California. See, Bompensiero knows this Sammy Ybarra who's the head of a big hotel chain in Mexico. Somehow or other years ago Bompensiero saved this guy's kid from getting killed in Tijuana and they became friends. Alioto was interested in that lard deal so Papale went to Mexico with Bompensiero. They paid all expenses, but Sammy Ybarra couldn't work it out."

The San Diego FBI office ended 1965 with this report:

Federal Bureau of Investigation
San Diego, California
December 16, 1965

Re: Frank Bompensiero, aka Frank Gavin

Frank Bompensiero, FBI Number 337240, has been involved for many years in the San Diego area in bookmaking, gambling, illegal union activities, extortion, and has been a prime suspect in three unsolved murders.

He is described as follows:
Sex: Male
Race: White
Nationality: American
Date of Birth: September 29, 1905
Place of Birth: Milwaukee, Wisconsin
Height: 5 feet, 6 inches
Weight: 160 pounds
Build: Medium
Hair: Brown—graying, bald on top
Eyes: Brown
Complexion: Medium-dark, round face, wide mouth
Appearance: Italian

"This subject has been a member of the La Cosa Nostra (LCN) for many years and at one time was leader of the San Diego family. He was widely feared for his strong-arm methods and has close contacts with hoodlums of Italian ancestry throughout California. He has also had close contacts with the gambling element in Southern California over the years.

"Since the end of his parole, Bompensiero has openly resumed contact with members of the Italian hoodlum element. He has been observed in contact with (**************) hoodlum leaders in Los Angeles. Investigation has also verified that he is in frequent contact with (**************) [Johnny Rosselli] of Beverly Hills, California, the LCN leader from Chicago who for several years has been operating out of Beverly Hills and Hollywood with numerous trips on LCN business to Las Vegas, Nevada.

"The subject is a cousin and close contact of (**************) who is emerging as one of the leaders of the Hoodlum society in the San Jose–San Francisco areas.

"In San Diego, he has been closely associated with (**************) hoodlum leader in the Detroit area.

"During the summer of 1965, the subject was observed traveling

> and in frequent telephone and personal contact with (★★★★★★★★★★★★★★★) [Frank La Porte], hoodlum leader in South Chicago, and with (★★★★★★★★★★★★★★★) [Fratianno] convicted extortionist, now residing in Sacramento, California.
>
> "His contacts with (★★★★★★★★★★★★★★★) [Frank La Porte] have been in California while (★★★★★★★★★★★★★★★) [La Porte] was vacationing here. (★★★★★★★★★★★★★★★) [La Porte] is very wealthy and is developing numerous financial investments in California and possibly Nevada.
>
> "During the past six months, investigation has indicated that Bompensiero has business interests in the Fratianno Trucking Company and Fratianno has been observed with subject in Southern California on numerous occasions.
>
> "Since the end of his parole in May, 1965, Bompensiero has remained residing in the San Diego area where he is living with Marie Adamo.
>
> "He drives a 1965 automobile and puts up a big front; however, informants report that he is broke most of the time. In view of his background, his very active associations with the hoodlum criminal element in Southern California, and his possible lack of money, it is indicated Bompensiero will now be making efforts to set something up.
>
> "The subject is a known braggart and at times exhibits possession of large amounts of pocket money and at other times his activities indicate he is broke. As a result of this, it is extremely difficult to assess his true financial condition or his true position in established hoodlum activities."

Mary Ann, when I read her this, said, "My dad used to say, 'If you have a dollar in your pocket or a thousand dollars, it doesn't matter. You don't cry the blues. You never say, "I can't afford to do this" or "can't afford to do that." You gotta be proud. Nobody has to know what you've got in your pocket.' That's what my dad told me."

**When Mary Ann opened her wide front door, I hope that my mouth did not fall open. I was shocked.**

CHAPTER FIFTY-FIVE

# FINALLY A BREAKTHROUGH

*The Last Mafioso: The Treacherous World of Jimmy Fratianno* portrays Bompensiero as an almost comic figure, a foul-mouthed Falstaffian cigar-puffing ruffian, a fat-bellied gunman whose every other word is "fuck." Jay Robert Nash in his *World Encyclopedia of Organized Crime* begins his entry on Bompensiero with this: "Bompensiero, Frank (aka: Bomp), 1905–77, U.S. A shifty, backstabbing character." Carl Sifakis, following Nash's and Demaris's leads, in *The Mafia Encyclopedia* writes: "In the treacherous world of Mafia hit men, few characters proved shiftier than Frank 'Bomp' Bompensiero.... For decades regarded as one of the most efficient hit men in the West Coast mob.... For double-dealing, Bompensiero was without peer."

In an elegiac mode, then–*San Diego Evening Tribune* columnist Neil Morgan turned Bompensiero into a Disneyesque troll whom he called Bompy. Morgan wrote the day after Bompensiero died:

> "Vignette: One night in 1955 at a restaurant here a bottle of champagne arrived at my table with a note: 'No hard feelings.' Across the room I saw Frank Bompensiero with his family. It was a farewell dinner on the night before he began a five-year prison term for bribery in a liquor license case. I'd broken the story in this column, tracing the origin of a license issued first to a non-address in a San Diego cemetery and then to Bompensiero at a Third Avenue bar with reputed Mafia connections. I sent the champagne away but went by his table to thank 'Bompy' and wish him well. It was the last time I saw him until we were alone in an elevator at 8 o'clock one morning last week in a medical building at 2850 Sixth Avenue. He quickly put out his hand with his old bright smile: 'I'm just an old man now, Mister Neil,' he said. 'No harm. No trouble. Just an old man.' They tell us we are free of organized crime in San Diego. Last night, on the sidewalk near his apartment in a quiet part of Pacific Beach, police found Bompy's body in a pool of blood."

Many aspects of what I read about the mob trouble me. What troubles me most is that the books' principal figures appear to have scant life outside thuggery. They may dazzle women, bet on horses, evade the FBI, but they remain one-dimensional. Reading about mob figures, you would think that all they did was plot the next union takeover, the next bribing of a judge, the next mob battle, and stir up a pot of spaghetti sauce when they went to the mattresses. These men inhabited lives as lavish with mundane detail as do any of us. They had "meaningful" relationships apart from their criminal connections. But you will read little about this.

Yet, try to learn about a mobster's family life! Even years after a husband or brother or grandfather has died, widows and sisters and grandsons greet one's gaze with terror—or, rage—when one mentions the late family member. The elderly sister of a San Diego "crime" name, after a lengthy interview embroidered with intimate detail, claimed that she could not tell me her maiden name. "It's confidential," she whispered, "confidential."

Ten years ago, when I became interested in Bompensiero, I telephoned Mary Ann and asked if I might interview her. She began to cry. She said that even though her father had been dead, by then, for more than a decade, that just the thought of him—gunned down in an alley in Pacific Beach—caused her to weep. She said, kindly, in the midst of throaty sobs, "No, honey, I just can't talk about my dad. I'm sorry."

I didn't feel good about that telephone call.

I went on to other things. Yet I always came back to Bompensiero. I would sit on my living room carpet and sort newspaper clippings. I gazed at photographs of Bompensiero sitting outside the Los Angeles federal courtroom, waiting to testify before the Kefauver Committee. He wore a dark gray suit, white shirt, and dark tie with white polka dots. The face that gazed back at me out of that photograph seemed almost sweet, and the mouth ready, any moment, to smile. I wondered what he thought that day. I wondered if he were rehearsing his testimony or deciding where he'd eat dinner in Los Angeles before driving back to San Diego. I walked many times into the lobby of the U.S. Grant and tried to imagine Bompensiero strolling across the polished floors. His bar, the Gold Rail, had been just across the street from the Grant. I walked—many times—past the block where the Gold Rail had been and tried to imagine that block before the buildings were torn down and the Westgate built. I found houses where he'd lived and sat outside them. I went many times to lunch at Tarantino's, where Bompensiero ate almost daily during the last ten years of his life. I sat at the table reputed to be his, a table in the bar area that offered a view out onto the bay. I went to Mass in the church where his sisters were married, his wife eulogized, his mother remembered. I visited San Quentin. I went on several February nights and stood where he stood when they killed him. I went to Holy Cross Mausoleum where he and his first wife are interred. The last time I went, I left flowers. More precisely, I left Parma violets—the strongly scented purple flowers wrapped in a white paper cone and tied with a purple ribbon.

On my computer I skimmed files of transcripts of taped interviews I conducted with retired lawmen and lawyers and judges and elderly Sicilians who knew Bompensiero. I began this so long ago that many people with whom I talked have died or suffered heart attacks or crippling strokes. I reread letters I had written to retired lawmen and elderly Sicilians, asking for interviews. Most of the letters were not answered. Several people did answer; they said no. In unpleasant fits of temper I had balled up those responses and tossed them out.

I read and reread trial transcripts. I studied hundreds of pages involved with probating Mary Ann's mother's estate. I ran my finger down lists of the inventory of the dress shop her mother owned when she died in 1955. I imagined what Mary Ann must have gone through—her mother dead, her father in prison—as she tried to save her mother's shop and the family home.

Every time a new Mafia book arrived in bookstores, I flipped to the back and looked for Bompensiero's name in the index. The rare times that the name appeared, all I found in the text was this fat-bellied, loud-mouthed caricature, this Bomp. He was always employing the old Italian rope trick, he was always gunning down Hooky Rothman and missing Mickey Cohen, he was always smoking his "big cigar," he was always saying "fuck."

He did smoke big cigars. A San Diego lawyer recalled, "Bompensiero smoked those big Berings, big round things about seven inches long. Like the Bering Immensas that you see now. Hell, maybe they were Bering Immensas that he smoked. Cigar store there on the corner of Third and Broadway, on the northwest corner, just three doors down from where his Gold Rail had been, sold them in the old days. He gave me a Bering at the racetrack one time. Back then, those things cost maybe 50 cents apiece, maybe a dollar. At the time you could get Santa Fe's for a nickel, a dime. He loved a cigar, though, he sure did."

After the day I called Mary Ann, I let five years go by. I decided, then, that I'd try one more time. I found Mary Ann's address. I wrote to her. I explained that I wanted to write something about her father that would not be all Mafia, Mafia, Mafia. I wrote that I had read books where her father appeared; I complained that I found "not one redeeming word anywhere." I wrote that I wanted to write the redeeming words. I begged Mary Ann to give me the opportunity to speak with her. "Please, please, please," I said, and dropped the letter into a mailbox.

Weeks passed, maybe two weeks, maybe three. Mary Ann called. Much had happened since the day we briefly talked. Her husband had died. She had retired from the job she held for two decades. She felt able to at least try to talk about her father. We agreed that I would come to her house.

I don't know what Mary Ann felt on the morning I was to arrive. I felt blessed. When a writer finds herself deeply interested in a story subject, that subject becomes like a lover. I'd been in love from afar. At last I was going to walk into the presence of someone who at least knew and loved the lover. I brought only my tape recorder and blank tapes and a notebook. The questions were all in my head. All I had was questions.

When Mary Ann opened her wide front door, I hope that my mouth did not fall open. I was shocked. Beneath beautifully kept blond hair Bompensiero's face greeted me; the face was a feminine, softened version, but nevertheless, his face. Later, Mary Ann would tell me that indeed she did look so much like her father that relatives often called her Little Frankie.

Our first meeting took place in the midst of a late summer heat wave. At nine in the morning the air already felt hot. Mary Ann wore a beige silk camp shirt and beige silk Bermuda-length shorts. She had a young woman's figure and a young woman's legs and a young woman's smooth hands. She drew me into the cool, airy house where she's lived since 1957, the house where her father came when he got out of San Quentin in 1960. The ample bedroom where he had slept in those days was being occupied, Mary Ann said, by a granddaughter who was attending college nearby. She showed me through the rooms. She pointed out family photographs. She indicated a lovely sofa that had been her mother's. Mary Ann poured coffee. We sat down at the round kitchen table where her father sat early in the morning and drank his coffee—"Lots of cream," she said. "He liked lots of cream. Every morning before he went anywhere else, he visited his mother. She always poured lots of cream into his coffee."

Mary Ann and I talked for many days. We looked at family photographs. Mary Ann said that she never knew much about her father's business life. "We never did. I remember that he used to say to my mother, 'What you don't know, honey, they'—he must have meant the police—'can't ask you.' That was how it was all his life. When my daughter Santa was still a young girl, after my dad got out of San Quentin, a little friend of hers asked her, 'What does your grandfather do?' Santa said, 'We never ask Papa what he's doing or where he goes. We don't ask Papa any questions like that.'"

An only child, Mary Ann had been protected, even cosseted, by her parents. The family's social life revolved around Mary Ann's family's families. The only "connected" people with whom Mary Ann's mother and Mary Ann were brought into contact were upper-echelon people—the Dragnas, Adamos, Frank La Porte, Leo Moceri, Johnny Rosselli, Frank Coppola, and other men and their wives from Kansas City and Chicago and Cleveland and Detroit whose names Mary Ann no longer remembered. When Mary Ann was a youngster, the Dragnas—Jack and his brother Tom and their wives and children—were almost as close as blood family. Mary Ann recalled only once meeting the Licatas, at a horse ranch that she believed they owned. She recalled meeting Frank Desimone on several occasions and recalled, too, that from girlhood on, she had not liked him. She frowned when I broached his name.

Mary Ann mentioned that "people from Chicago and Detroit and Cleveland, when their sons or daughters got married, often sent them out here to California for a honeymoon. My dad would entertain them. We'd have dinners at Tops or in the Mississippi Room at Imig Manor or later, for the time my father owned it, at the Algiers."

Mary Ann didn't always know her father's friends by the name that appeared on police blotters and in FBI files and newspapers. One afternoon as we sat in the shade by Mary Ann's pool, we talked and idly flipped through a stack of papers I'd brought. "There's Uncle Jimmy," Mary Ann said, pointing to the photograph of a man with large lips. "No," I said, "that's Leo Moceri, 'Leo the Lip' they called him because of his big lips."

Mary Ann knew that, she said. But, as a youngster, she was taught to call Leo Moceri "Uncle Jimmy" and Mrs. Moceri "Aunt Sally." Sally's name in fact was Marie. She was a tiny, gorgeous woman, said Mary Ann. She'd been a dancer. Perhaps a ballet dancer. Then Mary Ann laughed, as she would many times, and added, "Maybe she was a chorus girl. Who knows?"

*Tijuana, circa 1946, Three-fingered Frank, Frank La Porte, Diva, Mickey La Porte, Thelma Bompensiero, Mary Ann Bompensiero, Al (Frank La Porte's bodyguard), Frank Bompensiero*

**Every life Fratianno touched,**

**he dirtied.**

# CHAPTER FIFTY-SIX

# WHY DID FRANK GET MIXED UP WITH JIMMY?

Moceri was a member of the Sicilian and Jewish Cleveland underworld. In the early 1930s, he became aligned with Detroit bootleggers from the old Detroit Purple Gang who were attempting to gain control of Toledo, Ohio, illegal liquor sales. Moceri teamed up with a Detroit group that included Yonnie Licavoli, a dropout from a Christian Brothers college (Yonnie had been headed for the priesthood). In the midst of the gang war for control of Toledo, Licavoli and Moceri and eight of their companions shot and killed bootlegger/beer baron Jackie Kennedy, Kennedy's girlfriend, and three other men. Licavoli, together with four other gangsters, was sentenced to life in prison. Moceri escaped and went on the lam. He spent much of his time in California, and much of the time he spent in California, he spent in San Diego, jawboning with his old friend Bompensiero. Quite how the two men met, we will never know. Probably, they met through Dragna. Moceri and Bompensiero in 1937 did the messy Les Brunemann killing together. Moceri was old school, born, like Bompensiero, at the turn of the century. He was what younger *mafiosi* might call an "old mustache" : he believed in the old ways. He was one of the few men with whom Bompensiero did "underworld" business who was invited into Bompensiero's home.

Michael J. Zuckerman writes in *Vengeance Is Mine: Jimmy the Weasel Fratianno Tells How He Brought the Kiss of Death to the Mafia*: "Moceri wasn't merely a colorful Cleveland native. The man was a national legend. He had been suspected of murders committed throughout Ohio and on both coasts without ever being convicted. Most important, he was respected in every American mob stronghold."

Given what a small world the underworld is, or, was, Jimmy Fratianno, when he went to the Ohio State Penitentiary in 1938, came under the protective arm of Moceri's old friend Yonnie Licavoli. When Fratianno came out to California in 1946, it was in part through Licavoli's recommendation that Johnny Rosselli suggested Fratianno to Dragna as an LA family member. And because Fratianno became an LA family member, he met Bompensiero.

Every life Fratianno touched, he dirtied. Fratianno was a spoiler. He was as treacherous a friend as he was an enemy. I've never understood why Bompensiero in his later years permitted himself to become involved with Fratianno. But he did. Fratianno wasn't Sicilian. He was born near Naples,

Italy, in 1913. He was one of the non-Sicilian men "made" in the years after World War II, when the passage of years and underworld battles had obliged leaders like Dragna to initiate first- and even second-generation Neapolitans. Fratianno died in 1993, after suffering with Alzheimer's. When you think of all that Fratianno might have remembered, that disease's forgetfulness can only have been God's mercy. Mary Ann says, about Fratianno, "He had the reputation that he would kill his own mother, Fratianno did."

At some point in 1965, 60-year-old Bompensiero, finished with his five years' parole, got entangled in Fratianno's trucking business. Fratianno's wife Jewel, a pure platinum blonde but not a dumb blonde, oversaw the business out of the Fratiannos' Sacramento home. Under Jewel Fratianno's stewardship, this business ran on the up-and-up. Unlike the myriad Fratianno scams, the trucking business, for its first five years, dependably made money.

Fratianno obtained a contract in El Centro, where the state was building a 4.7-mile bypass for Interstate 8. The bypass was to run from Imperial Avenue to State Highway 111. Demaris explains this contract in *The Last Mafioso*. "It began routinely enough. Another trucking broker, Fred ReCupido, asked Jimmy to join him as a sub-hauler for Miles and Sons, the prime contractor, in the moving of two and a half million tons of earth for the construction of a freeway bypass in El Centro.... Jimmy put Bompensiero on the payroll at $150 per week and provided him with a leased automobile. One of his jobs was to ride up and down the highways to make sure the drivers kept moving at top speed. But mostly he was there as a companion for La Porte whenever he was in California and as a sounding board for Jimmy."

A retired policeman who knew Bompensiero and Fratianno once said to me, "Fratianno didn't have the class Bompensiero had. Bompensiero was a nice person. Fratianno wasn't."

A retired FBI agent who knew Fratianno in person and Bompensiero by reputation told me, "I think Frank and Jimmy were very close. They were both old school. They were real hustlers. I suspect they spent a lot of time talking about how to hustle a buck. Frank was not a womanizer. Jimmy was. Frank enjoyed his pasta and that was about all. I believe that in his early days Frank did participate in several killings with Jimmy. I do believe that. I think that Frank, later in life, had somewhat mellowed, but Jimmy respected him in the sense of Frank's being a fearful figure. I don't think Jimmy would have gone out of his way to cross Frank. And you have to remember that Jimmy was cautious but not particularly scared of anyone. I seem to vaguely remember that Frank always kept a bankroll in the house. He would have been one of those few people that Jimmy wouldn't take it away from. Jimmy always spoke of

Frank with great affection. But he spoke of him only in passing, because while Jimmy loved to tell stories, Jimmy liked most to talk about himself."

Mary Ann and I tried to figure why her father got mixed up in Fratianno's company. I had a theory about why Fratianno wanted Bompensiero's help. To fulfill the El Centro contract, Fratianno needed more trucks; to obtain more trucks he needed more money. Through Bompensiero, Fratianno was able to insinuate himself into the wealthy Frank La Porte's pockets. La Porte, for $304,000, purchased trucks to put into the El Centro job.

Why did Bompensiero wish to involve himself with Fratianno's trucking business in the hot, isolated little farming community of El Centro, population in those days, about 24,000? Why was he willing, week after week, to make that 120-mile drive along winding U.S. Highway 80 between San Diego and El Centro, a drive that could take as long as three hours? When I told Mary Ann how much Fratianno paid her father, she said, "Well, it wasn't just for the money, then." She added, "He did have to show income, so that may have been part of it. But also, my father wasn't the retiring type that would sit at home and take little fishing trips with Marie! No way in hell! Maybe he just wanted something at that point to do that got him out of the house. He couldn't stand to just sit around."

Her father, Mary Ann said, was aware that the FBI and local police kept an eye on him. He and other "underworld" figures also knew that law enforcement personnel lingered at the edges of family weddings and funerals, taking names and jotting down license plate numbers. Many avoided these occasions, for just that reason.

In the 1960s the San Diego office of the FBI was at 3211 Fifth Avenue, not far from Balboa Park and Mister A's. How many agents were stationed in San Diego and what their assignments were, I do not know. El Centro had two resident FBI agents during this period. But, apparently, they were not agents working what J. Edgar Hoover, in 1958, had dubbed the Top Hoodlum Program, as the memos I acquired through the Freedom of Information Act all originate from the San Diego office. At least two San Diego FBI SA's—special agents—took a particular interest in San Diego's "top hoodlums." These agents, I believe, were the men who wrote and filed surveillance reports of which I have copies.

On January 25, 1966, two FBI agents took a room at the Padre Trail Inn, in El Centro, next door to the rooms occupied by Fratianno and Bompensiero. Two locked doors separated Fratianno's room and the agents' room. The door to the agents' room was unlocked, and therefore some conversation in Fratianno's room could be heard through the remaining locked door.

The agents apparently stood with ears pressed against this locked door.

On the night of January 26, 1966, the agents heard Fratianno make a call in his room to Frank La Porte. Fratianno gave La Porte detailed advice regarding the purchase of earth-hauling equipment. He also asked if La Porte could come up with some more "scratch" to buy additional equipment. Fratianno, the agents reported, also seemed to be laughing along with La Porte, about Bompensiero, saying that "Bompensiero is worried about his loot." Fratianno added that Bompensiero had been promised an income of $150 per trailer, which was not being paid. Fratianno, the FBI memo noted, "then laughed long and loud."

On the morning of January 27, 1966, agents kept Bompensiero under surveillance. "He was observed driving to the Padre Trail Inn, where he contacted Fratianno for an hour and a half in Fratianno's motel room. During this period of time, Fratianno, who appeared to be supervising his earth-moving subcontract work, was seen in contact with someone driving a 1955 Ford station wagon, California license (★★★★★★★★★) which was determined registered to (★★★★★★★★★) Lakewood, California, and with someone driving a 1965 Chevrolet, California license (★★★★★★★) which car is registered to the Deer Leasing Company, 1616 I Street, Sacramento, California."

The memo continued:

> "At 8:55 am on the morning of January 27, 1966, Bompensiero joined Fratianno in his motel room, where they talked for 45 minutes. Fratianno was in the bathroom shaving and getting dressed, and only portions of conversation could be overheard. Fratianno referred to La Porte having $300,000 invested in tractors, trailers, and apparently other earth-moving equipment. Fratianno believes that La Porte will lose money on such an investment, and repeatedly made the remark that La Porte would get hurt. He seemed to blame (★★★★★★★★★) for talking (★★★★★★★★★) into purchasing all this equipment. Fratianno believed it would be wiser to sell much of this equipment now while they have the opportunity, working on some type of large construction jobs coming up in the near future.
>
> "During this conversation, Bompensiero mentioned to Fratianno that he was going to fly to San Francisco for the weekend of 1/29–30/66, and that he expected to return to San Diego on 1/30/66. He talked about meeting (★★★★★★★★★) and that (★★★★★★★★★) had an important meeting coming up over the weekend with some union people. In this connection, Bompensiero was heard to remark that they have known him for 35 years, and he has never gone back on his word.

"Later in the conversation, Bompensiero indicated to Fratianno that one reason he was going to San Francisco was to contact someone there who now has a lot of money and is connected with television and owns a 'string of TV...' He told Fratianno this person had been in prison with him.

"Bompensiero was to fly to San Francisco via Pacific Southwest Airlines Flight 111 on 1/28/66. Bompensiero [and Marie] flew under the alias Gavin."

— United Press International Telephoto

James Fratianno, once named as West Coast executioner for the Mafia, lights cigarette following his arrest at Los Angeles airport.

# Truck Fraud Case Figure Arrested

## Fratianno Seized At L.A. International Airport; Returned To El Centro, Jailed

By BOB WEAVER
San Diego Union Staff Writer

EL CENTRO — James (Jimmy the Weasel) Fratianno, a man once named as West Coast executioner for the Mafia, was

He said he was en route to El Centro to surrender to the charges.

Fratianno, manager of the

*From the San Diego Union, August 18, 1966*

**Fratianno could be heard on the telephone, complaining that the temperature in El Centro had been 120 degrees.**

CHAPTER FIFTY-SEVEN

# THE TRUCKING DEAL

After Marie Adamo Gavin's husband Patrick Gavin died, Bompensiero sometimes used Gavin's last name. He also on occasion told strangers that he was a retired military man. Telephoning friends or leaving messages for them, he might say, "This is the Colonel."

The FBI was waiting when Bompensiero and Marie arrived at the San Francisco airport. Angelo Marino, owner and founder of the California Cheese Company, accompanied by his wife, Precious, for whom Marino named his brand of ricotta cheese, met the Bompensieros at the airport. The four then drove to the Marinos' residence in San Jose, left off Precious (from whom Marino, later that year, would be divorced) and Marie, and then drove to Paolo's Restaurant in San Jose.

After leaving the restaurant, Bompensiero and Marino, the FBI report noted, "drove to the Continental TV Company, 3585 Stevens Creek Boulevard, Santa Clara, California. They remained at this location for approximately one hour. After leaving the Continental TV Company, they traveled to the Rocky Roost Lodging House at 145 North 13th Street in San Jose, where they were greeted by the management. Bompensiero brought in his suitcase and apparently planned to stay at that location. The surveillance was then discontinued."

I sometimes telephoned Mary Ann and read her sections of these FBI reports. We puzzled over blacked-out sections, wondering to whom the FBI referred and what, for instance, her father did at the Continental TV Company. The mention of the Rocky Roost Lodging House left Mary Ann laughing. We tried to imagine what sort of place it was and why her father had chosen to stay there.

Bompensiero was back home on Reed Avenue by February 7. The FBI continued its surveillance. On the evening of February 11, Frank La Porte showed up. For two days agents watched the apartment. And then, according to an FBI memo:

> "On the morning of February 13, 1966, La Porte and Bompensiero, while under surveillance, drove to nearby La Jolla, where they met with the following described person:

Race: White
Sex: Male
Nationality: American
Height: to 5 feet, 9 inches
Weight: 155 to 160
Hair: Black and wavy
Complexion: Medium
Age: Approximately 35 to 40

"This individual was driving a 1966 Lincoln Continental, black vinyl top with grayish-bronze-colored, metallic-painted bottom. The car had temporary California license (★★★★★) and from the license bracket it appeared to have been purchased through the Star Motor Company in Glendale, California.

"Bompensiero and La Porte joined this unknown person in his Lincoln Continental, and they drove around La Jolla for 45 minutes and then parked outside a beauty parlor operated by (★★★★★★★★★).

"This was on Sunday morning, and all establishments were closed; however, the unknown person had a key to the beauty parlor. He apparently conferred in the beauty parlor with La Porte and Bompensiero for about an hour. Upon leaving, the unknown person drove away in his Lincoln Continental and was lost in traffic. La Porte and Bompensiero continued driving around La Jolla, apparently sight seeing."

This beauty parlor in fact was a two-chair barbershop, owned by Harry Bianconi. A gentleman who owned a nearby gas station often went into the shop to pass the time. He recalled meeting Bompensiero there shortly after Bompensiero got out of prison in 1960. Harry Bianconi, previous to his shop in La Jolla, had barbered in shops all over town. "The U.S. Grant, the old El Cortez. They kicked him out of the old El Cortez because he talked too much. He was quite a talker," my informant remembered. He added that Bianconi was "one of those guys who would have liked to have been a *mafioso*, I think. These guys were a role model to him. Harry once told me that when he got out of the Army, that that's how he knew La Porte. He went to work for him in Chicago dealing cards."

Soon after Bompensiero came out of prison, he began visiting the barbershop. "Bompensiero," the gas station owner recalled, "was a very pleasant guy. He was a gentleman. Always dressed up nice and neat. Necktie. Clean-shaven. Always perfumed up a little bit. He was pretty dapper. He was smooth-skinned, red-faced. Thin up on top. He was very trim too. I understand that he used to be quite heavy but when he came out of prison, he was nice and trim and in good shape. He stayed that way. Very neat with his appearance and his fingernails buffed and the big cigar. He liked to smoke that big cigar. He never talked about any of his goings on at all. He would talk a bit about sports. The weather.

"Once in a while these fellows, they'd come in from Chicago and Detroit. One guy who came in was La Porte, and another was 'Leo the Lip' Moceri. Harry would be pretty excited. He'd say to me, 'You want to meet these guys?' Harry was taken in with all this stuff. It was a big thing with him."

Had Bompensiero and La Porte driven around downtown San Diego rather than La Jolla that afternoon, they would have noticed that changes were beginning to take place. In 1966 buildings on the square block bounded by Broadway and C, Second and Third Avenues, where Bompensiero's bars had been, were slated to be torn down. Harvey's Eat Shop, which first opened for business in 1914, was going out of business. The 37-year-old Heika Furs, on Third, where Bompensiero had bought gifts for Thelma, planned a new store at 1134 Seventh. Harold Clark talked of shifting his Saratoga Bar & Grill into the spot across the street from the U.S. Grant that had once been the home of Johnny Woo's Magic Shop. The little Greek grocery would set up shop in a new location. Varsity Clothiers was moving. The owner of the Black & Gold Room, where for many years you could place a bet with Boots DeKyser, thought he might open a go-go club at another site. Tommy Sheng, owner of Sheng Haw Low's, where judges and lawyers liked to eat lunch, for months held out against the wrecking ball. Finally, Tommy Sheng would give in.

Supplanting these establishments would be C. Arnholt Smith's Westgate California Corporation's $10 million high-rise hotel. "Smith," the *Union* reported, "president and board chairman of Westgate-California and the bank, said the structure will be named Westgate Plaza Hotel and will tie into city plans for converting Second Avenue into a mall-like development extending from the Community Concourse toward San Diego Bay. John S. Alessio, a Westgate director and longtime friend of Smith's, will develop Westgate management for the hotel, Smith said. Alessio interests own and operate the Kona Kai Club, Kona Inn, Fifth Avenue Financial Centre and Mister A's restaurant." Smith told the *Union* that the hotel would be "primarily for the executive trade," with "rooms that will feature baths of marble."

On February 18, 1966, the FBI observed in front of Bompensiero's apartment a white Oldsmobile Toronado, Ohio license P2892A. An agent noted that in the car was "clothing on hangers."

"Well," said Mary Ann, when I read her the February 18 report, "that must be Uncle Jimmy—Leo Moceri. He was from Ohio." Mary Ann told me a story, then, that her father once told her about Moceri. "Off and on, after my father got out of prison and was on parole, he would talk about Leo. 'Leo the Lip got arrested,' he said. 'The dumb son-of-a-bitch, he's so goddamn cheap. Guess why they got him? He's using the same telephone booth day after day, and he's so goddamn cheap he's putting slugs in.' So the telephone company put a detective on the booth, Leo makes a phone call, they go in and check, and they arrest him. So when they arrest him for this, they fingerprint him and they get all this other stuff. And that's how he went to jail again for a lousy few bucks. He had a thousand dollars on him, stuffed down in his pockets."

Surveilling agents noted that Moceri, beginning February 18, "was in constant contact with Bompensiero. Moceri went to El Centro with Bompensiero and remained there with him in his apartment, and appeared to be taking an interest in the trucking operations being supervised by Bompensiero."

During March, Moceri and his wife were seen going out with Bompensiero and Marie. They visited "the Black Widow Nightclub in San Diego managed by (★★★★★★★★★★)" and "on March 14, 1966, they were observed going to the Club Marina, 1310 Scott Street." During Moceri's stay in San Diego, "Bompensiero indicated to (★★★★★★★★★★) that Moceri was interested in moving to Southern California and investing in this area. Moceri offered (★★★★★★★★★★) $50,000 for the Coast Amusement Company, but his offer was refused as not being nearly enough."

April 1, a Friday, the report noted that Bompensiero and Moceri "were surveilled from El Centro, California, to Bompensiero's residence in San Diego. While under surveillance they were observed driving to the San Diego Testing Laboratory."

Bompensiero, Fratianno, La Porte, and Moceri had invested in a gold mine located in Mexico. The FBI reported, "At the San Diego Testing Laboratory they left off several samples of ore to be tested for gold and silver content. It was determined that the ore they left was practically worthless and the best sample assayed out to 3.65 worth of gold and silver content per ton, which according to laboratory testing people is practically worthless."

Bompensiero, by April, had moved into apartment 26A at the Jay L. Jay Apartments, El Centro, leased by the Fratianno Trucking Company. A woman who grew up in El Centro recalled the apartments and said, laughing, that they were "dumps, real dumps." Also using the apartment, in addition to Fratianno, was Nick Diacogianis, an ex-con whom Fratianno had met when he was incarcerated at Folsom. Diacogianis served as gofer. He picked up freight tickets, gathered parts, checked to see that drivers arrived at work on time.

Fratianno, by early 1966, had broken up with Jewel, and was involved with Jean Bodul, the woman whom, years later, he would marry. Bompensiero continued, every week, to drive on Monday mornings to El Centro, spend the week there, and drive back to San Diego on Friday afternoons.

Mary Ann, as we studied this period of her father's life, remained mystified by what tasks connected with the trucking company her father might have performed. He was, she said, a terrible driver, always scraping his cars. He knew nothing about car maintenance and "nothing," she said, "about running a trucking business."

FBI agents persevered in eavesdropping. Transcripts show myriad telephone calls in which Fratianno and Bompensiero complained to various unknown callers about how badly the trucking business was going. La Porte had been promised a 5 percent return on his $304,000. That was not being paid. On April 6, 1966, the FBI memo noted that "At 8:43 p.m. Fratianno was heard speaking with an unknown male and was heard to say, '304,000 in cold cash. This is my personal friend. I'm responsible to Frank but he's responsible for the $304,000. That's where Frank is stuck. He's stuck on the five percent.'"

April 4, 1966, Leo Moceri and his wife, the FBI surveillance report noted, stood outside Bompensiero's Pacific Beach apartment and "were seen loading all of their clothes into his car and saying goodbye to Bompensiero. They were observed by surveilling agents leaving San Diego and several hours later were observed leaving California heading east into Arizona on U.S. Highway 80."

Easter fell, in 1966, on April 10. Bompensiero returned from El Centro to San Diego for the weekend. I asked Mary Ann what the family did in those days on Easter. She said, "We would have had dinner in the afternoon. I would have baked a ham. That's not the Italian way, I know. But, by then, that's how I was doing things. And my father liked ham."

Easter Monday, Bompensiero drove back to El Centro. Demaris writes, in *The Last Mafioso,* "After moving equipment to El Centro, at a cost of $10,000, [Fratianno] discovered that Miles and Sons was not paying the PUC [Public Utilities Commission] rate of $14 an hour for truck and driver. Instead, ReCupido had agreed to haul dirt for twenty-four cents a ton. The drivers received 30 percent of the gross earned, and to meet state and federal regulations requiring an hourly rate, the amount earned was then converted into hours. A truck and driver working ten hours would end up receiving pay for seven or eight hours. The first month on the job, Jimmy's company lost close to $15,000."

FBI listeners reported:

> "A great deal of talk about trucking matters. Fratianno was heard to say to Bompensiero, 'Cheech, he's been going around me. From the bottom of my heart, if it hadn't been for me the Fratianno Trucks would not be working here—you know that.' Bompensiero and Fratianno were heard to mention 'precious metals.' Also, 'Bar or river bed in Northern California—$1000 a ton. Trucks can't get in there.'
>
> "Bompensiero was heard to say, '3000 pounds a day. I want something for the wife.... A little plant and a dump truck. I could make $75 to $100 a day. It would probably cost $10 a day for labor and a truck. Less than that in Mexico.... One of those Portland generators that work on gravity. You pick it up and it just washes away. Need plenty of water.'"

I asked Mary Ann about Fratianno's use of the name "Cheech" to address her father. "Cheech," she explained, "is a way in Italian, or the Sicilian version of Italian, to say Frank. And," Mary Ann added, "if you call someone 'Cheecheriado,' that's a particular term of endearment. When I was little, because I looked so much like my father, my aunt Annie, my mother's sister, used to call me 'my little Cheecheriada,' which meant 'my little Frankie.'"

The FBI memo continued, mentioning more talk about trucking operations. Late in the evening, agents heard Bompensiero on the telephone. "We got trucks breaking down. Some OL trucks [Orange Line Trucking Company of Huntington Beach, California, operated by Fred ReCupido] and some of yours. How should I know? I'm not a truck man. We need more trucks.... Starts tomorrow at the Desert Inn."

The listening agent hypothesized that Bompensiero referred to the Tournament of Champions Golf Match, to be played the next weekend in Vegas.

I asked Mary Ann if her father showed interest in golf. Mary Ann guffawed. She could not imagine that her father had any interest in golf. "He would never play golf. All the doctors told him, 'Frank, you got to get some exercise.' And he said, to us, talking to us with that big cigar in his mouth, 'All those doctors, they drop dead on the golf course of a heart attack.' And then he would laugh like hell. He'd say, 'Daughter of mine, I am going to live to be 105. Me and J.C., we talk all the time.' But golf? My father was not interested in golf."

Easter week, according to conversation overheard by FBI agents, was hellish for Fratianno's trucking business. Bompensiero is quoted as saying, on the telephone, "Everything goes to the shop. They don't fix anything themselves. I don't know how they make a business pay. But that's going to change because my buddy from Chicago Frank La Porte is flying down Monday." Bompensiero added that he was "running with a bunch of lunatics." But La Porte, he said, "will straighten this thing out."

At 5:40 a.m., Monday, the agents overheard Bompensiero in the apartment, talking with Diacogianis. Bompensiero, irritated with Fratianno, "exclaimed in agitated tones" that Fratianno wanted to take La Porte to Reno, "but La Porte wants to come here and see me. Fratianno wants to keep La Porte away from the trucks because he doesn't want La Porte to see them. La Porte hasn't seen the trucks since he bought them in Chino. Why should Fratianno want to go to Reno? The last time he was in Reno it cost him $10,000. I told Fratianno he better be down here on Monday or Tuesday. But he said he was trying to get a job in Reno."

The FBI listener observed that "Bompensiero then used obscene terms in regard to Fratianno and 'that Prince of Wales'"—perhaps a reference to Johnny Rosselli—and that Bompensiero, "again in obscene terms," accused Fratianno of "trying to trick La Porte."

Bompensiero was home on Friday, April 15. Agents watched. Saturday, they followed him to the Mission Valley Inn Hotel, where he joined La Porte and La Porte's nephew-bodyguard in the cocktail lounge. La Porte was "traveling with a blonde female, approximately thirty-eight, and a white male approximately forty-five, of Italian appearance. Monday, April 18, Bompensiero drove them all to El Centro where they checked into the TraveLodge Motel."

Agents overheard talk about gold and trucking. Bompensiero is reported as saying to La Porte, apparently about their gold mine efforts, "It's a long-range investment, Frank. Some months you will make money, other months you may go in the hole. It's like Jimmy Fratianno over there. If you're in legitimate business, it's hard to make good money."

After several days at the TraveLodge, "spending," the FBI agents noted, "the day around the swimming pool," La Porte, his "blonde female," and his bodyguard, on April 24, "traveled via Bonanza Airlines from El Centro to San Diego where they checked into rooms 200 and 221 at the Mission Valley Inn. They were picked up at the San Diego airport by Bompensiero."

On the afternoon of April 25, Bompensiero was back in El Centro. He chatted on the telephone about trucking operations. He made reservations, under Gavin, for "two doubles and a single at the Sands Hotel in Las Vegas for the coming weekend of April 30 to May 1, 1966." Later, Bompensiero called Vegas again, making reservations for *Hello, Dolly*. Bompensiero then dialed the person for whom he had made reservations, saying, "Be sure you thank (**********) for the tickets."

Mary Ann said that during this period when she and her girlfriends wanted to go to Vegas, her father made arrangements for them. "I got comped many times. I was always comped at the Sands and then, later, at the Dunes. My dad rarely went to Vegas. I don't think he was allowed at Vegas." The *Hello, Dolly* tickets, she said, "weren't for me. Sinatra, that was my thing in those days. Frankie. That's who I went to see."

Bart Sheela remembered that about this time Bompensiero came to see him. Sheela was no longer working in the DA's office and had opened his own practice. "Bompensiero said, 'I need some help. The FBI is putting pressure on me to talk to them.' He asked me to go with him and I did. I think he paid me 50 bucks. I went with him up to Fifth Avenue, at the corner of Fifth and Spruce where the FBI office used to be. I said, 'Look, he doesn't know anything, he doesn't want to talk to you about anything.' And then we left and he thanked me and that was that."

The FBI, in its April report on Bompensiero, wrote of that visit:

> "Subject interviewed 4/30/66 at San Diego and made statements concerning his present employment. Admitted money in Co-op Trucking put up by Frank La Porte of Chicago. Subject hopes to receive 20% interest in Co-op Trucking upon completion of payments to Chicago bank on purchase of trucks. Subject accompanied by his attorney and questions put to him limited mostly to his present activities."

Bompensiero on Monday, May 2, returned to El Centro. Tuesday afternoon, about noon, driving the Pontiac Grand Prix, Bompensiero left El Centro, drove to Palm Springs, and picked up Fratianno. They drove to Los Angeles and thence back to El Centro, arriving at 12:35 a.m. A woman knocked on their door, and asked for her money. The FBI report noted, "She told them they owed her $1.50 an hour for five hours (apparently for cleaning their apartment). They asked her to get them a rollaway bed. Woman departed 1:18 a.m. and the apartment remained quiet until 5:40 a.m. At 6:21 a.m. Bompensiero and Fratianno left in the Pontiac."

From the FBI surveillance report, it appears that Bompensiero spent much of this day in company with Nick Diacogianis, Fratianno, and a girl named Sandy. Sandy, riding with "a guy who owns the Cal-Neva," had come to El Centro to visit Fratianno. At 9:18 a.m., Bompensiero and Fratianno and Sandy arrived back in the Jay L. Jay Apartments. At some point Diacogianis arrived. Fratianno took and placed telephone calls. While Fratianno was on the phone, Bompensiero chatted with Sandy, who began to tell Bompensiero her problems. Fratianno finished his calls and joined the conversation. He suggested to Sandy, "You get your girlfriend. We'll need girls around to take care of things." Bompensiero suggested, then, that they have a spaghetti dinner that evening.

"Fratianno and Bompensiero," the FBI report stated, "then made numerous inferences to sex and made a lot of laughter and giggling. Bompensiero talked of Mexican girls hustling for $5.00. Fratianno was heard to say that he is against girls hustling but sees nothing wrong with girls making a little extra money on the side. Fratianno stated that he has a girl in Sacramento whom he 'sees' but she is not a prostitute. Bompensiero stated love has nothing to do with it and the two most important things are 'number one money and number two sex and that if a girl can make money on the side and her husband will never know, unless she tells him, she can run the house and pay the bills, etc., and that lots of girls do it.'"

All through the day, the telephone rang. Bompensiero and Fratianno gassed with various people about truck tires and trucking equipment. Fratianno telephoned his wife Jewel. People came and went. Bompensiero got into and out of the Pontiac, taking people here and there. Finally, about two in the afternoon, everyone left the apartment. Bompensiero took a nap. By four, Fratianno and crew returned. They awakened Bompensiero. The telephone rang and rang. Calls were taken. Calls placed. Sandy again began to fill Bompensiero in on her troubles. She was divorced. Her husband had the children in Sacramento. He wouldn't let her see them. He didn't answer her letters and let her know how the children were.

Bompensiero ferried people here and there in the Pontiac. Somewhere, the report did not make clear where, the spaghetti dinner was prepared and served. Several pages of transcript record telephone calls being made by Fratianno about trucking, about Vegas, about Reno. Fratianno and Sandy then leave the apartment. Bompensiero leaves. And then, the FBI report picks up, with this:

> "At 11:05 p.m. Bompensiero and Diacogianis were heard re-entering the apartment. They had a general discussion about bringing some unnamed doctor from Manila to Mexico. Diacogianis described this doctor as one who specializes in male sexual rejuvenation and they speculated how they could set him up in business and make a million dollars.
>
> "Bompensiero asked Diacogianis if (★★★★★★★★★★) was still a bookie and Diacogianis answered, 'No, he's a credit man.'
>
> "At 11:20 p.m. Bompensiero and Diacogianis quieted down,

apparently going to sleep."

May 9, Fratianno and Bompensiero moved from the Jay L. Jay Apartments to a three-room apartment, No. 75, at the American Motel, in El Centro, California. Diacogianis shared the apartment with them.

By mid-May, the El Centro job was going so badly that Fratianno was having trouble making his payroll. According to Fratianno's statements to Ovid Demaris, he not infrequently sent Diacogianis and another fellow to steal Fratianno equipment and "collect tax-free money from the insurance policy so generously provided by Allen Dorfman, who handled the Teamsters' insurance. A night's work of stealing 150 tires and wheels, valued at $18,000, did nicely to keep Jimmy in pocket money."

Fratianno, at about this time, took the step that would end by bringing down his trucking business. He offered to sell his trucks to the drivers. The drivers were asked to sign contracts, naming them as conditional lessees. They were not to pay anything down but were to receive 30 percent of the gross earnings. From the balance would come their payments on the trucks. This arrangement not only would permit Fratianno to pay his truckers less each week, but would also allow him to list them as owner-operators. That classification permitted Fratianno to no longer pay benefits. The majority of the truckers signed the contracts. Several did not and quit.

May 17, in midafternoon in the El Centro apartment, Fratianno and Bompensiero talked about trucking and Joseph Bonanno. Born in 1905 in Sicily, Bonanno was chief of one of New York's five Mafia families. In 1963 Bonanno planned to enlarge his holdings to include other New York families' territories, plus that of Southern California. Bonanno ordered his top enforcer to put out contracts on several New York family heads and Los Angeles' Frank Desimone. (When Desimone learned that Bonanno wanted him killed, Desimone became so frightened that he was reluctant even to leave his house, a situation that I am told vastly amused Bompensiero.) Anyone else engaging in such a plot would have been murdered, but the New York families decided to kidnap Bonanno. After meetings, the family heads decided that killing Bonanno would lead to years of Mafia warfare. Bonanno, promising that he would take early retirement in Tucson, was let go. On May 17, while Bompensiero and Fratianno fretted over the trucking business, Bonanno, who had not been seen since the 1964 kidnapping, surrendered in federal court in Manhattan to answer a subpoena.

The FBI report noted that "conversation then took place in low tones between Bompensiero and Fratianno. Fratianno said that he had been trying to hear the news all day. To which Bompensiero replied, 'You ain't going to hear nothing.'

"Fratianno answered: 'I ain't heard nothing.'

"Bompensiero: 'You ain't going to hear nothing, boy, you ain't going to hear nothing. That's it—you know?'"

The FBI reported that "more conversation took place in other parts of the apartment, which could not be overheard." And then Bompensiero was noted to say, apparently about Bonanno, "Well, that just goes to show you, one slip, one slip and they'll kill him, you understand? They'll kill him. Why will they kill him? The FBI—that's why." More conversation ensued which the agents could not overhear. And then Bompensiero was heard to say, "He is Italian, but they ought to give him back to the Indians."

May 18, Bompensiero and Fratianno discussed the trucking company's inability to make enough to enable Frank La Porte to get a return on his investment.

"Fratianno: 'If you do something with good intentions and you think you will do it right and I happen to shoot craps, and you tell me about something...as long as you tell me...I lose my money—so what?'

"Bompensiero: 'Frank didn't blame me.'

"Fratianno: 'That's what I mean. We did it with good intentions. He thought we were doing right. We thought we were going to make a buck...you didn't do it just for yourself. It was for everybody. You know a lot of these people they think I blame you.'

"Bompensiero then got quite upset at Fratianno, indicating that his feelings were hurt and what did they all want from him anyway, and stated, 'I didn't tell them it was going to be $50,000.'

"Fratianno: 'That's what I'm talking about. Now because (**********) introduced me to (**********) now do I blame (**********) because he blew my money over there? I don't blame him. He tried to do something good for me. If I tell you look, Cheech, there's a deal over here. Let's put in $3,000 apiece. I think this is all right. Look, if it ain't all right, well, Frank, it's not a bank, we're shooting craps. You don't win all the time. I know what he's hot about. The last couple of months he's making the payments but he's not getting anything back, but he doesn't have to take it out on us.'"

Later in this conversation, Fratianno sought to reassure Bompensiero about the truck drivers' becoming owner-operators. "They are never going to buy the trucks, Frank, can't be! I charge them for tires. I charge them $8 an hour when (**********) does welding. You understand, Frank? I murder them! At the end of the month they maybe get $200 in equity in the trucks. At the end of the year they maybe get $1,200 or $1,400 equity. When I get through with that truck he's got about $100 equity in the truck. Anything that's done I charge him $8 an hour. I charge him for tires, grease and everything. They are not going to buy the trucks, they know that. I am saving them $2.90 an hour. So am I doing right? I can't be calling him up every time I make a move. This is the way it looked when I got it. He said to me, you handle these trucks like you do your own. That's it and if he had told me any other way, you know what I would have told him. Frank, I can't do it. I can't be calling him up three times a week to make decisions because if I do call him, he doesn't know what it's all about. I know what I'm doing. I know what it's all about. I know how to run it to make a dollar. I might make a mistake."

"Bompensiero: 'We all do.'"

Bompensiero continued to drive to El Centro on Mondays and drive back to San Diego on Friday afternoons. Fratianno, deep in his flirtation with Jean Bodul, flew in and out of El Centro, made trips to Vegas and Reno and Sacramento. His truckers became increasingly restive. They often were forced to pay out of their own pockets for truck repairs. One of Nick Diacogianis's jobs, according to *The Last Mafioso*, was to see that the drivers were punctual in the morning. One driver persistently arrived late. Fratianno told Diacogianis to fire the man if he didn't show up on time. June 14, Diacogianis fired the driver. An altercation, at which Bompensiero was present, ensued, and Diacogianis ended by hitting the driver, who, almost immediately, went to the El Centro police. By afternoon a warrant was sworn out, charging Diacogianis with assault and battery.

Bompensiero had warned Diacogianis about his temper and further had told Fratianno that Nick needed reining in. Late on the afternoon of the 14th, Bompensiero must have felt exceptionally peeved when Fratianno lectured him about the truck tires. The FBI memo noted that Fratianno "instructed Bompensiero that tires should be at 85 pounds pressure and that the big tire should always be mounted on the inside." Tires, to Bompensiero, must have seemed the least of their problems.

The next day Fratianno found himself explaining to Bompensiero that the company was now "$236,000 in the hole." Fratianno, in a series of telephone calls, claimed that he was going broke. On the 16th, Fratianno confided in Bompensiero that the company "was being sued for two payments made on a truck involving a driver who claimed he had been fired. The driver wanted the two payments returned." Fratianno told Bompensiero that they "were in a spot and could not afford to lose any more drivers."

June 23, a Thursday, Fratianno could be heard on the telephone, complaining that the temperature in El Centro had been 120 degrees. While Bompensiero was out for dinner, several men, perhaps mechanics, were in the apartment with Fratianno. They grumbled to Fratianno that

Bompensiero did not know what he was doing. Fratianno told them "to be patient, that Bompensiero was learning." Fratianno added that his company was going broke. "We made $119,000 last year and made payments of $120,000. We lost $1,000. You figure it out."

The agents noted:

> "At 11:36 pm, Bompensiero returned to the apartment, and Fratianno told him that they had gotten a statement showing that from May, 1965, to May, 1966, they had netted $119,000. However, he claimed they were going in the hole, and Bompensiero talked to him about means of cutting overhead. Fratianno stated, 'When a truck is down it costs me fourteen bucks an hour. I don't like it.' He complained about the trucks breaking down as quickly as they came out of the shop. Fratianno then told Bompensiero about a driver who had run into the back of a private car, and Bompensiero advised that some drivers were 'tailgating.' Fratianno then said to Bompensiero: 'No one person can carry a heavy load all day. President Johnson—you know how many advisors he has? We got to get an organized system.'"

Bompensiero returned to San Diego on the afternoon of June 24. On June 27 agents observed Bompensiero driving to the airport and picking up Frank La Porte. "Immediately thereafter, the two proceeded in Bompensiero's automobile to the Palomar Inn located just off Highway 101 at Chula Vista, where the two had dinner with (★★★★★★★★★★) who has been identified as a former member of the LCN [La Cosa Nostra] from (★★★★★★★★★★)."

June 28, agents followed Bompensiero and La Porte while they visited Bompensiero's barbershop in La Jolla, and on the evening of June 28, agents noted, "Bompensiero and La Porte were together in Room 203 at the Mission Valley Inn, which room was occupied by La Porte during his stay in San Diego."

On the morning of June 29, agents observed Bompensiero and La Porte eating "breakfast together at King's Inn in the Mission Valley area of San Diego, and at 1:00 pm, La Porte left San Diego via American Airlines flight 268, which arrives in Chicago at 6:28 pm the same date."

Bompensiero returned to El Centro, arriving at about 3:00 p.m. Diacogianis, that morning, had been tried on charges of assault and battery in Judge Hugh Keating's El Centro courtroom. Diacogianis testified on his own behalf and on the stand admitted five felony convictions and other criminal activities. Fratianno testified for Diacogianis and admitted his criminal background and associations. Keating pronounced Diacogianis guilty and set sentencing for July 5.

That evening, in their apartment, Fratianno and Bompensiero were heard in discussion of Diacogianis's trial. Bompensiero, in the course of their conversation, remarked that he had broken the law since he was 14 years old and could not remember everything that he had done.

July 5, Bompensiero returned to El Centro after the Fourth of July holiday. He was heard by FBI agents in the apartment with an El Centro bail bondsman, getting details and information to arrange bail for Diacogianis pending his appeal from the sentence. Bompensiero complained about the judge having thrown the book at Diacogianis and stated that he would not sign bond for him because he did not have a chance to beat the case on appeal and it would not hurt him to lay out the three months in jail.

"July 6, at 12:30 pm, Bompensiero received a call from Diacogianis from the county jail. Bompensiero appeared to be very upset and told Diacogianis that Fratianno would arrive in El Centro that same day. When Bompensiero hung up he swore to himself for a long time.

"At 2:50 pm, Bompensiero received a call from Marie. He told her about Diacogianis's sentence. Bompensiero stated that Diacogianis was a fool, and they would only be throwing away money if they put up bond to get him out.

"At 3:45 pm, Fratianno arrived at the apartment driving his leased, green Pontiac station wagon. Bompensiero was very upset over Fratianno's late arrival, and Fratianno told him that he had stopped for three hours in Cabazon to see (★★★★★★★★★★). Bompensiero then wanted to know where 'the gun was.' Bompensiero told Fratianno he had heard that Diacogianis had a gun. Fratianno admitted he knew Diacogianis had a gun, but told Bompensiero that he had 'taken care of it.'

"Bompensiero was very upset with Fratianno and wanted Fratianno to let Diacogianis stay in jail and not pay his fine or bail him out. Bompensiero told Fratianno that Diacogianis was no good and would only cause him trouble.

"Fratianno indicated that he was going to have to have his bail bondsman in Los Angeles arrange to bail Diacogianis out that same night. He said he had already made arrangements. Bompensiero disapproved and was very upset about it all."

July 7, the *Imperial Valley Press's* front page, under a banner headline—"Mafia Present in Valley"—showed photographs of Fratianno, Bompensiero, and Moceri. "Neither Bompensiero nor Fratianno were aware of this article until after 8:30 pm, when a telephone call alerted them to it." The FBI report noted, "After they obtained a copy of the newspaper containing the article, Bompensiero burst into laughter and told Fratianno, 'After you spend all that money getting your nose fixed, they used an old picture.'"

Fratianno and Bompensiero, after reading the article, "were very much upset and threatened to sue the editor of the local paper."

Bompensiero and Fratianno continued, then, to try to keep the trucks hauling dirt. But it must have become apparent to both men that Fratianno's trucking business was falling apart and that Frank La Porte's $304,000 investment was lost. Either Bompensiero ceased driving over to El Centro or the FBI ceased surveilling him, or both. I lose all trace of Bompensiero until August 15, when charges of criminal conspiracy to defraud employees and the State of California were filed against Miles and Sons and Fratianno Trucking, as corporations. Charges also were filed individually against Fratianno, Bompensiero, Diacogianis, ReCupido, and Fratianno's foreman, Kenneth Bentley.

The *San Diego Union* for August 17 headlined its front page with:

Statewide Alert Put Out For Key Figure, Linked Earlier To Mafia

"A man once named as the West Coast executioner for the Mafia was charged in El Centro yesterday with defrauding truck drivers. James Fratianno, known as Jimmy the Weasel, was charged with criminal conspiracy following an investigation by the attorney general's office into contracts for construction of a new interstate freeway south of El Centro.... Fratianno late last night had not been arrested and a statewide alert had been broadcast. Bail was set at $55,000.

"Also charged were Frank Bompensiero, an associate of Fratianno's in operation of the trucking firm.... Bompensiero was arrested here yesterday at the home of friends. Deputies from El Centro took him in custody for return to El Centro. His bail was also set at $55,000."

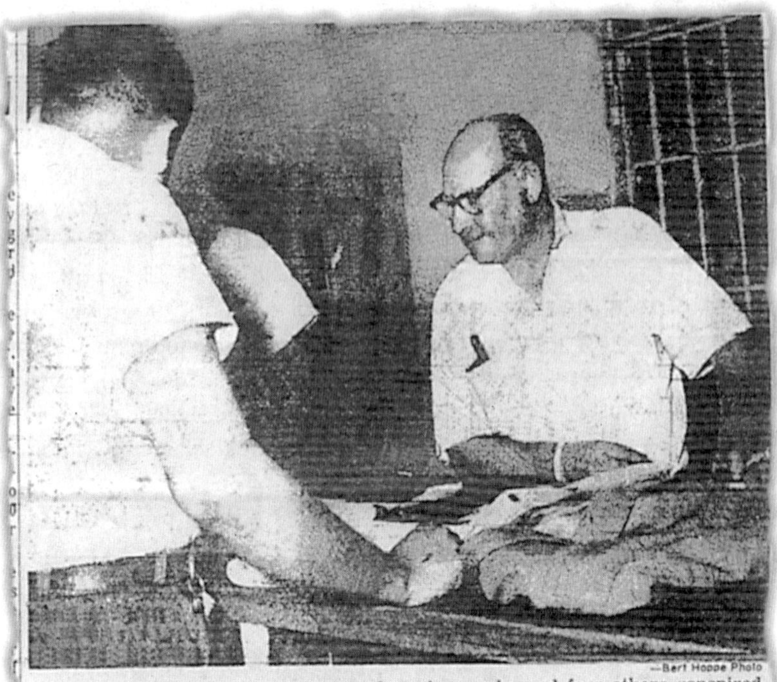


Frank Bompensiero (El Bompo) of San Diego is booked in El Centro on charges he and four others conspired to defraud truck drivers.

# $100,000 Trucker Loss Estimated In Fraud Case

By CHARLES ROSS

EL CENTRO — Drivers involved in an investigation of trucking operations here have lost an estimated $100,000 in wages and fringe benefits, Dis-

listed on company books as owners of trucks when actually they are employes.

"This plan was used to defraud the drivers of a minimum of about $1 an hour," said the

and Miles and Son Trucking C of Merced.

Charged as individuals a James Fratianno, manager Fratianno Trucking, Fred Re pido, of Huntington Beach,

*Bompensiero booked into El Centro jail - from the San Diego Union, August 18, 1966*

**Armstrong would testify in a Los Angeles federal courtroom that Bompensiero became his informant in 1966.**

CHAPTER FIFTY-EIGHT

# JAIL AGAIN

August 18, Fratianno's photograph graced the *Union*'s front page. The headline read: "Truck Fraud Case Figure Arrested, Fratianno Seized At L. A. International Airport; Returned To El Centro, Jailed."

The *Union* reported that Fratianno was booked on the night of the 17th into the Imperial County jail on charges of criminal conspiracy. "Sheriff's deputies brought him by car from Los Angeles after he was arrested about 12:30 pm at Los Angeles International Airport in company with his attorney. He said he was en route to El Centro to surrender to the charges." Bompensiero was relegated to the *Union*'s second page. Beneath his photo, the caption read, "Frank Bompensiero (El Bompo) of San Diego is booked in El Centro on charges he and four others conspired to defraud truck drivers." The photograph shows that Bompensiero wore a short-sleeved white shirt with a cigar sticking from its pocket.

Spectators crowded the 35-seat El Centro courtroom for the arraignment on August 18. Low bail was set for all defendants except Fratianno and Bompensiero. Judge Hugh Keating asked a $55,000 bail for the two men. All the defendants were ordered to appear for a preliminary hearing on August 25. Los Angeles lawyer Jimmy Cantillon, who served as Johnny Rosselli's attorney, pled for lower bail for Fratianno and Bompensiero, but Keating refused. The two were returned to the county jail. Fratianno apparently knew it was all over. He ordered his foreman to remove his trucks from Imperial County and get them back to Sacramento.

I talked one day with a woman who grew up in El Centro. She recalled that the jail had been built in the 1920s or 1930s. As she remembered the jail layout, there were four large iron-barred open cells that each held eight to ten people. These cells tended to fill up with drunks and men who'd become involved in fisticuffs. The jail had no air conditioning and the bathroom facilities were primitive.

The day's weather report for the Imperial Valley promised a high of 112, up from the previous day's 104. Mary Ann recalled that she drove to El Centro to visit her father. "That place was a real hellhole, the jail. The heat was awful. I was so worried about my father, there. He spoke to me very sternly, that day, and told me, in no uncertain terms that I was not to visit him there again. I was not to come again to El Centro. It broke my heart, I can tell you, to see him there. That place was dismal."

Meanwhile, Fratianno's trucks were idle. The trucking company soon would be bankrupt. On August 25, Jimmy Cantillon arrived from Los Angeles for the preliminary hearing. The weather report noted that the Imperial Valley's "torrid muggy weather is expected to continue." Temperatures were expected to rise to 112 degrees, up 6 degrees from the day previous. Cantillon argued unsuccessfully for lowered bail for his clients. Bompensiero and Fratianno were stuck. Imperial County's district attorney was busy interviewing drivers who had worked for Fratianno and ReCupido. He estimated that some 50 drivers had been defrauded of approximately $100,000 in wages and fringe benefits; he predicted that the preliminary hearing could take four weeks. Bompensiero must have wished that he'd never laid eyes on Jimmy Fratianno.

As Imperial Valley temperatures remained above 100 and on some days rose to 110, the preliminary hearing went on. August 31, Justice Vincent Whelan of the Fourth District Court of Appeals granted Jimmy Cantillon's motion to reduce bail for Fratianno and Bompensiero. Whelan ordered Fratianno's bail reduced to $15,000 and Bompensiero's to $10,000. A Los Angeles bail bondsman flew to El Centro to guarantee the bail.

Friday afternoon, September 2, Judge Keating adjourned the court at noon for Labor Day weekend, so that the Imperial Valley fall ritual—dove season's opening—might be observed. Fratianno and Bompensiero, that afternoon, were let out on bail. Eighteen days, Bompensiero had sweltered in El Centro's jail.

Bompensiero's La Jolla barber, Harry Bianconi, I was told, "had the job that day of going over and taking Frank clean clothes and getting him out of jail."

Quite what happened during the 18 days Bompensiero sweated in El Centro's jail, you and I will never know. FBI agents still alive today know. I wrote letters to two agents who are rumored to have been among the men who visited Bompensiero in El Centro. Both, when I first wrote them, were long retired. Both responded to my request with polite refusals to speak with me. One still lived in San Diego. Late afternoons, one year, when I took my daily hour's ramble for exercise, I made a point of walking past his home. I hoped that he might come out to stand on his lawn and gaze across the bay. I imagined I could stride right up to him and introduce myself. I imagined that after we shook hands and I explained that I needed to know what happened during those 18 days in El Centro, that he relented. On hot afternoons, I imagined that he invited me in, that he sat me down in his cool, dim living room. I imagined that he didn't stare at my ugly walking shoes. He said, "This is how it was. We went to see Bompensiero over there in El

Centro. Hotter 'n Hades, it was." As things turned out, no one would tell me anything much about those 18 days.

Whatever happened, Bompensiero, by the time Harry Bianconi picked him up for the drive back to San Diego, had been assigned FBI informant file number "SD-1064."

One retiree, a man who worked in several arms of local law enforcement, told me that "when that truck thing over in the valley came along, the state guys went in to talk to both Fratianno and Bompensiero. Fratianno, I don't know what happened with him. What I do know is that the state guys turned Bompensiero. It wasn't the FBI who first got to him. It was the state—guys from the attorney general's staff. The state guys then turned Bompensiero over to the FBI. I knew Bompensiero's first two handlers, the guys who were his handlers before Jack Armstrong came along."

I asked another law enforcement retiree about this business of handing off informants from one agency to another. He said that not infrequently the FBI stole other agencies' informants. "They had all the money, the FBI did. The PD paid peanuts. So informants would shit-can the PD and go over to the FBI."

John D. "Jack" Armstrong, a Massachusetts-born Irish Roman Catholic, originally came to the local FBI office in the late 1950s and at least for a time, worked interstate auto theft. He spoke "Boston," his vowels flattened in the manner that the Kennedy family made familiar to all America. Armstrong's appearance during the mid-1960s was described to me—"strawberry-blond hair, thinning and beginning to go gray; piercing blue eyes; sharp nose; florid complexion; about 180 pounds and six feet tall." Another person who knew Armstrong during this period said that he was afflicted with the photosensitive Irish complexion, that he had little sunspots on his forehead and the tips of his ears. His eyelashes, she said, were pale, almost colorless. She said that he wore what the FBI wore in those days—dark suits, white shirts, fedora, wing tips.

Many years after the El Centro debacle, Armstrong would testify in a Los Angeles federal courtroom that Bompensiero became his informant in 1966. He said Bompensiero was paid $250 a week plus expenses and he provided the FBI with leads which led to many arrests. Asked, "How many people did Bompensiero inform on?" Armstrong answered, "Hundreds."

Someone mentioned to me that behind Jack Armstrong's back, local lawmen sometimes referred to Armstrong, facetiously, as "the all-American boy." I badgered a retired lawman, an unusually perspicacious man, about why Armstrong was chosen as Bompensiero's handler. "Because Armstrong was righteous. Because he was close-mouthed to the nth degree. Because he was a J. Edgar Hoover man all the way. He was the kind of guy that you had a

30-second conversation with and you knew you wouldn't buy him off, trade him off, or get anything that hadn't already been cleared by J. Edgar Hoover. In those days that was the way they all were. Armstrong was not different. He simply was more rigid, more righteous. Everything was black-and-white. He didn't know gray. He was such a one-way bastard: he never shared, he would never tell you anything unless he was sure you already knew it. But that in those days was the FBI way."

Another law enforcement retiree told me that "Normally, when you get an informant that's got charges against him, you'd go to a DA and tell him what you had. If the guy was valuable enough, they would go through a sham thing on him. But I don't know what happened there in the valley between Armstrong and Bompensiero. And I don't know for sure why Bompensiero went over. Nobody now ever will. Maybe the FBI deal was kind of like a retirement plan for Bompensiero. He got money from the FBI, he got treated well. All his murders were forgiven. And they knew about the murders, you better believe they did. When they first put a guy to work, they shrink him. They get to know him, slow, but they get to know him. And he got protection. So he had all that going for him. But mostly, from what I know of Bompensiero, I believe that he was repenting for his sins of murder, trying to work them off. His life had been the bright lights, the fancy restaurants, the big cigar, down there on the streets with his *compares*. He owed something to society is what I think he thought. I really believe that from what I know of the guy."

Ovid Demaris writes in *The Last Mafioso* that for an FBI agent, "a high-level snitch could mean the difference between beating [your] brains out digging up gossip and rumors on the street and sitting smugly back like [Jack] Armstrong with a pipeline leading directly into the upper echelons of the organization." A law enforcement retiree agreed with Demaris's assessment. "Anyone," he said, "who had a real true-blue informant in organized crime was in hog heaven."

"What a guy like Armstrong," a man who knew him said, "was interested in was Armstrong. He wanted to get everything he could because Bompensiero, back then, was one of the few guys at that level who was snitching, and every word Jack Armstrong sent back East made Jack Armstrong look very, very good."

I found it peculiar that through the years, as I asked people locally and in other cities, about Armstrong and Bompensiero, that almost everyone with whom I spoke had something nice to say about Bompensiero and something not so nice to say about Armstrong. No one even intimated that Armstrong was not on the up-and-up, that he wasn't honest as the day was long, it wasn't that. It was that people did not seem to cotton to him, they didn't particularly enjoy being around him.

As things turned out, Bompensiero and Armstrong, an amiable and big-hearted murderer who had chats with "J.C." and a not-so-amiable and somewhat saturnine straight-arrow churchgoing Roman Catholic FBI agent would end up seeing each other as often as once a week for the next ten years. They ended up, my guess is, needing each other. You can't help but wonder what went on between them.

I did wonder. I tried to picture them at a table together. Bompensiero chewed his Bering Immensa. I didn't even know if Armstrong smoked. I did know that his jackets must have smelled of Bompensiero's cigar smoke. His jackets and his strawberry-blond hair and his colorless eyelashes, they must have smelled too. I tried to figure what they had in common. They were both interested in what you and I call "crime." They must have enjoyed gossip. What was Bonanno up to over there in Tucson? And Fratianno, flying in and out of San Francisco and Vegas and Los Angeles and Cleveland? And what was Trafficante doing in Tampa and Marcello in New Orleans? And what about Rosselli, who had he seen in Vegas and Beverly Hills and La Costa and Los Angeles and Miami and Tampa and Washington, D.C., and Chicago? And, in Chicago, what were Joey "Doves" Aiuppa and Jackie Cerone doing? Until 1968, when Frank Desimone keeled over after a heart attack, Armstrong and Bompensiero must have talked about Desimone's fear that Bonanno would have him killed. Armstrong's sun-scarred ear tips must have quivered with interest as Bompensiero schooled him in the nature of ties among and between various Matrangas and Mirabiles and Pepitones and Vitales and Priziolas. Perhaps Bompensiero told the All-American Boy stories of the villages from which these men's mothers and fathers came. Perhaps he told him about the boat his father had in Porticello and the house with the marble stairway. So they had that in common: they were interested in the same people.

*FBI surveillance photo of Bompensiero leaving for San Francisco, c. 1976*

*FBI surveillance photo of Larry Saunders, Chris Petti, and Bompensiero, Shelter Island Inn, San Diego, c. 1976*

**Mary Ann believes that her father strung Armstrong along.**

CHAPTER FIFTY-NINE

# SNITCH

I want to stop here and explain about how Aiuppa came to be called "Doves." Jay Robert Nash in his *World Encyclopedia of Organized Crime* writes that Aiuppa was "convicted in Fort Scott, Kansas, in 1962, and jailed for three months for illegally transporting 562 mourning doves from Kansas to Illinois. This last incident earned Aiuppa his strange sobriquet of 'Doves' Aiuppa. The gangster long fancied himself a gentleman hunter, and he encouraged his fellow mobsters to take out their aggressions on the fowl of the earth, holding hunting parties throughout the Midwest. He and some fellow gangsters drove to Kansas during the bird hunting season in 1962 and there blasted more than 1400 birds, mostly mourning doves, from the skies when the legal limit was 24. Officers arrested Aiuppa in his car when he crossed the Illinois line with the hundreds of illegal dead birds in his trunk. He was returned to Kansas where he was convicted before a federal judge who stated that Aiuppa's attack on the birds was nothing short of 'unconscionable slaughter.' Aiuppa persisted in his bird hunting, establishing the loftily-entitled Yorkshire Quail Club in Kankakee County, to the west of Chicago, enrolling dozens of high-ranking Mafia-syndicate members from around the country as members. The club's hunting permits were issued by the Illinois Department of Conservation, but these were later revoked when Aiuppa was revealed to be the president of the club."

Anyway, Armstrong and Bompensiero, when you think about it, had more in common than did, say, Bompensiero and Fratianno. Neither Bompensiero nor Armstrong was a womanizer. They were one-woman men. Both felt protectively toward women. Armstrong tended to behave in an avuncular fashion with female law enforcement personnel. Armstrong, apparently, liked a martini now and then; Bompensiero liked a cold beer; neither was a big drinker.

What this middle-aged Irishman and this aging Sicilian-American had most in common was a code of ethics, a way of life. Both the FBI agent and the old mustache were company men, each in his unique way bound by *onore* and *omertà*. In the tumultuous mid-1960s, as women burned bras and peaceniks burned draft cards and men who had never killed took over Jack Dragna's Los Angeles mob and men with longish sideburns and suspect politics came to work for the FBI, both Bompensiero and Armstrong must have seen themselves as men of honor forced to do battle against a dishonorable world.

September 6, 1966, an anonymous note in an unmarked envelope was discovered at the entrance of the San Diego FBI office. The note was typewritten in Italian. The Bureau noted that the type "resembles the Laboratory standards for Royal elite style of type, spaced 12 characters per inch." The local office sent the letter to Washington for translation. No request was being made "for fingerprint examination of the anonymous note because it was handled by numerous persons prior to submission, virtually eliminating possibility of successful development of latent fingerprints."

The San Diego office received from Washington the following translation:

> Dear Authority
> Last year I found myself at dinner in a restaurant, the place was dark and close to the table where I and a friend of mine sat down there was a table with six important persons beginning (?) to argue (?) and drink. They spoke Sicilian. They were speaking about having had a great loss of money and he who made them lose it was a television artist named "Linkletter." The persons were, the brothers Frank and Sam Bompensiero, (★★★★★★★★★★), Biaggio Bonventre, (★★★★★★★★★★)...this have produce business..., (★★★★★★★★★★). (★★★★★★★★★★) said to Frank Bompensiero, when we must we hurry and rid ourselves of the business of making disappear this rascal (or stronger) Linkletter, Frank answered saying, (★★★★★★★★★★) don't you think that the thing is all easy this is a big man and time and money is needed, this business is not like the Mexican that (★★★★★★★★★★) invited him to a banquet and they brought (?) him and they beat him and (★★★★★★★★★★) whose true name is (★★★★★★★★★★) made the hole and all was finished, with Linkletter we need time and patience. When I left the restaurant with my friend we said, when we kill among *didri* all is well but wanting to kill honest people it is necessary to investigate, and with the help of honest friends after many sacrifices we come to discover that about the year 1960 (★★★★★★★★★★) became a close friend with a Mexican and after many projects for making money they began a small commerce with Mexico, meanwhile from prison came Frank Bompensiero and as he was to have the position of boss as he was before, without making themselves known to the Mexican, they organized the commerce on a large scale, and in charged a Mafioso named (★★★★★★★★★★) with Mexico, father-in-law of one who is called in Los Angeles who is another big man, and with the syndicate of San Diego started I do not know what things, the business promised to the Mexican that if he behaved well and gave

> proof of being a man who keeps in his stomach they would admit him as an equal member in the syndicate, they said to the Mexican that the profit from the commerce must be given to the committee for giving help to all the brothers harassed by the law, but however the Mexican after much time discovered it was not true and began to resist with the five persons who were at the meal and with (**********), when he reported him to the brothers Bompensiero right away decided to invite him that it had become the time to admit him in the society of the Mafia and that there was to be a banquet prepared for him. He was going to meet the boss and at the same time the boss ordering all the brothers, to give to the Mexican a certain percentage of all the business that they had and in that manner the Mexican was convinced that he had secured an income for life, the rest as to the ending of the Mexican in 1962 in the month of July or August is written on the brothers (**********) and the remainder is that (**********) alias (**********) today has an Italian restaurant in Hemet, California and came…in America not legal attention and don't cause the shooting of Linkletter.

In January, 1962, Bompensiero had worked as assistant sales manager at the San Luis Rey Packing Company in Oceanside, with which the Linkletters, Art and his son Jack, were involved. The conversation related in the anonymous letter seems to make reference to that business.

The note's translator wrote: "In response to the request of the San Diego Office, it is felt that the writer of the letter is possibly past middle age, possibly attended three or four grades of elementary school in Italy and was possibly brought up in a Sicilian environment (most likely in Sicily). This is suggested by the good knowledge the writer displays of the Sicilian dialect (hardly contaminated by English) and by the fact that he shows a tendency to use school-taught spellings of the Italian language to express sounds which are typical of the dialect."

September 29, 1966, Bompensiero celebrated his 61st birthday. For his involvement with Fratianno's trucking business, Bompensiero had been charged with 36 counts of conspiring to cheat truck drivers on their wages and violate state laws in connection with freeway construction. These charges, even had Bompensiero not agreed to become an informant, would likely have been dropped. There just wasn't much there to show that Bompensiero acted illegally in his connection with Fratianno's trucking company. But, surely, he knew that his agreement to become an FBI informant meant those charges eventually would be dropped.

"Nobody," a man who knew Bompensiero said to me, "loves a snitch." This was his answer to a question I'd put to him. The question was, "Why does everyone who was at all close to Bompensiero seem to change the subject when I ask them about Bompensiero becoming an informant?"

"Nobody loves a snitch." When the man said that to me he looked me, hard, in the eye. His cold gaze hurt and the sentence hurt. "Nobody loves a snitch."

Two sets of deeds of which Bompensiero is accused make people uncomfortable. One is the murders. The other is that he became an informant.

About the murders, those close to Bompensiero offer a variety of opinions. "None of it was proved," some say. Others say, "They only killed each other." My answer to the murders is that for Bompensiero, the "murders" were not "murders" : they were his work as a soldier in Jack Dragna's army. I believe that as a soldier in Dragna's army Bompensiero instinctually felt himself to be fighting on the right side. My answer to the "murders" is that Bompensiero was no more and no less troubled by them than a soldier would be troubled after shooting up a foxhole filled with Nazis. Which is to say he was and he wasn't troubled. I do not think, however, that Bompensiero enjoyed killing.

Mary Ann says, about her father's role as an informant, that she does not believe that he told them anything useful. She believes that her father strung Armstrong along. I do believe that Bompensiero gave useful information to Armstrong. I believe that by the time Bompensiero found himself wiping sweat away from his broad forehead as he sat in the El Centro jail cell that he no longer felt like a good soldier in a valiant army, an army fighting for what was right. With Dragna's death and Frank Desimone's takeover of the Los Angeles family, this army to which Bompensiero had allied himself for almost four decades was no longer noble. It had outlived its reason for being. It had become something that was not in favor of justice. What remained must have seemed to Bompensiero not an army of Sicilian men of honor, but a backbiting crew of coarse American thugs and goons.

Bompensiero, in an odd way, became like protestors of the Vietnam War. Many protestors were deeply patriotic; they loved their country so much that they did not want to see America sully her honor in what seemed to them a dishonorable war. Bompensiero loved what we call the Mafia so much that he came to hate what the men who came after Jack Dragna were making of it.

When Bompensiero left San Quentin in May, 1960, the Los Angeles family was busying itself with its usual bookmaking, loan-sharking, and two-bit extortions. Simone Scozzari, Desimone's underboss, was deported back to Sicily in 1962. Nick Licata took Scozzari's place as Desimone's crew chief. Bompensiero liked Licata a bit better than he liked Desimone, which was not at all. Licata, someone told me, "was cheap. He was not one to cut up the money." About Desimone, Bompensiero would never feel that Desimone had done all he could to keep him out of San Quentin. Plus, Desimone's move to keep Momo Adamo from power and Desimone's rape of Marie, were, to Bompensiero, unforgivable acts. When Bompensiero left prison he kept clear of the Los Angeles family; some people might have believed that it was the stringencies of parole that kept Bompensiero from visiting Desimone and Licata and Jack Dragna's nephew, Louis Tom. It wasn't fear of violating parole that kept Bompensiero away, it was disgust and distaste. "*Pezzi de merde*," he called them, "pieces of shit."

But for all that Bompensiero detested and distrusted Desimone and the Licatas and Louis Tom Dragna and other LA family members, still, the first time he told a family secret to Armstrong must have been a painful moment. Nobody loves a snitch. When that first betraying sentence slipped off Bompensiero's tongue, he must have known that nothing again ever would be the same. Nothing was. Nothing would be.

Bompensiero now had two sets of secrets. He had the secrets he'd been keeping since he was 14 and began breaking the law and he had his secret relationship with Jack Armstrong. Bompensiero was good at secrets. He was good at keeping what he knew to himself.

**Marie was desperately jealous of Thelma, cold in her grave for more than ten years.**

CHAPTER SIXTY

# MARIE STEPS IN

Bompensiero also had many secrets from Marie, with whom he'd been living, by this time, for several years. Marie was accustomed to secrets. Her second husband, Bompensiero's friend Momo Adamo, forbade Marie from entering the living room when the men talked business. She was forced to sit in the kitchen. When she pried into Bompensiero's affairs, he told her, affably, "You take care of the house, I'll take care of business." He could not tell Marie how he missed Thelma, Mary Ann's mother. Marie was desperately jealous of Thelma, cold in her grave for more than ten years. He could say nothing to Marie of how little Santa, Mary Ann's daughter, reminded him of his dead wife. "You look just like your grandmother, honey" is what he used to say to Santa. He'd touch her hair, say, "Yes, you do, you look just like your grandmother." His grandson Frankie was a teenager, as old as his grandfather had been when he killed for the first time. He could not tell Marie about the evening he and Thelma stood by Frankie's crib and held hands; he could not tell Marie that tears streamed down Thelma's face, tears of joy. He could not tell Marie that Thelma looked up at him and said, "Our *vita nuova*, Frank, our new life." He could not tell Marie that he held himself responsible for Thelma's death. Thelma died, people said, of a broken heart; Bompensiero knew he broke that heart. What he brought on Thelma was the worst thing he ever did in his life. All the blood of however many men that stained his hands was nothing compared to what his way of life did to Thelma. Nothing.

January 6, 1967, Bompensiero made the 120-mile drive to El Centro. In a packed courtroom he heard his lawyer Jimmy Cantillon tell the court that no evidence heard in the preliminary hearing indicated Bompensiero was guilty of the charges against him. "If I were to be seen with you," Cantillon told Superior Court Judge Victor Gillespie, "and I happened to be a bookmaker, that would not make you guilty of a crime." Judge Gillespie ordered all charges against Bompensiero dropped. He continued until January 20 a decision on a motion to dismiss charges against Fratianno.

Bompensiero, after the hearing, was jovial. He told a *San Diego Union* reporter that he was "very happy to have the whole thing over with" and that his attorney did a "marvelous job." He said that Judge Hugh Keating, who had tried the preliminary hearing, "asked me if I planned to get into the trucking business again. I told him if I ever see a truck driver coming at me, I'm going to turn around and go the other way."

The last page of files on Bompensiero that I received through the Freedom of Information Act is this:

United States Department of Justice

Copy to: United States Attorney, San Diego (Attention: AUSA John A. Mitchell
Report of: (*******)
Date: April 28, 1967
Field Office File: San Diego 92-25
Title: Frank Bompensiero
Character: Anti-Racketeering
Synopsis:

Subject Frank Bompensiero continues to reside in San Diego, California. State felony charges against subject dismissed at El Centro, California, by Superior Court judge who ruled prosecution failed to show, at preliminary hearing, sufficient evidence of criminal conspiracy. Subject continues close contact with hoodlums. During investigative period, subject in contact with hoodlum leaders (**********) among others. subject should be considered armed and dangerous, as he is suspect in murders and has been arrested in possession of a gun.

Details:

I. Residence and Identification of Subject's Automobile

As of April 19, 1967, it was verified that subject Frank Bompensiero is still residing in Apartment 4, 1830 Reed Street in the Pacific Beach area of San Diego.

He continues to live there under the alias Frank Gavin. Subject's telephone number remains (**********).

The subject continues to maintain as his public residence the home of his daughter in San Diego. Subject Bompensiero operates only one car, a light blue 1965 Mustang bearing California license RDJ 155.

II. Employment

Investigation has revealed that subject Bompensiero remains unemployed since he left Imperial Valley in August, 1966, where he was last working for the Fratianno Trucking Company.

Try as I might, I was able to obtain through the Freedom of Information Act only a few more pages dated after the summer of 1966. I acquired a Washington, D.C., lawyer whose area of expertise was the Freedom of Information Act. For two years he tried to procure more Bompensiero documents. No luck. I tried extra-legal ways to gather more documents. Again, no luck. I wrote again to Jack Armstrong, who in 1978 had retired from the FBI and gone to work for the San Diego County District Attorney's office and then, in the early 1990s, retired there too. He had been divorced and returned to the East Coast. No luck.

From mid-summer, 1966 on, Bompensiero would have no visible means of employment. Fratianno claims in *The Last Mafioso* that in 1969 he gave Bompensiero several large sums—$15,000, and later, another $20,000. But who knows.

Mary Ann was working, full-time. Her children, then, were teenagers. Her father came by, afternoons, and checked on them. He often made dinner, his usual menu—steaks on the grill, pasta, mashed potatoes. He helped Mary Ann out with money. He made sure the children had clothes. "Then when I got home, we would visit a little and maybe he would watch the news with the kids. He always watched the news. He always liked Channel 10. I don't know who the news commentator was then. But he said, 'You can trust that guy.' He said that at Channel 10 they were nice to him. Anytime they ever talked to him, they respected him."

After the news, Bompensiero would say his good-byes for the evening. "Then," said Mary Ann, "my dad would go and eat at Marie's. I don't think he told Marie everything he was doing for us because she was such a jealous woman. She was always asking me if my father had bought this for me or that for me or the kids. She was so jealous. And jealous of my dead mother. My father made excuses for her, 'Ever since she got shot, you know, she hasn't been quite right.'

"I remember one time my father said to me, 'Honey, I want you to go pick out a car. You go pick out what you want and I'll make the payments.' I said, 'Daddy, what if something happens to you and I can't afford the payment?' I was afraid. They don't put anything in the bank you know, everything has got to be stashed and who the heck knows?

"To make a long story short, I get a phone call from Marie. My dad wasn't around. She'd never talk to me like that in front of my dad. I respected her always in front of my dad. Didn't pay too much attention to her, but respected her. She says, 'If you think you're going to get a car before I do!' I said, 'Marie, what are you talking about?' I said, 'You know, Marie, you're probably right. The reason I'm not going to get a car is because I don't want a car. You know why? My father supports you, he's got to give you everything you want, he wants to give me everything. I love my father and I don't want to see him stressed out. Otherwise I'd have a car, Marie.'"

Frank Desimone died. Seventy-one-year-old Nick Licata took over the Los Angeles family. He made Louis Tom Dragna his second-in-command. Licata, born in Camporeale, Sicily, in 1897, had come to the U.S. at 16. He became involved in the Detroit underworld. In his 20s he "got crosswise" with Detroit leader Joe Zerilli, who called for Licata's death. Licata fled to Los Angeles and Dragna, who talked Zerilli into forgiving young Licata, then took him into the Los Angeles group. Licata, albeit somewhat reluctantly, participated in the Cohen-Dragna battles. His son Carlo worked for a time in San Diego at a bar and suspected gambling joint, Nate Rosenberg's Navy Club, a 12-room suite on the second floor of 919 Fourth Avenue. Carlo had a reputation as something of a bumbler. Louis Tom Dragna, Jack Dragna's nephew, by this time was a wealthy man. Owner of Roberta Manufacturing in Los Angeles, a firm that made women's clothes, Dragna took scant interest in day-to-day management of the family. Bompensiero avoided contact with both men.

Fratianno, during the late 1960s and early 1970s, was in and out of courthouses and prisons. He and Bompensiero met several times, but they did not see each other frequently. The gas station owner who sometimes visited Harry Bianconi's barbershop remembered that at about this time, after the El Centro fiasco, Bompensiero began spending more time at the shop. "It seemed as if he had a lot of time on his hands. After lunch. Yeah. He'd wander around and end up there, sometime after lunch, and he'd be in there maybe a couple of hours or so. Came in about every other day or something. Drove an old Mustang. It wasn't a flashy car by any means. We would get together in the shop and Harry would cook up Italian sausage on a barbecue grill he kept in the back.

"Jack Armstrong was out there too. He'd come out and while away the time. I don't know what his game was at that time. Later I heard that Frank was a witness." The gas station owner knew that Armstrong was an FBI agent. He said that he thought Armstrong just came around "to see what he could find out." He didn't think it was all that unusual. "Everybody, I figured, was keeping an eye on Frank. Someone told me that the sheriff had people across the street at what then was the Security National Bank, taking photographs of people who went in and out of the barbershop." He recalled "a big, young, good-looking fellow who worked over there at the bank for a while. He'd come over and hang around the barbershop, and old Frank told him, 'You haven't got any business hanging around like this. You should be over there at the bank.' Frank told him that. And then, later on, the bank let the guy go."

The gas station owner said that he would have suspected Bompensiero was involved in things, even if Harry hadn't told him. "He never worked. And I wondered about that. Because he lived pretty good. There was no flashy car or anything but he never worked. He never mentioned that he'd been in prison. He mentioned being in the Army once, but not prison. He was pretty sharp in a lot of ways, not talking."

I asked if he remembered how Armstrong and Bompensiero behaved toward one another. "Just real friendly. Nothing special. They talked about how the weather was and who won the ball game. And this and that."

June 30, 1969, Bompensiero and Marie were married in Imperial County. Why they finally married, no one can tell me. Why they chose Imperial County, no one can say.

Mary Ann and I talked many times about why her father finally married Marie. Mary Ann believed, and I came to agree with her, that her father felt responsible for his old friend Momo's widow. "Someone," Mary Ann said, "had to look after her."

Late that summer, in 1969, Bompensiero's mother, born in 1877, fell in her kitchen on Columbia Street and fractured her left hip. Previous to her fall she had kept house, cooked meals, walked every morning to Our Lady of the Rosary for mass. After she broke her hip, she never walked again. November 22, she died. Mary Ann remembered that during the funeral Mass, tears flowed down her father's face. She remembered that during the mass two white doves flew into Our Lady of the Rosary, circled several times above the congregation, and then flew out.

Her father, Mary Ann said, began to seem a little older after that. He had problems with his eyes—cataracts. He wore heavy black-rimmed eyeglasses with thick lenses. He had several bouts with gout. He had high blood pressure, for which he began taking medication. "But his skin was still as smooth as a baby's. The Bompensieros don't wrinkle. They just don't."

November 21, 1970, William "Big Bill" Bonelli died in Hermosillo, Mexico. Seventy-five when he died—of emphysema—Bonelli had been on the lam since his failure to re-win election to his seat on the State Board of Equalization in November, 1954. Mary Ann still pulls a *funsha* at the mention of Bonelli's name. The net thrown out by the San Diego County DA's office that was intended, eventually, to catch Bonelli, of course also trapped her father. Bompensiero did five years staring out the bars into the San Francisco Bay. Bonelli lived freely in Mexico. "Bonelli," Mary Ann said, "had the gall, too, to want his state retirement sent to him in Mexico!" (Bonelli's retirement fund continued to accumulate. At the time of his death, the fund had grown to $91,187.)

San Diego District Attorney James Don Keller told the *San Diego Union* in a story related to announcement of Bonelli's death: "I always said Bonelli would be assured of a fair trial here. It's remarkable that this case closes at the time that I'm concluding my career—after all the years of investigation and prosecution in this matter." Keller, the *Union* noted, "will retire in January after serving 24 years as district attorney."

In 1972 Bompensiero's friend Frank La Porte died of a heart attack. Infamous for his gambling, prostitution, vending machine and other rackets, La Porte was denied a public funeral Mass by the Archdiocese of Chicago. I had wondered what happened between La Porte and Bompensiero after the El Centro calamity, but Mary Ann did not know.

Bompensiero and Marie had established a routine. "Marie," Mary Ann said, "could only see in one eye after Momo shot her. So she shopped in the morning, when it was light. She took my dad's dry cleaning and laundry out. She cooked in the afternoon. For my dad's dinner, she would warm something up. He didn't like his food steaming hot. He liked the flavors, when the food had set for a while. And, frankly, she would be drinking most of the day. She had been drinking for years. She was drinking when I was a girl. If my dad had company, he had to go out and buy a bottle of scotch. Because of Marie. He couldn't keep liquor in the house. Every day he'd buy her a six-pack of beer. He was embarrassed by her drinking. But he was kind to her. She'd get started on something and he'd just say, 'Marie…' He made excuses for her. When she got out of hand, he'd say, 'Well, it was that bullet.'"

The marriage didn't alter Bompensiero's routine. "My dad came by every day. By then I had married again, to Bill. My dad liked Bill, a lot. He wanted to be careful not to interfere. The kids were teenagers. Frankie drank Coca-Cola. My father asked Bill's permission to buy it for him. He wanted Bill to feel like the man of the house; he didn't want Bill to feel that he was intruding on our marriage. 'Bill, you don't care, do you?' he'd ask my husband, anytime he wanted to buy the kids something. My father would make a little bow and say to my husband that he'd like to do it. 'It's my pleasure,' my father would say."

Mary Ann said that she and Bill saw her father every weekend. "Saturday mornings, he'd come by. I would sit and have coffee with them. Then, I would move, get up and do laundry, that sort of thing, so the guys could talk. Bill, on weekends, liked to eat about ten or eleven o'clock in the morning. He'd grown up on Southern cooking and he'd fix things like fried eggs and fried pork chops, Southern cooking. My dad really liked this stuff. But when

Bill would make shit on the shingle, that's when my dad was happiest. When he was in the Army is when he first ate that and he always had a taste for it."

*Mickey Cohen and Frank Bompensiero, 1974*

**"I felt compelled to monitor Bompensiero. I owed it to all my fellow officers in other agencies."**

CHAPTER SIXTY-ONE

# LUNCH AT TARANTINO'S

After the El Centro incident had resolved itself, Bompensiero began to go every weekday to Tarantino's on North Harbor Drive for his lunch. Chris Petti, born Christopher Poulos in 1937 in Illinois, often came by and had lunch with Bompensiero. Pete Tenner, who for a time was in business with Petti, dropped in. Pete Marcos was often there. Marcos's mother for many years had run the Turk Café, a Greek restaurant not far from Bompensiero's Gold Rail. Occasionally Nicholas DePento, a lawyer, came in. DePento's office manager, Joe Stead came. These men were younger than Bompensiero. In later years it would be said that Petti was Bompensiero's bodyguard and driver, but the truth was that Petti didn't drive and Bompensiero never had a bodyguard.

Bruce worked as a waiter at Tarantino's from 1974 until 1977. He regularly waited on Bompensiero's table. I asked how Bompensiero looked in those years. "He was an older gentleman by then. He was stocky, balding, always had a cigar in his mouth or hand. He would wear suits or a jacket and trousers. When he sat down at the table, he would take off his jacket. He rarely wore ties."

Bompensiero sat at a table in the bar area, a table set between the bar and a row of tables that ran along the windows by the walkway. Bruce said, "It was lunch that he came for. It was pretty much a routine. I suspect that he was a creature of routine. He showed up a little before noon, about eleven-thirty. His stay would go on into the afternoon, after almost everybody else had left."

When Bruce first worked at Tarantino's, he addressed Bompensiero as "Mr. Bompensiero." After a short time, Bompensiero asked Bruce to call him Frank, and Bruce did. "When I was a kid I started at 12 working on tuna boats and I always looked up to the Portuguese and Italian fishermen as heroes, like Hemingway did—*The Old Man and the Sea*." Bruce said that Bompensiero reminded him of these men. "He seemed to be a real self-assured man. Dignified. You knew this was a guy people looked up to. People visited him. Usually four would be at the table. Sometimes as many as six or seven. Pete Marcos was around a lot. They called him 'Big Pete,' he was huge. He was maybe six-two. Chris Petti was almost always there. Nick DePento came in and out. He wasn't there all the time. There were people who came in from other places." Bruce recalled seeing Leo Moceri several times and Fratianno and Johnny Rosselli. He recalled that, at Bompensiero's table, "They spoke in English and then there were times they would switch into Italian."

Most of the time, said Bruce, Bompensiero was soft-spoken. "There were times when there was some growling going on. The majority of the time there wasn't. There was a lot of joking going on at the table. Laughter."

Bruce remembered that on occasion, maybe a dozen times, he saw Chris Petti bring in several guys, perhaps to receive a scolding from Bompensiero. On those occasions, said Bruce, "Chris would always stand up. He would never sit down. He would seem to be watching over the discussions that were going on between Frank and these men. During these discussions, these men always addressed Frank as 'Mr. Bompensiero.' My impression was that these people were being summarily chastised.

"It was out in the parking lot that they would get going. The only reason I would see this was that I was either leaving or outside, emptying things. But I remember that there were occasions when they would be out there and the conversation was heated and Frank would be holding his cigar in a stern way and jabbing it, perhaps to make a point. I knew at those times that something was not right, that he was annoyed."

Bruce said that he never knew that Bompensiero had anything to do with anything illegal until after he was in his senior year in law school. "It was really a shock. In a restaurant business a lot of what you hear is to be taken with not too much credibility. Since I was not a person to accept whatever I heard, I had dismissed it as just talk."

And what did Bompensiero order? "He loved calamari, cooked real special, in a certain way. Rather than cutting it in steaks, the squid was cut crosswise and lightly breaded. He liked it with lots and lots of pepper and lots of lemon. Otherwise, he almost always ate fish. Vince Tarantino would make special things for him. He liked a salad of tomatoes and cucumber with feta cheese—the feta cheese crumpled over the cucumber and tomato and lettuce. He didn't eat desserts."

Bompensiero sometimes stayed at the restaurant far into the afternoon. "The Tarantinos had a collection of old boxing films of Archie Moore, Marciano, Sonny Liston, Ali. They would show these. They would close off the back room and the guys watched these movies—Frank, Pete, Chris, and anybody else who happened to be there. There would be quite a few people. Usually that was in the late afternoon, always on a weekday. Always they enjoyed being there when there were less people. They showed them on an old home movie screen, you would hear the click-click of the projector, and the pictures as they showed up on the screen would be vibrating, like in the old newsreels. They didn't like to be bothered when that was going on. We would take things in before and after but while the movies were going on the doors were left closed."

Bruce said that unlike many people he waited on that Bompensiero took an interest in him, that he asked him about himself. Bompensiero knew that Bruce was in law school, that much of the time he rode a bicycle to work and to school. He left Bruce large tips. "And," said Bruce, "when I was out in the parking lot, getting ready to go home, he sometimes would walk out and hand me an envelope. 'Look,' he'd say, 'this is for your school.'" When Bruce opened these envelopes, he would find cash. How much, he said he preferred not to say.

I asked Bruce if there were anything else he wanted to say about Bompensiero. "Yes," he said, "he did have a big, big heart, Frank did. You always remember someone, who, when you are going through a time of need, they help. Lots of people will pass by a stranded dog or a homeless person in the rain and never notice. Frank Bompensiero was one of these guys who stop and notice."

Jimmy Fratianno was released from Chino state prison on August 27, 1973, after serving time for parole violation. Soon after he left prison, he, too, became an informer, chatting regularly with an FBI agent. He later would explain, "I got out of jail and I didn't have any money." The FBI offered him cash for information, he said, and over the next two years paid him $16,000.

At some point after Fratianno's release from prison, according to his account in *The Last Mafioso*, Bompensiero and Fratianno visited Frank Sinatra's home in Palm Springs. The occasion was a piece of madness engineered by Fratianno, in which Sinatra would be made a member of the Order of the Knights of Malta, a Roman Catholic organization with headquarters in Rome. The order's United Nations representative was present. Fratianno has Bompensiero say to the representative, "Excuse me, but while you're over there in Rome, could you get a papal blessing for my mother? Her name was Maria Anna." "Of course," the representative says, "I will see to it personally. I will have it mailed directly to your home."

Mary Ann recalled that on rare occasions her father attended large social events. She remembered that during this period there was a big New Year's Eve party. She thought that the party might have been held at the Kona Kai Club. "Chris Petti and his wife Virgie came. She was wearing a gorgeous black mink coat. She was a beautiful woman, Virgie was. Mickey Cohen was there. I didn't even realize at the time who he was. He looked like a shriveled-up old man to me. What I mostly remember about that party was that I had a godawful cold and had gotten up out of bed to go." Cohen, in 1972, was released from prison after serving ten years on McNeil Island for tax evasion.

By the time he began coming regularly to San Diego, he was ill, with stomach cancer, and seeing doctors at Scripps. He also attended the reception at the Bahia Hotel for Mary Ann's daughter's wedding, in 1974. By then, said Mary Ann, Mickey Cohen was a crippled-up old man. He walked with two canes and he had two bodyguards. "He gave her $450, in an envelope."

I asked someone who knew Cohen and Bompensiero if Cohen expressed hard feelings toward Bompensiero, given that Bompensiero, during the Dragna-Cohen bookmaking wars, apparently took a shot at Cohen. He didn't think so. He thought they were old men who had put all that behind them. He thought they both knew that trying to kill each other was just their way of doing business.

When Bompensiero's grandchildren married in the early 1970s, the number of stops on Bompensiero's morning route increased. He stopped first at the home of Frankie and his bride. And then he went by the home of Santa and her husband. He drank coffee with Frankie's wife and with Santa. He surreptitiously looked about to see if anything was needed. His grandson was just getting started in business. Bompensiero bought them a dining room set. Every week he picked up Frankie's young wife and drove her to Vons. He pushed the cart and gave advice on fruits and vegetables and fish and meat.

Mary Ann laughed, remembering this. "He would fill her cart. They had so much food they wouldn't know what to do. My kids were not going to want for anything. I don't mean Cadillacs, I mean comfort in the home. There's this saying, 'When you get 18, we are not going to break your plate.' Some families, when the kids turn 18, their parents make them pay rent or get out of the house. We weren't raised like that. Up until he died, up until they killed him, every week, he took Frankie's wife shopping. Frankie used to say, 'Papa, you don't need to do this,' and my dad would say what he always said, 'Frankie, I want to do it, no problem. When you are first getting started, it's not so easy.' After Frankie and his wife had little Frankie, my dad put a jar up on their kitchen counter. Every time he came by, he emptied the change out of his pockets into that jar. 'For my little great-grandson. For his college,' he said."

I talked one morning with a retired gentleman who, working in a department of local law enforcement, surveilled Bompensiero from 1975 until 1977. Bompensiero, he said, "was the key man in the 1970s." He remembered him as "a dapperly dressed gentleman. He always looked very sporty, dressed in what you might call 'the Southern California look.' Frank in his later years, as a bad guy, wasn't that much of a threat. What he was, was a draw for bad guys everywhere. In terms of a threat to society as an individual, he was no longer what he may have been back in the 1930s and 1940s and

1950s. But through his background and his status in the Mafia, he drew all these people in whom law enforcement was interested. That in itself was actually the draw card."

Few people, at the time, knew that Bompensiero and Armstrong talked. My retired friend said that he became aware of Bompensiero's informant status when he was advised by his superiors that he best not waste his time looking at him. It was then that he learned Bompensiero was an informant. But, he said, he believed that few if any local law enforcement people knew of Bompensiero and Armstrong's relationship. The federal authorities, he said, "were not sharing their information with us. So it was incumbent on us to conduct our investigations. I felt compelled to monitor Bompensiero. I owed it to all my fellow officers in other agencies. On a weekly basis, they wanted to know who it was he was talking to. They wanted to know who is he with, who is he meeting, what are they talking about. Our main concern was to monitor out-of-town OC [organized crime] types. So that whether he was a federal informant or not, did not matter." Local agencies, he said, as had many other local law enforcement retirees who worked during this period, did not have the money, manpower, and equipment that federal agencies had. "We had to depend upon a lot of legwork and a lot of guesswork.

"When I arrived on the scene, the first thing I was told by local investigators was that Frank was impossible to surveil. I, having come from a lengthy experience in surveilling, took that as a challenge. I quickly got a pattern on Frank, very early on. Without fail here is what he would do. He would leave the Lamont Street apartment between 9:00 and 9:30 each weekday morning. He arrived at his grandson's house at about 9:25, like clockwork. He would stay there for about ten minutes and then go on to his daughter Mary Ann's house. He would spend more time there. It got to the point that once I set up his pattern, I knew what he was going to do. It was rare that he changed his routine. So that soon, I didn't bother with him in the morning. I would pick him up at lunchtime." Typically, in these years, Bompensiero ate at Tarantino's, the Butcher Shop, or the Shelter Island Inn. The latter, said the retiree, "was the place they tended to go in the last six months of Bompensiero's life." Bompensiero's companions during those years were the same that Bruce, the waiter at Tarantino's, remembered—Chris Petti, Pete Marcos, Pete Tenner, a physician whose name the retiree did not wish to mention, because the man still is alive. "Sometimes," he said, "the doctor and Frank would go off alone and talk for a few minutes. They were talking, I think, about Frank's health." He added that he did not want to leave the impression that Bompensiero only took meals with people who were alleged to be organized crime figures or hangers-on to organized crime figures. "There would be many people who were not in any way involved in anything who ate lunch with Bompensiero and these guys.

"I would sit near them and eat lunch. I would look away but my ears were pricked up to try to pick up dialogue." The retiree noted that during this period he gained weight and his blood pressure went up, "just from the lifestyle. They would spend several hours over lunch. Bompensiero would go home in early afternoon and other than the shopping, the only other thing he would do was to go to the pay phone and make telephone calls. That became such a routine that after a while it was not all that valuable to me as a surveilling officer to watch him talk at the phone booth." Occasionally, they would use a camper when they followed Bompensiero. "We parked directly in front of his house." He recalled seeing Marie, gazing out from an open window. Many a day, he watched Bompensiero shop at Vons in Pacific Plaza. He did not recall that he ever saw Marie leave the apartment to go to the grocery store. "He seemed to do it all. You consider him an organized crime figure, but here he was at Vons, an everyday older gentleman, doing the grocery shopping."

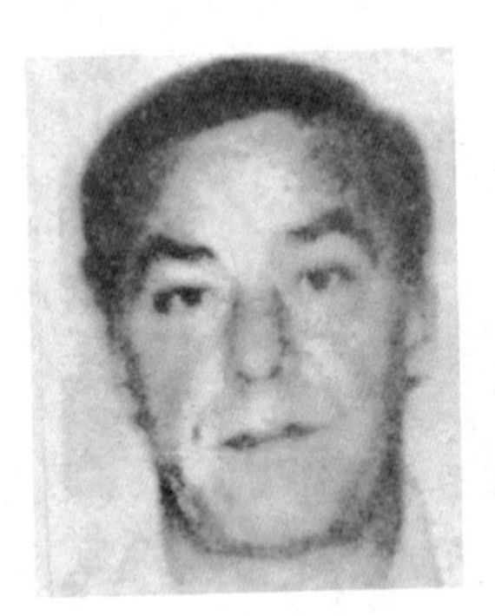

*Mike Rizzitello (aka Mike Rizzi)*

*Joey Aiuppa*

*Jack LoCicero*

*Dominic Brooklier*

*Thomas Ricciardi*

**Fratianno: "Don't you think if I wanted to kill him, I could have choked him and buried him somewhere?"**

CHAPTER SIXTY-TWO

# POLITICS

Nick Licata had died of natural causes in October, 1974. One hundred fifty people attended his funeral. Whether one of those in attendance was Bompensiero, I do not know. Dominic Brooklier succeeded Licata as Los Angeles headman. Brooklier, born Dominic Bruccoleri in 1913 in Palermo, as a young man did time in the Ohio State Penitentiary. Brooklier and Fratianno became friends at the tough Ohio prison. Brooklier came out to Los Angeles after World War II ended. Calling himself "Jimmy Regace," Brooklier worked for a time as a strong-arm thug for Mickey Cohen and then switched sides and worked as a strong-arm thug for Jack Dragna. According to Fratianno, he and Brooklier were "made" on the same evening in 1947. Again, according to Fratianno, Brooklier, on the Dragna side, participated in the Cohen-Dragna wars for control of LA's gambling outlets, shooting at and missing his old boss Cohen. After Dragna's death in 1956, Brooklier, who by then owned a used-car dealership in suburban Maywood, allied himself with Frank Desimone, and then after Desimone's death, with Licata.

"I don't know what it was," Brooklier's son, who became a prominent Los Angeles attorney, once told the *Los Angeles Times*. "I saw it when I was five years old. My father could walk into a place, and for whatever reason, the room would stop. It was as if every eye was on him. He just had an incredible charisma in a very subtle way. He wasn't loud, he wasn't fast-talking, he was understated. But men respected my father."

Frank Bompensiero did not respect Brooklier. What, precisely, had gone bad between them, I do not know. But Bompensiero had nothing good to say about Brooklier. Likewise, Brooklier had nothing good to say about Bompensiero. He was rumored to be concerned that Bompensiero might be trying to take over all California. Bompensiero was on easy terms with family members in San Jose and San Francisco, he was in communication with Joseph Bonanno in his Tucson exile. He kept up his connections with Chicago, Detroit, and Ohio. He had gotten to know Anthony "Tony the Ant" Spilotro, whom the Chicago family had sent to Vegas to keep watch over its holdings there. But for all this, it is unlikely that Bompensiero had anything as grandiose in mind as what Brooklier feared. It is more likely that Bompensiero was urged by his FBI handler to keep in touch with various families.

A retired FBI agent who knew Fratianno and had spent many days and nights talking with him, told me, about Bompensiero's attitude toward the post-Dragna Los Angeles family, "Frank was nontraditional in that he respected the rules of La Cosa Nostra but didn't pay much attention to the hierarchy. He didn't care if he was speaking to the Chicago family or the LA family, but he did believe in the organization. The LA group had treated Bompensiero, after he got out of prison in 1960, with benign neglect. Bompensiero far more so than Jimmy Fratianno, I think, held them all in contempt. Bompensiero was king of his own territory down there in San Diego, but he still paid lip service to the LA people and so did Jimmy. Jimmy was still a petty thief at heart in many ways and he wanted to be the big guy and for a while sort of was. Although late in the 1970s, Jimmy, who had been living in and was active in San Francisco in the mid-1970s, he really didn't have his own territory like Frank did, and he wanted that, wanted that bad, wanted to establish that separate family in San Francisco, and couldn't get it done. I think it could have been done. He could have worked something out with Jimmy Lanza at the time, who was about as senile as anybody ever was."

April 9, 1975, Brooklier and several Los Angeles family members, including Sam Sciortino and Peter Milano, were convicted of extorting money from Los Angeles bookmakers and businessmen. Sentences ranged from 15 months to four years. Brooklier's second-in-command, Louis Tom Dragna, was engrossed in his Roberta Manufacturing Company. Brooklier, concerned that the family would fall apart while he was in prison, named Fratianno as acting co-chief, with Dragna, of the LA family.

Fratianno later would testify in a federal courtroom to a meeting that took place between himself, Brooklier, Sciortino, and Peter Milano in April or May, 1975. Fratianno asked Brooklier why the family stayed away from shakedowns of out-of-state pornographers that were working in Los Angeles. Brooklier answered, "Nick Licata thought it was *por carilla*—dirt—and that we shouldn't fool with it." Fratianno testified that Brooklier then added, "From now on we are going to fool with it."

At that same meeting, according to Fratianno's sworn testimony, Brooklier mentioned Bompensiero. "Jimmy," he said, "I want you to take care of this guy. He's going around shooting his mouth off. Try to straighten him out while we're away in prison."

In June Brooklier and Sciortino entered prison. Fratianno took on the role of family co-don in his usual manic, heedless manner. Dressed in what he described as "dap threads," he began to fly about the United States, from one family center to another, introducing himself. He made deals first with one man and then the next. He gossiped and glad-handed. More than once he neglected to mention that he was only co-chief.

According to Fratianno's later sworn testimony, Louis Tom Dragna was the first LA family member who spoke to him about killing Bompensiero. In early summer, 1975, Dragna made Bompensiero the family *consigliere*, or counselor. "He told me," Fratianno testified, "'that way it will relax Frank and it will give us a good chance to clip him.'" Bompensiero was told of his promotion, Fratianno said, and "Frank was very, very delighted."

Dragna and Fratianno considered three ways to kill Bompensiero—a bomb in his Mustang, a drive into a remote area where they'd shoot the old man, or luring him out of the house at night to a phone booth and shooting him as he walked in the dark. Eventually, they abandoned the first two options. Fratianno later would testify that at Louis Tom Dragna's behest, "I called Frank one day, and I said, 'This is no good, talking on your home phone. Why don't you get a number of a pay phone where I can call you?'" Fratianno said that Bompensiero agreed, and began to walk down to the pay phone at the Arco station on the corner of Grand and Lamont. Bompensiero gave Fratianno the pay phone's number—273-9261. Fratianno later testified that he gave this number to Brooklier and Thomas Ricciardi. But Fratianno also later would testify that he didn't really want to kill his old friend Cheech. He said, "Don't you think if I wanted to kill him, I could have choked him and buried him somewhere? This man was my friend."

June 19, 1975, Sam Giancana, former head of the Chicago family, was shot to death in his Oak Park, Illinois, basement. July 30, 1975, former Teamsters president James R. Hoffa disappeared. Mary Ann recalled that her father said about Hoffa, "They'll never find him."

The retiree who for several years had surveilled Bompensiero said that he was aware that Joe Bonanno and Bompensiero were in touch during the 1970s. "Bonanno was communicating with Frank at that pay telephone." In Tucson, intelligence agents picked through Bonanno's trash. "I was privy to the materials that were coming out of that trash picking. The Bonannos were trying to reestablish themselves and they were attempting to accomplish this with the help of Frank." Bonanno, he said, "kept meticulous notes and had code names for people. His name for Frank was 'Cigaro.'"

Bonanno, the retiree said, had a cousin in Encinitas. During the Christmas holiday season of either 1975–76 or 1976–77, he was not sure which, "we heard that Bonanno and his wife were coming from Tucson to Los Angeles and then to Encinitas. Our objective at the time was to see if he made contact with Frank. Bonanno was in Encinitas on New Year's Eve—either 1976 or 1977. We watched him. He went to a pay phone and did his routine. We never knew if he called Frank. We followed Bonanno and his wife to Mass on New Year's Eve to a church in Solana Beach. The priest's sermon had to do with violence, with taking people's lives, and there was Joe Bonanno standing erect and looking very pious."

This story has been told so many times in law enforcement circles that it's taken on the glow of legend. An FBI agent—Jack Larson—on March 7, 1976, at the Murietta Hot Springs Hotel Coffee Shop, eavesdropped on a conversation between Fratianno and Louis Tom Dragna. Fratianno, per usual, was discussing his need for money. He said to Dragna, "Well, I want a piece of the porno." Dragna replied, "Don't worry about it. You'll get it."

"That conversation," writes Michael Zuckerman in *Vengeance Is Mine: Jimmy the Weasel Fratianno Tells How He Brought the Kiss of Death to the Mafia*, "when reported to [FBI agent] Jack Barron in Los Angeles, gave birth to Forex."

Jack Armstrong, according to Zuckerman's account, would later tell a Los Angeles jury that Bompensiero never knew that Forex was an FBI front. "Armstrong said that all he had told Bompensiero was that the FBI was interested in Forex, that it was a new company and it was making $100,000 or $200,000 annually selling pornography in South America; and anything Bompensiero could tell him about the company would be greatly appreciated. Armstrong said he knew Bompensiero could be counted on to take the bait and run to Fratianno."

Brooklier, at this time, was still in prison. Fratianno continued his manic travels about the country, insinuating himself into one after another family councils. June 6, 1976, he even took it upon himself to make a new member of the Los Angeles family. Mike Rizzitello, also known as Mike Rizzi, had attached himself to Fratianno during Fratianno's year as co-boss. Rizzi, in the worst way, wanted to be made. Fratianno arranged to meet Louis Tom Dragna and Bompensiero at the Murietta Hot Springs Hotel Coffee Shop. According to Fratianno's testimony to Ovid Demaris, this is what happened:

> "They ordered coffee and Jimmy said, 'Well, how're we going to do this?'
>
> "'Why don't we have Bomp say the words,' Dragna said. 'He can do it in Sicilian.'
>
> "'Okay, so where're we going to do it?' Bomp asked.
>
> "Jimmy shrugged. 'Let's do it in the car, find some deserted spot and park. We don't have a gun and knife, but I brought a pin.'
>
> "Dragna drove and Rizzi sat in front with him, with Jimmy and Bompensiero in the back. A few miles out of Murietta, Dragna swung onto a dirt road and stopped when they were out of sight of

> the highway. They held hands while Bompensiero quickly rattled out the strange-sounding liturgy....
>
> "Bompensiero said, 'That's it, now for the blood.'
>
> "'Mike,' Fratianno said, 'give me your right hand, the trigger finger.'
>
> "Jimmy punctured the skin and squeezed until he saw blood. 'Mike, this drop of blood's a symbol of your birth into our family. We're all as one until death.'"

There's more to this absurd story. Fratianno has Bompensiero, Dragna, Rizzi, and himself, then, kiss and hold hands and carry on about how now they are all *amici nostri*. I have no idea if this happened or if it did, if it happened this way. But if Bompensiero did drive out on a dark road and do all this, he must have had his tongue deep in his round cheek.

FBI agent Jack Barron, stationed in Los Angeles, had hoped to lure Fratianno with the Forex scam. But Bompensiero was unable to interest Fratianno in Forex. Instead, only Ricciardi and Jack LoCicero took the bait. Ricciardi and LoCicero met in Van Nuys with two FBI agents—Jack Larson and J.C. Fishbeck—who wore body wires while they posed as pornographers. The tapes later would be played in court. Ricciardi would be heard telling the agents: "Anything illegal done in California goes mostly through us because we represent the people in California here. You understand that?" LoCicero added his two cents: "We want a piece of the action and if you don't come across, you might as well pack and move, because we're gonna stop you doing business." And so on and on.

Forex came across. In a second meeting the two FBI agents handed over to the Los Angeles family members an initial payment of $5000.

The retired gentleman who surveilled Bompensiero recalled that in the summer of 1976 when he trailed Bompensiero, that "all of a sudden Bompensiero starts heading for the airport. We go, 'Oh, boy, he's going to catch a plane.' So we decide to follow him and see what he's up to. Turns out he's headed for San Francisco. We get on the plane. We get to the City. Lo and behold, Bompensiero meets Fratianno at the San Francisco airport. They go up to the Sky Room. We sat up there and had lunch and Frank was chewing the hell out of Jimmy. Poking that cigar, sticking out his finger. Jimmy just took it. Frank came back that same day and so did we." Later, he said, they learned the reason for Bompensiero's reprimand of Fratianno. "What had happened was that Fratianno and Mike Rizzi had in their infinite wisdom gone to Sidney Korshak's office in Century City to try to sell some contributions for a fundraiser. They muscled their way into the office and tried, in their way, to intimidate Korshak." Korshak, a prominent attorney, fell under the protection of the Chicago family, a family ruled then by Joey "Doves" Aiuppa and Jackie Cerone. Korshak apparently had contacted Aiuppa and Cerone and complained about Fratianno and Rizzi's call upon him. "California," the retiree explained, "was beholden to the Chicago syndicate and Frank had to answer up to that Aiuppa fellow and Jackie Cerone and the guys running things in Chicago at that time." Aiuppa and Cerone summoned Bompensiero to Chicago and, as the retiree put it, "chewed Frank up one side and down the other. They wanted Fratianno and Rizzi killed, right then. 'How dare they try to bamboozle Korshak!' Frank somehow talked them into not doing it."

Wednesday, July 28, 1976, 71-year-old Johnny Rosselli, who got his start with Capone and served as Jack Dragna's consigliere, drove away from his sister's Plantation, Florida, home. She would never see her brother alive again. Rosselli, in the 1950s, had suggested to Mary Ann and Bompensiero that Mary Ann's son was handsome enough to be in movies and that he'd be glad to get him a screen test. Bompensiero was outraged. He didn't want any relative of his in show business. Rosselli and Bompensiero had been on the outs for years. Rosselli in June, 1976, had suggested to Fratianno that Bompensiero had become a snitch. But Rosselli had been seen around Washington, D.C., talking to a Senate committee. He, himself, had been marked as a snitch. August 7, Rosselli's sister received a telephone call from the police. Her brother's corpse had been found. His body had been cut up and placed in a rusting 55-gallon oil drum and the drum had been tossed into the Intracoastal Waterway.

Charles Rappleye and Ed Becker conclude in *All-American Mafioso: The Johnny Rosselli Story*: "It seemed apparent early on that Rosselli's murder had indeed been ordered and sanctioned by the Mafia.... The primary sources for the detectives were underworld informants in Florida, and Frank Bompensiero in San Diego, who had overheard discussions of the murder by the leaders of the national crime syndicate."

September 2, 1976, Leo Moceri was reported missing and presumed dead after his damaged and bloodstained automobile was discovered in a motel parking lot in an Akron suburb. Not long after that Mary Ann asked her father if he'd heard from Uncle Jimmy lately. Her father, she said, looked troubled, and said, "No. Poor Leo, he had an accident."

Did Mary Ann think that her father feared he'd be next? "'Automobile accident, plane crash, or someone will shoot me,' that's what he used to say."

PHOTOGRAPH BY SANDY HUFFAKER, JR.

*Holy Cross Catholic Cemetery and Mausoleum*

**Mary Ann gets the last word.**

**"My dad always said, 'When I'm dead, baby, stick a cigar in my mouth.'"**

CHAPTER SIXTY-THREE

# FRANK CHANGES

Michael Zuckerman writes in *Vengeance Is Mine* that in November, 1976, Fratianno and Los Angeles family members Jack LoCicero, Mike Rizzi, and Thomas Ricciardi were served with subpoenas from the federal grand jury investigating pornography and pornographers. "The agents who served the subpoenas were the same men who had posed as pornographers; the men LoCicero and Ricciardi had shaken down on Bompensiero's recommendation."

"That's when we knew for sure that Frank was an informant," Fratianno said. Fratianno called Bompensiero and asked him how he learned about Forex. Bompensiero claimed that he'd been introduced to them by a person who ran a pornography store.

Bompensiero also was called to Los Angeles to testify before the grand jury. The gentleman who so often surveilled Bompensiero was at Tarantino's soon after the Los Angeles family and Bompensiero were subpoenaed. "Bompensiero's behavior," he said, "began during this time to change. Frank had never been much of a drinker. But during this period, he began to drink a lot. I told my cohorts about this. We knew that something was up. About a week before the grand jury was to meet, he was at lunch at Tarantino's. He ordered a mixed drink with a beer back. He was loud, which Frank never really was. He was going, 'Yeah, canary, tweet, tweet,' alluding to the fact that there was an informant, that someone had snitched him off. He was extremely loud. He was actually obnoxious. I followed him, leaving the place. He was driving about 55 mph in the Mustang. He almost hit the center divider. He was in those days very flushed. He must have been feeling very pressured. I saw a complete change in personality and actions. He was extremely nervous." He recalled that he followed Bompensiero to Los Angeles. Bompensiero's lawyer, Nicholas DePento, drove. When Bompensiero and the other Los Angeles family members arrived at the federal courthouse, he said that what he distinctly remembered "was Bompensiero's being separate from the other guys. They were rather distinctly away from him on the steps. They kept to themselves, which at the time I thought very interesting. They were inconspicuously away from him. There was just Frank and DePento, on the steps."

Fratianno reported that early in 1977, Sam Sciortino said to him, about Bompensiero, "That guy is a lying son of a bitch. We ought to kill him." And Brooklier, by then out of prison and in charge once again of the LA family, agreed. Brooklier, according to Fratianno, said, "Bomp is a wrong guy and he's no good. We got to do something about him. He's an informant."

I have heard from various sources that sometime in the first week of February, an attempt was made on Bompensiero's life. One man, long retired from local law enforcement, told it this way. "There was a dry run made on him a week before it happened. Two LA hoods were down here, to do him, they were staking him out. Some uniform car got on them. They were picked up a block away, sitting with shotguns. They got shook down. I knew a hit was out on him. I went to Armstrong and I said, 'These guys are going to sandbag him up there. Why the hell don't you pull him out?' Armstrong said, 'He's a fatalist. He doesn't want to be pulled. He figures he's going to die sometime anyway, and he's a fatalist.' I said, 'Well, you are going to have his blood on your hands when he goes, no matter what he is.'" The lawman continued, his face set in a deep frown. "Bompensiero wasn't any fatalist. He was a good-time Charlie, he liked his cigars, he liked his rare steak and his pasta, he liked to talk to people. I don't believe it for a minute that he was just a fatalist. But he signed his own death warrant by doing it, by talking to Armstrong and that bunch."

Armstrong later would testify in a court case that Bompensiero had regularly been counseled that his life was in danger. He would say that he had urged Bompensiero to place his car in private parking. He would say that Bompensiero declined to take precautions and expressed disdain for the Los Angeles family. He would say that Bompensiero was offered protection in the government's witness protection program, but turned all such suggestions aside.

Monday, February 7, Bompensiero met friends for lunch at Tarantino's. According to the *San Diego Union's* Mitch Himaka,

"From 12:55 p.m. to 1:30 p.m., five men sat in a booth at Tarantino's Restaurant in Point Loma enjoying their lunch and talking. The subject under discussion was a federal grand jury indictment which named two of the men."

At lunch that day with Bompensiero were Chris Petti, Robert Benjamin, David Gottlieb, and Larry Saunders. Himaka noted that "Benjamin and Gottlieb, along with Arthur F. Schulman and Earl John Rodde and Beach Cities Coatings and Construction Co., 722 Genevieve Street, Solana Beach, had been indicted three days earlier by a federal grand jury. They were charged with one count of conspiracy and 10 counts of causing false statements to be filed in loan applications to federally insured lending institutions. The five men were discussing the actions that would be taken with regard to the indictment, according to intelligence sources."

According to Zuckerman's *Vengeance Is Mine*, Fratianno later would testify that on February 9, 1977, he met Bompensiero, Chris Petti, Abe Chapman, and Jimmy Styles, who was connected to the Bonanno family. They met, Fratianno said, at the San Francisco Hilton. According to Fratianno, Bompensiero asked him to join them for dinner at Montefusco's Restaurant. Jimmy would forever insist that he did not know what they discussed that evening or why they met.

About that evening, Fratianno later said, "No, I didn't say nothing to Bomp. I knew this poor motherfucker was as good as dead while we were sitting there drinking wine and eating. But that was his fuckin' problem. If I warned him, it would become my problem."

Thursday, February 10, Bompensiero got up early. The sun was shining. It was going to be another pretty day. He dressed in dark green slacks, a white, short-sleeved shirt, and a rust brown cardigan. He walked around the neighborhood. He smoked his cigar. He didn't visit Frankie's house. He didn't visit Santa. Was he afraid that someone would follow him there? We will never know. At noon, he met DePento at Tarantino's. They sat at Bompensiero's usual table.

What Bompensiero did that afternoon, no one knows. The man who surveilled Bompensiero for the last two years of his life had been called into his office on another matter. "Otherwise," he said, "I might have been there." He wasn't there. Armstrong, someone told me, was back in Washington, D.C., that day. I don't know if he was or he wasn't.

Bompensiero may have watched Channel 10 news. He may have watched *Lassie*, the longtime favorite of his. A *Lassie* rerun was shown on television from 7:00 p.m. to 7:30 p.m. Marie, apparently, was dozing. He may have sat alone with his thoughts for a few minutes. He must have known that they were going to come for him. I think that he was a fatalist. He had once said to a friend, about killings he'd done, "If God didn't want them dead, he would've stopped the bullets." I think he believed that about himself. If God didn't want him dead, then God would stop the bullet. If God did want him dead, well.

Well. He had the appointment to call someone. We can be sure of that. Even if we do not know who that someone was. Fratianno swore it was Dominic Brooklier. But other people have said it was Fratianno himself who asked his old friend Cheech to call him. So Bompensiero, wearing the rust brown cardigan, carrying dimes in the pockets of the forest green trousers, walked downstairs and out the door and down Lamont to the Arco station. The temperature was in the mid-50s. The sky was cloudless. Lights were on in the small houses along Lamont Street. Television sets glowed from windows. Bompensiero strolled down to the pay phone by the Arco station and dialed whomever he dialed.

They were waiting. The wheel man and the shooter. I don't know what they were driving. No one does. The shooter had a .22, equipped, apparently, with a silencer.

Bompensiero turned, then, and started toward home. He had three dimes in his hand, the Bering in his mouth. You could see the stars that night and he must have looked up at them as he started walking south, on Lamont, from Thomas Avenue, back toward the Beach Club. I imagine that I can hear his footsteps against the cement. He soon arrived, only feet away from the tall picket fence. This would be the fence behind which Bompensiero's assailant was hiding. Gripping the .22-caliber automatic, he waits. What, for instance, goes through the gunman's mind? What does he see, as he stands here, maybe behind the fence, peering out perhaps, toward Grand Avenue. Can he see Bompensiero walk toward him? Can he hear his footsteps? Can he smell the smoke from Bompensiero's cigar? Does he think that soon he will do to Bompensiero what Bompensiero did to so many men?

Bompensiero steps from the curb at the intersection of the alley that runs west from Lamont Street, about halfway between Thomas and Reed Avenues.

The gunman fires his first shot into Bompensiero's head from behind.

The first shot is followed quickly by three more. The shots are fired into the side of his balding head, high, above the ear.

Fratianno would later testify that Jack LoCicero drove the car and Thomas Ricciardi shot the gun. Fratianno testified that Ricciardi said to him, "You know, when I clipped Bomp he gave me a little struggle. But it was beautiful. There was no noise. It went along beautiful."

We don't want to leave Ricciardi with the last word. We don't.

Mary Ann gets the last word. "My dad always said, 'When I'm dead, baby, stick a cigar in my mouth. I want a cigar.' So I wanted to put a cigar in his mouth for the viewing. The funeral director didn't like the idea. He put a cigar in his hand and folded his hand around it. And he stuck several cigars in his pocket. My father's face looked awful. I didn't want anyone to see him. He looked like a wax museum. After the family viewing, we had the casket locked. I didn't want anyone to see my dad like that. After the Rosary, we went over to Marie's. A guy came over to me, a friend of my father's, I'd rather not say his name. He whispered in my ear, 'Mary Ann, I want you to know that your father didn't go down begging. He went down like a man.'"

Mary Ann paused. "My dad when it happened, he probably didn't say, 'Don't shoot me, don't shoot me.' He probably said, 'Go ahead, you son-of-a-bitch, shoot me. I know I'm going to get it anyway.'"

# ABOUT THE AUTHOR

From the *New York Times*, May 25, 2006:

"Judith Moore, the author of *Fat Girl,* a searingly angry and widely praised memoir about being overweight, died on May 15 in Berkeley, Calif. She was 66. The cause was colon cancer, said her daughter Rebecca Moore.

"At the heart of *Fat Girl* is the story of a brutal childhood. Ms. Moore was born in Stillwater, Okla. Her parents divorced when she was young. Her father, a lawyer, was obese, her mother slender. As a child Ms. Moore was shuttled between her mother and her maternal grandmother, both of whom beat her, she said. But her grandmother liked to cook, and so Judith devoured food, desperate to fill the emptiness inside her. And as she grew fat, both women derided her.

"Writing in *The New York Times Book Review*, the author Jane Stern called the book 'brilliant and angry and unsettling.'

"With her mordant humor and tart style, Ms. Moore was sometimes compared to another California writer, Joan Didion.

"Ms. Moore published two earlier books. *The Left Coast of Paradise: California and the American Heart*, a collection of essays published in 1987, included pieces on the political philosopher Herbert Marcuse, on a neurotic elephant and on a philosophically minded pimp. *Never Eat Your Heart Out*, in 1997, was also a memoir about her life and food, though without the anger of *Fat Girl.*

"Ms. Moore was also a senior editor at the *San Diego Reader*, a weekly newspaper, where she was known for her almost uncanny intuition about how to bring out the best in writers.

"Ms. Moore married and divorced twice. In addition to Rebecca, of Dunedin, Fla., she is survived by a second daughter, Sarah Sullivan of Tacoma, Wash., and a grandson."